T0261746

CLOSING THE CANCER DIVIDE:
AN EQUITY IMPERATIVE

Based on the work of the
Global Task Force on Expanded Access
to Cancer Care and Control in Developing Countries

Edited by:

Felicia Marie Knaul
Julie R. Gralow
Rifat Atun
Afsan Bhadelia

Forewords by:

Harvey V. Fineberg
Amartya Sen
Nobel Laureate

Published by:

Distributed by:
Harvard University Press

Closing the Cancer Divide: An Equity Imperative

ISBN-13: 978-0-9829144-0-3
Published in the United States of America

President and Fellows of Harvard College acting through
the Harvard Global Equity Initiative

Distributed by Harvard University Press
Copyright © 2012 by the President and Fellows of Harvard College

www.hgei.harvard.edu

Harvard Global Equity Initiative is an inter-faculty initiative at Harvard University that seeks to advance the understanding and tackle the challenges of equitable development.

Suggested citation: Knaul FM, Gralow JR, Atun R, Bhadelia A (Eds). Closing the Cancer Divide: An Equity Imperative. Based on the work of the Global Task Force on Expanded Access to Cancer Care and Control in Developing Countries. Cambridge, MA: Harvard Global Equity Initiative, 2012. Distributed by Harvard University Press.

See Table of Contents for authorship of specific chapters and text boxes.
Additional information on the GTF.CCC is available at http://gtfccc.harvard.edu

Editorial advisor: **Mary Hager**
Cover design and layout: **arte¡diseño** - www.arteidiseno.com
Printer: **Flagship Press**, North Andover, Massachusetts, United States of America

To Amanda J. Berger

May your memory forever be for a blessing to us all

ACKNOWLEDGEMENTS

The Global Task Force on Expanded Access to Cancer Care and Control in Developing Countries (GTF.CCC) and the Harvard Global Equity Initiative (HGEI) gratefully acknowledge the financial and in-kind support received for both the research and events that made this volume possible from: Harvard University, Lance Armstrong Foundation, Susan G. Komen for the Cure,© American Cancer Society, China Medical Board, EMD Serono, Fogarty International Center, Fundación Mexicana para la Salud, GlaxoSmithKline, Hoffman & Hoffman PR, Johnson and Johnson, King Hussein Cancer Foundation and Center, Management Sciences for Health, Sanofi, Seattle Cancer Care Alliance, and Union for International Cancer Control, as well as anonymous donors.

The GTF.CCC and HGEI would like to further thank collaborators within Harvard University, including President Drew Faust, Dean Jeffrey S. Flier, Steven Hyman, Barbara J. Grosz, as well as members of the HGEI Steering Committee including its Chair Amartya Sen and members Sudhir Anand, Harvey Fineberg, Paula Johnson, Jennifer Leaning and Tony Saich. Further, we thank the Office of the Provost, including Provost Alan M. Garber, Doreen Koretz, Patricia Harrington and Radha Suraj, the Department of Global Health and Social Medicine at the Harvard Medical School, particularly Jennifer S. Puccetti, Debra Keaney and Emily Durrant, the Francois-Xavier Bagnoud Center, the Dean's Office at the Harvard School of Public Health (HSPH), including Linda Brady McDonald, HSPH Operations Office, including Mary Jane Curran, the Office of General Counsel, the Connors Center for Women's Health and Gender Biology, the information technology (IT) departments in HSPH, Harvard Medical School and Central Administration, and last but certainly not least, Harvard University Press, particularly Mary Ann Lane.

In addition to all authors and contributors as listed in the table of contents, many more were instrumental in bringing this work to fruition. Numerous patients and many other contributors gave of their time to help make this volume a reality. From the report that served the basis of this book, the GTF.CCC and HGEI take this opportunity to specifically list some of the many individuals and institutions who collaborated and contributed to this volume and to whom we are indebted for generous support and partnership.

To name but a few, these individuals include, Marian Affarah, Marcella Alsan, Ala Alwan, Ana María Amaris, Islene Araujo de Carvalho, Martha del Socorro Arias Novoa, Larry Bagley, Emily Bahnsen, Anna Barker, Janine Barnaby, Matthew Basilico, John Beard, Sarah Bearse, Shenieque Bennett, Vinona Bhatia, Morgan Binswanger, Barri M. Blauvelt, Kelly Bogaert, Silvana Bouhlal, Donna Bowers, Nancy Brinker, Lori Buswell, Francisco Caballero García, Victor Manuel Caballero Solano, Christopher Cahill, Miguela Caniza, Emily Carwell, Gail Cassell, Héctor Castro, Franco Cavalli, Eduardo Cazap, Tia Chester, Lilian Cheung, Lee Chin, Shu-Ti Chiou, Tea Collins, Michael Constantine, Gerard Cunningham, Diana Currea, Isabel Davis, Sara Day, Fausta Debones, Jenny Diaz, Elizbeth De Ocampo, Javier Dorantes, Richard Downing, Henry Drew, Dean Eastwood, Robin Eisner, Lena El-Malek, Martha Embrey, Amy Kate Eussen, Sophia Faris, Rebecca Firestone, James Fitzgerald, David Forman, Harold Freeman, Francis D. Fuller, Kathryn Galvin, Oliver Gantner, Pat García-González, Atul Gawande, Gary Ginsberg, Jennifer Goldsmith, Luz María González, María Cecilia González, Chris Gray, Sarah Hagan, Mary Hager, Laurie Hall, Gregory Harper, Ana Cecilia Hidalgo, Susan Higman, Marshall Hoffman, Richard Horton, James Hospedales, Anne Hubbard, Claudine Humure, Omar Ishrak, Salma Jaouni, Prabhat Jha, Mercedes Juan López, Ilana Kadmon, Hugh Kelleher, Chelsea Kelley, Patrick Kelley, Heidi Kleedtke, Garrett Krik, Richard Laing, Mary Ann Lane, Jeremy Lauer, David Lee, Leslie Lemann, Daisy Leo, Ana Ley, Guohong Li, Tatiana Lingos, Yuanli Liu, Amalia Lizárraga, Douglas Lowy, Silvana Luciani, Roberto Rivera Luna, Jing Ma, Maricela Macías, Laura Magaña, Joanne Manrique, Angela Marmo, Jaime Andres Giraldo Marmolejo, Mario Márquez, Sarah Marsh, Bethany Maylone, Jarred Mcateer, Miguel Angel Mejía, Terri McDonald, Kathryn McNaught, Oscar Méndez Carniado, Fortunate Mendlula, Andy Miller, Mary Lisa Miller, Beth Minnich, Vickie Monta, Nour Nasif, Esperance Ndenga, Fidele Ngabo, Andrew Norden, Jason Obedzinski, Meg O'Brien, Faith Oliver, Olufunmilayo Olopade, Sonia Xochitl Ortega Alanis, James Ossman, Sheena Patel, Erin Pearson, Sonia Peña, Gerardo Pérez, Teresa Pérez, Mirta Roses Periago, Alfonso Petersen Farah, Malebogo Pusoentsi, Ibrahim Qaddoumi, You-Lin Qiao, Yuri Quintana, Taghreed Rabaa, Astha Ramaiya, Jim Rankin, Scott Ratzan, Elizabeth Reid, Joseph Rhatigan, Chie Ri, Herb Riband, Dee Dee Ricks, Gaston Rivera, Jospeh Roberts, Julie A. Roberts, Rusty Robertson, Horacio Robles, Danielle Rodin, Daniel Rodríguez, Abish Guillermina Romero Juárez, Erin Ross, Debasish Roychowdhury, Imara Roychowdhury, Greg Ruisi, Francis Saba, Jasmine Samuel, Silvia Sánchez, Ramon Sánchez Pina, Mahmoud Sarhan, Zaina Sarhan, Peer M. Schatz, David Scheer, Ellen Sheets, Maria Schenider, Erin Schwartz, Edna Senato, Jacqueline Sherris, Ana Shuler, Blaine Smith, Claudia Smith, Patricia Spellman, Butch Staley, Anna Standertskjold,

Bettina Stevens, Paul Stoffels, Katy Stout, Kathleen Stover, Jeff Sturchio, Ana Teasdale, Christopher Ternan, Elizabeth Thompson, Amber Thomson, Julie Torode, Doug Ulman, Leopoldo Valentín Vargas, Marcela Vallejo, Wim Van Damme, Cassia van der Hoof Holstein, Harold Varmus, George Vélez, Jesús Zacarias Villarreal Pérez, Ludmila Vite Torres, Kim Vitols, Claire Wagner, Rebecca Weintraub, Yelena Wetherill, Christopher Wild, Iain Wilson, Eric Winer, Scott Wittet, Kevin Wnek, Hyun Ju Wooh, Jerome Zeldis, Miri Ziv.

The GTF.CCC efforts have significantly benefited through collaboration with many institutions and initiatives, including but not limited to, the American Society of Clinical Oncology, Avon Foundation, Axios International, Ben-Gurion University of the Negev, Beth Israel Deaconess Medical Center, Breast Health Global Initiative, Brigham and Women's Hospital, Center for Social Protection and Health Economic (PROESA), China Medical Board, Clinton Global Initiative, Dana Farber Cancer Institute, Earth Institute (Columbia University), Equal Right to Life, FEMAMA, Family, Women's and Children's Health Cluster at the World Health Organization, Forum of African First Ladies Against Breast & Cervical Cancer, Fred Hutchinson Cancer Research Center, Fundación Plenitud, Global Access to Pain Relief Initiative, Global Alliance for Vaccines and Immunization, The Global Fund to Fight AIDS, TB and Malaria, Global Health Council, Harrington Memorial Hospital, Harvard University Press, Imperial College, Institute of Medicine of the National Academies, Instituto Jalisciense de Cancerología, International Agency for Research on Cancer, International Network for Cancer Research and Treatment, International Society of Pediatric Oncology, Jordan Breast Cancer Program, London School of Hygiene and Tropical Medicine, Medtronic, Milford Regional Medical Center, Ministry of Health of Mexico, Ministry of Health of Rwanda, Ministry of Health of the State of Jalisco, Ministry of Health of the State of Morelos, Ministry of Health of the State of Nuevo León, National Cancer Institute of Mexico, National Cancer Institute of the US, National Commission for Social Protection in Health (Seguro Popular) of Mexico, National Institute of Public Health of Mexico, NCD Alliance, NCD Child, Non-Communicable Diseases Cluster at the World Health Organization, Pan American Health Organization, Partners in Health, PATH, Pediatric Oncology Group of Ontario, Princeton University, Public Health Foundation of India, RTI International, Sheikh Mohammed Hussein Al-Amoudi Center of Excellence in Breast Cancer, Stand up to Cancer, St. Jude's Children's Research Hospital (International Outreach Program), The Lancet, Tómatelo a Pecho, A.C., Uganda Cancer Institute, Union for International Cancer Control (UICC), Universidad del Pacífico, University of Washington, University of Wisconsin School of Medicine and Public Health, World Economic Forum.

TABLE OF CONTENTS*

PART I: MUCH SHOULD BE DONE — 1

CHAPTER 1 — 3

CLOSING THE CANCER DIVIDE: OVERVIEW AND SUMMARY

Felicia Marie Knaul, Julie R. Gralow, Rifat Atun, Afsan Bhadelia,
Julio Frenk, Jonathan Quick, Lawrence Shulman, and Paul Farmer

---

* All text boxes listed without authorship were drafted by chapter authors.

CHAPTER 2 _____ 29

THE GLOBAL CANCER DIVIDE: AN EQUITY IMPERATIVE

Felicia Marie Knaul, Hans-Olov Adami, Clement Adebamowo,
Hector Arreola-Ornelas, Amanda J. Berger, Afsan Bhadelia,
James Cleary, David J. Hunter, Nancy Keating, Anthony Mbewu,
Oscar Mendez, Claire Neal, Meg O'Brien, Peggy Porter,
Isabel dos Santos Silva, Rola Shaheen, Julio Frenk

CHAPTER 3 _____ 71

INVESTING IN CANCER CARE AND CONTROL

Felicia Marie Knaul, Hector Arreola-Ornelas, Rifat Atun,
Oscar Méndez, Ramiro Guerrero, Marcella Alsan, Janice Seinfeld

PART II: MUCH COULD BE DONE   93

PART III: MUCH CAN BE DONE   167

CHAPTER 6 _____ 169

INNOVATIVE DELIVERY OF CANCER CARE AND CONTROL
IN LOW-RESOURCE SCENARIOS

Felicia Marie Knaul, Afsan Bhadelia, Rashid Bashshur,
Amanda J. Berger, Agnes Binagwaho, Erin Blackstock,
Amy Judd, Ana Langer, Doug Pyle, Mounica Vallurupalli,
Julie R. Gralow

CHAPTER 7 _____ 197
ACCESS TO AFFORDABLE MEDICINES, VACCINES, AND HEALTH TECHNOLOGIES

Niranjan Konduri, Jonathon Quick, Julie R. Gralow, Massoud Samiei, Philip Castle, Ramiro Guerrero

CHAPTER 8   257

INNOVATIVE FINANCING:
LOCAL AND GLOBAL OPPORTUNITIES
Rifat Atun, Felicia Marie Knaul

CHAPTER 9 _____ 289

EVIDENCE FOR DECISION-MAKING: STRENGTHENING HEALTH INFORMATION SYSTEMS AND THE RESEARCH BASE

Nancy Keating, Elena Kouri, Julie R. Gralow, Kathy Cahill, Jo Anne Zujewski, Peggy Porter, Gustavo Nigenda, Rifat Atun, Felicia Marie Knaul

CHAPTER 10 _____ 311

STRENGTHENING STEWARDSHIP AND LEADERSHIP TO EXPAND ACCESS TO CANCER CARE AND CONTROL

Felicia Marie Knaul, George Alleyne, Rifat Atun, Flavia Bustreo, Julie R. Gralow, Mary Gospodarowicz, Peter Piot, Doug Pyle, Julio Frenk

STORIES THAT INSPIRED THIS VOLUME

Abish

My name is Abish Guillermina Romero Juárez and I am 24 years old. I have always considered myself very lucky to be a member of a close-knit family where my parents always worked hard to educate and provide for our development and necessities. I would say that I had the perfect childhood: I only had to worry about playing, attending school, and obeying my parents. I always knew that I could count on them because they were my best friends. Throughout my adolescence, things did not change and me and my brother received their complete support. When it was time for us to attend university, one of our greatest desires, I studied Hotel Administration and Tourism for 4 years in the Banking and Accounting School in Mexico City, and I was very happy during this time.

I never imagined that in a few months my life, and that of my family, would drastically change.

Our family suffered the attacks of that terrible and painful disease, breast cancer, in one of our most loving family members, my mother. Even though she had self-examined herself, no one listened to her. The doctors did not adequately examine her and told her that the mass she had was only fatty substance, and that it was not necessary to do any testing. Over the months to come, my mom noticed that the lump grew and began to feel light stinging, but relying on her doctor's advice, we let time pass, allowing the disease to make threatening advances, and when she was finally diagnosed with breast cancer, it was already in stage III. We fought it and suffered every instant during this time until the cancer was apparently eliminated. It returned with fury three years later in that woman who was so sweet and loving to us and to all to those who knew her. Together with my father and brother we lovingly cared for her day and night in the last few months. After a long and painful struggle, my mother died.

In September of 2010, right after suffering the death of my loving mother and having finished my studies, I decided to register in a cultural exchange program to work and study in the US for a year. When I lived in Boston for 7 months everything looked okay. It seemed that I was recovering from such great suffering, but having been raised in the habit of self-examination and learning about my breasts, one day I discovered a lump in one of them. Since I had insurance from my job in the USA I called and explained the situation. They said they would cover the cost of diagnostic tests so I went to the doctor and had an ultrasound. They observed that the image was suspicious, gave me a mammogram and a biopsy, and then things began to get more serious than I wanted. Finally I got the results and one of my worst fears came true. The nightmare returned. I was being diagnosed with breast cancer, stage II, and my world seemed to collapse. Why me? Why again?

I talked to my insurance agent who told me that because of my diagnosis they could not cover my treatment and that I would also have to leave my job because I was no longer going to be able to do it. That was the worst part, seeing the plans I worked so hard for months go to the trash. At that time I was not only concerned about the fact that I was sick, but also that I did not have any insurance in Mexico either to cover me in this situation. I knew that cancer treatment is expensive and that it can have many implications. I talked to my employer in the US and she contacted some friends to see if anyone could inform me of a place or a doctor that I could see in Mexico. I was fortunate to meet Felicia Knaul (Director of HGEI, who works on issues of health and breast cancer in Mexico) to whom I will be forever grateful for all the help and information she gave me when I needed it most.

She told me about the social health protection system, Seguro Popular, and the National Cancer Institute (INCAN) which is a tertiary level care center under the Ministry of Health, which provides specialized cancer care. Before that, I was not aware of these institutions, but Felicia told me that breast cancer was totally covered by Seguro Popular and not to worry. In that moment, and after all the anguish I had lived through, I had a bit of good news. She connected me with Seguro Popular and so I went back to Mexico, very sad but hopeful that I would receive treatment. I went to register at the Seguro Popular office – I only needed my basic identification, to be a Mexican citizen and to not be affiliated to social security institutions such as IMSS, ISSSTE, PEMEX, SEDENA, etc. In less than an hour I was being registered. They explained to me that there is a fund that is part of the social health protection system that seeks to provide highly specialized medical services to people who do not have Social Security and that are affected by expensive illnesses that may put at risk their lives and family property. The fund, called the Catastrophic Expenses Protection Fund, allows me to access everything I need in order to receive full treatment. I was relieved to know that all expenses would be covered by my new insurance, and that I would be treated at the National Cancer Institute of Mexico. Some people have access to health insurance institutions such as IMSS, ISSSTE, PEMEX, SEDENA, etc, or pay for private health insurance, and now we all have the option of enrolling in Seguro Popular, which covers many illnesses, including breast cancer since 2007.

Approximately mid May 2011, I started to have tests again to confirm the previous diagnosis and to learn in what condition my body was in order to receive treatment. There were ultrasounds, blood tests, some nuclear medicine tests, placement of a catheter, and a study called a BRCA1 genetic study, which would be useful for determining the type of surgery I would require in a few months.

I had a couple of consultations with my INCAN oncologist to determine my treatment plan. My plan indicated 16 rounds of chemotherapy, 12 of which would have to be weekly with medication to prevent side effects caused by Taxol. I must confess that I did very well with the exception of a neuropathy that occurred after the 4th infusion for which I took a special medication (Gabapentin) that reduced the annoying sensations. I finished this first stage and about 2 months ago I started the second and final round, consisting of 4 infusions every 21 days which have been aggressive. My body has suffered considerably with these infusions but, fortunately, I have been prescribed various medications for nausea, headaches and other symptoms that have come up. I am also receiving a drug called Herceptin which raises the cost of treatment but at the same time promises better results.

At the end of this year the chemotherapy treatment will end and with the help of my oncologist, we will determine what the best surgical procedure for me will be. I know that many women do not have the choice at the end of the treatment to have reconstructive surgery due to the high cost of the procedure. Thanks to Seguro Popular, I have that choice. I would like to have the bilateral mastectomy and reconstruction at the end of radiation. All these surgical procedures are covered by Seguro Popular, too. I feel relieved as otherwise it would have been much more complicated to receive treatment. One of the objectives of this initiative is to reduce the number of women detected in advanced stages (III and IV), and to expand access to care and quality treatment for women with breast cancer. No doubt this is being met and I am a witness to it.

It is very stressful to make decisions for people who have no knowledge on health issues, from knowing what hospital to go to, to the type of studies we need to have in order to have the proper diagnosis of the disease we suffer, what drugs can be best in response to treatment or to simply choose a doctor in whom we can trust our care; it is a long process. I admit it is hard to accept the illness and especially at such a young age as mine. But I believe it is even more stressful to think that you don't have the means to seek treatment, and have nowhere to go for treatment. I feel deeply grateful and fortunate that I have Seguro Popular, an initiative that has been driven and supported by my country, Mexico. Thousands of women like me are being saved and with that, also the well-being of our families. I know that with initiatives like this one, access to health services will be expanded to all sectors of Mexico's society that do not have social security.

I have met extraordinary people that have survived this illness and they inspire me to forge ahead and help others. Information is and will be the most important tool to avoid thousands of deaths worldwide. The authorities of every country must continually train their doctors and nurses so that they are able to make correct diagnoses, like in the case of my breast cancer. It is extremely important for all of us to become promoters of self-examination and of Seguro Popular in order to save thousands of lives with this information.

Our economic status should not be an impediment to obtaining access to treatment. I wish every country would guarantee financial protection and health coverage so that no more mothers, children, spouses or any other family members suffer death due to lack of resources.

**Life is beautiful and this war,
despite the difficulties we encounter,
is worth fighting.**

Abish Guillermina Romero Juárez

October 25, 2011
Mexico City, Mexico

Anite

A WOMAN IN SEARCH OF CARE
WILL SPEND ALL SHE HAS AND MORE[1]

A young woman takes my arm... in rural Haiti. "Look at this, doctor." She lifts a left breast mass. This lesion... has almost completely replaced the normal breast. It is a "fungating mass," in medical jargon, and clear yellow fluid weeps down the front of a light-blue dress. Flies are drawn to the diseased tissue, and the woman waves them away mechanically. On either side of her, a man and a woman help her with this task, but they are not kin, simply other patients waiting in the line.

"Good morning," I say, although I know that she is expecting me to say next to nothing and to be the speaker. She lifts the tumor toward me and begins speaking rapidly.

"It's hard and painful," she says. "Touch it and see how hard it is." Instead, I lift my hand to her axilla and find large, hard lymph nodes there –likely advanced and metastatic cancer– and I interrupt her as politely as I can... I need to know how long this woman has been ill.

But the woman, whose name is Anite... is going to tell the story properly... We are surrounded by hundreds... I think to pull her from the line, but she wants to talk in front of her fellow sufferers... She carries, in addition to a hat and a small bundle of oddments, a white vinyl purse. Please, I think, let there be useful information in there. Surely she has seen other doctors for a disease process that is, at a minimum, months along?

...We do not have a surgeon on staff just now. We have been promised, a weary functionary at the Ministry of Health has told me, that the Cuban government will soon be sending us a surgeon and a pediatrician. But for this woman, Anite, time has run out.

...She has let go of my arm to lift the mass, but now she grips it again. "I am from near Jeremie," she says, referring to a small city on the tip of Haiti's southern peninsula – about as far from our clinic as one could be and still be in Haiti.

---

1. Excerpt from: Farmer P. An anthropology of structural violence. In: Partner to the Poor. Berkeley, CA: University of California Press, 2010; 350-375.

To reach us, Anite must have passed through Port-au-Prince, with its private clinics, surgeons, and oncologists.

"I first noticed a lump in my breast after falling down...

"How long ago was that?" I ask again.

"I went to many clinics," she says in front of dozens of people she has met only that morning or perhaps the night before. "I went to 14 clinics." Again, many nod assent...

"Fourteen clinics," I respond. "What did they say was wrong with you? Did you have an operation or a biopsy?" The mass is now large and has completely destroyed the normal architecture of her breast; it is impossible to tell if she has had a procedure, as there is no skin left to scar.

"No," replies Anite. "Many told me I needed an operation, but the specialist who could do this was in the city, and it costs $700 to see him. In any case, I had learned in a dream that it was not necessary to go to the city."...

...I think uncomfortably of the privacy of a US examination room and of the fact that I have never seen there a breast mass consume so much flesh without ever having been biopsied. But I have seen many in Haiti, and almost all have proven malignant.

...[when] she discovered the mass. It was "small and hard," she says. "An abscess, I thought, for I was breastfeeding and had an infection while breastfeeding once before."

...Anite returns to the real tale. She hurt her back in the fall. How was she to care for her children and for her mother, who was sick and lived with her? "They all depend on me. There was no time."

And so the mass grew slowly "and worked its way under my arm." I give up trying to establish chronology. I know it had to be months or even years ago that she first discovered this "small" mass. She had gone to clinic after clinic, she says, "spending our very last little money. No one told me what I had. I took many pills."

"What kind of pills?" I ask.

Anite continues. "Pills. I don't know what kind." She had given biomedicine its proper shot, she seems to say, but it had failed her. Perhaps her illness had more mysterious origins? "Maybe someone sent this my way," she says. "But I'm a poor woman – why would someone wish me ill?"

... "...The mass was growing, and there were three other small masses growing under my arm. I had a dream in which a voice told me to stop taking medicines and to travel far away for treatment of this illness. "She had gone to a voodoo priest for help in interpreting this dream. ...

..."In order to cure this illness, he told me, I would have to travel far north and east." It has taken Anite over a week to reach our clinic. A diagnosis of metastatic breast cancer is later confirmed.

Claudine

I lost both my parents when I was six years old. I was taken to an orphanage with my older brother and younger sister. In the orphanage, I played all sorts of games, especially soccer. I was also a choir member. I loved spending my time with friends and going to school. In the orphanage I did activities any child might do, like laundry and fetching water. During my childhood, I always dreamed of becoming a doctor or a teacher, even though at that point I had never met a doctor. Then I got sick...

When I was finishing fourth grade, while I was playing soccer, the ball hit my knee. It wasn't a heavy shot that could break the bone, but it was very painful. I went to the nurse from the orphanage who gave me pain killers, thinking that I had a simple fracture. He told the care takers from the orphanage to put a compress on my leg since the swelling kept getting worse. This nurse treated me for months, and instead of getting better, I got worse.

The orphanage sent me to several hospitals including one in Kigali, the capital city of Rwanda. There, they did surgery to try to reduce the swelling, but they didn't explain this to me. After my recovery I was taken back to the orphanage where I started getting ready for school, since another year had already started. I managed to go to school for one day, but then I got sick again. Things became even more serious. I could not eat, walk or do anything. I could only sit up and lie down because the pain had gotten so severe. It was then that I got a visit from Dr. Joia Mukherjee and others from Partners In Health. They came and told me how they were going to help me get better, but by that time I didn't know what to believe anymore.

They asked me what I thought was wrong with me. I told them that I thought I had AIDS. I knew that AIDS was the only disease that had no cure, and all the doctors I saw had a hard time figuring out what I had. They assured me that I didn't have AIDS. At first they thought that I had TB and left me with some medicine, but there was no progress. I kept getting more and more sick. The woman who ran the orphanage decided to take me to a hospital in Congo, there I spent a long time. Dr. Paul Farmer visited me, but I didn't know who he was at that time and I couldn't understand anything he said because he spoke in English.

During my time in Congo, the doctors put a cast on my leg which did nothing but cause more pain. They took it off in less than a week due to the pain it was causing. Later, another surgery was done and I was sent home. The nurse from the orphanage took care of my stitches but my leg wasn't getting better. Finally, the orphanage invited some other doctors to come look at me. It was a Sunday evening. Those doctors told me that I had cancer and that there was nothing they could do to save my leg. They had to amputate it. When I heard what they said, I felt lost and confused. I didn't know what to say to them. I screamed and yelled at them, thinking that they hated me. I could not believe what my ears were hearing. I started thinking of all that I have been through. I could not understand why they were unable to save my leg. I was faced with the most difficult decision of my life. I didn't know that I would ever have to choose between life and death. Of course I had no choice, other than letting my leg go. The amputation was done the next day. After my amputation, it was discovered that the cancer had gone into my lungs.

In May 2005, Partners In Health sent me to Massachusetts General Hospital in Boston for chemotherapy because there was no hospital in Rwanda that could treat cancer. I spent 11 months at MGH. There, I went through more surgeries in my lungs and my leg. I was given a prosthetic leg which felt like a dream to me, because I never thought of being able to walk again. While going through my treatment, I lived with a host family who helped me get used to the American culture and acted as my parents. When I recovered, I came to realize that having cancer could not stop me from following my dreams.

After my recovery, I returned back home to Rwanda in 2006, where I got to see my siblings and friends once again. It felt so wonderful to see their surprised faces. It seemed as though they could not believe I was the one standing with them. I cannot explain the joy I felt.

PIH helped me get into one of the best boarding schools in Rwanda, where I excelled in my studies. This year, Dr. Sara Stulac helped me come to the USA where I am a junior at Dana Hall School in Wellesley, MA. I hope to go to college and medical school in the USA, and to become a pediatric oncologist in Rwanda, so that I can help other kids with cancer.

I know I was one of the lucky few children in Rwanda who was able to receive treatment for my cancer. Most people with cancer in Rwanda and in Africa die without ever receiving treatment. I know from my experience that cancer can be treated, and my life is now full of hope and possibility. I want these same opportunities to be available to other children in Rwanda who are suffering from cancer.

Since I returned to Rwanda after my cancer treatment, I have seen doctors begin treating children with cancer in Rwandan hospitals, with medications and advice from doctors and hospitals in the USA. I hope that more doctors in Rwanda can be trained to provide cancer care, since most kids with cancer would never have the opportunity to leave Rwanda for treatment.

**I hope to see kids with cancer in Rwanda
finding treatment more quickly and easily than I did,
by doctors in their own country, and being able
to stay near their homes and families
while they are sick.**

Claudine Humure

October 17, 2011
Greenwich, Connecticut

Francine

Francine was 11 years old when she arrived at Rwinkwavu Hospital in Rwanda in 2005. This was just a few months after the hospital opened with support from Partners In Health.

She and her father had traversed Rwanda looking for a cure for the enormous tumor protruding from Francine's right cheek. It was obvious that left untreated the cancer would eventually take her life. In Francine's own words, "My parents had nearly given up hope". Before coming to Rwinkwavu, the family consulted numerous physicians and traditional healers. But lacking diagnostic equipment or expertise in oncology, the medical community could offer few answers. And even when a doctor did make a tentative diagnosis, Francine's family –poor, subsistence farmers– could not afford the fees for treatment.

At Rwinkwavu, Francine sat in the pediatric ward for months as her tumor grew and as hospital doctors and nurses tried to determine if cancer treatment, never before provided there, was possible in their small, rural hospital. Eventually, treatment was made possible through links with colleagues at institutions in the US. A tissue sample was sent to the Centres for Disease Control and Prevention laboratory for diagnosis, a pediatric oncologist at Dartmouth-Hitchcock Medical Center advised on creating a treatment regimen that was safe in the local setting, and Partners In Health purchased chemotherapy and other medications.

After several family meetings and training of local staff by a PIH pediatrician on site –Dr. Sara Stulac, who is also the author of this summary of Francine's story– she began receiving chemotherapy. Her tumor shrank each week, and after nine weeks of chemotherapy, she was able to have surgery to remove the residual tumor. The surgery was performed at Rwanda's national referral hospital.

Francine subsequently returned to Rwinkwavu for a total of 48 weeks of chemotherapy. Her father was employed at the hospital farm and so was able to support his family even during his daughter's lengthy hospitalization. The hospital doctors, nurses, and social workers developed close relationships with Francine and her family as they accompanied her through treatment.

As of 2011, 6 years after her arrival at Rwinkwavu, Francine remains cancer-free, and is a happy and healthy student at her local elementary school. She returns often to the Rwinkwavu Hospital pediatric ward to visit patients and her friends among the hospital staff, and often mentions how important it is that other kids who are suffering find access to medications just as she did.

Francine's story continues to provide inspiration and guidance for programs to expand access to cancer care and control in LMICs.

MESSAGES

When I was first asked to be the Honorary Co-President of the Global Task Force for Expanded Access to Cancer Care and Control in Developing Countries (GTF.CCC) two years ago, I immediately accepted, because beyond the long and prestigious title and the ambitious goals, this Task Force struck a deep chord. Every item the GTF.CCC sought to address, we had experienced or were experiencing at the King Hussein Cancer Foundation and Center in Jordan. Whether it was the high cost of drugs or the access to care, we faced it. Whether it was the use of telemedicine or doable solutions within constraints, we faced it. These challenges were all extremely real to us, and remain real to us today as we continue to provide international quality cancer care in a resource-poor, middle income country and in a region where many countries still do not have access to quality cancer care.

What is unique about the GTF.CCC is that it applies a two pronged approach: First, the idealist prong, which pushes for best practices in global funding and sustainable international support for cancer – similar to the support afforded to AIDS, Malaria and TB. And second, the realistic prong, which recognizes the limitations on the ground and works despite them, through them, and around them to reach its objectives. One of the many examples of this is Rwanda where, rather than leave a patient untreated, chemotherapy was safely prepared, administered, and monitored despite the lack of an on-site oncologist, but with backup from off-site specialists internationally through coordination between the Government of Rwanda and Partners in Health. This is a concrete example of how collaboration and international partnerships are at the core of achieving any success against cancer.

Cancer, a disease plagued by stigma and discrimination within many communities, itself displays no discrimination in how it targets its victims. It affects everyone, all ages and all races. However, today, with approximately two-thirds of the annual cancer mortality worldwide in low and middle income countries (LMICs), it is clear that the burden of the disease is disproportionately faced by the poor who either have no access to cancer care at all or cannot afford the exorbitant costs associated with such catastrophic illnesses.

I witnessed this harsh inequity and disparity between the developed and developing world in a very personal way when, just two days shy of his second birthday, my son was diagnosed with leukemia. Rather than the joys of celebration, we faced a cancer diagnosis and the paralyzing fear that we could lose what is most precious. Fortunately, I was one of the privileged few able to travel the distance necessary to provide my son with life-saving treatment at Dana Farber, one of the best cancer centers in the United States. Others are not so lucky.

The reality of leukemia cure rates is sadly reflective of the inequity in care; children with leukemia in the developed world have a 90% chance of a cure, while 90% of their counterparts in the world's 25 poorest countries will die. While cancer patients in the developed world are asking "Where will I be treated?" their counterparts in the developing world are asking "Will I be treated?" I firmly believe that it remains every individual's right to receive the best possible treatment – regardless of where they live.

This is why the GTF.CCC's work is so critical. This volume, following the 2011 GTF.CCC report, contains and expands on the real examples of successfully achieving cancer care in resource-poor settings. The lessons documented in this volume about Jordan and other countries such as China, Mexico and Rwanda provide the groundwork for cross-country exchanges and serve as a guideline on best practices, expertise and resource sharing that will benefit any LMIC struggling not only with cancer care but with the care of other noncommunicable diseases. Moreover, this volume highlights the fact that there is no "one size fits all," and therefore, an analysis of each country's capabilities, competing priorities, national key actors, and long-term and short-term needs is necessary to better delineate appropriate strategies that should be applied.

I am delighted to serve as Honorary co-President of the GTF.CCC alongside the unconquerable Lance Armstrong who has done and continues to do so much for cancer worldwide. I also cannot thank the GTF.CCC members, co-Chairs, both current and former, and Secretariat enough. This volume culminates almost three years of intense efforts and hard work to garner evidence and distill recommendations for on-going and coordinated action on cancer care and control in LMICs. The GTF.CCC is currently being guided in its efforts by our wonderful co-Chairs, Dr. Julio Frenk and Dr. Lawrence Corey, and carried out through the dual Secretariat at the Harvard Global Equity Initiative, led by the unstoppable Dr. Felicia Knaul, and the Fred Hutch Cancer Research Center, led by the incredible Dr. Julie Gralow. We are so fortunate to have a membership that is a diverse and unique merger of extraordinary leaders from the cancer and global health communities. Their diversity of expertise, innovative thinking and strong commitment to the issue have been instrumental in producing the result embodied in this volume, the seminal product of the GTF.CCC. I am thrilled to share this volume as a starting point to a unified vision and as a testament that change is within our grasp. Our success story at the King Hussein Cancer Foundation and Center in Jordan lends me the complete confidence to say that cancer care and control can be achieved in low and middle income countries. Despite the many challenges faced along the way our center stands tall, a beacon of hope in the region and a real-life example of how, despite the backdrop of a low-resource middle income country, cancer care is feasible.

However, in most of the developing world, the landscape for cancer care remains bleak. There is no time to waste; we must act now. We have an epidemic on our hands. It is our moral responsibility to not only save lives, but also alleviate undue suffering. We, the GTF.CCC, challenge the global community to seize the momentum generated by the UN High Level Meeting on the Prevention and Control of Non-Communicable Diseases and garner the political will needed to ensure that cancer receives its own line item on the global agenda and obtains the support and funding needed to make it a disease of the past.

I hope that this volume serves as a springboard to help produce the necessary action needed to end this disparity. The chance for a cure, the chance to live, should no longer remain an accident of geography.

Her Royal Highness Princess Dina Mired,
Honorary co-President, GTF.CCC
Director-General, King Hussein Cancer Foundation
Hashemite Kingdom of Jordan

August 12, 2012
Amman, Jordan

Unity is strength and knowledge is power in the fight against cancer. We are entering a time of great hope for our cause and one in which we can envision a more equitable future. The change we envision can only be accomplished through coordinated and informed action. The combined efforts of the Global Task Force on Expanded Access to Cancer Care and Control in Developing Countries (GTF.CCC) and the cancer and global health communities are leading to increased awareness of the truth about cancer. We have begun to dispel the misconceptions that have impeded our progress. No longer is the perception of cancer as a low-impact disease in the developing world tenable. We have shown that cancer control is both affordable and achievable, even in remote and modest settings. And we are making progress with efforts to cement the idea that a disease-centric approach to health must become a thing of the past.

As a cancer survivor and Honorary co-President of the GTF.CCC, alongside the leadership of Her Highness Princess Dina Mired of the Hashemite Kingdom of Jordon, I am pleased to have been a part of the effort to launch this timely volume and its critical recommendations to address the challenge of cancer in low and middle income countries. I am grateful for the commitment of each of the GTF.CCC co-Chairs, members and Secretariat, among others, to make the report a reality. This commitment transcends the words written herein on paper and serves to propel the wider movement for change, fueled with evidence and determination to act.

We celebrated the attention brought to cancer and other noncommunicable diseases at the United Nations High Level Meeting in September 2012. Hundreds of disparate groups spoke with one voice in their call for action by governments and world leaders. United, we challenged member states to end the gap between what we know saves lives and what we are willing to do to save them.

It was a significant moment in our fight.

We must end the inefficient use of global health investments. Our resources must be used to build health systems that serve people and all of our various health needs. Only then will we turn the tide of the cancer epidemic which threatens to claim 17 million of us every year by 2030.

If we fail, the cost in human and economic terms will be more devastating than the toll taken by any previous plague in human history. Failure, therefore, is not an option. Survivorship is the only option.

The progress we make today will save millions of lives in years to come. With this and future such efforts, we must continue our urgent calls for policy reform and effective investment. We must embrace the hope promised by our current successes. And we must stand together, calling for change with one powerful, indelible voice.

Lance Armstrong
Honorary co-President, GTF.CCC
Founder, LIVESTRONG, Lance Armstrong Foundation

August 15, 2012
Austin, Texas, USA

FOREWORDS

This volume of the Global Task Force on Expanded Access to Cancer Care and Control in Developing Countries (GTF.CC) promises much, and it delivers. If you believe that cancer is not a severe and growing problem in poor countries, your misconception will be corrected. If you suspect that programs to prevent, detect, diagnose and treat cancer are unaffordable in low and middle income countries, this volume will show the opposite. If you believe that high quality care is unattainable in non-affluent settings, examples in these pages will demonstrate that it is possible to deliver effective, high quality care even in relatively poor countries. This volume dispels every excuse for inaction against cancer in low and middle income countries, and it makes a powerful case that the time for action is now.

The Task Force lays the foundation for its case on three levels: the burden of cancer on health, disproportionately borne in low and middle income countries; the economic consequences of inaction, and the gains in productivity and income that follow from effective cancer prevention and treatment; and the inequity of circumstance that exposes those who live in economically disadvantaged settings to heightened risks of cancer and diminished chances of successful treatment. Rejecting any contradiction between disease-based approaches and strategies to improve the health system generally, the Task Force adopts a diagonal strategy, where improvements in cancer strategies and strengthening of the health system are mutually reinforcing. The approach proposed here is comprehensive, encompassing prevention, detection, diagnosis, treatment, survivorship, and palliation. The volume covers the spectrum of major cancer threats and leading opportunities for intervention, and it uses a combination of data, illustrative examples, and analysis to convey a persuasive and encouraging message: the burden of cancer in the world can be dramatically reduced if we are willing to do what it takes.

It will take a five-part strategy, outlined in these pages: first, innovation in delivery systems to get preventive services and treatment to those who need it; second, increased access to affordable vaccines, medications, and technologies; third, innovative financing mechanisms to make care accessible and affordable; fourth, strengthened analysis of evidence to inform decision making about cancer policies and practices; and fifth, leadership for a sustained and successful effort. As the volume demonstrates, virtually nothing is required that has not already been demonstrated somewhere in low and middle income countries. The global challenge is to make what has been proven somewhere available everywhere.

In 2007, an Institute of Medicine report on *Cancer Control Opportunities in Low and Middle Income Countries* called on international organizations, bilateral aid agencies, national agencies, and academic institutions all to contribute to a concerted effort to reduce the burden of cancer in the world. The goal is achievable. This volume of the Global Task Force serves as a valuable guide to all who are willing to do their part to convert the attainable reduction in cancer in low and middle income countries into a reality.

Harvey V. Fineberg, MD, PhD
President, Institute of Medicine

August 15, 2012
Washington, D.C.

The world in which we live is characterized by many terrible problems, but it also produces deeply enlightened and visionary attempts to tackle these adversities. The suffering and mortality that cancer causes around the globe are immense, and the fact that the disease is severely neglected in the poorer countries in the world makes it a monumental tragedy as well. There is much needless agony and preventable death that make the tragedy especially intense. What the massive global affliction demands is a well thought out and well planned response to the calamity that has gone unchallenged too long. In providing a sharply reasoned and powerfully analyzed volume on cancer care and control in the developing countries, the Global Task Force on Expanded Access to Cancer Care and Control in Developing Countries (GTF.CCC) has provided an extraordinarily important service to the suffering humanity. It is a great privilege for me to have the opportunity of welcoming this deeply informed volume that shows how we can reduce the human distress and the loss of lives that cancer causes in the developing world.

The Task Force is not only endowed with remarkable expertise, it is fortunate in having the leadership of Julio Frenk and Lawrence Corey as co-chairs, aided by Her Royal Highness Princess Dina Mired and Lance Armstrong as honorary co-Presidents. Their superb knowledge of the problems to be encountered, combined with their human understanding –to invoke David Hume's well-chosen expression– has helped to give clear-headed direction to the work of the Task Force. And that, along with the very insightful and penetrating research that the members of the team (with 115 authors and contributors) have done for this volume has made it a truly major step forward in dealing with an extremely difficult but urgent global problem.

The institutional affiliations on which this volume draws are, of course, stellar, with the Medical School and the School of Public Health at Harvard joining hands with Dana-Farber Cancer Institute, as well as Fred Hutch Cancer Research Center. The Harvard Global Equity Initiative, under its Director Felicia Knaul, has been able to play a valuable coordinating function in what is a new –and extremely fruitful– direction for the Initiative. Just as global problems arise from a combination of circumstances, and involve the shortcomings of many institutions, the solutions to these problems also call for coordinated efforts of experts in many different fields, drawing on a range of expertise that needs to be harnessed together. This the Task Force has done with great perspicacity and success.

The adversities of poverty are pervasively relevant to the curse of cancer, since people who also suffer from serious social deprivations are hit much harder by cancer. This happens in a variety of ways: through their lack of opportunity to have regular medical check ups; through their inability to arrange and pay for the needed diagnostics and to get professional medical advice; through the lack of means for securing appropriate treatment; through the unaffordability of expensive drugs (indeed sometimes any drugs at all); through the lack of freedom of the poor patient to withdraw from normal duties of job, family work or child care in order to concentrate on treatment and healing; and –not least– through the way unnecessary pain and agony are taken as inescapable in societies that have come to tolerate adversity as something that is impossible to overcome. But each one of these problems, this volume shows, can be addressed, with immense benefit to the quality of human life across the world.

This volume of the GTF.CCC has broken fresh ground in many different areas related to expanding access to medical care, and to related social support, to overcome, or at least blunt, the cruelty of a supremely powerful disease that causes so much misery and demise in every continent of the earth. New knowledge has been skillfully combined with better use of already known connections to provide a state-of-the-art answer to the agonizing question: What can we practically do to prevent the unnecessary agony and avoidable mortality caused by cancer in the developing countries?

Nothing is as heartening for humanity as the recognition that the terrifying problems we have to encounter can be met with astute answers. We cannot make the world perfectly just, but we certainly can do a lot more than is being done to make it far less unjust than it is. *Closing the Cancer Divide: An Equity Imperative* is a wonderful contribution in that positive and constructive direction.

Amartya Sen, PhD
Nobel Laureate, Economics, 1998
Lamont University Professor, Harvard University

August 10, 2012
Cambridge, MA

PROLOGUE

Closing the Cancer Divide: An Equity Imperative is devoted to demonstrating the many necessary, affordable and implementable opportunities that exist to reduce the burden of cancer in low and middle income countries (LMICs). Taking up these opportunities is a moral, equity, and economic imperative that will contribute to closing the cancer divide.

The history of this volume

"Expansion of cancer care and control in countries of low and middle income: a call to action," an article signed by the members of the Global Task Force on Expanded Access to Cancer Care and Control in Developing Countries (GTF.CCC)[1] was published by the Lancet in 2010. The paper argued that much could be done to prevent and treat cancer by deploying primary and secondary caregivers, using global financing mechanisms effectively, making off-patent drugs available and all drugs and inputs more affordable, and by using global and regional procurement mechanisms. Further, the paper asserted, increasing access to cancer care and control (CCC) can strengthen health systems to also meet the challenges of other diseases.

A report, on which this volume draws heavily, entitled *Closing the Cancer Divide: A Blueprint to Expand Access in Low and Middle Income Countries,*[2] was published by Harvard University through the Harvard Global Equity Initiative and on behalf of the GTF.CCC in October of 2011. The report presents the evidence that supports the case for expanded access to CCC, describes innovative models of financing and delivery for achieving this goal, and provides a blueprint for future action in resource constrained settings as part of broader efforts to strengthen health systems. Originally in English, the report is being made available in Spanish, Russian, and Arabic.

This volume extends and updates the work presented in that report.[3] It focuses on opportunities for expanded vaccination, secondary prevention, diagnosis, treatment, survivorship, and palliation. These topics have been underserved in both research and policy spheres. The need for continued and increased investment in population-based primary prevention programs associated with tobacco control, physical activity, and nutrition is emphasized throughout.

The research in this volume draws on the work of more than 144 authors and contributors, including members of the GTF.CCC and its Technical Advisory Committee, as well as patients and representatives of academic, civil society, private sector, multi-lateral and governmental institutions from countries at all resource levels. The work is an outcome of many discussions with members of the GTF.CCC and of international working meetings held in February, June, and November of 2010 and May of 2011. It is based on work with clinicians, researchers, policy makers, civil society organizations, private sector and patients in, or working with institutions from LMICs that span all regions of the developing world. The volume includes and summarizes information from 56 countries. While this is not an exhaustive account of the innovative projects and programs currently underway, it offers a large and encompassing sample and a wealth of lessons learned.

This book also draws on an extensive literature review based on more than 400 search terms (available in the web annex at gtfccc.harvard.edu) that uncovered some 2850 published reports, journal articles, books, and web-based information that are cited throughout the text. Several earlier reports provided the basis from which to develop much of the analysis in the book. This included the 2007 *"Cancer Control Opportunities in Low and Middle Income Countries"* report from the Institute of Medicine,[4] and the World Health Organization's *"Global Status Report on Noncommunicable Diseases 2010."*[5]

Organization of the volume

The information and research presented in this book is divided into three parts, each with a set of separately authored chapters:

Part I - MUCH SHOULD BE DONE;
Part II - MUCH COULD BE DONE; and,
Part III- MUCH CAN BE DONE.

The first part of the volume, "Much should be done," includes three chapters. The opening chapter introduces the volume and presents the overarching arguments that support a call for action to increase access to cancer care and control in LMICs. Chapter two demonstrates why preventing, treating, and palliating cancer is an equity imperative and reviews the global, epidemiological evidence. The third chapter identifies the significant economic costs of failure to increase investment in cancer care and control and in other noncommunicable (NCDs) diseases and chronic illnesses. It includes an analysis of avoidable mortality from cancer and the costs associated with this preventable loss of life.

The second part of the volume, "Much could be done," begins with chapter four, which describes the diagonal approach to health system strengthening across the CCC continuum –primary and secondary prevention, diagnosis, treatment, survivorship and palliation– with an emphasis on chronicity. Chapter four includes a hypothetical case study of a patient and the application of the diagonal approach across the CCC continuum. Chapter five outlines the possible strategies and key elements for CCC programs in LMICs focusing on those cancers which are most amenable to prevention, early detection, and treatment – the essential core of national cancer plans. This chapter includes a list of the essential anti-neoplastic agents required to treat adult and pediatric cancers in LMICs, the vast majority of which are off-patent.

The third part of the volume, "Much can be done," includes five chapters, each of which deals with a specific area of action related to strengthening health systems: delivery; pricing and procurement; global and national financing; evidence; and, stewardship and leadership. Chapter six reviews opportunities to innovate in delivery, especially on improved use of human resources and technology. This analysis is based on examples of projects undertaken by civil society and various ministries of health, often through international partnerships. Chapter seven provides an analysis of opportunities for improving access to vaccines, medicines and other health technologies in order to prevent and treat cancer by strengthening health systems and removing price and non-price barriers. The analysis demonstrates that treatments for several cancers are not financially onerous for individual health systems or globally. Financing, both global and national, is a major challenge for expanding access and this is taken up in chapter eight, which includes a set of case studies from LMICs that have implemented social insurance programs using domestic financing and cover treatment for at least some cancers. The critical issue of improving data, health information systems and research capacity is discussed in chapter nine. The final chapter reviews opportunities to renew stewardship and leadership capacity, both globally and within countries, building on the opportunities presented by the United Nations High Level Meeting on NCDs and the declaration that emerged from that meeting. The findings stress the benefits of involving all stakeholders, including the private sector, civil society, patients, academia, bilateral and global institutions, donor organizations, and national governments in implementing solutions to increase access to CCC.

Each chapter draws on global and national experiences, most of which are described in cases studies and text boxes. A summary of key messages is provided at the beginning of each chapter.

This volume is very much inspired by the experience of patients and opens with their stories. These include contributions from two young women who have lived with cancer in an LMIC and become outspoken advocates, striving to increase access for fellow patients.

Global Task Force on Expanded Access to Cancer Care and Control in Developing Countries

The mandate of the Global Task Force on Expanded Access to Cancer Care and Control in Developing Countries (GTF.CCC) is to design, promote, and evaluate innovative, multi-stakeholder strategies for expanding access to cancer prevention, detection, and care in LMICs. Working with local partners, the GTF.CCC participates in the design and implementation of innovative service delivery models to scale up access to CCC and to strengthen health systems in developing countries.

GTF.CCC brings together cancer and global health leaders from all regions of the world. It is directed from the Harvard Global Equity Initiative, the Harvard School of Public Health, the Harvard Medical School, the Fred Hutchinson Cancer Research Center and the University of Washington. Originally convened in 2009 by four Harvard-based institutions including the Dana-Farber Cancer Institute, the GTF.CCC forms a network of more than 30 leaders in the fields of cancer and global health. GTF.CCC also draws on more than 50 technical and strategic advisors, who serve on private sector engagement, strategic advisory and technical advisory committees. GTF.CCC includes researchers, members of civil society, patients and family members, and the private sector, in addition to clinicians and policy makers who contribute invaluable support for advocacy, research, and action.

Her Royal Highness Princess Dina Mired of the Hashemite Kingdom of Jordan and Lance Armstrong, founder of LIVESTRONG, serve as honorary co-Presidents of the GTF.CCC, which is chaired in its second phase by Drs. Larry Corey, President of the Fred Hutchinson Cancer Research Center, and Julio Frenk, Dean of the Harvard School of Public Health. The initiative is managed by a dual secretariat of staff based at the Harvard Global Equity Initiative and led by Dr. Felicia M Knaul, and at the Fred Hutchinson Cancer Research Center led by Dr. Julie R Gralow.

In addition to strongly supporting efforts to prevent the cancers of tomorrow by reducing risk factors, especially tobacco use, the GTF.CCC proposes and supports actions to improve treatment and palliation.

The GTF.CCC applies the knowledge and ability of its members, combining expertise in global health and cancer, to:

- Raise awareness of the impact of cancer on developing countries at the global, regional, and national levels through an evidence-based call-to-action;

- Expand the stewardship and evidence base for implementing the most efficient approaches to CCC in low and middle income countries;

- Dentify suitable packages of essential services and treatments to provide care in low-resource settings for cancers that can be cured or palliated with currently available therapies;

- Reduce human suffering from all cancers by promoting universal access to pain control and palliation, and increased access to the best treatment for cancer through the procurement of affordable quality assured drugs and services;

- Support development and implementation of multi-sectoral, multi-stake-holder plans to expand access to CCC through health systems that provide comprehensive health coverage;

- Develop and evaluate innovative service delivery models that effectively utilize existing human, physical and technological resources in different economic and health system settings, and to share the lessons and evidence gained.

The GTF.CCC is predicated on the conviction that solutions to access barriers exist and that the reasons for scaling-up cancer care rapidly are compelling enough to merit an immediate and vigorous global response. Many of these solutions can be built into existing programs and platforms by harnessing health systems and involving multiple stakeholders.

Using the evidence garnered for its *Closing the Cancer Divide*[vi] report, GTF.CCC developed a series of recommendations with global implications for resource-constrained settings. The overarching recommendations are presented below. The full report includes a detailed review and list of specific actions.

1. PROMOTE prevention policies that reduce cancer risk.

2. EXPAND access across the cancer care control continuum through universal financial protection for health, an explicit package of guaranteed benefits, and efficient use of all levels of care.

3. STRENGTHEN national health systems to effectively respond to cancer and other chronic illness by integrating interventions into existing programs and institutions and by translating evidence into policy through strong information systems, research, and monitoring and evaluation frameworks.

4. LEVERAGE global institutions and in particular those that could offer financing, pricing and procurement, evidence generation, capacity building, and stewardship and leadership for cancer care and control.

5. MOBILIZE all public and private stakeholders in the cancer arena, through new and existing global and national forums and networks dedicated to improving health outcomes and equity.

Felicia Marie Knaul, MA, PhD
Director, Harvard Global Equity Initiative
Associate Professor of Medicine, Harvard Medical School
Founder, Tómatelo a Pecho, A.C.

Julie R. Gralow, MD
Director, Breast Medical Oncology, Seattle Cancer Care Alliance
Jill Bennett Endowed Professor of Breast Cancer, University of Washington School of Medicine
Full Member, Fred Hutchinson Cancer Research Center

Rifat Atun, MBBS, MRCGP, MBA, DIC, MFPHM
Professor of International Health Management, Imperial College London

Afsan Bhadelia, MS
Research Associate and former Research Director, Harvard Global Equity Initiative

DEDICATION

To Amanda Jaclyn Berger

Amanda devoted herself to the cause of global equity and health. She was a tireless force and source of insight, spirit, inspiration and kindness.

At the time of her tragic passing on April 14th, 2012 at the age of 25, she was pursuing her Masters Degree in Public Health at the London School of Hygiene and Tropical Medicine (LSHTM). Her thesis was to be dedicated to improving capacity of Mexican nursing and medical students in early detection of breast cancer and in promoting breast health – a project that emerged directly out of the research in this volume.

Amanda began as an enthusiastic intern and then became Research Assistant at the Harvard Global Equity Initiative where she worked with the Global Task Force on Expanded Access to Cancer Care and Control in Developing Countries (GTF.CCC) in 2010 and 2011. The Report *Closing the Cancer Divide: A Blueprint to Expand Access in Low and Middle Income Countries* was largely her work as she contributed to each chapter and to all aspects of the research. Most importantly, she directed and personally undertook all of the background literature review that uncovered almost 2850 publications and generated a library of materials on cancer in low and middle income countries that will serve as a key input for research and policy for many years to come. The breadth and depth of this review serves as example of her promise and capacity as a young researcher, but also of her dedication to quality in all the work she undertook. She also wrote several of the background cases and edited and reviewed each and every section of the Report and took part in producing the original versions of many of the chapters in this volume. Her contributions were always insightful, keeping perspective of the overall goal –help those most in need– and all her work demonstrated a love of learning and meticulous attention to detail.

Dedicated forever to the cause of expanding access to cancer care and control in developing regions, Amanda continued to work with the GTF.CCC while undertaking her degree and in December 2011 was instrumental in the launch of *Closing the Cancer Divide: A Blueprint to Expand Access in Low and Middle Income Countries* at LSHTM.

Amanda dreamed. One of her dreams was of doing an internship at the World Health Organization in Geneva in the Summer of 2012 on women's cancer as the next stage of her work on global health equity.

Amanda was a person who always gave and supported others through tiring and difficult moments both as a friend and as a colleague. There were many, many wee hours of the morning when she worked to make the *Closing the Cancer Divide: A Blueprint to Expand Access in Low and Middle Income Countries* and hence this book into a reality.

Her dedication to global health was inspired in great part by a moment when she, working with GTF.CCC, came very close to perceiving suffering and peace in death. She wrote of a visiting a Bedouin dying of cancer in an open tent and resting on the ground and how through the Ben Gurion University of the Negev it was possible to offer palliative care. This was one of the experiences that cemented her decision to dedicate her career to global health.

Amanda demonstrated a maturity uncommon at such a young age and continually sought knowledge to guide her on her quest to help those in need. Her energetic spirit and genuine compassion touched all of her colleagues on a daily basis. She had a certain sparkle and it was rare to not be uplifted by her presence as she radiated light, brilliance and much kindness. Her delightful humor was sure to bring a smile on any day. All who worked with her and counted her as a friend, and indeed the many who have and will benefit from her work yet will never have the opportunity to meet her, are fortunate to be illuminated by this light.

We can only think of how much more we wished we had given to Amanda. She is the quintessential example of a person to whom one always wanted to have given more and taken less. This is a wonderful way to be remembered – as a person who gave and to whom others wanted to have given more.

As often happens in journeys with disease and with losses, it is a child that provides comfort and insight for the unexplainable. Speaking of losing Amanda, a child she had befriended said: I think God needed an Angel and that there was no one better than Amanda to be God's Angel.

May Amanda's memory be forever a blessing to us all. May it guide us in our efforts to improve the fate of the many who struggle with illness and disease. This was and is her calling and for this reason the authors and all who worked with Amanda, dedicate this volume, **Closing the Cancer Divide: An Equity Imperative**, to her memory.

EDITOR'S ACKNOWLEDGEMENTS

As the editors of this volume, we offer our thanks to the members of the GTF.CCC and its Technical Advisory, Private Sector Engagement and Strategic Advisory Committees, and especially to Honorary co-Presidents HRH Princess Dina Mired of the Hashemite Kingdom of Jordan and Lance Armstrong, co-Chairs Drs. Julio Frenk and Lawrence Corey, and former co-Chair Dr. Lawrence Shulman for their dedication, encouragement, investment, and belief in this project.

We are most grateful to those who worked with us especially closely in preparing the report that guided this book: Julio Frenk, George Alleyne, Paul Farmer, Mary Gospodarowicz, Nancy Keating, Ana Langer, Peter Piot, Peggy Porter, Jonathan Quick, Magdalena Rathe, Rocio Saenz, and David Scheer.

It is impossible to adequately express our thanks in these short paragraphs to staff, based at the Harvard Global Equity Initiative and the Department of Global Health and Social Medicine of the Harvard Medical School and the Fred Hutchinson Cancer Research Center, and our collaborators at the Mexican Health Foundation and Tómatelo a Pecho. They include Héctor Arreola-Ornelas, Kathy Cahill, Grace Cho, Isabel Davis, Emily Durrant, Ana Cecilia Hidalgo, Debra Keaney, Oscar Méndez, Gustavo Nigenda, Sonia Xochitl Ortega, Maja Pleic, Jennifer Puccetti, Abish Romero Juarez, as well as collaborators Zaid Bitar from the King Hussein Cancer Foundation and Claire Neal of the Lance Armstrong Foundation. Our personal thanks also to all those listed in the Acknowledgments and the supporting institutions, and especially Harvard University. We are also very grateful to Harvard University Press and particularly Mary Ann Lane for her ongoing guidance and support. For making this publication possible in all its components and especially the tedious details, our gratitude to Oliver Gantner and the staff of arte i diseño for design and layout of the publication, and to Mary Hager for invaluable work editing the volume with patience and care. Further, our sincerest thanks to Imara Roychowdhury and Ali Carter for research assistance, particularly on reference review and proof reading each of the chapters. We also extend our gratitude to Jenny Diaz, Danielle Rodin, and Erin Ross for timely and crucial support during the final stages of the publication process.

The Task Force also recognizes with great respect and admiration the work of the many patients whose experiences provided invaluable insights, as well as that of the healthcare providers based in LMICs who struggle daily to expand access to CCC in resource constrained environments. On behalf of the members of the GTF.CCC, we further thank each and every one of the many people and institutions that contributed to making this book a reality, especially those who did so while facing the adverse effects of illness.

Closing the Cancer Divide: An Equity Imperative is dedicated to the memory of Amanda Jaclyn Berger who died tragically on April 14th, 2012 at the age of 25, just a few months after the launch of the report *Closing the Cancer Divide: A Blueprint to Expand Access in Low and Middle Income Countries*, a work that was made possible by her unflinching dedication and inspiration.

1. Global Task Force on Expanded Access to Cancer Care and Control in Developing Countries – http://gtfccc.harvard.edu.
2. Knaul F, Frenk J, Shulman L for the Global Task Force on Expanded Access to Cancer Care and Control in Developing Countries. Closing the cancer divide: a blueprint to expand access in low and middle income countries. Harvard Global Equity Initiative, Harvard University, Boston, MA, October 2011.
3. Ibid.
4. Sloan FA, Gelband H (Eds.). Cancer control opportunities in low-and middle-income countries. Washington DC: National Academy Press, 2007.
5. World Health Organization. Global Status Report on noncommunicable diseases 2010. Geneva, Switzerland; World Health Organization, 2011.
6. Knaul F, Frenk J, Shulman L, 2011.

Much should be done

Part I

Chapter 1

CLOSING THE CANCER DIVIDE: OVERVIEW AND SUMMARY

Felicia Marie Knaul, Julie R. Gralow, Rifat Atun,
Afsan Bhadelia, Julio Frenk, Jonathan Quick,
Lawrence Shulman, Paul Farmer

1.i Introduction

The burden of increasingly prevalent noncommunicable diseases (NCDs) is a largely unrecognized challenge for low and middle income countries (LMICs). This burden is layered onto the backlog of infectious diseases and preventable maternal deaths driven by abject poverty and underdevelopment.[1] Yet, health systems in developing regions are largely unprepared to respond to this confluence of challenges.

Cancer epitomizes the complexities and inequities of the epidemiologic challenge faced by LMICs. Both a cause and an effect of poverty, cancer also poses a substantial challenge to economic and human development. The long-term disability and ongoing costs of cancer impoverish families and health systems while worsening social exclusion and diminishing overall well-being.

There are glaring disparities in the way cancers affect rich and poor. Unbalanced nutritional intake, limited educational opportunities, and lack of access to health care services expose the poor to increased risk of cancer. Death from preventable and treatable cancers, as well as the pain, suffering, and stigma associated with the disease, are concentrated among the poor. These disparities constitute an unacceptable cancer divide; an issue of equity that must be addressed by increased access to prevention, care, and treatment.

The first section of this introductory chapter provides an overview of the findings of this volume. The second section presents some of the arguments against expanding access to cancer care and control (CCC) in LMICs. These arguments helped prevent an adequate global response to cancer as well as to other chronic and NCDs. The third section summarizes the epidemiological and economic evidence in favor of action to close the cancer divide – the idea that much should be done. The fourth section provides an overview of the diagonal approach to health systems strengthening and a framework for national cancer planning in LMICs, which includes a summary of high-priority cancers and interventions. This summary motivates the argument that much could be done. The final section briefly summarizes all that can be done: the recommended spheres of action in delivery, pricing and procurement, financing, evidence and research, and stewardship and leadership.

This book presents recent evidence that supports the case for expanded access to CCC, describes innovative models for achieving this goal, and provides a blueprint for future action in resource-constrained settings as part of efforts to strengthen health systems. The volume draws heavily on *Closing the Cancer Divide: A Blueprint to Expand Access in Low and Middle Income Countries*, produced by the Global Task Force on Expanded Access to Cancer Care and Control in Developing Countries (GTF.CCC).[2]

1.ii Myths and opportunities

The evidence presented in this volume demonstrates that there are significant opportunities to reduce the burden of cancer in LMICs via affordable and pragmatic measures. Acting on these opportunities is a moral, equity, and economic imperative that will contribute to closing the cancer divide.

Yet myths persist that meeting the challenge of cancer in LMICs –with the exception of some basic prevention– is: (1) unnecessary, (2) unaffordable, (3) unattainable, and (4) inappropriate because such an effort would take resources away from other pressing development priorities. Evidence disproves these four myths, and is presented in the panel below:

Cancer care and control – well-focused and appropriate to the needs of LMICs is:

Necessary because cancer is a health priority (Chapter 2):

- There is a misperception that the burden of cancer is not large in LMICs and therefore does not warrant global action, yet each year over half of all new cancer cases and two-thirds of cancer deaths occur in these countries.

- Tobacco use, which accounts for at least 30% of all cancer deaths, will kill an estimated one billion people in the 21st century – the vast majority in LMICs, where 80% of current smokers live.

- Breast cancer is the second leading cause of death among Mexican women aged 30-54.

- For children aged 5-14, cancer is the third leading cause of death in upper-middle, fourth in lower-middle, and eighth in low income countries.

- Just two cancers –breast and cervical– account for almost the same number of deaths among women in reproductive age in LMICs as does death in pregnancy and childbirth.

- 50-60% of cancer mortality in LMICs could be averted with country-specific strategies for prevention and treatment.

Affordable, with a high return on investment (Chapters 3 and 5):

- The global value of lost productivity from cancer far outstrips the estimated cost of prevention and treatment.

- Tobacco use alone reduces gross domestic product by as much as 3.6% per year. Between 2020 and 2030, the global economic costs of tobacco use are expected to double. Accelerated implementation of tobacco control would cost less than US$ 0.16 per person per year for countries like China and India.

✦ Many CCC interventions are less costly than assumed: 26 of the 29 key agents for treating many of the most prevalent, treatable cancers in LMICs are off-patent. For most drugs, treatment is relatively low cost at less than US$ 100 per course. The total cost of covering drug treatments for unmet needs for cervical cancer, Hodgkins lymphoma, and acute lymphoblastic leukemia in children 0-14 in LMICs is approximately US$ 115 million.

✦ There are successful examples of expanding access to innovative vaccines and treatments: the prices of human papilloma virus (HPV) and Hepatitis B vaccines have been reduced by up to 90% in some low income countries.

✦ Only 5% of global spending on cancer occurs in LMICs, although these countries account for almost 80% of the global cancer burden.

Possible even in resource-constrained settings (Chapter 6-10):

✦ Early detection programs for breast and cervical cancer can be integrated into anti-poverty, maternal and child health, sexual and reproductive health, and HIV/AIDS programs. These improve women's health across the life course and beyond reproduction.

✦ The King Hussein Cancer Center in Jordan is Joint Commission-certified as a specialty treatment center.

✦ Telemedicine has been effectively used to expand capacity for treatment of cancer, especially children's cancers, in LMICs. In El Salvador, links between St. Jude hospital in Memphis and local hospitals helped achieve an increase in survival rates for children with acute lymphoblastic leukemia from 10% to 60% during the first five years of collaboration.

✦ Global partnerships in cancer pathology can provide immediate and critical interim support alongside efforts to build local infrastructure and human resource capacity.

❧ In extremely resource-poor settings such as Haiti, Malawi, and Rwanda, primary and secondary care providers and facilities with no on-site oncologist can safely provide some chemotherapy with links to specialists and specialty centers.

❧ Since including childhood cancers in *Seguro Popular* in Mexico to eliminate financial barriers to accessing treatment, 30-month survival has increased from approximately 30% to almost 70%.

❧ For the estimated 5.5 million terminal cancer patients who needlessly suffer moderate to severe pain with no pain control, effective national programs can increase availability and accessibility of this essential and inexpensive intervention.

❧ Around 50-60% of cancer mortality in LMICs can be averted through country-specific strategies for prevention and treatment.

Appropriate and complementary to investment in other health priorities (Chapter 3, 4 and 6-10):

❧ Expanding CCC can strengthen health systems and increase capacity to benefit all populations. An example is pain control, which is crucial for many patients, including an estimated 5.5 million terminal cancer patients.

❧ As mentioned in the previous section, early detection programs for breast and cervical cancer can be readily integrated into existing health and development initiatives.

❧ Since including childhood cancers in *Seguro Popular* in Mexico to eliminate financial barriers to accessing treatment, adherence to treatment has increased significantly.

❧ The distinctions between communicable and noncommunicable disease are increasingly irrelevant. Many cancers that burden LMICs are associated with infections: Kaposi sarcoma (HIV/AIDS); cervical cancer (human papilloma virus); liver cancer (hepatitis B); gastric cancer (H. pylori); and bladder cancer (schistosomiasis).

❧ Failure to protect populations from preventable health risks associated with cancer and other chronic illness will hinder economic development and efforts to reach many Millennium Development Goals (MDGs).

Indeed, these four myths are familiar to the global health community because they were the arguments used only a decade ago as justifications for inaction on HIV/AIDS. Fortunately, each of the myths was dispelled, and HIV has been transformed from an acute and fatal disease to a chronic illness effectively managed in a large number of LMICs.[3]

The evidence presented in this volume proves that these myths also do not apply for many cancers and for many types of interventions for combating cancer. Control of risk factors and prevention of cancer are of the highest priority in LMICs. Effective low-cost treatment, financial protection programs, and innovative care delivery and pain control models exist and can be applied in resource-constrained settings to address cancer. Indeed, many of these findings also apply to a broad range of NCDs and chronic illnesses.

Developing programs to meet the challenge of cancer and other chronic and NCDs in low-resource settings is especially complex due to the diversity of cancers, the special procedures needed for diagnosis, and the many specialists and medications required for treating them.

Despite these complexities, many opportunities exist for reducing cancer incidence, improving survival and survivorship, and offering better palliative care.[4] This book focuses on these compelling opportunities and on evidence for successful approaches that can enable scale-up of cancer services in LMICs. This steers policy toward all that can be accomplished at different resource levels, rather than stressing what cannot be done.

This volume is in the spirit of the 2011 High-level Meeting of the General Assembly of the United Nations on the Prevention and Control of Noncommunicable Diseases (UNHLM on NCDs), which set the stage for the action that is required to reduce global inequities in access and outcomes for cancer as well as other NCDs. The Declaration positioned NCDs as a priority for both development and health.[5]

Although the Declaration stressed the importance of research, international cooperation and trade, it fell short of establishing targets and goals for reducing the burden of NCDs. It did, however, set out a number of specific short-term tasks. These include the development of a comprehensive global monitoring framework that includes voluntary global targets and national indicators, proposals for carrying forward multisectoral action by the end of 2012; the strengthening of multisectoral national policies by 2013, and the production of a report on these commitments by 2014.[6] Indeed, the World Health Organization (WHO) recommendation for a 25% reduction in premature deaths from NCDs by 2025 was adopted as a voluntary, overarching target by the World Health Assembly in May 2012. Still, the specific targets that would make this overall goal attainable were not agreed on and continue to be the subject of international negotiation.[7]

The road from commitment to success requires sustained evidence generation and advocacy. Indeed, ongoing efforts by entities established around the UNHLM continue to generate results. NCD Child, for example, is invigorating entities such as UNICEF to take up this neglected cause in children. The Task Force on NCD and Women's Health, conceived at the UNHLM, continues to integrate these two communities and apply a gender perspective to the NCD policy, research, and practice dialogue.

This book seeks to contribute to the global milestones set in the Declaration of the UNHLM on NCDs and stresses the need to identify, develop, evaluate, and scale-up evidence-based policies through an inclusive multi-stakeholder process. The proposals in this book include actions specific to cancer that can concurrently further the agenda on NCDs and chronic illnesses, especially in establishing a global monitoring framework and partnerships for multisectoral action.

Advocacy for increased access to CCC in LMICs need not –and should not– jeopardize other health priorities.[8] Cancer care, and the effective communication of the outcomes of that care, has the potential to catalyze the NCD agenda and to invigorate advocacy and activism around diseases and issues that, in contrast to HIV/AIDS, have failed to create a sense of urgency.[9-11] Advocacy around cancer has successfully galvanized communities through movements led by patients and their families[12] and mobilized stakeholders in unique ways that can be leveraged to bridge the false divide between communicable diseases and NCDs. The approaches proposed in this book design CCC in ways that reinforce health systems to simultaneously meet the challenge of NCDs and promote broad economic and human development.

Controlling risk factors must be at the core of any NCD control effort in LMICs. A set of high-priority, effective, and low-cost interventions must be immediately put in place to avoid an impending NCD crisis and its attendant negative impact on social, economic, and human development. Tobacco control is a key priority and requires an accelerated implementation of the WHO Framework Convention on Tobacco Control (FCTC) as indicated in the Declaration of the UNHLM on NCDs. In addition, preventing harmful alcohol use and promoting healthy diets and physical activity must be established as priorities for LMICs.[13-15]

At the same time, managing risk factors will not be sufficient to effectively meet the challenge of cancer in LMICs. Indeed, the risk factors for many cancers are not well established, especially in the case of childhood cancers. It brings to mind a lesson from the early years of the HIV/AIDS epidemic: "The belief that treatment may be reserved for those in wealthy countries whereas prevention is the lot of the poor might be less repugnant if we had highly effective preventive measures."[16] The HIV/AIDS movement successfully fought these, and other, unfounded arguments about the affordability of treating AIDS in LMICs. In fact, expanded access to prevention and care for HIV/AIDS has to be considered one of the greatest achievements in the history of global health. Thus, in addition to prevention efforts and risk factor reduction, this book calls for immediate action around early detection, diagnosis, treatment, and palliation.

1.iii Much should be done: The cancer divide

The cancer landscape has changed dramatically in less than a generation. While the challenge of cancer is far from met, many cancers which were once considered death sentences can today be prevented or cured. For many people, cancer is now a chronic illness, one that they live with rather than die from. With a large proportion of patients surviving both the disease and the treatment to enjoy a healthy life, a flourishing survivorship movement has helped reduce the stigma of the "C" word.

The gains in survival and the reductions in stigma are revolutionary for a disease that, not so long ago, was synonymous with suffering, stigma, and death.[17] Yet, the opportunity to survive and the reduction in the hardships faced in trying to do so are far from universal, enjoyed primarily by wealthy countries and individuals. However, in 2008, LMICs were home to more than 55% of the 12.7 million cancer cases and 64% of the 7.6 million cancer deaths in the world.[18] By 2030, LMICs will bear the brunt of an estimated 27 million new cancer cases and 17 million cancer deaths.[19-21] The same is true of NCDs overall. For women aged 15-49 living in sub-Saharan Africa, death or disability from an NCD is four times more likely than for women who live in high income countries.[22,23]

Increasing access to CCC in LMICs is an equity imperative. While the better off are often able to live with cancer, the poor die –painfully– from the same diseases. A "protracted and polarized epidemiologic transition" –through which populations simultaneously face emerging chronic and NCDs while still battling other diseases traditionally associated with poverty and underdevelopment– is also occurring with cancer.[24] This cancer transition is widening the divide between rich and poor (Chapter 2).

Preventable cancers such as cervical, liver, and lung cancers, that are declining in incidence in high income countries, are almost universally poorly controlled in LMICs. As policies to reduce risk factors, provide access to vaccination, and emphasize early detection become universal in high income countries, the burden of these cancers in LMICs will become more pronounced. This backlog of preventable yet unaddressed cancers, combined with the burden of cancers that cannot be prevented, generates a double cancer burden for LMICs.

The disparity in cancer outcomes between rich and poor –which we refer to as the cancer divide– directly relates to inequities in access to health care and to differences in underlying socio-economic, nutritional, environmental, and health conditions (Chapter 2).[25] The cancer divide is fueled by the higher levels of preventable risk, disease, suffering, impoverishment from ill health, and death among poor populations. Further, the divide is likely to continue to widen and deepen over the coming decades if the fruits of modern medicine are not available to LMICs.

Five facets of the unacceptable cancer divide are further elaborated in Chapter 2:

i.   Risk factors associated with cancers amenable to prevention through behavior change (e.g., smoking and lung cancer) or reduced exposure to environmental risk (e.g., indoor air pollution and lung cancer).

ii. Preventable infections for which no vaccine exists that are associated with cancer (e.g., HIV/AIDS and Kaposi sarcoma) and infections that can be prevented through vaccination or detected and controlled in pre-cancerous stages (HPV and cervical cancer).

iii. Cancers for which treatment exists and is often made more effective by early detection (e.g., breast cancer).

iv. Suffering associated with the social and psychological aspects of disease or survivorship, including discrimination and stigma.

v.   Pain and physical suffering associated with all cancers, including those for which neither effective treatment nor prevention is possible.

Access to services, state-of-the-art treatment, advocacy, and financial protection create an environment in rich countries where healthy survivorship is now possible for patients with many cancers. The opposite is true in LMICs where cancer is often considered a death sentence and the stigma around the disease and the effects of treatment –compounded by discrimination associated with gender, ethnicity, and socio-economic status– too often prevent care-seeking, almost guaranteeing a fatal outcome even when cure is feasible.

Pain control, an issue common to all cancers and many other diseases, offers the most distressing and insidious example of the cancer divide. Controllable pain is considered unacceptable in most high income countries, at least for the wealthy. Despite the generally low cost of pain control, many populations lack access to this fundamental health intervention, one which should be considered a basic human right.

When quantified, these disparities are appalling (Table 1). For the poorest decile of countries, the average mortality rate for adult women from cervical cancer –which is highly preventable if detected in pre-cancerous stages– is 36 compared to 3 per 100,000 adult women in the richest decile of countries. Approximately 90% of cervical cancer occurs in LMICs. More than half of women who develop breast cancer in LMICs die, compared to less than a quarter of women in the developed world. In Canada, roughly 90% of children with acute lymphoblastic leukemia are cured, but the inverse is true in the poorest countries of the world: more than 90% of children will die of the disease. High income countries account for less than 15% of the world population, yet more than 94% of global morphine consumption for pain control.[26] In 2008, Sub-Saharan Africa recorded 1.3 million deaths in pain and yet uses enough medicinal opioids to treat just 85,000 people.[27,28] Patients who die in pain from cancer or AIDS-associated illness in the poorest decile receive only 54 milligrams of opioid per death; patients in the richest decile receive almost 97,400 milligrams per death in pain.

The differences within income regions, however, are also significant. The level of economic development is not the only determinant of outcomes or access. Some countries, despite low income, are better able to meet the challenge of cancer than others. For example, 90% of children are likely to die from childhood cancers in the low income countries with the worst outcomes, compared to 40% in the low income countries where treatment options are more readily available.

The cancer divide is also large across different geographical regions of LMICs. In the African region, all of the averages are relatively poor. In Asia, the spread in the indicators is especially large for cervical, breast, and childhood cancers. In Latin America and the Caribbean, differences in cervical cancer mortality are high and lethality varies by a factor of more than 2 for childhood cancers. For pain control, there is less variation, but the average level even for the countries with the highest consumption is only 6,600 milligrams per death in pain from cancer or HIV/AIDS-associated illness.

Table 1.1

Cervical Cancer Mortality, Ratio of Mortality to Incidence for Childhood and Breast Cancer, and Non-methodone Opioid Consumption per Death from HIV/AIDS or Cancer in Pain; Averages by Income and Geographic Region.

			Cervical cancer[b] (15 or more years of age)	All cancers in children (0-14 years of age)[b]	Breast cancer (40 - 69 years of age)[b]	Non-methadone opioid consumption[c] (morphine-equivalents)
			Mortality (rate per 100,000)	Mortality/ Incidence	Mortality/ Incidence	Per death from HIV or cancer in pain (mg)c
	Decile 1 (poorest 10% of countries)		36	0.80	0.60	54
	Decile 10 (most wealthy 10% of countries)		3	0.28	0.25	97,396
Country Income	Low income	Average of Bottom 5	57	0.9	0.7	31
		Average of Top 5	6	0.42	0.35	522
	Lower middle income	Average of Bottom 5	35	0.98	0.64	148
		Average of Top 5	1	0.29	0.30	4,716
	Upper middle income	Average of Bottom 5	24	0.88	0.56	964
		Average of Top 5	4	0.19	0.25	8,970
	High income	Average of Bottom 5	16	0.83	0.61	7,456
		Average of Top 5	1	0.05	0.14	150,869
Geographic Region	Africa	Average of Bottom 5	57	0.93	0.66	19
		Average of Top 5	13	0.69	0.47	1,724
	Asiad	Average of Bottom 5	25	0.94	0.58	358
		Average of Top 5	7	0.42	0.25	9,656
	Eastern Mediterranean[d]	Average of Bottom 5	15	0.82	0.62	422
		Average of Top 5	2	0.71	0.45	7,136
	Europe[d]	Average of Bottom 5	16	0.61	0.53	330
		Average of Top 5	5	0.20	0.30	11,332
	Latin America and the Caribbean[d]	Average of Bottom 5	29	0.68	0.39	748
		Average of Top 5	10	0.30	0.25	6,612

a) World Development Indicators, 2008. World Bank.
(http://data.worldbank.org/data-catalog/world-development-indicators/).

b) Source for cervical cancer mortality 15+; M/I cancers in 0-14; M/I breast cancer 40-69; and M/I NHL 15+ Globocan 2008; http://globocan.iarc.fr/. Taken directly from the online data base.

c) Source for opioid consumption per capita and per HIV or cancer deaths: GAPRI methodology available at (http://www.treatthepain.com/methodology) and University of Wisconsin Pain & Policy Studies Group (http://www.painpolicy.wisc.edu/). See Appendix 1, Section 2 of the full Report and full GAPRI methodology available at (http://www.treatthepain.com/methodology).
    dExcluding high-income countries.

d) Including high income countries.

These differences between rich and poor are hardly surprising. LMICs account for 80% of global cancer burden in terms of years of life lost, yet only 5% of global spending on cancer is in LMICs.[29,30] Inequitable funding means LMICs face a severe shortage of human and physical infrastructure to confront cancer.[31-34] In Honduras, for example, fewer than twenty oncologists serve a country with a population of eight million. In Ethiopia, four oncologists care for more than 80 million people.[35] High income countries account for 70% of the world's cancer radiotherapy facilities. Thirty countries, fifteen of them in Africa, do not have a single radiation therapy machine. These inequities tend to disproportionately affect women, who constitute the majority of patients requiring radiotherapy.[36] Similar shortages are faced in other specialty services that are essential to treat cancer, such as pathology.[37]

Treating health care as an investment rather than a cost is now a predominant philosophy that inspires human, economic, and environmental development agendas (Chapter 3). Human life and well-being have intrinsic and immeasurable value. Illness, especially chronic and catastrophic diseases such as cancer, cause much human suffering, drive families into poverty, reduce productivity, and detract from economic growth and human development.[38] Failure to protect populations from preventable health risks associated with chronic illness will inevitably and severely detract from both economic development and social well-being.[39] Still, this investment framework remains largely ignored in global and national policymaking surrounding cancer and other chronic illness.

Cancer, chronic illness, and NCDs are both an outcome and a cause of poverty. According to Amartya Sen, "The poorest groups not only bear higher risks for noncommunicable diseases but, once they develop such a disease, they also face larger medical and economic adversity. The poor have less resources and less access to medical care, and often have delayed diagnosis. Diseases like cancer tend, as a result, to progress to more advanced states than in the case of the rich, and this leads to higher levels of mortality and disability. The costs and economic handicaps related to these diseases are also a major cause for tipping already poorer households further into abject poverty."[40]

The cancer divide will further worsen economic disparities between and within countries. Each year, the nearly 13 million new cases of cancer in the world create an enormous burden, both in years of life lost and human suffering, as well as in economic terms.[41] The economic consequences of each cancer case include the direct and indirect costs of treatment, the income forgone by patients and their families as a result of being unable to work during treatment, and, most importantly, the lost productivity of the patient and the family from premature death and disability and the demands of care-giving that often fall hardest on young women. The World Economic Forum (WEF), which considers chronic diseases one of the three leading global economic risks based on their potential impact on global productivity and economic growth,[42] cautions against taking a short-term view of the benefits of investing in chronic disease prevention and management.[43]

Tobacco is a huge economic risk for LMICs. Tobacco's estimated US$ 500 billion drain –mainly from tobacco-related illness and treatment costs– exceeds the total annual health expenditure of all LMICs combined. Tobacco's total economic costs reduce gross domestic product by as much as 3.6% per year. And the trend is grim: from 2020-2030, the global annual economic costs of tobacco-related illness are expected to reach US$ 1 trillion.[44]

This book identifies a subset of cancers that can be prevented or treated successfully in low-resource settings using current knowledge and medical advances. Between 2.4 and 3.7 million deaths from cancer could be avoided each year with effective prevention and treatment.[45] LMICs account for approximately 80% of these deaths, many of which occur in women and children. Overall, 50-60% of cancer mortality in LMICs is avoidable, compared to 35% in high income countries.

The total cost of lost productivity due to premature death and disability from cancer in the world is estimated at US$ 921 billion,[46] based on the total Disability Adjusted Life Years (DALYs) lost and the value of lost individual productivity from early death. The global economic cost of new cancer cases, including medical costs, prevention costs, the time of caregivers, transportation to treatment facilities, and prevention is US$ 310 billion dollars.[47]

Using a Value of Statistical Life (VSL) approach, the value that individuals place on lost income, out-of-pocket spending on health, and pain and suffering is US$ 2.5 trillion – more than 4% of global GDP.[48] A more conservative estimate, combining costs of treatment and productivity losses, places the total annual economic cost of cancer at close to US$ 1.16 trillion, approximately 2% of total global GDP. This figure does not include the substantial longer-term costs to patients, families and caregivers that are not directly related to the treatment period. (All US$ amounts are as of 2010).

Regardless of which estimate is used, the economic value of the human life (the value of lost years of healthy, productive life to both the economy and the individual) that could be saved far exceeds the cost of effective CCC. A reasonable estimate of what the world could have saved in 2010, based on the economic value of lost DALYs and by investing in CCC, is between US$ 100 and US$ 200 billion. Potential savings are much higher – over US$ 500 billion and up to almost US$ 1 trillion – taking into account the individual perception of the value of lost life and human suffering.

The estimated total economic burden from NCDs and cancer far exceed health costs experienced from other diseases, including those from HIV/AIDS, tuberculosis and malaria.[49] Yet the cost of implementing a core set of NCD interventions is comparatively low. The cost of reducing risk factors such as tobacco use and harmful alcohol use is estimated at US$ 2 billion per year for all LMICs – less than US$ 0.40 per person. Including a limited set of individual cancer interventions (for example, Hepatitis B immunization to prevent liver cancer and measures to prevent cervical cancer), the cost increases to US$ 9.4 billion per year. Overall, this amounts to an annual per capita investment that is less than US$ 1 in low income, US$ 1.50 in lower-middle income, and US$ 3 in upper-middle income countries.[50]

There has been success in achieving reductions in prices of key vaccines for infections that underpin many cancers. For example, the price of Hepatitis B vaccine declined from a launch price in 1982 of over US$ 100 per dose to US$ 0.20, enabling LMICs to dramatically increase vaccination rates with support from the Global Alliance for Vaccines and Immunizations (GAVI). Similarly, the price of human papilloma virus (HPV) vaccine declined from US$ 32 per dose in 2010 to US$ 14 per dose in 2011 for eligible countries. GAVI was able to achieve further reductions in June 2011 when Merck offered the vaccine at US$ 5 per dose for low income countries[51] (Chapter 7).

Expanding coverage of prevention, detection, and treatment, especially in LMICs, requires additional investment. The evidence presented here demonstrates that this investment will be more than compensated for by the projected reductions in the economic burden of the disease.

1.iv Much could be done: A solution-oriented framework

The growing burden of chronic disease, epitomized by cancer, requires health systems to replace the conventional "either-or" model of treating specific diseases with systems that create synergies to benefit all diseases.

Strong health systems are needed to prevent, diagnose, and treat cancer and other chronic illness. Similarly, CCC can be expanded in ways that strengthens health systems to address multiple conditions.[52] This "diagonal approach" mutually reinforces CCC and health system strengthening by simultaneously considering the overall goals of health systems in addition to disease-specific priorities and interventions (Chapter 4).[53,54] The either-or debates –prevention versus treatment, infectious versus NCDs– provide excuses for inaction, foster destructive competition rather than complementarity, and detract from effective mobilization of all stakeholders to mount urgent action.

The distinctions between chronic and acute and communicable and non-communicable that have been used for decades are increasingly irrelevant. These false dichotomies that shaped public health in the past place a heavy burden on research and on policy. The nomenclature stifles the most effective translation of research into advocacy and policymaking. Health systems must not become trapped in static thinking and thus fail to respond to epidemiological change, medical breakthroughs, or opportunities for innovation in delivery and financing of care. Global health requires a framework that embraces the neglected area of work on NCDs and at the same time bridges the false divide between communicable diseases and NCDs.[55]

Using the diagonal approach, priority interventions can drive necessary improvements in the health system. Rather than focusing on disease-specific "vertical" programs or on "horizontal" initiatives that address system-wide constraints, a diagonal approach seeks to do both. Applications of the diagonal approach to CCC include: tobacco control to help prevent certain cancers as well as reduce cardiovascular and respiratory diseases; promoting increased physical activity and healthy eating to reduce the risk of several NCDs; empowering women through better knowledge of cervical cancer prevention and early detection of breast cancer with interventions implemented through sexual and reproductive health programs; and, strengthening health systems to support access to pain control medication for all patients (Chapter 4).

Health systems in LMICs were designed to respond to acuity. Consequently, these systems manage chronic disease as a series of unrelated episodes of acute illness, not as conditions with continuing and long-term care needs. Health systems need to be redesigned to respond to the ongoing needs of cancer and other chronic conditions. Health system innovations must address the six overlapping components of the cancer-control continuum and develop integrated programs that incorporate primary prevention, early detection, diagnosis, treatment, survivorship, and palliation.

Applying the diagonal approach across the cancer care continuum is a response to the challenges of chronicity. Existing horizontal, population-wide systems and programs –such as education, infrastructure, reproductive health initiatives, regulatory structures for pain control, health insurance, and surgical equipment– can be used in ways that also respond to the health needs of a variety of disease groups.

Identification of the most effective treatments and the cancers most susceptible to these treatments is needed in order to set priorities. This will define a set of candidate cancers and compelling CCC opportunities for immediate action to expand prevention and/or treatment. For example, lifestyle-related prevention interventions to reduce tobacco use will help reduce the incidence of lung, head, neck, bladder, and throat cancers. Preventing infections of HPV, Hepatitis B, and Helicobacter pylori will reduce incidence of cervical, hepatocellular, and stomach cancers, respectively. Early detection and treatment of retinoblastomas in children and cervical and breast cancers in women is possible. Childhood acute lymphocytic leukemia, along with Burkitt, Hodgkin and non-Hodgkin lymphomas can be effectively treated at relatively low cost. Systemic therapy for Kaposi sarcoma and chronic myelogenous leukemia can provide effective life extension and palliation. Pain control and survivorship management can be applied to all cancers (Chapter 5).

Resource stratification aids in defining the most useful and appropriate interventions at different income levels, and a careful analysis should be applied to each cancer for each country setting.[56,57] A particular challenge in cancer treatment is the recognition that treatments span a spectrum from highly effective, low-cost options to minimally effective and sometimes even experimental or unproven high-cost treatments. Of course, this is not to say that some highly effect treatments are also high cost. This spectrum of interventions contrasts with the scale-up of antiretroviral therapy for HIV, where most of the applicable medications had rapid and visible initial effect. Care should be taken to avoid ineffective treatments, especially if they detract from palliative care that could improve the quality of life for the patient and the family, and sometimes even prolong survival.[58]

The proposals and recommendations around core elements of a CCC strategy for LMICs set forth in this volume are anchored in five key assumptions presented in detail in Chapter 5:

i. Many cancers are preventable through infection control, risk factor reduction, and lifestyle modifications, especially eliminating the use of tobacco.

ii. Accurate diagnosis is critical to determine an appropriate and successful treatment plan.

iii. Many cancers are highly curable with affordable drugs, which means denial of therapy for diseases for which effective, affordable treatments exist is unacceptable.

iv. Treatment of more complex, less curable diseases requires evaluations specific to each country and available resources.

v. Palliation of pain and suffering from cancer is a basic human right. Such programs should not be based on cost-benefit calculations that are measured in extending life. Dignity and equity are equally as important as efficiency.

Each country should define an appropriate set of candidate cancers and specific strategies to address them, establishing priorities through a national cancer strategy that also identifies the investments needed for research and evidence generation. This framework can be used by LMICs to develop cancer plans by delineating the foundations of adequate CCC and the core components for essential effective cancer control. National cancer plans should apply a diagonal approach to create synergies with other health programs. International agencies such as IARC and the International Agency for Atomic Energy through the Program of Action for Cancer Therapy can play an important role in providing support to develop national cancer plans.[59]

CCC implementation will require support from broad coalitions of actors, including local stakeholders. National and sub-national task forces or commissions on CCC can be especially effective; Rwanda and Mexico are examples.

While it will take time in many countries, the goal should be to establish a national center of excellence in each LMIC. Examples from several countries that have established centers provide both lessons and encouragement. The Cancer Institute at Chennai in India, the Ocean Road Cancer Institute in Tanzania, and the National Institute of Neoplastic Disease of Peru have been highlighted.[60] This volume adds the examples of the King Hussein Cancer Center and Foundation of Jordan, the Uganda Cancer Institute, and the network in Mexico of the National Cancer Institute of Mexico and regional centers such as the Jalisco Cancer Institute (Chapter 6).

This volume proposes a series of innovations that seek to bridge gaps in delivery, including international partnerships (so-called "twinning"), which will utilize communications technology such as telemedicine and telepathology. Models that have been developed based on experiences in pediatric oncology can inform scale-up globally.

National plans or strategies can help identify priority cancers and interventions in LMICs and dispel the myth that "little can be done" (Chapter 5). For example, 26 of the 29 key agents for treating many of the most prevalent, treatable cancers in LMICs are off-patent, making drug treatment relatively low cost. For candidate cancers, the estimated cost of increasing access to treatments in LMICs is far lower than many fear (Chapter 7): less than US$ 500 per patient for cervical cancer, Kaposi sarcoma, and Burkitt lymphoma. Many of the off-patent generic cancer medicines required for LMICs are available for less than US$ 100 per course of treatment, and nearly all for under US$ 1,000.

The total cost of unmet drug treatments in LMICs for cervical cancer, Hodgkin lymphomas, and acute lymphoblastic leukemia in children 0-14 is roughly US$ 115 million; for one year of incident cases the price is US$ 280 million (GLOBOCAN 2008 data). While these estimates do not include diagnostics, surgery, or radiation therapy, they are relatively low given the quantum of external investment in health. Breast cancer treatment, by contrast, is orders of magnitude more costly, especially if using highly effective, on-patent drugs for HER2-positive cases. It is important to note that early detection not only increases the probability of cure but also significantly reduces the cost of treatment by decreasing the total medication requirements (Chapters 5 and 7).

Remarkable opportunities for action exist –at relatively low cost– to close the cancer divide. Prevention of risk factors, beginning with tobacco control, must be a high priority. Several highly curable cancers affecting children, youth, and women, along with cancers associated with preventable infections, are among the most obvious targets. Reducing stigma, improving survivorship, and providing pain control and palliative care are necessary and feasible for all patients in LMICs. All of these interventions can and should be mutually reinforcing, strengthen health systems, alleviate unnecessary suffering, and promote economic and human development.

1.v Much can be done: Spheres of action

A diagonal approach can significantly narrow the cancer divide by targeting delivery, pricing and procurement, financing, research, and stewardship. Innovations in delivery should optimize the use of human and physical resources, utilize information and communication technologies both across and within countries, and involve the primary and secondary levels of care to the fullest extent. Improvements in access to affordable medicines, vaccines, and health technologies can be achieved through global and national strategies that reduce price and non-price barriers. Innovations in financing that link social protection to health can incorporate CCC. Health information systems and decision-making research should be conducted to develop better frameworks for monitoring and evaluation, as well as performance measures that promote accountability and results. Effective national cancer plans must take full advantage of the global energy around NCDs and galvanize multi-stakeholder action, including communities, patients, and the private sector.

We summarize below each area for strategic action that is in turn presented in more detail in Chapters 6 to 10 of this book. A set of specific, enabling recommendations for each area of action is presented in the GTF.CCC Report.[61]

INNOVATIVE DELIVERY (CHAPTER 6)

This chapter identifies a number of innovative service delivery models and mechanisms that could be implemented in LMICs to improve CCC, even where specialized services are not available. Examples from Mexico, Uganda, Jordan, Partners In Health sites, and the St. Jude International Outreach Program illustrate these innovations. The examples are further supported by a comprehensive literature review on innovative delivery for other diseases and health services.

Telemedicine can be used and non-specialized medical personnel can be trained in order to shift components of CCC to less specialized facilities. This strategy can bridge the distance between the patient and the point of care to ensure accessibility and uptake. While much more can be accomplished with available resources, additional investment is required to diagnose and treat most cancers, particularly in low income countries. Building local human resource capacity is crucial, as is the creation of comprehensive centers.[62] Further, on-site facilities are essential to improve diagnostic capacity, especially in processing pathology. While telemedicine can help to build this capacity, investment is also required to develop capacity on-site.[63,64]

ACCESS TO AFFORDABLE MEDICINES, VACCINES, AND HEALTH TECHNOLOGIES (CHAPTER 7)

Expanding access requires a systems approach that links cost-effective selection, vigorous price reduction, transparent information on prices and sources, reliable procurement, assured quality, engagement of key stakeholders, actions to address barriers to palliation and pain control, and "frugal" innovation.

For a range of diseases, LMICs regularly receive reductions of more than 90% from the launch price for drugs. This practice should be extended to cancer. For example, most chemotherapy and hormonal medicines considered essential for low-resource settings are off-patent. For these products, the best price and quality will be obtained through competitive pooled procurement and bulk purchasing from qualified suppliers with well-organized supply.

Expanding access in LMICs will require three levels: financial resources, political will, and a health systems approach. Multilateral agencies, the international community, national governments, the private sector, civil society, and patient groups should collaborate to ensure:

- "Frugal innovations" for new bioavailable oral chemotherapy and low-cost radiation therapy.

- International guidelines for all components of CCC and an expanded WHO model list of essential medicines and vaccines.

- Optimal pricing to reduce the variations faced by LMICs for off-patent generics.

- Transparent, web-based information on prices and sources of medicines.

- Engagement of middle income country producers of both finished products and active pharmaceutical ingredients for off-patent chemotherapeutic agents.

- An expanded range of cancer agents for global, regional and national procurement agencies.

- National cancer plans that incorporate global guidelines to strengthen procurement and distribution systems, ensure regulation of quality and safety, and establish effective regulatory strategies for pain medicines to break down non-price barriers.

INNOVATIVE GLOBAL AND DOMESTIC FINANCING (CHAPTER 8)

Innovative global and domestic health system financing mechanisms are needed to meet the growing burden of cancer and other NCDs and chronic illness.

Expanding and improving global financing: To date, international support for cancer and NCDs has been very limited despite the rapidly increasing health burden in LMICs. Mobilization and investment of new international funding is required for CCC in low income settings. New funding must leverage existing international and domestic investments for CCC without diminishing local efforts. New funding also must be synergistic and non-duplicative by: 1) channeling through existing innovative global financing mechanisms to reduce costs, 2) by leveraging investments for both disease control and health system strengthening using the diagonal approach, and 3) by remaining stable and predictable over time.

Innovative, integrated financing mechanisms that have worked at scale for disease- and population-specific initiatives such as the Global Fund and GAVI, could be utilized to create synergies for CCC. Since 2006, significant growth in financing for maternal and child health has come not from direct funding, but through cross-investments by GAVI and, indirectly, the Global Fund. These investments strengthen health systems in ways that could benefit efforts around CCC and other NCDs and chronic illnesses. New financing commitments for reproductive, maternal, newborn and child health, and the Pink Ribbon Red Ribbon initiative on cancer and HIV/AIDS provide additional opportunities for engagement and for channeling funds.

Strengthening domestic financing through universal social insurance: The majority of health care in almost all LMICs is financed from domestic sources; much of this is direct out-of-pocket spending that often leads to financial catastrophe for families, especially with chronic illness like cancer. Novel health financing mechanisms are needed to expand existing benefit packages to include cost-effective CCC interventions.

Several LMICs, cognizant of the need to reduce out-of-pocket financing, have established universal financial protection programs alongside significant additional investments in health. Many of these initiatives include CCC in the package of covered services. The level of investment made by many of these LMICs contrasts starkly with the lack of global financing for cancer and other NCDs.

Important lessons can be learned from the experiences of a select group of countries that have embarked on achieving universal health coverage with financial protection. We review lessons from Colombia, China, Dominican Republic, India, Mexico, Peru, Rwanda, and Taiwan, each of which has successfully included cancers in the package of services covered by universal social insurance funds. Their experiences with innovative domestic financing demonstrate that:

- Social protection in health, based on pre-payment and pooling, reduces catastrophic health spending by families.
- Establishing entitlements around a guaranteed benefits package that includes cancer leads to improved access.
- Financing can be used to balance cost-effective prevention, early detection, and treatment interventions across the care continuum.
- Investments in treatment are made much less effective if prevention and early detection are neglected; separate funds for health promotion services should be established.

- Financial protection for health care is less effective if other financial and nonfinancial barriers, such as transportation costs, care-giving for the patient, and stigma, are neglected.
- A strong evidence base, including rigorous evaluation, is needed to develop innovative financing mechanisms for CCC.

EVIDENCE AND RESEARCH FOR DECISION-MAKING (CHAPTER 9)

High-quality evidence to support decision-making is essential for allocation of resources among competing needs and priorities. Evidence also provides the core of accountability. Yet, most LMICs lack both the health information systems (HIS) and the research capacity to generate the kind of evidence necessary for effective decision-making on cancer.

Several strategies can be followed globally and in LMICs to strengthen HIS and the research base for CCC, thereby contributing to the global monitoring framework proposed by the UNHLM on NCDs. These strategies are low-cost and will produce global public goods that should be financed by international and bilateral agencies:

- Strengthen cancer registries through additional investment by the International Agency for Research on Cancer (IARC), participating states, and bilateral agencies.
- Expand training opportunities for researchers, evidence-builders, and decision-makers from LMICs.
- Apply novel methodologies and metrics to improve measurement within and evaluation of CCC programs.
- Establish a clearinghouse of programs, policies, and projects implemented by multiple stakeholders (governmental, civil society, and private sector), and make this information widely accessible to improve cross-learning.
- Ensure that national cancer plans include specific indicators and time-bound targets for reducing morbidity and mortality.

The lessons learned from accountability frameworks in women's and children's health should be applied to CCC and NCDs. The World Cancer Declaration of the Union for International Cancer Control (UICC) provides a base for establishing these targets and goals.

STEWARDSHIP AND LEADERSHIP (CHAPTER 10)

Weak heath systems leadership is a key limitation to increasing access to CCC in LMICs. This stewardship gap has hindered the production and dissemination of essential global and local public goods. Stronger stewardship can be accomplished by mobilizing stakeholders through new and existing global and national forums and networks dedicated to improving health outcomes and equity.

At both the national and international levels, players have emerged who are actively and successfully swaying leaders. The key to moving forward and taking full advantage of this opportunity for generating stable and sustainable programs will be identifying additional spaces for collective action that span government, academia, civil society, the private sector, and patients. One example, spurred by the 2011 UNHLM on NCDs, is the formation of the NCD Alliance, in which the Union for International Cancer Control (UICC) actively represents the cancer community.

The Declaration crafted at the UN meeting provides a host of recommendations and proposals to improve global stewardship and leadership. The focus is rightly on the World Health Organization as the global entity charged with health. Yet, an effective response must be whole-of-government and whole-of-society. The Declaration calls for proposals by the end of 2012 for partnerships that will strengthen and facilitate global multisectoral action. In the future, all relevant international and national organizations must actively ensure that NCDs are treated as an integral part of a development agenda. The cancer community can play a leadership role in implementing the proposals set out in the Declaration of the UNHLM on NCDs to:

- Better position the WHO to take on a stewardship role with the global cancer agenda, and the IARC to provide evidence for decision making.
- Strengthen UICC as a global umbrella and stewardship organization.
- Better engage key multilateral agencies with links to specific cancers (such as UNICEF and the children's rights community for childhood cancers; UNFPA for women and health, empowerment, sexual and reproductive health and maternal and child health programs for cancers of women).
- Support governments to formulate national cancer strategies and integrate cancer into national health plans.
- Actively engage the private sector in the production of solutions and knowledge.

- Encourage and support in-country, multistakeholder commissions on CCC to coordinate with other disease groups and system-wide initiatives.
- Identify agencies, working with IARC and WHO, to develop a system of measurable and implementable targets and goals specific to cancer that can be integrated into global targets for NCDs.

1.vi Moving forward

A range of evidence-based interventions that are necessary, affordable, feasible, and appropriate can begin to close the cancer divide. We propose the following as guiding principles as we seek to achieve that goal:

i. It is necessary and feasible to extend cancer prevention, treatment, and care opportunities to LMICs as they seek to meet the challenge of cancer.

ii. If people in rich countries have the opportunity to live healthy and productive lives after cancer, those same opportunities should be extended to people living in poor countries.

iii. As survivorship is the standard of care in developed countries, survivorship also should be the standard of care in poor countries.

As Kofi Annan, then UN Secretary General, remarked in reference to HIV/AIDS, "people no longer accept that the sick and dying, simply because they are poor, should be denied drugs which have transformed the lives of others who are better off."[65] The same must be true for cancer and all diseases for which effective interventions exist. Achieving an effective response will require concerted action from global health community.

Closing the cancer divide is an equity imperative. There is a compelling case to invest in CCC and thereby prevent millions of unnecessary deaths. In this book, we hope to identify the key drivers of the cancer divide, highlight the looming challenge of cancer in LMICs, and show the huge cost of failure to address this challenge. Closing the cancer divide –meeting this equity imperative– requires an immediate, inclusive, and large-scale global response. It is what we would expect for our own families, and it is what we must demand for our global family.

References

1. Frenk J, Bobadilla JL, Sepúlveda J, Cervantes ML. Health transition in middle-income countries: new challenges for health care. *Health Policy and Planning* 1989;4(1):29.

2. Knaul F, Frenk J, Shulman L for the Global Task Force on Expanded Access to Cancer Care and Control in Developing Countries. Closing the Cancer Divide: A Blueprint to Expand Access in Low and Middle Income Countries. Harvard Global Equity Initiative, Harvard University, Boston, MA, October 2011.

3. Atun R, Bataringaya J. Building a Durable Response to HIV/AIDS: Implications for Health Systems. *Journal of Acquired Immune Deficiency Syndrome* 2011; 57(Suppl 2):S91-S95

4. Sloan FA, Gelband H (Eds.). Cancer control opportunities in low-and middle-income countries. Washington DC: National Academy Press, 2007.

5. Beaglehole R, Bonita R, Alleyne G, Horton R. NCDs: celebrating success, moving forward. *Lancet* 2011; 378(9799):378.

6. Ibid.

7. Gulland A. World leaders agree to cut deaths from non-communicable diseases by a quarter by 2025. *British Medical Journal* 2012; 344:e3768.

8. Institute of Medicine. The US Commitment to Global Health: Recommendations for the public and private sectors. Washington, DC: The National Academies Press, 2009.

9. Judt T. Night. Letter. The New York Review of Books, 2010

10. Stuckler D, Basu S, McKee M. Commentary: UN high level meeting on non-communicable diseases: an opportunity for whom? *British Medical Journal* 2011; 343:d5336.

11. Reardon S. A world of chronic disease. Science 2011; 333(6042): 558-9.

12. Mukherjee S. The emperor of all maladies: a biography of cancer. New York: Scribner (simon & Schuster?), 2010.

13. U.N. General Assembly, 66th Session. Political declaration of the High-level Meeting of the General Assembly on the Prevention and Control of Non-communicable Diseases: Draft resolution submitted by the President of the General Assembly (A/66/L.1). 16 September 2011.

14. World Economic Forum and the Harvard School of Public Health. From Burden to "Best Buys": Reducing the Economic Impact of Non-Communicable Diseases in Low- and Middle-Income Countries. Geneva, Switzerland: World Health Organization. 2011.

15. World Health Organization. Global Status Report on noncommunicable diseases 2010. Geneva, Switzerland; World Health Organization. 2011.

16. Farmer P, Léandre F, Mukherjee JS, et al. Community-based approaches to HIV treatment in resource-poor settings. *Lancet* 2001; 358:404-9.

17. Mukherjee S, 2010.

18. GLOBOCAN 2008. Cancer fact sheet: all cancers (excluding non-melanoma skin cancer) incidence and mortality worldwide in 2008, 2010. http://globocan.iarc.fr/factsheets/cancers/all.asp (accessed July 23 2011).

19. Sloan FA, Gelband H (Eds.), 2007.

20. Beaulieu N, Bloom D, Bloom R, Stein R. Breakaway: the global burden of cancer-challenges and opportunities. Economist Intelligence Unit. 2009.

21. Kanavos P. The rising burden of cancer in the developing world. *Annals of Oncology* 2006; 17(Suppl 8): viii5-viii23.

22. Stuckler D, Basu S, McKee M, 2011.

23. Alwan A, Galea G, Stuckler D. Development at risk: addressing noncommunicable diseases at the United Nations high-level meeting. *Bulletin of the World Health Organization* 2011; 89(8):546-546a.

24. Frenk J, Bobadilla JL, Sepulveda J, et al., 1989.

25. International Atomic Energy Agency. Inequity in cancer care: a global perspective. Vienna, Switzerland; International Atomic Energy Association. 2011.

26. Liberman J. O'Brien M, Hall W, Hill D. Ending inequities in access to effective pain relief? *Lancet* 2010;376(9744):856

27. Global Access to Pain Relief Initiative (GAPRI). Understand the problem. Facts about access to pain relief. http://www.gapri.org/understand-problem (accessed August 12, 2012).

28. O'Brien M. Global Access to Pain Relief Initiative. Presentation for the Union of International Cancer Control. http://www.africacncl.org/HIV_AIDS/initiative_activities/NCD_Session_3_Obrien.pdf (accessed September 20, 2011).

29. Farmer P, Frenk J, Knaul FM, et al. Expansion of cancer care and control in countries of low and middle income: a call to action. *Lancet* 2010; 376(9747):1186-93.

30. Sloan FA, Gelband H (Eds.), 2007.

31. Frenk J, Chen L, Bhutta ZA, et al. Health professionals for a new century: transforming education to strengthen health systems in an interdependent world. *Lancet* 2010; 76(9756):1923-58.

32. World Health Organization. The World Health Report 2006: working together for health. Geneva, Switzerland: World Health Organization, 2006.

33. Ferlay J, Shin H, Bray F, Forman D, Mathers C, Parkin D. GLOBOCAN 2008: cancer incidence and mortality worldwide. *International Journal of Cancer* 2010; 127(12):2893-917.

34. Joint Learning Initiative, Global Equity Initiative. Human resources for health: overcoming the crisis. The President and Fellows of Harvard College 2004. http://www.who.int/hrh/documents/JLi_hrh_report.pdf (accessed October 4, 2011).

35. American Society of Clinical Oncology/Health Volunteers Overseas. International Cancer Corps needs assessment reports on Honduras. 2008.

36. International Atomic Energy Agency, 2011.

37. Knaul FM, Shulman LN, Gralow J, et al. Improving pathology for better cancer care and control in countries of low and middle income. *Lancet* 2012; 371(9831): 2052.

38. World Health Organization. Macroeconomics and health: Investing in health for economic development. Report of the Commission on Macroeconomics and Health. Geneva, Switzerland: World Health Organization, 2001.

39. World Economic Forum. Global Risks 2010: A global risk network report: Geneva, Switzerland: World Economic Forum, 2010.

40. Amartya Sen. Personal communication, October 17th, 2011.

41. John RM, Ross H. The global economic cost of cancer. The American Cancer Society and LIVESTRONG, 2010. http://www.cancer.org/acs/groups/content/@internationalaffairs/documents/document/acspc-026203.pdf (accessed July 30, 2011).

42. World Economic Forum. Global Risks 2010: A global risk network report: Geneva, Switzerland: World Economic Forum, 2010.

43. Ibid.

44. Shafey O, Eriksen M, Ross H, Mackay J. The tobacco atlas, Third Edition. American Cancer Society. 2009. http://www.tobaccoatlas.org/downloads/TobaccoAtlas_sm.pdf (accessed September 27, 2011).

45. Castelli A, Nizalova O. Avoidable mortality: What it means and how it is measured. Centre for Health Economics (CHE) Research Paper 63. 2011. http://www.york.ac.uk/media/che/documents/papers/researchpapers/CHERP63_avoidable_mortality_what_it_means_and_how_it_is_measured.pdf (accessed September 27, 2011).

46. John RM, Ross H, 2010.

47. Beaulieu N, Bloom D, Bloom R, Stein R, 2009.

48. Bloom DE, Cafiero ET, Jané-Llopis E, et al. The global economic burden of non-communicable diseases. Geneva, Switzerland: World Economic Forum. 2011.

49. WHO. Global Status Report on noncommunicable diseases 2010. 2011.

50. World Economic Forum and the Harvard School of Public Health. From Burden to 'Best Buys': Reducing the economic impact of non-communicable diseases in low- and middle-income countries, 2011.

51. Global Alliance for Vaccines and Immunization. GAVI welcomes lower prices for life-saving vaccines. Press Release; 6 June, 2011. http://www.gavialliance.org/media_centre/press_releases/vaccine_prices.php (accessed June 10, 2011).

52. Institute of Medicine, 2009.

53. Sepúlveda J, Bustreo F, Tapia R, et al. Improvement of child survival in Mexico: the diagonal approach. Lancet 2006; 368(9551): 2017-27.

54. Frenk J. Bridging the divide: global lessons from evidence-based health policy in Mexico. *Lancet* 2006; 369(9539): 954-61.

55. Knaul F, Frenk J. Strengthening Health Systems to Address New Challenge Diseases (NCDs). Harvard Public Health Review. Fall 2011. http://www.hsph.harvard.edu/news/hphr/fall-2011/new-challenge-diseases.html (accessed October 15, 2011).

56. Sloan FA, Gelband H (Eds.), 2007.

57. Anderson BO, Yip CH, Ramsey CD, et al. Breast Cancer in Limited-Resource Countries: Health Care Systems and Public Policy. *The Breast Journal* 2006;12(Suppl. 1): S54-S69.

58. Sullivan R, Purushotham A. The Goldilocks' problem of cancer medicines. *Lancet Oncology* 2010; 11(1 1):1017-8.

59. International Atomic Energy Agency. Programme of Action for Cancer Therapy (PACT). 2011. http://cancer.iaea.org/ (accessed October 15, 2011).

60. Sloan FA, Gelband H (Eds.), 2007.

61. Knaul M, Shulman LN, Gralow J, et al., 2012.

62. Sloan FA, Gelband H (Eds.), 2007.

63. Roberts DJ, Wilson ML, Nelson AM, et al. The good news about cancer in developing countries – pathology answers the call. *Lancet* 2012; 371(9817): 712.

64. Knaul FM, Shulman LN, Gralow J, et al., 2012.

65. Médecins sans Frontières South Africa, the Department of Public Health at the University of Cape Town, the Provincial Administration of the Western Cape, South Africa. Antiretroviral therapy in primary health care: Experience of the Khayelitscha programme in South Africa: Case Study. Genva, Switzerland; World Health Organization. 2003.

Chapter 2

THE GLOBAL CANCER DIVIDE: AN EQUITY IMPERATIVE

Felicia Marie Knaul, Hans-Olov Adami, Clement Adebamowo, Hector Arreola-Ornelas, Amanda J. Berger, Afsan Bhadelia, James Cleary, David J. Hunter, Nancy Keating, Anthony Mbewu, Oscar Mendez, Claire Neal, Meg O'Brien, Peggy Porter, Isabel dos Santos Silva, Rola Shaheen, Julio Frenk

2.i Introduction

Cancer, sometimes thought to be a disease mainly of developed countries, is in fact a complex set of distinct health challenges, many of which are associated with poverty. The cancer transition[1] mirrors the overall epidemiological transition, which means that low and middle income countries (LMICs) increasingly face cancers associated with infection as well as all other cancers. Suffering from cancer –a disease widely assumed to be exclusive to the wealthy– will in fact be increasingly concentrated among the poor.

A protracted and polarized epidemiologic transition is occurring in cancer and generating a divide that reflects the inequity in access to all components of cancer care and control (CCC).[2,3] This cancer divide refers to the disparities in incidence, mortality, and all other outcomes between the poor and the rich –both countries and individuals– that are directly related to inequities in access as well as to differences in underlying socioeconomic, environmental, and health conditions; but are unrelated to biological or genetic factors.

The cancer divide has five facets, and these are associated with specific types of interventions. The facets are not mutually exclusive as certain cancers may contribute to more than one of the five categories. The facets are:

1. Cancers associated with preventable behavioral and environmental exposures:
   a) cancers amenable to prevention with behavior change (smoking and lung cancer), or
   b) reduced exposure to environmental risk (workplace contamination and associated cancers; indoor air pollution/stoves and lung cancer).

2. Cancers associated with preventable infection:
   a) associated with, or worsened by, existing infections for which no vaccine exists (HIV/AIDS and Kaposi sarcoma), and
   b) from infections that can be prevented through public health measures or vaccination, cured with medication, or detected and controlled in pre-cancerous stages (human papillomavirus (HPV) and cervical cancer; schistosomiasis and bladder cancer).

3. Cancers for which treatment exists and is often made more effective by early detection (e.g. breast cancer, colorectal cancer). some of these cancers are also preventable (e.g. cervical cancer).

4. Suffering associated with the social and psychological aspects of disease or survivorship, including discrimination and stigma.

5. Pain and physical suffering associated with all cancers, including those for which neither effective treatment nor prevention is possible.

The divide is the result of a concentration among poor populations of preventable risk, disease, and suffering from cancer-related ill health and death. Further, the divide is likely to continue to widen and deepen over the coming decades, fueled by the progress in cutting-edge science, and medicine in high income countries that is largely unavailable in LMICs.

Indeed, social determinants of health –differences in income, education, occupation, gender, and ethnicity– correlate highly with risk of death and disability associated with noncommunicable diseases (NCDs), including cancer.[4,5] Further, poverty intensifies lack of access, and the costs of the disease itself are compounded by the burden of financing the treatment and management of the illness.[6] This led the 2011 WHO report to conclude that: "Vulnerable and socially disadvantaged people get sicker and die sooner as a result of NCDs than people of higher social positions."[7]

Closing the cancer divide is a glaring equity imperative. Yet, even the existence of that divide remains shrouded in ignorance. The first step in closing the divide is to generate global awareness of its existence, and that is the purpose of this chapter.

The first section describes the protracted and polarized cancer transition, focusing on the complexity and overlapping nature of the burden in LMICs. The next section describes each facet of the cancer divide. The final part summarizes the major findings.

2.ii The cancer transition

The term "protracted" describes a pattern of epidemiological transition typical of countries where the process of change in levels of mortality and fertility, and hence life expectancy, is non-linear. The coexistence of pre- and post-transitional diseases leads to an epidemiological polarization where the poorer population groups not only experience higher rates of diseases associated with infections and nutritional disorders, but also of many NCDs.

As a result, diseases that were once considered diseases only of the poor cease to be the only diseases of the poor.[8] Similarly, there are cancers that are today almost exclusively seen among poor populations. Yet, cancers that were once thought to be diseases of the rich are now affecting all populations, so that "cancers of the poor" are no longer the only cancers of the poor.

The cancer transition is emblematic of the "double burden" of disease faced by less developed countries. Cancers that are uncommon and sometimes even declining in (person-time) incidence in high income countries –for instance, cancers of the cervix, liver, and stomach– are far from controlled, while cancers historically less common, such as breast and colorectal cancer, are increasing in (person-time) incidence. Thus, LMICs face a cancer burden that includes both the backlog of preventable cancers and the emergence of other cancers that cannot be prevented with existing scientific knowledge. The summary table illustrates the transition for several tracer cancers (Table 2.1).

The cancer transition is most clearly shown by comparing breast and cervical cancer. Based on data from GLOBOCAN,[9] in all parts of the world other than the poorest countries of sub-Saharan Africa and Southeast Asia, breast cancer (an NCD for which primary prevention is very difficult) kills more women than cervical cancer (a cancer associated with an infection that can be prevented by vaccination and for which pre-cancerous lesions can be detected and treated). Further, age-adjusted breast cancer mortality has risen over time, while cervical cancer has declined in many middle and even low income countries.

Table 2.1

The Cancer Transition: Summary Table*

	% cancer of infectious origin		Childhood cancers			Childhood Leukemia			Cervical			Breast		
									15 or older					
	I	M	I	M	M/I	I	M	M/I	I	M	M/I	I	M	M/I
Norway	12%	10%	6	0.9	15%	2.4	0.3	14%	7.2	2.4	34%	72.5	17.3	24%
Canada	9%	8%	7	1.1	15%	2.4	0.3	12%	5	1.9	38%	81.7	18	22%
Saudi Arabia	10%	9%	4.7	3.3	69%	1.2	1.1	90%	1	0.4	36%	11.6	4.9	42%
Costa Rica	23%	26%	6.6	1.9	29%	2.5	0.8	32%	12.3	4.8	39%	28.3	8.3	29%
Colombia	25%	26%	4.4	2.1	48%	1.9	1	55%	14.5	6.6	45%	20.4	6.5	32%
Egypt	17%	16%	5	4	80%	1.1	1.1	99%	0.9	0.5	58%	22.9	11.9	52%
India	24%	22%	4	1.9	46%	1.3	0.7	53%	17.2	9.3	54%	14.7	6.8	46%
Uganda	46%	45%	8.6	7	81%	0.3	0.3	100%	22	15.1	69%	12.5	7	56%
Zimbabwe	50%	50%	5.2	4.3	83%	0.8	0.8	100%	23.6	16.3	69%	8.1	4.6	56%

* Rates are per 100,000 population.
Source: Author calculations based on GLOBOCAN 2008. Selection of countries included in Cancer Incidence in Five Continents.
http://www-dep.iarc.fr/

Comparisons of mortality across populations, or over time within the same population, are affected not only by changes in the occurrence of newly diagnosed cancer cases (incidence) but also by differences in the probability of surviving the disease. Reassuringly, however, data from long running population-based cancer registries clearly demonstrate how the cervical–breast cancer transition began in high income countries and slowly spread to LMICs. For example, in Denmark, the age-standardized incidence of breast cancer already exceeded that of cervical cancer in the early 1950s, but the gap between the two cancers increased markedly over the following 50 years. In contrast, the age-adjusted incidence of breast cancer surpassed that of cervical cancer much later in Asian populations – only in the early 1970s in Singapore, and in the early 1990s in urban India (e.g. Chennai and Mumbai).[10]

The mortality time series for Mexico and Costa Rica demonstrate a similar transition in Latin America (Figure 2.1). For Costa Rica the data span the period 1995 to 2008 and throughout this period age-standardized breast cancer mortality exceeds cervical cancer mortality. Breast cancer mortality has fluctuated

Liver			Hodgkin lymphoma (Rate*100000)			Testicular			Colorectal			GNI per capita (2005 USD)
			15 or older									
I	M	M/I	I	M	M/I	I	M	M/I	I	M	M/I	
3.5	3.4	98%	2.9	0.3	11%	14.3	0.4	3%	91.1	42	46%	$58,810
6.7	6.5	97%	3.1	0.4	12%	6.7	0.2	4%	83.8	28.2	34%	$38,668
2.6	2.5	96%	1.7	1.2	69%	0.6	0.3	44%	9.8	6.7	68%	$24,726
6.9	6.8	98%	2.3	1.1	46%	3.1	0.7	21%	18.8	11.4	61%	$10,870
2.9	5.8	200%[a]	1.4	0.5	35%	2.6	0.5	21%	13	7.5	58%	$8,589
10	9.7	97%	1.4	1.1	84%	0.7	0.4	55%	5.3	4	76%	$5,889
2.4	2.2	91%	0.7	0.4	58%	0.9	0.4	45%	4.5	3.2	70%	$3,337
7.4	7.3	99%	0.8	0.7	90%	0.1	0.1	100%	4.8	3.9	80%	$1,224
6.4	6.4	100%	0.6	0.6	93%	0.3	0.2	73%	5	4	80%	$176

a) M/I over 100 is likely a reflection of the small number of cases and the very high lethality of the disease, especially if registered/diagnosed late, as well as problems with quality of data.

minimally, while cervical cancer deaths dropped dramatically. Thus the difference in mortality rates gap has steadily widened from about 1 per 100,000 women to approximately 8 per 100,000. In Mexico, a time series spanning more than 50 years shows how cervical cancer deaths reached a high of approximately 16 per 100,000 women in the late 1980s and subsequently fell to below 8 per 100,000 in 2008. By contrast, breast cancer death rates show an increasing trend over the entire period and finally surpassed cervical cancer death rates in 2006.[11]

For Mexico, data disaggregated by state also supports the transition hypothesis. Trends from 1979 -2008 for wealthier states (e.g. Nuevo Leon) differ from poorer states (e.g. Oaxaca). In many of the wealthier states, age-standardized breast cancer mortality surpassed cervical cancer mortality early on, while in the poorer states, cervical still exceeds breast cancer mortality, although the gap is narrowing.

Figure 2.1

Transition in Breast and Cervical Cancer Mortality, Mexico and Costa Rica

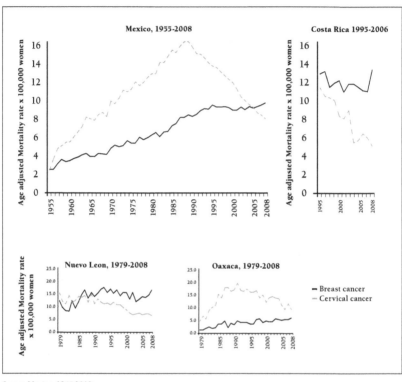

Source Mexico, 1955-2008:

Knaul et al. Reproductive Health Matters, 2008; and updated by Knaul, Arreola-Ornelas and Méndez based on WHO data, WHOSIS (1955-1978), and Ministry of Health in Mexico (1979-2006).

Source Costa Rica, 1995-2006:

Instituto Nacional de Estadística y Censos, Ministerio de Salud, Unidad de Estadística, Registro Nacional de Tumores de Costa Rica.

The country-specific results are borne out by global data, covering the period 1980- 2010, generated by the Institute for Health Metrics and Evaluation.[12] In the case of breast cancer, both age-specific incidence and mortality are increasing in all income regions. Yet, the increase is more pronounced in LMICs. In developing regions, breast cancer incidence increased 60% and mortality 53%, compared to 47% and 20% in high income countries. The proportion of deaths from breast cancer that occur in LMICs increased from 49% to 63%.

In the case of cervical cancer, age-specific incidence increased by 24% and mortality by 19% between 1980 and 2010 in low and middle income regions.

By comparison, there was an impressive decline in high income countries of approximately 30% in both incidence and mortality. As a result, cervical cancer is becoming a disease much more concentrated in poor countries. In 1980, LMICs accounted for approximately 80% of both age-adjusted incident cases and deaths from cervical cancer. In 2010, both figures were close to 90%.

As of 2010, breast cancer deaths (~262,700) surpassed cervical cancer deaths (~174,500) in LMICs. By contrast, in 1980 cervical cancer (~142,000) accounted for more deaths than breast (~122,500). Even in the lowest income countries, the gap is closing as breast cancer incidence and mortality are increasing at a faster rate. In high income countries, breast cancer deaths outnumbered cervical cancer deaths by a factor of 4:1 in 1980, and by 2010 this factor was approaching 7:1.

The transition in cancer that is clearly illustrated by contrasting trends in breast and cervical cancer also applies to several other cancers. For instance, a similar transition is occurring for digestive cancers whereby declines in the age-standardized (person-time) incidence of stomach cancer (an infection-related cancer) are paralleled by rises in the age-adjusted (person-time) incidence of colon cancer (a cancer known to be associated with unhealthy diets, excessive weight and lack of exercise). In Europe, this stomach-colon cancer transition began in the north (e.g. in Denmark and Finland colon rates overtook stomach cancer rates in the 1970s), reaching the south only a few decades later (e.g. rates in Italy and Spain crossed-over only in the mid-1990s). The epicenter of this transition has now moved to LMICs, as illustrated by data from selected Chinese populations. In men, the incidence of colon cancer surpassed that of stomach cancer in the early 1980s in Hong Kong, and in the early 1990s in Singapore. The cross-over in rates has yet to happen in Shanghai, but the gap between stomach and colon incidence narrowed considerably between 1988 and 2002.[13]

The patterns in the cancer transition demonstrate trends that can be generalized. Low income countries will face increasing burdens in all groups of cancers –infection-associated and otherwise– with little access to the tools and resources needed to meet these challenges.

Middle income countries are in an intermediate position. Preventable cancers associated with behavior, lifestyle, environment and occupation (Facet 1 of the cancer divide) are likely to increase in incidence and mortality. At the same time, these countries will face a rising incidence of treatable cancers, many of which are not amenable to primary prevention, but where early detection is key (Facet 3). In comparison, cancers associated with preventable infections (Facet 2a) are relatively low in incidence, and cancers for which vaccines exist (Facet 2b) have declined and are likely to continue to do so.

By contrast, most high income countries have effectively evaded or controlled the majority of the infections that are associated with particular cancers. Further, and as discussed in greater depth below, wealthier countries tend to have solid screening programs, substantially more access to treatment options, the social structures to promote survivorship and combat stigma and discrimination, and face few restrictions on providing pain control.

Text Box 2.1
CCC in high income countries: elements of progress

Identifying the cancers most amenable to prevention, early detection and treatment, and assessing incidence and mortality patterns in LMICs versus high income countries, can initiate a roadmap for action. A first step for estimating the burden of avoidable cancer in LMICs is to examine what high income countries have achieved through prevention and little restriction on access to best care practices. The site-specific changes in cancer incidence and mortality that have been achieved in developed countries over the last 50 years provide a framework to identify the potential range scope for action in LMICs.[14]

Cancer is the second leading cause of death in the US, after heart disease. Although heart disease death rates have declined dramatically over the last 50 years, total cancer mortality rates have remained remarkably constant, despite high levels of spending in a country where more than 17% of GDP is devoted to health.[15]

Cancer mortality in the US —for men and, more recently, for women— is dominated by lung cancer. A steep increase in lung cancer deaths associated with increased rates of smoking, was followed by declines for men and a leveling-off for women, reflecting the fact that smoking rates, too, have declined.[16-18] *(Figure 2.2).*

Figure 2.2

Cancer Mortality Rates by Site, US 1930-2005

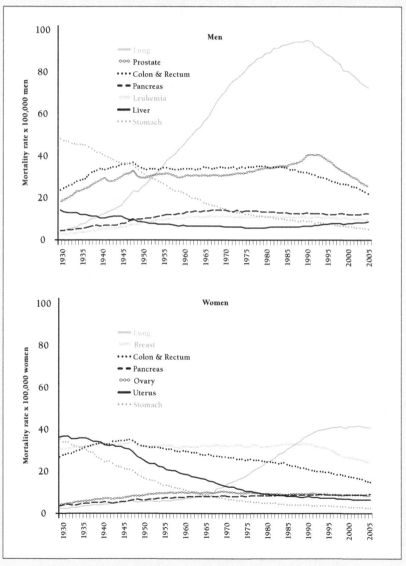

Source: Health, United States, 2005, with chartbook on trends in health of Americans; 2005.
http://www.cdc.gov/nchs/data/hus/hus05.pdf

For many cancers, particularly those that are infection–related, large and impressive reductions in mortality over the past decades can be attributed to reduced incidence or earlier detection. Some of the greatest reductions in mortality have been for cervical cancer, where incidence and mortality have decreased sharply with the availability of screening and the treatment of pre-cancerous lesions. Incidence and mortality are likely to decline even further with the availability of the HPV vaccine. Deaths from stomach cancer have decreased substantially for reasons that are not completely understood.

Other cancers are registering declines in mortality due to earlier detection and more effective treatments. Breast cancer death rates were constant until the last decade of the 20th century, when they began to decline as a result of both earlier detection due to education and mammographic screening, and the availability of more effective systemic adjuvant treatments.[19,20] Deaths from colorectal cancer for men and women also show some recent decline.

Figure 2.3

Age-standardised (European) Mortality Rates by Cancer Site, UK 1971-2008

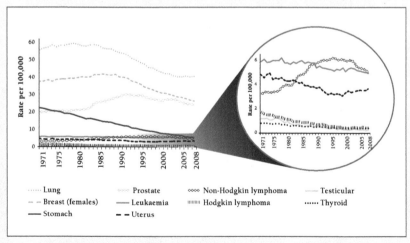

Lung	Prostate	Non-Hodgkin lymphoma	Testicular
Breast (females)	Leukaemia	Hodgkin lymphoma	Thyroid
Stomach	Uterus		

Source: Statistics on the most commonly diagnosed types of cancer in the UK. Cancer Research UK. http://info.cancerresearchuk.org/cancerstats/types/index.htm.

The other cancer sites for which improved treatment is responsible for large reductions in mortality are less common. Data for three decades from the UK show impressive declines in testicular and thyroid cancers, as well as Hodgkin lymphoma (Figure 2.3).

Dramatic improvements have also occurred in cancer survival for children. Whereas the vast majority of cases ended in death until a few decades ago, survival from acute lymphoblastic leukemia is now more than 80% overall, and close to 90% in high income countries.[21,22]

By contrast, for several types of cancer (lung, esophagus, liver, brain, and pancreas), even optimal and cost-unfettered treatment has failed to delay disease morbidity and mortality, and is far less likely to provide long-term remission, control, or a cure. For many of these cancers, even the ability to prolong life with the disease is very limited and extremely costly. Thus, for some cancers –for example, pancreatic– little change has been seen in mortality over time, even in high income countries.[23] For some, but not all, of these cancers, prevention is possible and constitutes the optimal policy response.

In sum, the historical evidence of cancer mortality from high income countries demonstrates major success for an important subset of cancers through treatment and for another subset through primary and secondary prevention. This historical evidence helps define the set of candidate cancers on which LMICs could focus resources to reduce both incidence and mortality. Reduction of suffering, by contrast, should be considered an important area for action for all cancers in LMICs.

2.iii Facets of the cancer divide and sources of disparities

FACET 1
RISK FACTORS AND PRIMARY PREVENTION

The first dimension of the cancer divide is the distribution of risk factors and their prevention. As was the case in high income countries, much of the increasing incidence of cancer in developing countries is due to an increase in the number of people living to older ages. At the same time, cancer incidence rates vary substantially around the world, and these disparities are due chiefly to differences in the prevalence of risk factors for specific cancers. Some of these are not readily modifiable. For example, increased breast cancer risk is linked to early age at menarche and late age at menopause. Others, such as behavioral risk factors, are theoretically modifiable, although not necessarily easy to change (examples are alcohol consumption, weight gain after menopause, fewer births, and late age at first birth).[24-26]

Risk factors for some cancers are increasingly prevalent among the poor (e.g. smoking and obesity). By contrast, smoking is declining in some wealthy populations. Unless behaviors are modified significantly in LMICs, the burden of cancers associated with these risk factors will increase disproportionately.

The major modifiable risk factor for cancer is tobacco use, which is causally associated with 15 different types of cancers and estimated to cause some 20% of cancers worldwide.[27] The rise in prevalence of cigarette smoking has made lung cancer the most common form of cancer and cause of death in LMICs. The epidemic of cancers associated with such well-established risk factors has contributed significantly to the large increase in the absolute numbers of cancer deaths.[28] Approximately 6 million people die annually from tobacco use and exposure, and the figure is projected to rise to 7.5 million by 2020.[29]

Countries can implement effective policies for reducing tobacco use inexpensively.[30] Recognizing this, most high income countries have developed and institutionalized a series of policies to reduce tobacco consumption over the past several decades.[31] These policies include education and social communication. Many effective tobacco control interventions are legal or regulatory in nature, including taxes, smoke-free spaces, and bans on advertising and promotion.

As a result, tobacco consumption has declined, measured both in terms of cessation among older populations, and the increase in the proportion of younger adults who have never smoked), especially among men.[32-34] By contrast, poorer countries show persistent and increasing rates of tobacco consumption. Among men, the prevalence of smoking declines as income rises; with the highest prevalence of smoking seen in LMICs. For women in LMICs, smoking rates are lower and preventing them from rising is an important public health goal.[35] As a consequence, tobacco-related deaths and lung cancer rates are declining in high income countries, while they are predicted to rise in LMICs.[36] Declining tobacco consumption in high income countries may also be an important reason for the dramatic fall in cardiovascular mortality. Similar public health success could be achieved through tobacco control in LMICs, which might prevent the expected increase in mortality in future decades.

Obesity is a more recently recognized risk factor for certain cancers.[37] According to predictions, slowing the worldwide epidemic of obesity would substantially reduce future cancer incidence. Again, high income countries have developed credible policy tools that include promoting physical activity, healthier food at schools, and education about the nutrient content of packaged foods. Within high income countries, weight is negatively associated with socio-economic status.[38] By contrast, overweight is positively associated with income across LMICs, and the rates are high and increasing.[39] Obesity rates are particularly high in upper middle income countries. This contributes to the cancer divide as well as to the increased risk for and concentration of several other NCDs (e.g. diabetes mellitus and cardiovascular disease), placing enormous strains on already overburdened health systems.[40]

Environmental pollution and lack of safety in the home, workplace, and community are other preventable sources of disparity that fuel the cancer divide. Indoor air pollution from reliance on solid fuels, including biomass and coal, in cramped living conditions, is intimately linked to poverty.[41] With regards to occupational risk, some authors posit a risk transition: populations in developing countries are exposed to both traditional and emerging workplace risks. Further, these groups of risks are often cumulative and interactive (e.g. asbestos and tobacco).[42] Further, for many families, the workplace and the home are one, which means that any contamination from pesticides or other agents quickly comes in contact with young children.

Knowledge gained from experience makes the divide in risk factors between the poor and rich especially insidious. Decades ago, many of the same behavioral, workplace, and environmental risks were prevalent in high income countries. Yet, at the time when high income populations were exposed, little was known about the effects of many risk factors. Today, laws and policies to reduce exposure and share information that can change behavior increasingly protect the wealthy. In Norway, for example, the ILO lists 97 general and 42 specific laws against occupational health hazards, compared to 12 and 4, respectively, in India.[43] The poor are being exposed at a time when the consequences of many risk factors are well-known, and effective, low cost policies exist to mitigate those risks.[44,45]

Many of the risk factors for cancer overlap with other diseases, such as CVD and diabetes, as mentioned above. The diagonal approach to health system strengthening highlights these overlapping and often undervalued benefits.[46,47]

The risk factors for cancer also detract from overall economic and social development. They lead to declines in workplace productivity and may contribute to climate change, which affects the global community. Further, there are implications for the wellbeing of vulnerable groups, such as children who are exposed to second-hand risks of tobacco. Thus, policies to reduce risk factors for cancer can have important benefits for the broader goals of economic and human development. Indeed, the magnitude of 5-year cancer prevalence is directly related to a country's level of human development.[48]

FACET 2

CANCERS ASSOCIATED WITH INFECTIONS
THAT ARE AMENABLE TO PRIMARY PREVENTION[49]

A majority of infections associated with cancers today are diseases of the poor – in terms of both incidence and mortality. This is due to lack of access to the kind of prevention that is increasingly the norm in high income populations.

In 2008, 16.1% of new cancer cases globally were attributable to infection-related disease. In low income countries, however, 22.9% of cancers were infection-related, compared to just over 7.4% in high income countries. In sub-Saharan Africa, 32.7% of cancer cases were caused by infections, with the fraction reaching over 80% for specific infections.[50] In fact, seven of the ten most common cancers in Uganda are attributable to infectious diseases.[51,52] In the majority of LMICs, especially the poorest of Africa and Asia, cervical cancer continues to rank among the top three causes of death, especially in young women. In South Africa, cervical cancer is reported to be the leading cause of death among adult women, and is especially concentrated among the poorer, black population.[53] These findings are similar to and supported by previous analysis.[54]

Kaposi sarcoma is basically restricted to low income countries and the Africa region. HIV/AIDS infection emerged in the last few decades as an important risk factor for cancer, particularly in Africa, where 70% of the 33 million people living with HIV reside.[55] Since its origin, HIV/AIDS infection has been closely associated with increased incidence of certain cancers like cervical cancer, non-Hodgkin lymphoma, and Kaposi sarcoma, which were collectively described as AIDS-defining cancers because of their association with untreated HIV/AIDS infection.[56] The role of HIV/AIDS infection appears to be permissive in most cases. The exception is cervical cancer, where shared risk factors are important.

Thus, with the advent of effective anti-retroviral treatment, the incidence of AIDS-defining cancers, except for cervical, has been reduced. The incidence of other cancers among people living with HIV/AIDS, such as anal, oropharyngeal, and lung, now often referred to as Non-AIDS-Defining cancers, started to rise at about the same time, and has continued to do so.[57] In countries with mature epidemics, one third of all deaths among people living with HIV/AIDS are cancer related, but the picture is less clear in other LMICs because of incomplete treatment coverage and a lack of good quality data.[58]

There are striking differences by country income-level in the distribution of age-adjusted (person-time) incidence for cancers related to infection compared to other cancers (Figure 2.4). While for most cancers, incidence increases by country income-level, for cervical cancer and Kaposi sarcoma, incidence declines as income increases. The incidences of liver and stomach cancer tend to be unrelated to income. This relationship between income and incidence varies by geographic region for some cancers. The epidemiology of liver cancer, for example, is different in high and low income countries, and within developing regions in Asia.

The inequity of the cancer divide is well illustrated by the distribution of screening and vaccination for cervical cancer. A study of survey data from 57 countries indicates that coverage of cervical cancer screening in developing countries is, on average, 19%, compared to 63% in high income countries. The figures for LMICs range from 1% in Bangladesh to 73% in Brazil. Further, the highest risk groups —older and poor women— are the least likely to be screened. In China, crude coverage is 70%, yet effective screening coverage (periodicity, inclusion of PAP smear) is only 23%.[59] In general, the highest risk groups —poor and younger women— are the least likely to be screened. Coverage of the HPV vaccine is similarly skewed, although recent reductions in price to LMICs should help to close part of this divide.[60]

Important opportunities exist for meeting the challenge of several infection-related cancers, especially if prices of vaccines are brought down for LMICs.[61] Increased investment in HIV/AIDS treatment and better and more disease management will eliminate a significant proportion of the HIV/AIDS–associated cancers that threaten countries with a large burden of HIV/AIDS infection. Further, controlling the spread of the infection will produce the added benefit of preventing cancer.

Figure 2.4

Cancer Incidence by Country per Capita Income, 15 or More Years of Age

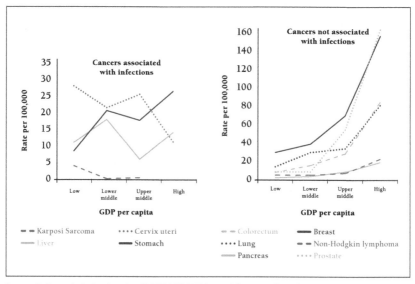

Source: Authors calculations based on GLOBOCAN 2008 http://globocan.iarc.fr/, and World Bank, World Development Indicators, 2010. http://data.worldbank.org/data-catalog/world-development-indicators

Cervical cancer is one of the few viral-induced diseases with an effective vaccine as well as a public health intervention that can dramatically reduce the probability of disease advancement and mortality. Screening and vaccination could have a major impact in LMICs, especially if used in combination in a non-overlapping, dual approach.[62] Effective, widespread screening programs for cervical cancer in LMICs could substantially reduce morbidity and mortality in the short- and medium-term.[63] Population-based screening has been proven to be an effective public health intervention for preventing cervical cancer in women who are infected with HPV. The recent development and validation of inexpensive HPV-based testing with minimal visits can make screening programs more easily implementable and cost-effective in low-resource settings. Further, screening is proven to reduce incidence and mortality over a short time interval if followed with effective measures for treatment, as documented by evidence from a number of developing countries, including Mexico and India.[64-66] In addition, the widespread deployment of a vaccine against HPV could eventually prevent up to two-thirds of future cervical cancer cases.[67,68] Vaccination will be increasingly effective as interventions become better informed by epidemiological research on the prevalent strains of HPV in each country.[69]

Another example of successful prevention of infection-associated cancer is vaccination of young children against Hepatitis B. In Taiwan, universal vaccination has nearly eradicated pediatric liver cancer, which was previously one of the most common cancers in Taiwanese children.[70]

Taken together, the focus on infectious agents in the primary prevention of cancer could lead to enormous gains in the fight against infection-related malignancies. Results would be evident in both the short- and medium-term.

FACET 3

CANCERS AMENABLE TO TREATMENT, WHICH ARE OFTEN MADE MORE EFFECTIVE WITH EARLY DETECTION[71]

While income and geography should not determine the probability of dying from a disease, in large part they do. LMICs suffer a larger share of global mortality, as compared to global incidence, for almost all cancers that are screening-detectable or treatable, whether or not they are of infectious origin. Indeed, as science uncovers new methods for early detection, treatment, and cure, the suffering and death from these cancers becomes more "exclusive" to the poor.

Certain cancers that were once uniformly fatal, now have high potential for many years of remission, and possibly cure with treatment. Testicular cancer, childhood leukemia, thyroid cancer, Hodgkin lymphoma, and chronic myeloid leukemia were all once uniformly fatal, but current treatments have produced higher survival rates, at least in wealthy countries. For those cancers where early detection makes a difference –including cancers of the breast, prostate, and colon– the opportunities to achieve remission or cure are especially broad.[72]

Breast cancer is the leading cause of death for women below age 60 in high income countries, and among the top five causes in LMICs. Age-adjusted incidence and mortality rates from breast cancer are higher in wealthy countries due to differences in risk factor distribution and the stage of demographic transition. Yet, both age-standardized incidence and mortality are rising rapidly in poorer countries. Evidence from 1990 to 2010 shows a cumulative increase of more than 30% in many parts of Africa, Asia, and the Middle East, and a decline in North America.[73]

Breast cancer cure rates are closely associated with stage of detection. Yet, late stage presentation is the norm in most LMICs. Between 60 and 70% of cases in LMICs are detected in late stages with regional disease and metastasis, compared to less than 20% in most high income countries.[74,75]

According to GLOBOCAN data, more than 85% of pediatric cancer cases and 95% of deaths occur in LMICs. At the same time, LMICs account for 90% of the global population of children aged 0-14. For children aged 5-14, cancer is the third leading cause of death in upper middle, fourth in lower middle, and eighth in low income countries. It is the second leading cause of death in high income countries. The fact that cancer has become a leading cause of death among children in developing countries reflects the substantial gains in preventing childhood mortality from communicable diseases and underdevelopment.

Figure 2.5

Ratio of Mortality to Incidence by Cancer Type and Country per Capita Income

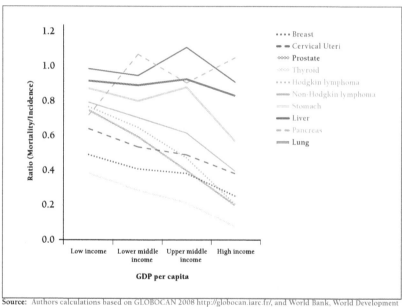

Source: Authors calculations based on GLOBOCAN 2008 http://globocan.iarc.fr/, and World Bank, World Development Indicators, 2010. http://data.worldbank.org/data-catalog/world-development-indicators.

Variation in the probability of surviving a treatable cancer (beyond those associated with factors directly related to the specific type of disease) is caused by differences in access to quality treatment and early detection. For adults aged 15 and over, lethality varies significantly by country income level. This is true for all cancers other than those cancers for which no effective treatments exist and early detection is not possible (Figure 2.5). For all other cancers, where early detection and/or treatment can significantly affect outcomes, the lines slope downward and are particularly steep for cancers such as testicular. In the case of thyroid and prostate cancer, the comparison between low and high income countries could be confounded by diagnostic intensity, as well as screening, in the case of prostate cancer.

For cancers in children aged 15 and under, the lethality gradient is particularly steep (Figure 2.6). For leukemia, which is the most common childhood cancer by far, the rate of mortality to (person-time) incidence is over 70% in low income countries, compared to below 20% in high income countries. The survival inequality gap is almost as large when childhood cancers are viewed as a whole. When broken down by geographic region, the high rates for sub-Saharan Africa, Middle East and North Africa, and East Asia and the Pacific are evident when compared to other parts of the developing world and to high income regions. Using data from hospitals and in-depth country reviews, Ribeiro et al. also demonstrated the inverse relationship between lethality and health spending, per capita.[76]

Figure 2.6

Ratio of Mortality to Incidence by Cancer Type, Country per Capita Income and Geographic Region; Children 0-14

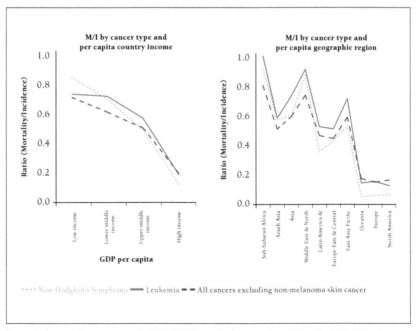

Source: Authors calculations based on GLOBOCAN 2008 http://globocan.iarc.fr/, and World Bank, World Development Indicators, 2010. http://data.worldbank.org/data-catalog/world-development-indicators.

Although the limitations of the data make it unreasonable to claim precision in measuring the slope of each line and the levels for each country or group of countries, the trends are clear. Further, data are robust to excluding countries for which incidence, mortality, or both, are projected in the GLOBOCAN database, as well as to replacing per capita country income with level of education and per capita health spending. Even so, significant differences exist within regions and between countries at similar levels of income. These differences merit further review to isolate those countries that are particularly good performers for their income level, and to analyze why and how this good performance has been achieved.

FACET 4
SOCIAL AND PSYCHOLOGICAL ASPECTS OF LIFE WITH DISEASE AND AFTER TREATMENT

Eliminating the social and psychological elements of suffering should be a core component of reducing the burden of all cancers in LMICs. Often, these elements are associated with long-term disability that is intensified by social exclusion and neglect. Further, these aspects of suffering tend to be poorly measured and greatly undervalued, and they receive little recognition in resource allocation and decision-making.

Cancer is still one of the world's most stigmatized diseases.[77] Stigma refers to the perception that the person affected by cancer differs from the norm in a negative or undesirable way. This perception often leads to discrimination, which, in turn, results in a loss of status, and rejection or isolation.[78] Further, stigma exacerbates the social, emotional, and financial devastation that all too often accompany a diagnosis of cancer.[79]

Although too often acute and rapidly fatal, cancer can be a chronic illness and the effects of treatment long-term. Indeed, recognizing this represents a fundamental change in how cancer is perceived in many communities, and can provide important incentives for prevention and early detection.

People living with cancer may encounter numerous physical, psychological, social, spiritual, and financial difficulties during their diagnosis and treatment, and then throughout their lives. The after-effects of cancer and its treatment may be medical or physical, along with non-medical or practical concerns.[80] The specific late medical effects that cancer survivors experience vary, but can include physical impairments, psychological distress, sexual dysfunction, infertility, impaired organ function, cosmetic changes, and limitations in communication, mobility, and cognition.[81] Non-medical late effects can include issues such as unemployment, poverty, debt, and loss of insurance.[82]

These effects –forms of disability that vary in severity– change the capability of persons diagnosed with cancer to manage daily life, and, often, to earn income. When fully taken into account, they exacerbate the cancer divide and constitute a tremendous source of inequity, particularly for families that are already poor or vulnerable.[83]

In LMICs where protective legislation is weaker and ignorance about the etiology, prevention, and treatment of cancer is widespread, cancer patients, and often their family members, face discrimination and exclusion. A historical analysis of the United States and England demonstrates that risk factors also have been concentrated in the poor and that legislation has tended to protect and benefit the wealthy.[84,85] Populations that already suffer discrimination both inside and outside the home –women, children, certain ethnic groups, and the poor in general– have to face yet another layer of obstacles. Social exclusion can exacerbate the lack of basic freedoms to choose and achieve a state of well-being, and can cause families to fall into poverty.[86,87] Illness compounds exclusion, especially with diseases like cancer where treatment often makes the disease impossible to hide and requires physical mutilation.

The dearth of survivorship care and the lack of protection from stigma at home, in the community, and in the workplace combine to intensify the long-term hardships and costs of the disease. By contrast, addressing survivorship issues from the moment of diagnosis can help to prevent secondary cancers and recurrence of cancer. It can also promote disease management following diagnosis and treatment to ensure the maximum number of years of healthy life for those surviving with cancer, minimize preventable pain, disability, and psychosocial distress, and help cancer patients obtain support and resources to cope with life, both during and after treatment.[88]

Without greater access to treatment, cancer will remain a stigmatized disease not to be discussed. Greater access to treatment can lead to more humane treatment of cancer patients by their communities because the disease will not be seen as inevitably fatal, and this greater optimism will translate to an increased awareness. The history of cancer and its awareness in high income countries tends to support this hypothesis.[89]

In LMICs, survivorship care is sorely lacking and has not been adequately incorporated into health systems as an integral part of treatment. It is an area of caregiving rarely considered since cancer continues to be equated with a death sentence. A further barrier is that health care systems are designed to manage acute illnesses, not chronic diseases.[90]

At the same time, most cancer patients –and indeed most people– in LMICs, are uninsured and lack any form of financial protection for health care. Just as with any health shock, cancer can drive a family into, or deeper into, poverty.[91-94] The chronic nature of the disease intensifies this phenomenon as care is ongoing. Unemployment and the inability to work compound the costs of treatment and the risks that a family will fall into poverty.

Stigma can hamper advances in the struggle with cancer. For example, people may be detracted from engaging in practices that reduce their cancer risk, and diagnosis may be delayed if fear of stigma creates a barrier to getting symptoms checked by a doctor. At a population level, governments are less likely to devote resources to reduce their cancer burden if individuals affected by the disease fail to express their needs or to advocate for themselves and others.[95,96]

While stigma is a global problem, it is a greater obstacle in LMICs and among poorer populations. For these groups, the stigma of cancer is layered onto other forms of discrimination associated with gender, age, ethnicity, religion, and poverty.[97]

Further, policies and institutions to cope with stigma tend to be weak in LMICs. Advocacy movements are relatively new and not well developed, although they are evolving.[98-100] Legislation to prevent workplace discrimination and to protect and promote the rights of women, for example, is more frequently found in higher income countries. Most LMICs have few laws or services for disabled workers, and even where these laws and services do exist, they do not apply to the majority of the labor force who work in the informal sector.[101]

Finally, survey evidence shows that the ignorance about cancer that causes stigma is more pervasive in LMICs. For example, between one-fifth and one-third of respondents from Mexico, India, China, South Africa, and Argentina reported concerns about "catching cancer" from people who have it, compared to approximately 5% in Italy, Japan, and France.[102] In another study, 55% of women living inside Gaza consider breast cancer to be contagious, as compared to 14% of Gazan women residing in countries with greater access to services.[103]

Stigma and exclusion may be particularly severe for patients who suffer uncontrolled pain or live with a terminal illness.[104] This is another reason to advocate for increased access to pain control and palliation, especially at end of life.

Text Box 2.2
Understanding and combating stigma:
A LIVESTRONG research and outreach program[105]

The LIVESTRONG global cancer research study sought to give people affected by cancer a chance to share their experiences and perspectives in order to gain a better understanding of stigma. The research draws on multiple sources of data – including media coverage, public opinion surveys, and semi-structured interviews describing how cancer is portrayed and perceived. Argentina, Brazil, China, France, India, Italy, Japan, Mexico, Russia, and South Africa were sites for the study. The study included more than 4,500 interviews with health care practitioners, cancer survivors, organization leaders, and community members investigating the nature of the stigma associated with cancer and its impact. The data illustrated that stigma is pervasive across countries, cultures, and communities.

Six "lessons learned" were derived from the global research results:

1. Around the world, cancer continues to carry a significant amount of stigma; however, there are opportunities to capitalize on shifting perceptions for positive change.

2. Awareness of cancer prevention, early detection, treatment, and survival are on the rise; however, too many people still report that they feel uninformed, when it comes to cancer.

3. Communication is essential to decreasing cancer-related stigma, raising cancer awareness, and disseminating cancer education. People with a personal history of cancer –especially well-known or celebrity survivors– and multiple mass media channels are key resources for raising awareness and disseminating cancer education.

4. The school system represents a potential venue for cancer education, and increasing cancer awareness among children may be an investment with high returns.

5. When facing cancer, people around the world want information and emotional support for themselves and for their families.

6. *Tobacco use and obesity are widely acknowledged cancer risks. Programs and policies that help people translate awareness into action are needed.*

*Based on these findings, LIVE**STRONG** developed the Cancer Anti-Stigma Initiative and chose South Africa as the first pilot nation. This effort was aimed at raising awareness, improving knowledge about treatment, and challenging stigma. Over a period of 18 months, the initiative conducted focus groups and interviews, empowered survivors to share their stories, held community events, launched a door-to-door campaign, trained community health workers and media figures, and created SMS, TV and radio interventions. These efforts produced significant results among the target audience, including a 4% increase in knowledge of radiation, a 21% increase in knowledge of chemotherapy, and a 9% decrease in those who said cancer patients are in "constant pain." In addition, 45% of those who had heard cancer messages in the last year responded that they learned something new or did something differently about cancer.*

The success of the initiative was also described in words. At the beginning of the project, respondents' views on cancer often included, "Cancer is a death sentence." Just 18 months later, respondents' views had shifted to, "I learned that cancer can be treated" and "I learned to be strong and not feel guilty about the disease I have."

*LIVE**STRONG** is continuing its anti-stigma work in Mexico with the Comparte tu Historia Campaign.*

FACET 5
PAIN AND PHYSICAL SUFFERING

Pain control and palliation create an abyss in the global cancer divide. Even for the cancers where neither treatment nor prevention is possible, a crater of controllable pain and suffering separates the poor and rich. Much can be done to remedy this most unacceptable of inequities.

Yet, the importance of investing in pain control and palliation is omitted from the outcome measurements that typically guide health policy-makers. The focus on income, incidence of disease, or mortality as metrics for fairness, equity, and efficiency excludes or severely undervalues the control of pain. This is because neither income nor extension of life are the primary purpose of palliation, and because the impact on productivity and other health outcome measures is assumed to be nil.[106] Yet, in addition to the obvious and tremendously important function of reducing pain, especially at end of life, palliative care has been associated with improved quality of life, reduced symptoms of depression, and longer survival.[107] Palliative care at end of life has, in fact, been given insufficient attention in both high and low income countries.

The lack of access to pain relief, and specifically to opioids, represents one of the most appalling and unnecessary global health disparities between rich and poor countries. These inequities repeat themselves within countries, including the United States, across socio-economic groups.[108]

WHO estimates suggest that the majority of terminal cancer patients worldwide have no access to pain-relieving medications, despite their low cost.[109] High income countries account for less than 15% of the world population but more than 94% of global morphine consumption.[110] Sub-Saharan Africa in 2008 experienced an estimated 1.3 million deaths in pain, yet consumed enough medicinal opioids to treat just 85,000 people (<1% of the global total).[111,112]

Over the last decade, consumption of opioids for pain treatment has more than doubled worldwide, but very little of the increase has occurred in low income countries.[113] A 2011 study demonstrated that access to adequate pain management is exceptionally rare. In the case of strong opioid analgesics, and considering a wide spectrum of types and causes of pain, including cancer, 83% of the world's population (5.5 billion people) lives in countries with low to non-existent access, 4% has moderate access, and only 7% has adequate access.[114]

Country-specific data are available for several key indicators of opioid consumption and demonstrate the huge range in access as well as use. Non-methadone, morphine-equivalence opioid consumption in mg per capita, per death from HIV/AIDS or cancer, and per death from HIV/AIDS or cancer in pain are reproduced in Appendix 1, with permission from UICC-Global Access to Pain Relief Initiative and the University of Wisconsin Pain and Policy Studies Group. These are multi-year averages, making the data less subject to single-year variations, and are based on annual opioid consumption reported by governments to the International Narcotics Control Board.

These data show tremendous variation in access across countries and regions. There is an almost 580-fold difference in morphine-equivalence opioid consumption per death from HIV/AIDS or cancer in pain between the 20% poorest countries of the world and the 20% richest countries of the world.

There is also variation in access that is only partially explained by income, and must also be related to health system weaknesses and cultural barriers. In many low, and even in a few lower middle income countries, consumption per death from HIV/AIDS or cancer in pain is extremely low – less than 100 mg. In these cases, there is likely to be almost no access to pain control for patients, and even surgical pain control is often lacking.[115] By contrast, Uganda, Ghana, Bangladesh, Viet Nam and Uzbekistan –all low income countries– report consumption between 450 and 790 mg per death from HIV/AIDS or cancer in pain.

Jordan is the highest of all lower middle countries at over 9,900 mg per death from HIV/AIDS or cancer in pain. Other lower middle income countries with similar levels of per capita income have much lower levels of consumption and access, with Armenia at just over 600 mg and Egypt at just below 2,000 mg. China has a higher per capita income, yet a consumption level that falls below 1,300 mg. Botswana, Mexico, Chile, and Turkey are all upper middle income countries with similar levels of per capita income. Yet, there is a 10, 25, and 50 fold difference in use of pain control medication – approximately 250 versus 2,400, 6,200 and 11,900 mg respectively.

Wealthier countries consume pain control medication at higher rates but there is still great variation for similar income levels. Portugal, with an income of approximately US$ 22,000, registers close to 32,000 mg per death from HIV/AIDS or cancer in pain, compared to the Czech Republic at 23,000 mg. Hungary, with a somewhat lower level of income, consumes 21,500 mg. Japan registers a low level of consumption at just over 9,100 mg, compared to 35,400 in the UK, 57,100 in Ireland, 83,350 in Sweden, and 155,000 in Germany. All of these countries have an income per capita in the US$ 35,000 range. Spain, with an income per capita of US$ 29,600, consumes almost 70,000 mg, while the level in Italy, with a similar level of income, is approximately 18,800 mg. Canada and Australia have similar income levels per capita, yet Canada consumes more than double what Australia consumes. The US and Canada register similar levels of approximately 270,000 mg per death from HIV/AIDS or cancer in pain.

In addition, the gap between LMICs and high income countries has been increasing. In 1980, consumption was approximately 10-20 mg/capita (morphine equivalence) for high income countries, compared to less than 1 mg/capita, and close to zero, for most developing countries. In the USA and Canada, in 2007, opioid consumption was close to 650 mg/capita, compared to 100 in the UK, and less than 1 in most countries of Africa, as well as in India, Pakistan, Bangladesh, and Indonesia, among others. In China, Brazil, Mexico, and South Africa, consumption was around 5-7 mg/capita (Figure 2.7).[116]

At least in the case of opioids, price should not be the issue since essential pain medicines are largely off-patent. And yet the global divide in access to pain control is compounded by differential prices for the poor and rich that are the result of lack of competition in developing country markets. An immediate release, 1 mg tablet of morphine sulfate should cost less than one cent, and a one-month supply between US$ 1.80 and US$ 5.40. Yet, the documented costs in some developing countries range between US$ 60 and US$ 180.[117] Even in the high-end, middle income countries of Latin America, the cost of a month of morphine or its equivalent can reach 200% of average monthly income.[118]

Lack of medical personnel to prescribe and monitor analgesics plays a large role in determining access, as do government policies and the interpretation of international treaties designed to limit the illicit use of opioids and curb the potential for trafficking while ensuring access for medical purposes. Outdated regulations at both the national and international levels also affect both opioid availability and accessibility.[119] Weak and inappropriate –excessive and poorly defined– regulatory frameworks in many developing countries make it difficult to get adequate pain medication to patients. In these countries, it is illegal to dispense opioids, dosage and duration are limited in ways that do not match the needs of patients, or extensive licensing requirements make it impossible for most pharmacies, clinics, and medical personnel to dispense opioids.[120] Too often, some population groups, such as children or those with cancer, are excluded under the false assumptions that pain is less severe, other drugs will suffice, or that opioid use will generate addiction.[121] International agencies dedicated to managing the legal framework and implementing the 1961 Single Convention on Narcotic Drugs, appear to have worked harder on preventing illicit use than on guaranteeing access where required for the relief of pain and suffering.[122] Indeed, the International Narcotics Control Board consistently approves government quotas for controlled narcotics that are far below the epidemiological prevalence of clinical pain, leaving patients legally prohibited from access to pain control.[123]

Access to pain relief is also hampered by market failures. The low price and low demand for morphine are disincentives for pharmaceutical companies to register and sell morphine in LMICs, particularly when doing so exposes them to increased regulations and inspections by government authorities. In several countries, pharmaceutical distributors have stopped importing morphine, preferring instead to import more expensive products with higher profit margins, such as fentanyl or less potent analgesics that are not subject to strict controls but are also not appropriate for the treatment of moderate or severe pain.

Figure 2.7

Country Opioid Consumption by Human Development Index, 1980 and 2007

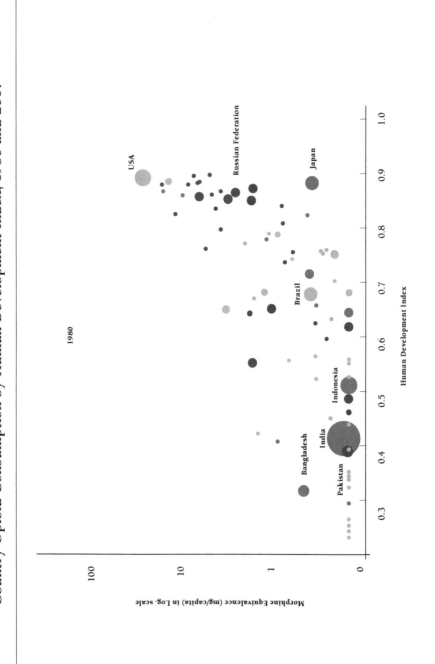

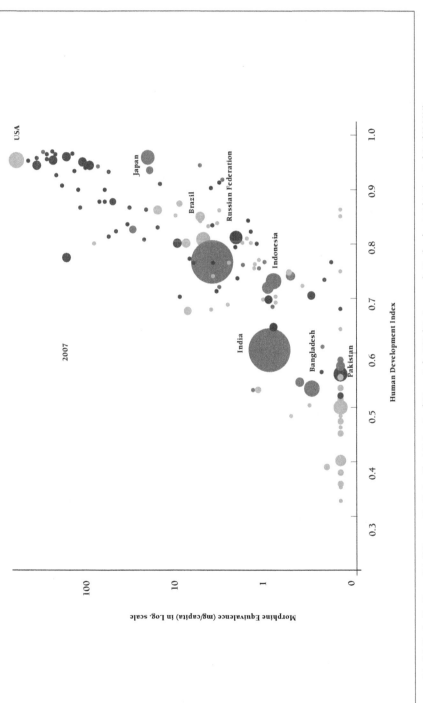

Source: Pain & Policy Studies Group. Opioid Consumption Motion Chart. University of Wisconsin for 2007. http://ppsg-production.heroku.com/chart (accessed April 22 2011).

In the case of pain control, much can be done with relative ease and speed, compared to many other aspects of the cancer divide. Given the low price, availability of proven interventions, existence of international legal treaties and agencies, availability of global data and evidence resulting from the strong controls to avoid illicit trade, relative ease of administration, and few human and infrastructure requirements, dealing with this piece of the divide is an obvious area for immediate action.[124-128] Pain control might even be considered an absolute minimum requirement at any level of economic development, even with severe resource constraints. Moreover, access to appropriate pain medication is an effective horizontal strategy[129] that can improve quality of life for all patients.[130] Thus, improving pain control represents an opportunity to impact across-the-board on all diseases, and expanding access to pain control and palliation through better access to opioids is a good starting point for applying a diagonal approach[131,132] to achieving better CCC.

2.iv Conclusions

The cancer divide is a result of disparities in access to CCC that include prevention, early detection, diagnosis, treatment, survivorship care, and palliation. The evidence presented in this chapter demonstrates the breadth and depth of the cancer divide, and why closing this gap is an equity imperative.

All facets of the cancer divide are increasingly concentrated in LMICs. As a result, avoidable morbidity, mortality, and suffering from disease that can be prevented, treated, or palliated will become even more concentrated among the poor. It is the poor who contract preventable cancers and die from them. They will also become the most likely to die of treatable cancers and the most exposed to becoming impoverished by the costs of trying to manage the disease. The concentration of suffering among the poor is most poignantly illustrated by the lack of access to pain control, which should be considered a fundamental human right.

Even as many of the diseases that are associated with cancers, as well as specific cancers, become better understood and increasingly preventable and treatable, the global divide will continue to widen, especially if risk factors continue to spread globally and remain unfettered among poorer populations.

Options exist to begin to close each facet of the cancer divide. Evidence from high income countries demonstrates that increased coverage of cancer prevention strategies, access to early detection, and effective treatments result in decreased incidence, morbidity, and mortality for a set of targetable, candidate cancers for CCC in LMICs. CCC efforts in resource-poor settings, guided by the explicit needs of each country, should focus existing resources on the specific cancers and interventions that would maximize reductions in cancer incidence and mortality, as well as improve access to palliation and pain control.

First, risk factors, beginning with tobacco consumption but also including obesity and unhealthy lifestyles, as well as environmental and safety risks in the workplace and in the home, are prime targets for interventions in LMICs. The policies that have been effective in high income countries to reduce risk factors, especially around tobacco consumption, need to be adapted and applied in LMICs.

Second, the technologies to prevent those cancers that are produced by known infections need to be made widely available, and new technologies need to be developed. A focus on infectious agents in the primary prevention of cancer can produce enormous gains in the short and medium term, the most obvious being Kaposi sarcoma and cervical cancer, but also stomach and liver cancer.

Third, treatments for cancers that are curable with effective and often low-cost interventions, combined with earlier detection, should be expanded. This is true for the cancers, such as breast cancer, that are increasingly affecting populations in LMICs at all income levels. This is especially the case for several of the most common cancers of children, Hodgkin disease, and testicular cancer. These malignancies have several features in common: the disparities in treatment mean differences in cure rates are enormous; they are highly curable without the need for major surgical resources; they affect young people; and the life years gained would be substantial relative to the modest investment made in treatment. Also, this could prove to be one of the areas where early success stories are easiest to generate.

Fourth, stigma and discrimination need to be eliminated in the context of improving survivorship care and reducing social and psychological suffering. Countering stigma and discrimination can reduce suffering and increase the impact of health policies around prevention, early detection, and treatment. This can be a virtuous cycle as greater access to early detection and effective treatment can translate into increased awareness.

Finally, pain control and palliative care for all patients must be guaranteed, but especially for those for whom cure and meaningful prolongation of survival is not possible. Indeed, the most insidious example of the cancer divide is pain palliation. The glaring gap in access to pain control and palliation can, and must, be closed by strengthening health systems and regulatory frameworks.

Opportunities to reduce the cancer divide exist, and many of the lowest-cost interventions and treatments can be the most useful. Without policies to close each facet of the divide, death from cancer will increasingly become the painful lot of the poor. Immediate action on all available opportunities is an equity imperative.

APPENDIX 2.1

Non-methodone Opioid Consumption
(Morphine Equivalent), 2008
Ordered by "per death from HIV or cancer in pain"

Income Region (World Bank)[4]	Country[1]	GNI per capita (PPP 2008)[4] $	Non-methadone opioid con-sumption (morphine-equivalents)[2]		
			Per capita (mg)	Per death from HIV or cancer (mg)	Per death from HIV or cancer in pain[3] (mg)
Low Income	Tanzania	1,344	0/NA	–	–
	Rwanda	1,190	0.0	10	18
	Mali	1,171	0.0	16	23
	Myanmar	1,596	0.0	16	24
	Burkina Faso	1,215	0.0	17	26
	Central African Republic	758	0.1	18	31
	Chad	1,067	0.0	19	31
	Ethiopia	992	0.0	21	35
	Cambodia	1,868	0.0	26	39
	Niger	675	0.0	31	42
	Haiti	949	0.0	28	47
	Malawi	911	0.1	26	49
	Burundi	402	0.1	29	50
	Sierra Leone	809	0.1	39	57
	Madagascar	953	0.0	46	58
	Senegal	1,816	0.0	52	68
	Democratic Republic of Congo	291	0.1	42	70
	Togo	844	0.1	45	75
	Mozambique	854	0.2	44	80
	Zimbabwe	176	0.7	43	85
	Zambia	1,359	0.3	45	86
	Benin	1,499	0.1	87	130
	Tajikistan	2,020	0.1	134	170
	Eritrea	643	0.1	117	182
	Lao PDR	2,321	0.1	198	249
	Kenya	1,628	0.6	149	280
	Mauritania	2,118	0.2	211	283

APPENDIX 2.1 *(continued)*

Non-methodone Opioid Consumption (Morphine Equivalent), 2008

Ordered by "per death from HIV or cancer in pain"

Income Region (World Bank)[4]	Country[1]	GNI per capita (PPP 2008)[4] $	Non-methadone opioid con-sumption (morphine-equivalents)[2]		
			Per capita (mg)	Per death from HIV or cancer (mg)	Per death from HIV or cancer in pain[3] (mg)
Low Income	Yemen	2,387	0.2	309	388
	Nepal	1,201	0.2	313	394
	Kyrgyzstan	2,291	0.2	319	400
	Uzbekistan	3,085	0.2	360	451
	Uganda	1,224	0.9	243	452
	Ghana	1,385	0.5	318	513
	Bangladesh	1,587	0.2	416	520
	Viet Nam	2,995	0.6	597	792
	Democratic Republic of Korea	–	0.8	825	1,032
Lower-middle Income	Bolivia	4,357	0/NA	–	–
	Honduras	3,750	0/NA	–	–
	Nigeria	2,156	0.0	6	10
	Cote d Ivoire	1,625	0.0	11	19
	Lesotho	2,021	0.4	44	85
	Sudan	2,051	0.1	57	87
	Republic of Congo	3,258	0.1	51	⁻92
	Pakistan	2,678	0.1	107	135
	Indonesia	3,957	0.1	159	199
	Iraq	–	0.2	181	226
	Azerbaijan	8,747	0.2	209	261
	Turkmenistan	7,052	0.2	294	369
	Angola	4,941	0.4	268	407
	Armenia	5,495	1.1	505	634
	Guyana	3,302	0.7	438	671
	India	3,337	0.4	542	717
	Bhutan	5,607	0.4	637	797
	Philippines	4,002	0.4	656	820
	Mongolia	3,619	1.1	710	888
	Paraguay	4,585	0.7	702	911
	Thailand	8,001	1.6	703	1,039

APPENDIX 2.1 (continued)

Non-methodone Opioid Consumption
(Morphine Equivalent), 2008
Ordered by "per death from HIV or cancer in pain"

Income Region (World Bank)[4]	Country[1]	GNI per capita (PPP 2008)[4] $	Non-methadone opioid con-sumption (morphine-equivalents)[2]		
			Per capita (mg)	Per death from HIV or cancer (mg)	Per death from HIV or cancer in pain[3] (mg)
	Sri Lanka	4,886	0.8	837	1,049
	Albania	7,976	1.5	1,016	1,271
	China	7,258	1.4	1,016	1,276
	Republic of Moldova	3,149	1.6	1,028	1,287
	Guatemala	4,694	0.9	1,106	1,487
	Morocco	4,628	0.6	1,246	1,585
	Ecuador	7,931	1.2	1,255	1,628
	Nicaragua	2,567	1.0	1,335	1,704
	Ukraine	6,535	2.9	1,336	1,737
Lower -middle Income	Egypt	5,889	0.8	1,508	1,890
	Islamic Republic of Iran	11,764	1.0	1,570	1,991
	Cape Verde	3,306	0.8	1,635	2,057
	Papua New Guinea	2,227	1.2	1,992	2,664
	Georgia	4,902	2.1	2,290	2,863
	El Salvador	6,498	2.1	2,221	3,050
	Samoa	4,126	1.8	3,002	3,759
	Vanuatu	3,908	2.0	4,155	5,197
	Syrian Arab Republic	4,760	1.5	5,428	6,787
	Tunisia	7,979	3.1	7,014	8,873
	Jordan	5,956	4.8	7,917	9,924
	Botswana	13,204	1.1	126	244
	Dominican Republic	8,273	0.7	470	660
	Namibia	6,323	2.0	379	723
	Kazakhstan	10,234	0.9	578	725
Upper -middle Income	Belarus	12,926	1.5	714	906
	Russian Federation	15,258	1.5	738	937
	Suriname	7,093	0.9	747	1,041
	Romania	12,844	1.7	850	1,065
	Peru	8,424	1.1	819	1,071
	Algeria	8,320	0.5	878	1,108

APPENDIX 2.1 (coninued)

Non-methodone Opioid Consumption
(Morphine Equivalent), 2008
Ordered by "per death from HIV or cancer in pain"

Income Region (World Bank)[4]	Country[1]	GNI per capita (PPP 2008)[4] $	Non-methadone opioid con-sumption (morphine-equivalents)[2]		
			Per capita (mg)	Per death from HIV or cancer (mg)	Per death from HIV or cancer in pain[3] (mg)
	South African Republic	9,812	7.1	977	1,817
	Cuba	–	2.6	1,503	1,883
	Jamaica	7,207	2.6	1,522	2,111
	Uruguay	13,808	4.5	1,862	2,347
	Mexico	13,971	1.4	1,846	2,363
	Venezuela	11,846	1.5	1,973	2,536
	Mauritius	13,344	1.8	2,314	2,916
	Panama	13,347	2.6	2,443	3,362
	Costa Rica	10,870	2.5	2,673	3,381
	Malaysia	13,927	2.6	2,804	3,619
	Libya	17,068	1.8	3,561	4,633
Upper -middle Income	Lebanon	13,475	3.5	4,285	5,462
	Chile	13,561	6.6	4,920	6,196
	Bulgaria	11,139	10.7	4,957	6,199
	Bosnia Herzegovena	8,222	8.5	5,173	6,471
	Brazil	10,607	5.8	5,130	6,612
	Argentina	14,603	8.9	5,493	6,936
	Colombia	8,589	5.1	5,395	7,101
	Latvia	12,944	17.1	6,574	8,226
	Lithuania	14,824	21.1	9,003	11,258
	Turkey	13,359	7.7	9,508	11,893
	Poland	17,803	38.2	15,041	18,811
	Montenegro	12,491	15.3	–	–
	Serbia	10,449	20.0	–	–
High Income	Equatorial Guinea	22,218	0/NA	–	–
	Oman	25,653	1.3	2,920	3,708
	Trinidad and Tobago	24,233	4.6	2,978	4,236
	Brunei	49,915	1.8	3,414	4,268
	Singapore	48,893	4.8	3,915	4,916
	Malta	21,004	11.9	6,469	8,093

APPENDIX 2.1 *(continued)*

Non-methodone Opioid Consumption (Morphine Equivalent), 2008

Ordered by "per death from HIV or cancer in pain"

Income Region (World Bank)[4]	Country[1]	GNI per capita (PPP 2008)[4] $	Non-methadone opioid con-sumption (morphine-equivalents)[2]		
			Per capita (mg)	Per death from HIV or cancer (mg)	Per death from HIV or cancer in pain[3] (mg)
	Estonia	17,168	19.7	7,283	9,124
	Japan	34,692	18.5	7,308	9,135
	Saudi Arabia	24,726	3.5	7,450	9,336
	Bahamas	25,201	10.9	7,278	10,597
	Bahrain	26,664	4.7	8,738	11,150
	Cyprus	21,962	11.4	10,092	12,615
	Republic of Korea	29,518	18.9	10,843	13,559
	Kuwait	55,719	2.4	11,022	13,828
	Barbados	21,673	23.0	11,741	15,536
	Croatia	16,389	37.1	13,049	16,313
	Qatar	79,426	2.3	12,883	17,408
	Italy	29,619	41.1	14,985	18,769
	Hungary	17,472	56.6	17,235	21,546
	United Arab Emirates	58,006	3.1	17,444	22,531
High Income	Czech Republic	22,678	53.4	18,572	23,216
	Portugal	22,105	61.0	25,374	32,073
	United Kingdom	35,087	75.5	28,315	35,411
	Slovakia	21,658	62.4	28,443	35,557
	Greece	27,580	76.8	31,047	38,817
	New Zealand	25,438	62.3	32,142	40,196
	Slovenia	25,857	105.5	38,700	48,383
	Israel	27,831	64.4	45,219	56,588
	The Netherlands	40,658	113.6	45,299	56,673
	Luxembourg	51,109	98.5	45,614	57,108
	Ireland	33,078	93.6	45,655	57,137
	France (metropolitan)	34,341	132.9	48,438	60,702
	Norway	58,810	154.9	63,354	79,261
	Sweden	36,936	152.2	66,647	83,350
	Iceland	22,917	128.6	71,753	89,709
	Belgium	34,873	222.6	79,798	99,835

APPENDIX 2.1 (continued)

Non-methodone Opioid Consumption
(Morphine Equivalent), 2008
Ordered by "per death from HIV or cancer in pain"

Income Region (World Bank)[4]	Country[1]	GNI per capita (PPP 2008)[4] $	Non-methadone opioid con-sumption (morphine-equivalents)[2]		
			Per capita (mg)	Per death from HIV or cancer (mg)	Per death from HIV or cancer in pain[3] (mg)
High Income	Finland	33,872	161.6	80,098	100,151
	Switzerland	39,849	194.1	87,044	109,131
	Australia	38,692	174.2	90,237	112,913
	Denmark	36,404	278.1	94,800	118,586
	Germany	35,308	324.3	123,894	155,014
	Austria	37,056	345.8	146,319	183,096
	Canada	38,668	449.8	213,586	267,645
	United States of America	47,094	428.6	216,229	272,612

1) Countries/territories not included due to lack of data: Chinese Taipei, France (La reunion, Guadaloupe, Martinique), French Guyana and Polynesia, Guam, Maldives, New Caledonia, Puerto Rico, Timor-Leste, Wesern Sahara, Fiji, Gabon, Belize, Cameroon, Djibouti, Gaza Strip and West Bank, Solomon Islands, Swaziland, Afghanistan, Comoros, Guinea, Guinea-Bissau, Liberia, Somalia, The Gambia. Tanzania, Bolivia, Honduras and Equatorial Guinea report an absolute zero for consumption which is treated as missing data. FYR Macedonia is excluded for lack of classification on income per capita.

2) Full GAPRI methodology available at http://www.treatthepain.com/methodology. Morphine equivalent is a metric to standardize doses of opioids and allow combination and comparison of different medicinal opioids. It is calculated as Mor Eq=(1*morphine)+(83.3*fentanyl)+(5*hydromorphone)+(1.33*oxycodone) +(0.25*pethidine)+(4*methadone). This equation is taken from the ratios of the defined daily dose (oral dosing for all except fentanyl, which is transdermal) as described by the WHO Collaborating Centre for Drug Statistics Methodology. Because of methadone's widespread use as opioid substitution therapy, non-methadone morphine equivalent is also used in some instances and is calculated as Non-meth Mor Eq= (1*morphine)+(83.3*fentanyl)+(5*hydromorphone)+(1.33*oxycodone)+(0.25* pethidine). Opioid consumption data are taken from the International Narcotics Control Board annual report for narcotics consumption in 2008 that was published in 2009. Where data are missing in the 2009 report, values are taken from the International Narcotics Control Board report for 2007 that was published in 2008 (3). For estimates that are reported as below ½ of the unit of measure, a value that is 0.25 of the unit of measure is used. For each drug, the average of non-missing consumption data over the last 3 years (2006-2008) is used.

3) Full GAPRI methodology available at http://www.treatthepain.com/methodology. Deaths in Pain: It is assumed that 80% of cancer deaths and 50% of HIV/AIDS deaths require morphine and that the morphine required for each death in pain is 67.5mg/day for 91.5 days. The number of deaths due to cancer and HIV/AIDS is estimated by applying the mortality rates from the 2008 update of the WHO 2004 cause of death dataset to national population estimates for 2008 from the WHO. Untreated deaths in pain: It is assumed that all of the morphine is used for deaths in pain due to cancer and HIV. The number of untreated deaths in pain is calculated by subtracting the number of deaths in pain that could be treated with the total morphine equivalent in the country from the total number of deaths in pain.

4) World Development Indicators, 2008. World Bank. (http://data.worldbank.org/data-catalog/world-development-indicators/).

References

1. Gersten O, Wilmoth JR. The cancer transition in Japan since 1951. *Demographic Research* 2002; 7(5):271-306.

2. Omran AR. The Epidemiologic Transition: A theory of the epidemiology of population change. *Milbank Memorial Fund Quarterly* 1971; 49(4): 509-38.

3. Frenk J, Bobadilla JL, Sepúlveda J, Cervantes ML. Health transition in middle -income countries: new challenges for health care. *Health Policy and Planning* 1989; 4(1): 29-39.

4. Marmot M, Friel S, Bell R, Houweling T, Taylor S. Closing the gap in a generation: health equity through action on the social determinants of health. *Lancet* 2008; 372(9650):1661-9.

5. World Health Organization. Global Status Report on Noncommunicable Diseases 2010. Geneva: World Health Organization, 2011.

6. See Chapter 8 of this volume for a more detailed discussion.

7. World Health Organization. Global Status Report on Noncommunicable Diseases 2010. Geneva: World Health Organization, 2011.

8. Frenk J, Bobadilla JL, Sepulveda J, et al., 1989.

9. International Agency for Research on Cancer. GLOBOCAN 2008. Cancer incidence, mortality and prevalence worldwide in 2008. http://globocan.iarc.fr/ (accessed January 18th, 2012).

10. Ferlay J, Parkin DM, Curado MP, Bray F, Edwards B, Shin HR, Forman D. Cancer Incidence in five continents, Volumes I to IX: IARC CancerBase No. 9 [Internet]. Lyon, France: International Agency for Research on Cancer; 2010. http://ci5.iarc.fr (accessed on August 10, 2012)

11. Knaul FM, Nigenda G, Lozano R, et al. Breast Cancer in Mexico: a pressing priority. *Reproductive Health Matters* 2008; 16(32): 113-123.

12. Forouzanfar MH, Forman KJ, Delossantos AM, et al. Breast and cervical cancer in 187 countries between 1980 and 2010: a systematic analysis. *Lancet* 2011; 378(9801):1461-84.

13. Ferlay et al 2010.

14. Doll R, Peto R. The causes of cancer: quantitative estimates of avoidable risks of cancer in the United States today. *Journal of the National Cancer Institute* 1981; 66(6):1191-308.

15. National Center for Health Statistics. Health, United States, 2005, With Chartbook on Trends in the Health of Americans. Hyattsville, Maryland: National Center for Health Statistics, 2005.

16. Thun MJ, Wingo PA. Chapter 23: Cancer Epidemiology. In Bast RC, Kufe DW, Pollock RE, et al. (Eds.) Holland-Frei Cancer Medicine. 5th Edition. Hamilton (ON): BC Decker, 2000.

17. Cancer: On-Line Information. Table of Contents and Programmed Study: Oncology Content, Practice Questions and Practice Exams. 2011. http://cancer2000.net/. (accessed September 30, 2011).

18. Mukherjee S. The emperor of all maladies: a biography of cancer. New York: Scribner; 2010.

19. Berry DA, Cronin KA, Plevritis SK, et al. Effect of screening and adjuvant therapy on mortality from breast cancer. *New England Journal of Medicine* 2005; 353:1784-92.

20. Shulman LN, Willett W, Sievers A, Knaul FM. Breast Cancer in Developing Countries: Opportunities for Improved Survival. *Journal of Oncology* 2010; Article ID 595167. doi:10.1155/2010/595167: 1-6.

21. Ribeiro RC, Pui CH. Saving the children – improving childhood cancer treatment in developing countries. *New England Journal of Medicine* 2005; 352(21):2158-60

22. Mukherjee S, 2010.

23. Cancer Research UK. Statistics on 27 common types of cancers, 2011. http:info.cancerresearchuk.org/cancerstats/types/index.htm (accessed on September 30, 2011).

24. Smith-Warner SA, Spigelman D, Yuan SS, et al. Alcohol and breast cancer in women: a pooled analysis of cohort studies. *Journal of the American Medical Association* 1998; 279(7): 535-40.

25. Key TJ, Schatzkin A, Willett WC, Allen NE, Spencer EA, Travis RC. Diet, nutrition and the prevention of cancer. *Public Health Nutrition* 2004; 7(1a):187-200.

26. Hunter DJ, Willett WC. Diet, body size, and breast cancer. *Epidemiological Reviews* 1993; 15(1): 110-32.

27. Thun MJ, DeLancey JO, Center MM, Jemal A, Ward EM. The global burden of cancer: priorities for prevention. *Carcinogenesis* 2010; 31(1):100-10.

28. Thun MJ, Wingo PA. Cancer Epidemiology. In: Bast RC, Kufe DW (Eds.) Cancer Medicine. Hamilton, ON: B.C. Decker Inc., 2000.

29. World Health Organization. Global Status Report on Noncommunicable Diseases 2010. Geneva: World Health Organization, 2011.

30. Sloan FA, Gelband H. Cancer control opportunities in low-and middle -income countries. Washington DC: National Academy Press, 2007.

31. Mukherjee S, 2012.

32. Jha P, Chaloupka FJ, Moore J, et al. Chapter 46: Tobacco Addiction. In: Jamison DT, Breman JG, Measham AR, et al. (Eds.). Disease Control Priorities in Developing Countries. 2nd ed. Washington, DC: World Bank, 2006.

33. Ames BN, Gold LS, Willett WC. The causes and prevention of cancer. Proceedings of the National Academy of Sciences of the Unites States of America 1995; 92(1): 5258-65.

34. Thun MJ, DeLancey JO, Center MM, et al., 2010.

35. World Health Organization. Global Status Report on Noncommunicable Diseases 2010. Geneva: World Health Organization; 2011.

36. Jha P, Chaloupka FJ, Moore J, et al., 2006.

37. Calle EE, Thun MJ. Obesity and cancer. *Oncogene* 2004; 23:6365-78.

38. Flegal KM, Carroll MD, Ogden CL, Curtin LR. Prevalence and trends in obesity among US adults, 1999-2008. *Journal of the American Medical Association* 2010; 303(3):235-41.

39. Subramanian S, Perkins JM, Özaltin E, Davey Smith G. Weight of nations: a socioeconomic analysis of women in low-to middle -income countries. *American Journal of Clinical Nutrition* 2011; 93(2):413-21.

40. World Health Organization. Global Status Report on Noncommunicable Diseases 2010. Geneva: World Health Organization, 2011.

41. Bruce N, Rehfuess E, Mehta S, Hutton G, Smith K. Chapter 42: Indoor Air Pollution. In: Jamison DT, Breman JG, Measham AR, et al. (Eds.). Disease Control Priorities in Developing Countries. 2nd ed. Washington, DC: World Bank, 2006.

42. Rosenstock L, Cullen M, Fingerhut M. Chapter 60: Occupational Health. In: Jamison DT, Breman JG, Measham AR, et al. (Eds.). Disease Control Priorities in Developing Countries. 2nd ed. Washington, DC: World Bank, 2006.

43. International Labour Organization (ILO). NATLEX database. http://www.ilo.org/dyn/natlex/natlex_browse.home?p_lang=en (accessed September 30, 2011).

44. Rosenstock L, Cullen M, Fingerhut M, 2006.

45. World Health Organization. Global Status Report on Noncommunicable Diseases 2010. Geneva: World Health Organization, 2011.

46. Sepúlveda J, Bustreo F, Tapia R, et al. Improvement of child survival in Mexico: the diagonal approach. *Lancet* 2006; 368(9551): 2017-27.

47. See Chapter 4 of this volume for a more detailed discussion of the diagonal approach.

48. Bray F, Jemal A, Grey N, Ferlay J, Forman D. Global cancer transitions according to the Human Development Index (2008-2030): a population-based study. *Lancet Oncology* 2012; 13(8): 790-801.

49. All data are based on Globocan 2010 (http://globocan.iarc.fr/) to allow for comparisons across cancers and by age group. Somewhat different estimates of mortality and incidence are presented in Forouzanfar MH, Forman KJ, Delossantos AM, et al. Breast and cervical cancer in 187 countries between 1980 and 2010: a systematic analysis. *Lancet* 2011;378(9801):1461-84.

50. de Martel C, Ferlay J, Franceschi S, Vignat J, Bray F, Forman D, Plummer M. Global burden of cancers attributable to infections in 2008: a review and synthetic analysis. *Lancet Oncology* 2012; 13(6):607-15.

51. Curado MP, Edwards B, Shin HR, et al. (Eds.). Cancer incidence in five continents. Volume IX. Lyon: IARC Scientific Publications 160, 2007.

52. Casper C, Sessle E, Phipps W, Yager J, Corey L, Orem J. Uganda Program on Cancer and Infectious Diseases. GTF. CCC Working Paper Series, Paper No. 2. Boston: Harvard Global Equity Initiative, 2011.

53. Denny L. Cervical cancer in South Africa: an overview of current status and prevention strategies. *Continuing Medical Education* 2010; 28(2):70-3.

54. Boyle P, Levin B. (Eds.). World cancer report 2008. Lyon: International Agency for Research on Cancer Press, 2008.

55. UNAIDS. Report on the global AIDS epidemic 2008. Geneva: Joint United Nations Programme on HIV/AIDS. 2008.

56. Patel P, Hanson DL, Sullivan PS, et al. Incidence of types of cancer among HIV-infected persons compared with the general population in the United States, 1992-2003. *Annals of Internal Medicine* 2008; 148:728-36.

57. Casper C. The Increasing Burden of HIV-Associated Malignancies in Resource-Limited Regions. *Annual Review of Medicine* 2010; 62:157-70.

58. Bonnet F, Burty C, Lewden C, et al. Changes in cancer mortality among HIV-infected patients: the Mortalité 2005 Survey. *Clinical Infectious Diseases* 2009; 48(1):633-9.

59. Gakidou E, Nordhagen S, Obermeyer Z. Coverage of Cervical Cancer Screening in 57 Countries: Low Average Levels and Large Inequalities. *PLoS Medicine* 2008;5(6):e132.

60. See Chapters 3 and 7 for more detail on the cost of HPV vaccines.

61. Casper C, Sessle E, Phipps W, et al., 2011.

62. Lowy DR, Schiller JT. Reducing HPV-associated cancer globally. *Cancer Prevention Reserach* 2012; 5: 18-23.

63. Sahasrabuddhe VV, Groesbeck PP, Mwanahamuntu MH, Vermund SH. Cervical cancer prevention in low- and middle-income countries: feasible, affordable, essential. *Cancer Prevention Research* 2012; 5:11-7.

64. Knaul FM, Nigenda G, Lozano R, et al., 2008.

65. Lazcano-Ponce E, Tibor Lorincz A, Cruz-Valdez A, et al. Self-collection of vaginal specimens for human papillomavirus testing in cervical cancer prevention (MARCH): a community-based randomised controlled trial. The *Lancet* 2011; 378(9806): 1868 – 73.

66. Sankaranarayanan R, Nene BM, Shastri SS, et al. HPV screening for cervical cancer in rural India. *New England Journal of Medicine* 2009; 360:1385–94.

67. Lowy DR, Schiller JT. Reducing HPV-associated cancer globally. *Cancer Prevention Research* 2012; 5: 18-23.

68. Sahasrabuddhe VV, Groesbeck PP, Mwanahamuntu MH, et al., 2012.

69. Garland SM, Hernandez-Avila M, Wheeler CM, et al. Quadrivalent vaccine against human papillomavirus to prevent anogenital diseases. *New England Journal of Medicine* 2007; 356(19):1928-43.

70. Chang MH, Chen CJ, Lai MS, et al. Universal hepatitis B vaccination in Taiwan and the incidence of hepatocellular carcinoma in children. *New England Journal of Medicine* 1997; 336(26):1855-9.

71. All data are based on Globocan 2010 released data for 2008 (http://globocan.iarc.fr/) to allow for comparisons across cancers and by age group. Somewhat different estimates of mortality and incidence are presented in Forouzanfar MH, Forman KJ, Delossantos AM, et al. Breast and cervical cancer in 187 countries between 1980 and 2010: a systematic analysis. *Lancet* 2011;378(9801):1461-84.

72. Cancer Research UK. Statistics on 27 common types of cancers, 2011. http:info.cancerresearchuk.org/cancerstats/types/index.htm (accessed on September 30, 2011).

73. Forouzanfar, M. Estimating trends in mortality of cancers in the world: the case of breast cancer. Presentation at Global Health Metrics and Evaluation 2011 Conference. Seattle, WA, March 14, 2011.

74. American Cancer Society. Breast Cancer Facts & Figures 2009-2010. Atlanta, GA: American Cancer Society, 2010.

75. Shulman LN, Willett W, Sievers A, et al., 2010.

76. Ribeiro RC, Steliarova-Foucher E, Magrath I, et al. Baseline status of paediatric oncology care in ten low-income or mid-income countries receiving My Child Matters TM support: A descriptive study. *Lancet Oncology* 2008; 9:721-9.

77. Sontag S. Illness as metaphor; and, AIDS and its metaphors. New York: Picador, 2001.

78. Link BG, Phelan JC. Stigma and its public health implications. *Lancet* 2006; 367:528-9.

79. Lagnado, L. In some cultures, cancer stirs shame. *The Wall Street Journal* 2008; Oct 4 Sec A1. http:ionline.wsj.com/article/SB122304682088802359.html (Accessed on September, 30 2010).

80. Hoffman KE, McCarthy EP, Reckiltis CJ, Ng AK. Psychological distress in long-term survivors of adult-onset cancer: Results from a national survey. *Archives of Internal Medicine* 2009; 169 (14):1274-81.

81. Hewitt M, Greenfield S, Stoval E. From cancer patient to cancer survivor: Lost in transition. Washington, D.C: National Academies Press, 2006.

82. Wolff SN, Nichols C, Ulman D, et al. Survivorship: An unmet need of the patient with cancer – implications of a survey of the Lance Armstrong Foundation. Poster presented at the American Society of Clinical Oncology Annual Meeting, Chicago, IL, 2005.

83. Sen A. The Idea of Justice. Cambridge, MA: Belknap Press of Harvard University Press, 2009.

84. Walls HL, Walls KL, Loff B. The regulatory gap in chronic disease prevention: a historical perspective. *Journal of Health Policy and Planning.* 2012; 33(1): 89-104.

85. Walls HL, Walls KL, Loff B. The regulatory gap in chronic disease prevention: a historical perspective. *Journal of Public Health Policy* 2012; 33(1): 89-104.

86. Sen A. Social exclusion: concept, application, and scrutiny. Social Development Papers No. 1. Office of Environment and Social Development: Asian Development Bank, June 2000. http://www.adb.org/documents/books/social_exclusion/Social_exclusion.pdf (accessed October 1, 2011).

87. Sen A. Inequality Reexamined. Cambridge, MA: Harvard University Press, 1992.

88. Centers for Disease Control and Prevention and the Lance Armstrong Foundation. A National Action Plan for Cancer Survivorship: Advancing Public Health Strategies. 2004.

89. Faust DG. Opening Session: Breast cancer in the developing world: meeting the unforeseen challenge to women, health and equity. Harvard University. Joseph B. Martin Conference Center, Harvard Medical School, Boston, MA. November 4, 2009.

90. See Chapter 4 for more information on the chronicity of cancer.

91. Knaul F, Arreola-Ornelas H, Mendez-Carniado O, et al. Health system reform in Mexico 4. Evidence is good for your health system: policy reform to remedy catastrophic and impoverishing health spending in Mexico. *Lancet* 2006; 368(9549):1828-41.

92. World Health Organization. World Health Report 2010, Geneva: World Health Organization, 2010.

93. Krishna A. Pathways out of and into poverty in 36 villages of Andhra Pradesh, India. *World Development* 2006; 34(2):271–88.

94. Anand S. Human security and universal health insurance. *Lancet* 2012; 379(9810):9-10.

95. Keusch GT, Wilentz J, Kleinman A. Stigma and global health: developing a research agenda. *Lancet* 2006: 367:525-7.

96. Castro A, Farmer PE. Understanding and addressing AIDS-related stigma: from anthropological theory to clinical practice in Haiti. *Public Health Matters* 2005: 95(1).

97. Sen A. Development as Freedom. New York: Random House, 1999.

98. Durstine A, Leitman E. Building a Latin American cancer patient advocacy movement: Latin American cancer NGO regional overview. *Salud Publica de Mexico* 2009; 51(Suppl 2):s316-s323.

99. Koon K, Soldak T, Gralow J. Breast cancer advocacy: Changing perceptions. *Salud Publica de Mexico* 2009; 51 (Suppl 2):s323-s329.

100. See Chapter 10 of this volume for additional discussion.

101. International Labour Organization (ILO). NATLEX database. http://www.ilo.org/dyn/natlex/natlex_browse.home?p_lang=en. (accessed on September 20, 2011).

102. Neal C, Beckjord E, Rechis R, Schaeffer J. Cancer stigma and silence around the world: A LIVESTRONG report. 2010. TX: LIVESTRONG. Available at http://livestrong.org/pdfs/3-0/LSGlobalResearchReport (accessed September 20, 2011).

103. Shaheen R, Slanetz P, Raza S, Rosen M. Barriers and opportunities for early detection of breast cancer in Gaza women. *Breast* 2011; 20(2):s30-s4.

104. Epley RJ, McCaghy CH. The stigma of dying: attitudes towards the terminally ill. *Journal of Death and Dying* 1978; 8(4): 379-393.

105. Neal C, Beckjord E, Rechis R, Schaeffer J. Cancer stigma and silence around the world: A LIVESTRONG report. 2010. Austin, TX: LIVESTRONG. Available at http://livestrong.org/pdfs/3-0/LSGlobalResearchReport (accessed September 20, 2011).

106. Sen A. The Idea of Justice. Cambridge, MA: Belknap Press of Harvard University Press, 2009.

107. Temel JS, Greet JA, Muzikansky A. Early palliative care for patients with metastatic non-small-cell lung cancer. *New England Journal of Medicine* 2010; 363:733-42.

108. Taylor AL, Gostin LO, Pagonis KA. Ensuring effective pain treatment: a national and global perspective. *The Journal of the American Medical Association* 2008; 299(1):89-91.

109. Scholten W, Nygren-Krug H, Zucker HA. The World Health Organization paves the way for action to free people from the shackles of pain. *Anesthesia and Analgesia* 2007; 105:1-4.

110. Liberman J, O'Brien M, Hall W, Hill D. Ending inequities in access to effective pain relief? *Lancet* 2010; 376(9744):856.

111. O'Brien M. Global Access to Pain Relief Initiative. Presentation for the Union of International Cancer Control. http://www.africacncl.org/HIV_AIDS/initiative_activities/NCD_Session_3_Obrien.pdf (accessed September 20, 2011).

112. Global Access to Pain Relief Initiative (GAPRI). Understand the problem. Facts about access to pain relief. http://www.gapri.org/understand-problem (accessed August 12, 2012).

113. International Narcotics Control Board. Report of the International Narcotics Control Board for 2009. New York: United Nations, 2010.

114. Seya MJ, Gelders SFAM, Achara OU, Milani B, Scholten WK. A first comparison between the consumption of and the need for opioid analgesics at country, regional, and global levels. *Journal of Pain & Palliative Care Pharmacotherapy* 2011; 25:6-18.

115. Murthy S, Antwi-Kusi A, Jabir AR, Ofori-Amanfo G. Patient and healthcare practitioner perspectives of postoperative pain control in Kumasi, Ghana. American Society of Anesthesiologists, 2010. http://www.asaabstracts.com/strands/asaabstracts/abstract.htmjsessionid= 2D9F6DB208 9C25D23ABF47CC0AD0FFCC?year=2010&index=17&absnum=1361 (accessed October 1, 2011).

116. Pain & Policy Studies Group. Opioid Consumption Motion Chart. University of Wisconsin for 2007. http://ppsg-production.heroku.com/chart (accessed September 22, 2011).

117. Brennan F, Carr DB, Cousins M. Pain management: a fundamental human right. *Anesthesia and Analgesia* 2007; 105(1):205-221.

118. Ibid.

119. Joranson DE, Ryan KM. Ensuring opioid availability: methods and resources. *Journal of Pain and Symptom Management* 2007; 33:527-32.

120. Anderson T. The politics of pain. *British Medical Journal* 2010; 341:328-30.

121. Taylor AL, Gostin LO, Pagonis KA, 2008.

122. Liberman J, O'Brien M, Hall W, et al., 2010.

123. Nickerson JW, Attaran A. The inadequate treatment of pain: collateral damage from the war on drugs. *PLoS Medicine* 2012; 9(1): e1001153.

124. Mosoiu D, Ryan KM, Joranson DE, Garthwaite JP. Reforming drug control policy for palliative care in Romania. *Lancet* 2006; 367 (9528):2110-7.

125. Bosnjak S, Maurer MA, Ryan KM, Leon MX, Madiye G. Improving the availability and accessibility of opioids for the treatment of pain: The International Pain Policy Fellowship. *Journal of Supportive Care in Cancer* 2011; 19:1239-47.

126. World Health Organization. Ensuring balance in national policies on controlled substances: Guidance for availability and accessibility of controlled medicines. 2nd and revised Edition. Geneva: World Health Organization, 2011.

127. Gilson AM, Maurer MA, Ryan KM, Skemp-Brown M, Husain A, Cleary JF. Ensuring patient access to essential medicines while minimizing harmful use: a revised WHO tool to improve national drug control policy. *Journal of Pain and Palliative Care Pharmacotherapy* 2011; 25(3):246-51.

128. Joranson DE, Ryan KM, Maurer MA. Opioid policy, availability and access in developing and nonindustrialized countries. In: Fishman SM, Ballantyne JC, Rathmell JP (Eds.). Bonica's Management of Pain. 4th Ed. Pages 194-208. Baltimore, MD: Lippincott Williams & Wilkins, 2010.

129. See Chapter 4 of this volume for a discussion of the horizontal strategies.

130. Taylor AL, Gostin LO, Pagonis KA, 2008.

131. Sepulveda J, Bustreo F, Tapia R, et al., 2006.

132. See Chapter 4 of this volume for a discussion of the diagonal approach.

Chapter 3

INVESTING IN CANCER CARE AND CONTROL

Felicia Marie Knaul, Hector Arreola-Ornelas,
Rifat Atun, Oscar Méndez, Ramiro Guerrero,
Marcella Alsan and Janice Seinfeld

Key messages

- Chronic disease is a leading global economic risk. Planning for chronic illness prevention and management must be integrated into health and economic development agendas.

- Tobacco's estimated $US 500 billion drain –mainly from tobacco-related illness and treatment costs– exceeds the total annual expenditure on health of all low and middle income countries (LMICs).

- Between one-third and one-half of cancer deaths can be avoided with prevention, early detection and treatment – between 2.4 and 3.7 million avoidable deaths each year, 80% of which are in LMICs.

- The total annual economic cost of cancer was approximately $1.16 trillion in 2010 – the equivalent of more than 2% of global GDP. Even this impressively high figure is a lower bound as it does not include the substantial longer-term costs to families and care givers.

- Investing strategically in cancer care and control (CCC) more than pays for itself and is likely to even 'payoff'. A reasonable estimate shows that the world could have saved between $US 100 and $US 200 billion in 2010 by investing in cancer control and care in ways that prevent disease and cover effective treatment. Potential savings are much higher – over $US 500 billion and up to almost $US 1 trillion – taking into account the individual perception of the value of lost life and human suffering.

- Cost of prevention and treatment of cancer will likely decline over time. The ability to prevent, detect and treat many cancers has improved over time, and many of these advances have led to reductions in costs. Harnessing markets and increasing access can also bring down prices.

- Investments that generate system-wide improvements benefit cancer, but also accrue gains for other diseases, thereby achieving greater health outcomes per capita investment. This is part of a diagonal approach to planning.

- The "economics of hope" foresees a future when drugs and other forms of treatment for cancer will become more accessible to wide population groups in LMICs.

3.i Introduction

Human life and well-being have intrinsic value to individuals and countries. They also have economic value. Viewing health as an investment, rather than a cost, is now the philosophy that inspires human, economic, and environmental development agendas. Still, this investment philosophy –with a few notable exceptions described later in the report– remains largely ignored in the global and national policy-making that deals with cancer and other chronic illness.

This chapter presents a series of economic arguments for investing in CCC. The first section reviews the literature to highlight the most compelling arguments for investing in CCC. The next section presents an analysis of premature and avoidable mortality and provides estimates of the avoidable cancer burden in LMICs. The third section of the chapter presents estimates of the economic value of the avoidable cancer burden, and compares potential savings to estimates of the current costs of CCC, generating potential economic value from investing in CCC. These estimates draw heavily on existing calculations of lost productivity from cancer and other noncommunicable diseases (NCDs). The final section of the chapter reformulates thinking about the potential cost of CCC using a framework of resource optimization that considers both projections of potential price declines and how investment in treatment and prevention are spread across diseases within health systems – strategies that are discussed in greater detail in later chapters of this volume.

3.ii The economic burden of chronic and noncommunicable disease

The World Economic Forum (WEF) identified chronic disease (including cancer, diabetes, cardiovascular disease, and chronic respiratory disease) to be one of the three leading global economic risks.[1] This assessment by the Forum was based on the potential severity and likelihood of the impact of these diseases on global productivity and economic growth, as well as the risks posed to the global economic system. Similarly, the World Bank highlighted the negative economic consequences of NCDs on countries due to adverse effects on worker productivity and competitiveness, fiscal balance, and other health outcomes due to pressure on health systems from NCDs, with obvious ramifications for poverty, financial security, and inequity.[2] A recent Chatham House report suggests the beneficial impact of the low incidence of NCDs on sustainable and balanced economic policy.[3]

The economic impact of NCDs on LMICs will become more severe over time, as a result of the increasing burden on younger and working-age populations. Although globally the proportion of NCD deaths that occur among 15-59 year-olds is expected to fall globally by 2030, this proportion is likely to increase in LMICs. Further, LMICs are facing higher NCD burdens –age standardized NCD-related disability adjusted life years (DALYs) per capita– at lower levels of economic development, compared to high income countries, while facing other challenges such as rising food prices.[4]

Tobacco is a huge economic risk for LMICs. Tobacco's estimated $500 billion[5] drain –mainly from tobacco-related illness and treatment costs– exceeds the total annual health expenditure of all LMICs. Tobacco's total economic costs reduce gross domestic product by as much as 3.6% per year. Further, the future does not portend well if trends in smoking continue. At current smoking trends, between 2020-2030, the global annual economic costs of tobacco are expected to reach $1 trillion.[6]

The WEF and WHO estimate potential income loss of $558 billion in China and $237 billion in India, between 2005 and 2015, due to stroke, heart disease, and diabetes, alone.[7] Overall, the economic costs of loss of life and productivity are estimated to be as much as 400% higher than the costs of treatment. For the US, the $1 trillion in lost economic output from NCDs, compared to $300 billion in health expenditures, suggests an avoidable impact on GDP of $700 billion.[8] In Egypt, the projected loss from the impact of NCDs on the work force is placed at 12% of GDP.[9,10]

One study estimated that a 50% rise in chronic disease incidence and mortality, such as that projected for Latin America from 2002 to 2030, could produce a slowdown of more than 2% in annual economic growth.[11] This decline would widen the existing economic divide and the disparities between high income countries (HICs) and LMICs, as the increases in NCD mortality and morbidity will be concentrated in poor countries. WHO notes that this projected economic burden dwarfs any experienced to date – including from malaria and HIV/AIDS.[12]

A variety of studies demonstrate the impact of chronic illness on the economic well-being of families. Noncommunicable diseases, and especially cancer, increase the risk of catastrophic health expenditure, which in turn increases the financial vulnerability of families and impairs their ability to invest in areas such as education and nutrition. In South Asia, the chances of catastrophic expenditures from hospitalization are 160% higher for cancer patients, compared to those with a communicable disease requiring hospitalization.[13] Both the patient and their family members are often forced to leave the labor force or reduce their hours of work. In Egypt, for example, people with NCDs have a 25% lower probability of being employed.[14] Further, the burden of care giving may fall especially heavily on women and girls, reducing both their labor force participation and their access to educational opportunities, thereby further exacerbating existing gender inequities.[15]

The WEF Global Risk Assessment Report also cautions against making shortsighted and misguided decisions about investing in health.[16] In the face of resource constraints, a short-term view would encourage LMICs to focus only on achieving the MDGs. Yet, ignoring NCDs places many countries at further risk of not meeting many of the MDGs because of escalating health costs and the health risks to mothers, infants, and young children.[17] Failure to protect populations from preventable health risks will inevitably and severely detract from both economic development and social well-being.[18] Planning for chronic disease prevention and management must therefore be integrated into both health and economic development agendas, to reach beyond the existing MDGs and meet broader development goals.

3.iii The "avoidable" cancer burden[19]

A significant proportion of the cancer burden is avoidable through prevention, early detection, and treatment. In addition, though difficult to measure, better access to pain control would alleviate tremendous suffering.

Analysis of avoidable mortality assumes a goal for life expectancy of a population and identifies all deaths from specific causes that occur before that age. For a cause of death to be considered "avoidable", it must produce premature deaths – i.e. it must be responsible for death within an age range considered as early or untimely compared to the life expectancy of that individual. These deaths may be due to lack of prevention, or a lack of early detection and treatment.

The literature on avoidable deaths has typically established premature death using an empirical approach to set an upper limit, usually taken as 64 years. Under this scenario, a death that occurred in any of the 12 cancer causes listed in Table 3.1 is considered potentially avoidable if the age at which death occurred is before 65 years of age (or any other upper limit). The exception to this rule is death from leukemia, for which the age limit in the literature is prior to 40.

The selection of cancers that are considered either preventable or treatable or both preventable and treatable is based on earlier research[20-24] as well as on Chapters 2 and 5 of this volume.[25,26] The cancer groups considered are: stomach, colorectal, liver, lung, melanoma of the skin, breast, cervix-uterus, Hodgkin lymphoma, leukemias (in children), larynx, oral cavity, pharynx, thyroid, bladder, prostate, endometrial, and non-Hodgkin lymphoma. Notably, the estimates presented here include Kaposi sarcoma – a cancer that could be prevented to the extent that HIV/AIDS can be prevented or managed.[27]

The analysis in this chapter uses three distinct scenarios to establish the age limit below which a cancer death could be considered avoidable. These are presented in Table 3.1. Estimates consider only the cancers where prevention should have been possible, or where treatment, with or without earlier detection, might have resulted in either a cure or an increase in life expectancy. Each scenario corresponds to a specific framework.

1. The **empirical approach** establishes a normative minimum as the lower bound on life expectancy. A 'world average' is used and applied to all countries. The approach sets a threshold that all countries should be able to achieve. The analysis presented here follows the majority of the literature and uses the age limit of 65.

2. The **feasibility approach** considers as the norm for life expectancy the best attainable level in a given group of countries. The idea is that any country should be able to do as well as other countries in a group that faces similar challenges and restrictions. The analysis in this chapter uses the World Bank, country income levels (low, lower-middle, upper-middle and high) to establish the reference group for each country. The average age of death in the best performing country of each region for each preventable or treatable cancer is taken as the threshold for what can be feasibly achieved. Another option that would reduce the threshold is to use the average or median life expectancy in each region for each cancer. This approach might indeed be closer to a concept of feasibility and will be part of future analysis.

3. **Social Justice:** Under this scenario, the threshold for life expectancy is set at the highest attainable level: the average age of death in the countries of the world with the highest age of death for each preventable or treatable cancer. This approach focuses on the maximum achievable life expectancy that is possible based on the best performing countries in the world, and reflects the view that residents of poorer countries should be able to expect the same as those of rich countries. In the analysis this chapter presents, a simpler approach is provided, where the threshold is set at 75 years as this age is close to levels observed in the top performing countries.[28-31]

Each life expectancy scenario is applied to countries' income-group-specific GLOBOCAN estimates of mortality and age at death by cancer type. The analysis is based on estimates of cancer incidence and mortality from the International Agency for Research on Cancer (IARC) published in its GLOBOCAN 2008 database.[32] Information from the World Bank was used to build the income regions from per capita GDP at purchasing power parity or international dollars reported in the 2010 World Development Indicators.[33]

Using life expectancy of 75 years as the standard (scenario 3), an estimated 49% of cancer deaths are considered avoidable with prevention, early detection, and/or treatment. Setting the standard at the level of the best performing countries in each income region (scenario 2), the figure is lower but still shows that 36% of deaths could be avoided. Using the minimum standard of life expectancy at 65 years (scenario 1), produces a figure of 32%.

These estimates suggest, respectively for each scenario, that there are 3.7, 2.7 and 2.4 million avoidable deaths from cancer each year. LMICs account for approximately 80% of this avoidable mortality in each life expectancy scenario.

Table 3.1

Avoidable Cancer Mortality, by Income Region

		Scenario 1: Normative minimum (LE: 65 years)		Scenario 2: Feasibility (LE: Best in each income region)		Scenario 3: Social Justice (LE: 75 years; close to LE of high income countries)	
		% of all avoidable deaths	% of deaths considered avoidable as a % of all cancer deaths	% of all avoidable deaths	% of deaths considered avoidable as a % of all cancer deaths	% of all avoidable deaths	% of deaths considered avoidable as a % of all cancer deaths
Low income	%	11.5	46.5	11.6	52.0	9.7	60.2
	Number of deaths	277,480		310,090		358,969	
Lower middle income	%	56.4	38.7	56.7	43.5	53.6	56.5
	Number of deaths	1,356,424		1,522,597		1,978,640	
Upper middle income	%	14.8	30.1	14.6	33.2	15.3	47.8
	Number of deaths	355,653		392,243		564,960	
High income	%	17.3	18.5	17.1	20.5	21.4	35.2
	Number of deaths	414,787		458,652		788,532	
Global	%		32.0		35.7		49.1
	Number of deaths	2,404,344		2,683,583		3,691,101	

1/ LE: Life Expectancy.

2/ Estimates Knaul and Arreola-Ornelas (2011) based on GLOBOCAN 2008 data. Methodology: Tobias and Jackson, 2001; Franco-Marina, Lozano, et al., 2006. Castelli A. Nizalova O. 2011. http://gtfccc.harvard.edu/icb/icb.do?keyword=k69586&pageid=icb.page420088.

There is a clear gradient from low to high income countries in the proportion of deaths that can be considered avoidable. A much larger proportion of deaths in LMICs could be prevented, approximately twice as many in low as in high income countries. Many of these deaths are associated with infection-related cancers. Using the age-of-75 definition, 60%, 57%, and 48% of all cancer mortality is avoidable in low, lower middle, and higher middle income countries, respectively.

Even in high income countries a considerable proportion –between one-fifth and one-third– of deaths from cancer could potentially be avoided with prevention and/or treatment.

Many deaths due to cancers that strike children and young adults –notably cervical cancer, testicular cancer, and certain leukemias and lymphomas– can be avoided with relatively low-cost treatment or prevention options.[34,35] These cancers account for many potential years of healthy life lost. Wealthy countries have been able to prevent many of these deaths, while lower income countries have not. These "candidate" cancers make ideal targets for advocacy and action in LMICs.

3.iv The economic value of investing in CCC[1]

Each year, the world's nearly 13 million estimated new cases of cancer lead to enormous economic cost as well as human suffering.[36,37] Much of the cost could be avoided by expanding coverage of prevention, early detection, and treatment services. The additional investments needed to achieve expanded coverage would be more than counterbalanced by reductions in the economic toll caused by the disease.

Human life and well-being have an intrinsic and immeasurable value. They also have an economic value, which can be approximated by the income individuals would have generated had they lived, their lost contributions to family and community, and the value they place on lack of well-being and on suffering.

The economic consequences of each cancer case include the direct and indirect costs of treatment, the income forgone by patients and families unable to work during treatment and illness periods, and most importantly in economic terms, the productivity lost due to premature death, disability, and suffering. Broader estimates of economic consequences also, and appropriately, take into account the losses from catastrophic health spending that undermine the economic stability of families, as well as perceived costs of human suffering.

The annual, global economic cost of *new* cancer cases has been estimated at $310 billion for 2010[2,38] taking into account all incident cases for 2009.[3] Of this cost, 53% ($164 billion) is due to medical costs, and 24% to productivity losses due to time spent in treatment and disability associated with treatment. The remaining 23% is attributed to the time of caregivers and the cost of transportation to treatment facilities.

Estimates for costs of prevention are low, as suggested by the findings from a WHO study of scaled-up implementation of a core set of NCD "best buy" intervention strategies, which estimates the cost of reducing risk factors such as tobacco and harmful alcohol to be $2 billion per year, for all LMICs – less than $0.40 per person. Including a limited set of individual-based NCD "best buy" interventions –in the case of cancer, Hepatitis B immunization to prevent liver cancer, and measures to prevent cervical cancer– the cost increases to $9.4 billion per year. Overall, this sum amounts to an annual per capita investment that is less than $1 in low income, $1.50 in lower middle income, and $3 in upper middle income countries.[39]

For the estimates presented below on total costs and potential savings, we apply a cost of prevention at $11.4 billion, which is equal to 7% of total treatment costs. As one comparison of the scale, this amount corresponds to the proportion of total health spending that Canada devotes to prevention.[4,40]

The total global economic cost of premature death and disability from cancer has also been estimated at $921 billion for 2010;[5,41] based on DALYs (losses due to death and disability) for 17 categories of cancer covering all cancer sites.[6]

A first approximation to the total annual economic cost of cancer is the sum of costs of incident cases, plus the costs of prevalent cases, plus the costs of investing in prevention. Summing the two estimates mentioned above and accounting for overlap[7] provides an approximation of total, annual economic cost of almost $1.16 trillion, which is approximately 2% of total global GDP. This cost represents the sum of lost DALYs including the first year of treatment, direct treatment costs in the first year, the cost of the time of caregivers during the treatment year, costs of transportation to treatment facilities, and an estimated cost of prevention at $11.4 billion.

The figure of $1.16 trillion underestimates total annual economics costs for many reasons. The most important factor is lack of data on the substantial longer-term costs to families and caregivers, which often extend well beyond the first year of treatment. The figure also fails to account for the value that patients and families place on human suffering that may be well above productivity losses.

An alternate way to calculate the cost of cancer is to use a use a Value of Statistical Life (VSL) approach. This methodology accounts for the value individuals place on lost income, out-of-pocket spending on health, and pain and suffering. Based on a recent study, the total 2010 VSL estimate for cancer is $2.5 trillion. Of this sum, close to $1.7 trillion is in high income countries, and the remaining $800 billion in LMICs.[42]

To arrive at a VSL estimate of the total costs of cancer that can be compared to the cost of preventing and treating cancer, it is necessary to account for out-of-pocket health spending by families that is part of the cost of care.[8] Subtracting the out-of-pocket spending by families, the VSL estimate of losses for cancer is $2.37 trillion.[43]

Total costs of cancer, as estimated by direct and indirect costs or through VSL method, can be compared to the total costs of investing in preventative services, medical treatment, and care giving during treatment to derive a figure for the expected return on investing in CCC. These calculations require an assumption about the proportion of deaths that can be avoided and then applying this figure to the estimate of the economic value of DALYs. Analysis of avoidable deaths is provided in the previous section of this chapter.

The available estimates of the costs of treatment do not account for the possibility of more effective primary and secondary prevention becoming available. Several of the cancers that generate significant global investment in treatment are preventable, either by reducing exposure to risk factors such as tobacco or by vaccination, as for cervical cancer.

Cancers with a high burden in LMICs for which a considerable proportion of cases are potentially amenable to prevention or detection in pre-cancerous stages –and hence for which costs of treatment can be avoided– are Kaposi sarcoma, and cancers of cervix, liver, and (most importantly in terms of burden) lung. Prevention can extend to other cancers with a lower overall burden such as head and neck cancer, as well as stomach cancers (by treating Helicobacter Pylori).[9] Preventing the majority of these cancers means avoiding a considerable proportion of treatment costs. For Kaposi sarcoma, cervical, liver, and lung cancers, a 90% reduction in cases implies a reduction of at least 20% in the total estimated costs of treating cancer – or approximately $65 billion. Hence, with more effective prevention, the total cost of treatment for cancer could be less than what is actually spent: rather than the estimated $310 billion, approximately $246 billion. Adding the cost of prevention ($11.4 billion) to the remaining treatment costs produces an overall figure of almost $257 billion.[10] Including prevention for bladder, esophagus, head and neck, and stomach cancers, would reduce treatment costs by approximately 25%.

The estimates in Table 3.2 compare the economic value of lives saved in DALYs and VSL to the total costs of treatment and prevention. The driving factor in these calculations is the value of lost years of healthy, productive life to both the economy and the individual. The economic value of avoiding deaths and reducing pain and suffering –comparing potential savings to costs– are estimated under different scenarios of avoidable deaths and total treatment costs. The estimates are based on the most optimistic estimate of avoidable deaths of 49% using the scenario of life expectancy of 75 years (see previous section of this chapter), and a more conservative estimate of avoidable deaths of 36%. The VSL figures less out-of-pocket spending ($2.37 trillion) are compared to the estimated value of lost DALYs ($921 billion) plus costs of treatment and prevention. Further, costs of treatment are considered applying an optimistic 90% reduction in cases to two different sets of cancers (cancers of lung, liver, cervix and Kaposi sarcoma; and an expanded list of preventable cancers).

These estimates provide approximations of what the world could have saved in 2010 by investing in CCC. They range from the most optimistic returns of $230 million and almost $1 trillion in terms of DALYs and VSL, respectively, to the lower bound of $10 million and $531 million. Thus, even under the most pessimistic scenario of avoidable deaths, no effective prevention beyond current levels and considering only gains in terms of DALYs, investing is CCC more than pays for itself.[11]

Further, estimates of the total value of lost output from cancer, based on macroeconomic modeling for 2011 to 2030 –a different approach to the ones presented above– show an even higher cumulative economic loss of $2.9 trillion to LMICs and of $5.4 trillion for high income countries.[44] The same study shows that between 2011 and 2030, NCDs –including cancer, CVD, chronic respiratory disease, diabetes, and mental health– represent a global, cumulative output loss of up to $47 trillion, based on macroeconomic models.[45] Applying these estimates of cumulative loss would yield even higher rates of returns on investment in prevention and treatment.

Even interventions that are cancer-specific can have positive economic returns, especially with early detection. Reports from the International Atomic Energy Agency complement the analysis presented above. These suggest that the productivity gains from radiotherapy for cancer, for example, can exceed the fractional costs of treatment because of years of healthy life gained. The mean break-even point on the financial investment of radiotherapy for low income, low middle and upper middle income countries is 12.1, 4.5 and 1.9 years, respectively.[46] When analysing results from treatment in high income countries, it is found that 60% of adult cancer patients are still alive five years after treatment, making the prospect of reaching these break-even points quite attainable.[47]

Table 3.2

Sensitivity Analysis of Economic Returns to Investing in Cancer Treatment and Prevention

Cost of treatment and prevention[1]	Economic cost of cancer			
	DALYs: $921 billions		VSL less OOP: $2.37 trillions	
	Avoidable deaths		Avoidable deaths	
	49%[3]	36%[4]	49%[3]	36%[4]
(1) Assuming full cost of treatment based on Bloom (2010) + cost of prevention: 310+11 = $321m	130	10	839	531
(2) Scenario (1) with reduced costs of treatment based on preventing 90% of liver, lung, cervix and Kaposi sarcoma: (310-64)+11=$257m	194	75	904	596
(3) Scenario (1) with reduced costs of treatment based on preventing 90% of all potentially preventable cancers: (310-100)+11 = $221m)[2]	230	110	940	632

1) Each cell equals: [[economic cost of cancer]*[% mortality avoided with treatment or prevention]] - [Medical and non-medical costs of treating new cancer cases + costs of prevention]

2) 90% reduction in incidence and hence treatment costs for cervix uteri, Kaposi sarcoma, Larynx, Liver, Lung, Nasopharynx, Other pharynx and Stomach.

3) 49% of cancer mortality is assumed avoidable using a scenario of achieving levels of best performing countries - social justice approach.

4) 36% of cancer mortality is assumed avoidable using a scenario of achieving levels of best performing country in each income region.

This again highlights the importance of early detection of cancers – which is seldom the case in LMICs – where treatment can significantly extend life and in some cases offer cure.[48]

3.v A longer-term view

Both costs and benefits of interventions can change over time, or can be changed by taking advantage of markets. This suggests that prices should not be taken as given. Rather, the appropriate approach is to consider how much prices or costs would need to decline or how much expected benefit would need to increase for an intervention to be adopted within a health system.

For similar reasons, effectiveness cannot be taken as a given. Innovations in delivery and financing can increase DALYs averted and the effectiveness of interventions, even if unit costs remain unchanged. Scientific innovations for preventing and treating cancer, while often costly, emerge quickly, changing both the field and the cost structure.

All components of the cancer care control continuum (primary and secondary prevention, diagnosis, treatment, survivorship and palliation) have costs that vary over time and are prices that are sensitive to market changes and new discoveries, as well as patent expiration. The price tag on the total cost of prevention and treatment for cancer care for incident cases is highly permeable, even with the increasing costs of new technologies and drugs. New discoveries, including specific drugs or therapies but also their delivery, can reduce costs and increase the options for implementing cost-effective interventions (Chapter 7).

Prevention is clearly the most desirable outcome for any cancer, from both the economic and the human perspective. Effective prevention and early detection avoids unnecessary morbidity and mortality, and thereby helps reduce costs and achieve significant savings.

WHO recommends a series of "best buys" that are high-impact and cost-effective, even in the poorest countries.[49,50] Many of these interventions will affect a number of NCDs simultaneously, thus spreading costs over a number of diseases. Reduced consumption of tobacco is the most obvious example. Further, prices of some preventive interventions—most recently the HPV vaccine – have declined substantially.

In practice, the dimensions and boundaries of prevention and treatment change over time. Cancers such as those of the liver that is largely untreatable, and cervix that was once amenable only to early detection or treatment, can now be prevented. Hence, estimates of future costs of cancer care may be overstated as science progresses and identifies new options for prevention that are less costly than treating cancer.

Further, the costs of care for several prevalent cancers like breast, colorectal, and cervical –and hope for cure– depends on the stage in which they are diagnosed. Thus, investing in earlier detection reduces the cost per year of life saved (Text box 3.1). At the same time, population-based screening can be very costly, making it a priority to develop innovations for earlier detection.

Optimizing the use of scare and costly health inputs for delivery of cancer interventions can also lead to cost savings. Innovative delivery solutions –such as working with community health workers, nurses, and primary care physicians– can lead to the most effective use of human and physical resources. Further, effective use of information and communication technology can expand the boundaries for providing high quality care, and reduce its price (Chapter 6).

Text Box 3.1
The economic benefits of early detection and prevention: cervical, breast and colorectal cancer

Janice Seinfeld, Arlette Beltrán, Edmundo Morocho

A background study for the Closing the Cancer Divide report analyzed total economic cost –including medical costs and DALYs averted– for cervical, breast, and colorectal cancers across WHO regions, comparing a "prevention + early detection + treatment" strategy with a "treatment only" strategy (with no early detection or prevention).[51] The study draws on existing literature and reconfirms that cost savings are significant with the preventive scenario,[52] compared to the non-prevention scenario, in all WHO regions.

Results coincide with studies that recommend implementing vaccination for HPV –depending on cost per dose and duration of efficacy– and global screening programs to reduce the burden of disease from cervical cancer.[53] For cervical cancer, prevention (3-dose vaccination plus screening with PAP and coloposcopy) represents a 55% to 65% savings, with the greatest savings in WHO regions where the HPV type 16/18 is most widespread. The total economic cost of cervical cancer-medical costs and the value of DALYs lost- is significantly higher than the cost of prevention and early detection, especially in WHO regions where the HPV type 16/18 is most widespread.

The results are similar for colorectal and breast cancer. Prevention of colorectal cancer (sigmoidoscopy every 5 years, for every person between 50 and 80 years, and, if positive, colonoscopy and lesion removal), is cheaper than the scenario of treatment with no investment in early detection. The figures vary substantially for breast cancer, from 40% to close to 70%.

For breast cancer, the economic saving of the prevention-plus-treatment-scenario, is approximately 60%, across all regions (without considering the cost of Herceptin).

Figure 3.1

Total Economic Costs Reduction of "Prevention/Early Detection/Treatment" Compared to "Treatment Only" Scenarios for Cervical, Breast and Colorectal Cancers; by WHO Geographic Regions

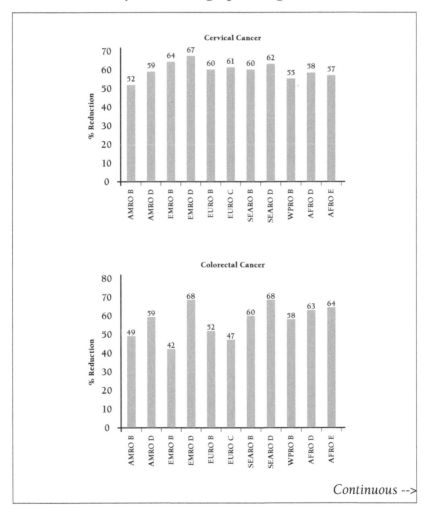

Continuous -->

Figure 3.1 *(continued)*

Total Economic Costs Reduction of "Prevention/Early Detection/Treatment" Compared to "Treatment Only" Scenarios for Cervical, Breast and Colorectal Cancers; by WHO Geographic Regions

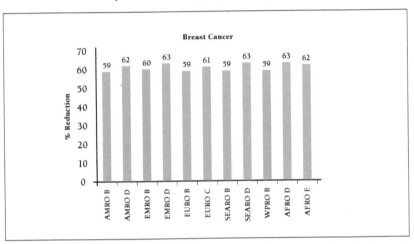

Notes: 1. Based on Seinfeld J., Beltran A. and Morocho E. Cost-benefit analysis of cancer care and control: The case of cervical, colorectal and breast cancer in LMIC. GTF.CCC Working Paper and Background Note Series, No. 7, Harvard Global Equity Initiative, 2012.
http://gtfccc.harvard.edu/icb/icb.do?keyword=k69386&pageid=icb.page420088

2. For each cancer type, the bar graph represents the cost savings -medical costs and DALYs averted- from prevention, early diagnosis and treatment when necessary, versus just treating the cancer.

3. The results are based on a disease and protocol model for each cancer type. Then, cost information was used for a person-type for each WHO region. Information on DALYs provided by WHO where also considered.

4. WHO classifies Member States into 6 geographic regions: AFRO (Africa), AMRO (Americas), EMRO (Eastern Mediterranean), EURO (Europe), SEARO (South-East Asia) and WPRO (Western Pacific). These 6 WHO regions are also divided based on patterns of child and adult mortality in groups ranging from A (lowest) to E (highest).

Source: 1. Ginsberg G. M., Tan–Torres T., Lauer J. A. and Sepulveda C. (2009). "Screening, prevention and treatment of cervical cancer–A global and regional generalized cost–effectiveness analysis."

2. World Health Organization (2008). "The global burden of disease: 2004 update."

Non-medical costs account for almost 50% of total costs of cancer treatment and must be considered when seeking to reduce the costs of investing in CCC.[54] For example, families spend large sums to pay for transport, lodging, and child-care during treatment, often for the patient and a friend or family member. Bringing care closer to home through task and infrastructure shifting, as described in Chapter 6, can reduce costs faced by patients. Many trips are made for adjunct therapy, which could be provided in a nearby clinic or secondary level hospital. Further, innovation in prevention and early detection can reduce the number of visits by combining interventions and using mobile units.

The cost of producing and delivering drugs can drop, as shown by the experience with ARVs for HIV/AIDS and MDR-TB among others, and prices can be reduced. This is true even for drugs that are off-patent as LMICs often pay higher prices than larger purchasers. The GAVI-spurred 96% drop in the price of the HPV vaccine in June 2011, from $120 per dose in 2006 to $5, is a recent and notable example. Earlier, the PAHO Revolving Fund garnered an 88% reduction to $14 per dose. While still unaffordable for many countries, this price reduction marks a huge step forward, and was accomplished in only half a decade (Chapter 7).

New techniques for marketing and packaging agents, such as oral chemotherapy or patches for pain relief, can ease production, transportation, and provision of care. Expanding demand is one way to drive down prices. Pooled purchasing, negotiated rates for low income countries, and frugal innovation are other interventions that can help reduce prices. Further, many older variants of drugs and inputs are only marginally less effective, yet far less costly than new front-line technologies and medications. Finally, pooling funds can generate more secure financing for population groups, reducing the prices for individual patients. All of these options are discussed in greater detail in Chapter 7 and 8.

The diagonal approach[53,56] –presented in Chapter 4 of this volume– is a strategy for optimizing resources that calls for the identification of the horizontal applications and vertical interventions that spread costs and benefits, and decrease the cost-effectiveness ratio for many services. Synergistic investments that generate system-wide improvements are possible, and benefits apply not only for cancer, but also for other diseases and population groups. For these interventions, costs are spread across diseases and beneficiaries, reducing unit costs. One example are pulse oximeters which are used extensively in surgery.[57]

In the case of prevention, the fact that some diseases share common risk factors, can lead to important savings. For example, smoking and diet are risk factors for both cancer and cardiovascular disease. This means that the return on investment for prevention and health promotion is higher when more than one NCD is considered. This "diagonal approach" to prevention and health promotion is particularly important for LMICs that have higher cost constraints.

Future studies on the economic impact of cancer and other chronic diseases should evaluate the expected rate of return on investments in prevention, treatment, and control of a full range of illnesses. These calculations, though complex to undertake, should account for the many opportunities for shared benefits across diseases from specific investments using the diagonal approach as a framework.

Often ignored, are the positive economic benefits that accrue from establishing CCC systems for cancer. These include increased local employment for health care personnel and expanded local industries and should also be incorporated into any analysis of the real value of investing in CCC.

Resource stratification techniques offer options for selecting the most appropriate interventions for the level of resources and the development of each country. To date, a complete analysis and effective tools are available only for breast cancer. A high priority for future research should be the extension of this analysis and resource stratification exercise to other cancers.[58] Further, resource stratification should also be infused with a diagonal approach to ensure that joint costs and benefits are considered.

3.vi Conclusions

Health is an investment, rather than a cost. Yet, this idea has not sufficiently permeated the discussions on CCC or other chronic diseases. Planning for chronic illness prevention and management must be integrated in a forward-looking manner into all policy agendas in order to achieve the most effective investment of health dollars. Adopting an investment approach to health reshapes human, economic, and environmental development agendas.

Given the huge and avoidable suffering caused by cancer, meeting the unmet need for CCC in LMICs is a moral imperative. From an economic standpoint, expanding prevention, detection, and treatment of cancer yields benefits that exceed the costs, making investment in many CCC interventions financially attractive as well.

Between one-third and one-half of cancer deaths can be avoided with prevention, early detection and treatment. Thus between 2.4 and 3.7 million deaths are avoidable each year, 80% of which are in LMICs. Yet, even in high income countries, the proportion of avoidable deaths is significant and as high as 30%.

Chronic disease, including cancer, is a leading global economic risk. The drain of tobacco alone on the global economy exceeds the total annual expenditure on health of all LMICs. This makes investment in both prevention and treatment a priority for health and for economic development.

The total annual economic cost of cancer –not including longer term costs to families and care givers– was approximately $1.16 trillion in 2010, reaching more than 2% of global GDP. By contrast, investing in CCC yields a positive annual return on prevention and treatment because of the number of deaths that are potentially avoidable. Global economic savings of at least $100-200 billion could be achieved by avoiding deaths and hence lost healthy years of productive life through treatment and prevention. Taking into account the human cost of suffering –the value that individuals place on reduced suffering and illness– the savings are at least $500 million and could reach $1 trillion.

Planning for the future requires harnessing markets in ways that can stimulate innovation, encourage savings that reduce prices, investments that generate system-wide improvements benefit cancer that also accrue to other diseases, spread benefits and reduce costs. These economic benefits could be much greater if the potential cost savings from innovative delivery and financing, combined with more equitable pricing of drugs and other therapies, could be achieved. A diagonal approach to planning ensures that joint benefits of interventions are fully taken into account.

A future where prevention, early detection and treatment become more accessible to patients and health systems in LMICs is one that builds on the "economics of hope." Neither the costs of prevention nor the potential benefits of CCC should be taken as fixed given the opportunities that exist to increase access.

References

1. World Economic Forum. Global Risks 2010: A global risk network report: Global Risk Network of the World Economic Forum. 2010.
2. Nikolic IA, Stanciole AE, Zaydman M. Health, Nutrition and Population (HNP) Discussion Paper: Chronic Emergency: Why NCDs Matter. The International Bank for Reconstruction and Development. World Bank. 2011.
3. Chand S. Silent Killer, Economic Opportunity: Rethinking Non-Communicable Disease. Centre on Global Health Security, Briefing Paper, January 2012. http://www.chathamhouse.org/publications/papers/view/181471 (accessed August 10, 2012).
4. Nikolic IA, Stanciole AE, Zaydman M, 2011.
5. All monetary values in this chapter are in US dollars.
6. Shafey O, Eriksen M, Ross H, Mackay J. The Tobacco Atlas, Third Edition. American Cancer Society. 2009. http://www.tobaccoatlas.org/downloads/TobaccoAtlas_sm.pdf (accessed September 27, 2011).
7. World Health Organization. Global Status Report on noncommunicable diseases 2010. World Health Organization. 2011.
8. DeVol R, Bedroussian A, et al. An Unhealthy America: The Economic Burden of Chronic Disease. Charting a New Course to Save Lives and Increase Productivity and Economic Growth. Santa Monica: Milken Institute. 2007.
9. Rocco L, Tanabe K, Suhrcke M, Fumagali E. Chronic Diseases and Labor Market Outcomes in Egypt. Policy Research Working Paper 5575. Washington DC: World Bank. 2011.
10. Nikolic IA, Stanciole AE, Zaydman M, 2011.
11. Stuckler D. Population Causes and Consequences of Leading Chronic Diseases: A Comparative Analysis of Prevailing Explanations. The Milbank Quarterly 2008; 86(2): 273-326.
12. World Health Organization. Global Status Report on noncommunicable diseases 2010, 2011.
13. Engelgau MM, El-Saharty S, Kudesia et al. Capitalizing on the Demographic Transition: Tackling Noncommunicable Diseases in South Asia. The International Bank for Reconstruction and Development. World Bank. 2011.
14. Rocco L, Tanabe K, Suhrcke M, Fumagali E, 2011.
15. Nikolic IA, Stanciole AE, Zaydman M, 2011.
16. World Economic Forum. Global Risks 2010: A global risk network report: Global Risk Network of the World Economic Forum. 2010.
17. World Health Organization. Global Status Report on noncommunicable diseases 2010. World Health Organization. 2011.
18. Ibid.
19. A more detailed description of the methodology and cancer-specific estimates are provided in a background note. Knaul F, Arreola H. Estimates of avoidable cancer deaths by country income. 2011. http://gtfccc.harvard.edu/icb/icb.do?keyword=k69586&pageid=icb.page420088 (accessed January 30, 2012).
20. Gispert R, Serra I, Barés MA, Puig X, Puig A, Freitas A. The impact of avoidable mortality on life expectancy at birth in Spain: changes between three periods, from 1987 to 2001. Journal of Epidemiology and Community Health 2008; 62: 783-789.
21. Gómez-Arias RD, Nolasco Bonmatí A, Pereyra-Zamora P, Arias-Valencia S, Rodríguez-Ospina FL, Aguirre DC. Diseño y análisis comparativo de un inventario de indicadores de mortalidad evitable adaptado a las condiciones sanitarias de Colombia. Revista Panamericana de Salud Pública 2009; 26(5): 385-97.
22. Humblet PC, Lagasse R, Levêque A. Trends in Belgian premature avoidable deaths over a 20 year period. Journal of Epidemiology and Community Health 2000; 54: 687-691.
23. Weisz D, Gusmano MK, Rodwin VG, Neuberg LG. Population health and the health system: a comparative analysis of avoidable mortality in three nations and their world cities. European Journal of Public Health 2007; 18(2): 166-172.
24. de Martel C, Ferlay J, Franceschi S, Vignat J, Bray F, Forman D, Plummer M. Global burden of cancers attributable to infections in 2008: a review and synthetic analysis. *Lancet Oncology* 2012; 13(6):607-15.
25. Knaul FM, Adami HO, Adebamowo C, et al. The global cancer divide: an equity imperative. In Knaul FM, Gralow JR, Atun R, Bhadelia A (Eds.) for the Global Task Force on Expanded Access to Cancer Care and Control in Developing Countries. Closing the Cancer Divide: An Equity Imperative. Boston, MA: Harvard Global Equity Initiative, 2012.
26. Gralow GR, Krakauer E, Anderson BO, et al. Core elements for provision of cancer care and control in low and middle income countries. In Knaul FM, Gralow JR, Atun R, Bhadelia A (Eds.) for the Global Task Force on Expanded Access to Cancer Care and Control in Developing Countries. Closing the Cancer Divide: An Equity Imperative. Boston, MA: Harvard Global Equity Initiative, 2012.
27. The calculations were also undertaken excluding KS, bladder; prostate; endometrial; and, non-hodgkin lymphoma. The pattern of results was similar.
28. Franco-Marina F, Lozano R, Villa B, Soliz P. La Mortalidad en México, 2000-2004 "Muertes Evitables: magnitud, distribución y tendencias". México, D. F. Dirección General de Información en Salud, Secretaría de Salud. 2006.
29. Nolte E, McKee CM. Does health care save lives? Avoidable mortality revisited. London: The Nuffield Trust. 2004.

30. Castelli A, Nizalova O. Avoidable Mortality: What it Means and How it is Measured. Centre for Health Economics (CHE) Research Paper 63. 2011. http://www.york.ac.uk/media/che/documents/papers/researchpapers/CHERP63_avoidable_mortality_what_it_means_and_ how_it_is_measured.pdf (accessed September 27, 2011).

31. The social justice approach assumes that people living in poorer countries should have the right to be able to achieve the same life expectancy as high -income countries, or at least what is feasible in the best-performing country in terms of life expectancy in the income group to which a country belongs.

32. International Agency for Research on Cancer. GLOBOCAN 2008 Cancer Incidence, Mortality and Prevalence Worldwide in 2008. http://globocan.iarc.fr/ (accessed on August 10, 2012).

33. World Bank. World Development Indicators 2010. Washington DC: World Bank, 2010. http://data.worldbank.org/sites/default/files/wdi-final.pdf (accessed August 10, 2012).

34. Konduri N, Quick J, Gralow JR, et al. Access to affordable medicines, vaccines, and health technologies. In Knaul FM, Gralow JR, Atun R, Bhadelia A (Eds.) for the Global Task Force on Expanded Access to Cancer Care and Control in Developing Countries. Closing the Cancer Divide: An Equity Imperative. Boston, MA: Harvard Global Equity Initiative, 2012.

35. Gralow GR, Krakauer E, Anderson BO, et al., 2012.

36. Beaulieu N, Bloom D, Bloom R, Stein R. Breakaway: the global burden of cancer challenges and opportunities. Economist Intelligence Unit. 2009.

37. John RM, Ross H. Economic value of disability-adjusted life years lost to cancers, 2008. http://media.marketwire.com/attachments/EZIR/627/18192_FinalJournalManuscript.pdf (accessed September 27, 2011).

38. Beaulieu N, Bloom D, Bloom R, et al., 2009.

39. World Health Organization. From Burden to "Best Buys": Reducing the economic impact of non-communicable diseases in low- and middle -income countries. World Health Organization. 2011. http://www.who.int/nmh/publications/best_buys_summary.pdf (accessed September 27, 2011).

40. OECD Stat Extracts. 2010. http://stats.oecd.org/Index.aspx (accessed September 27, 2011).

41. John RM, Ross H, 2008.

42. Bloom DE, Cafiero ET, Jané-Llopis E, et al. The Global Economic Burden of Non-communicable Diseases. Geneva: World Economic Forum. 2011.

43. Out of pocket spending on health tends to be over 50% in many LMICs. In some countries it can be much higher. In order to avoid any bias, an exaggerated estimate of 80% is used for these calculations.

44. Bloom DE, Cafiero ET, Jané-Llopis E, et al. 2011.

45. Ibid.

46. Rosenblatt, Datta, Samiei and Camacho Presentation (IAEA internal review).

47. Curtiss and Haylock 2006

48. Sen, A. Inequality Reexamined. Cambridge, MA: Harvard University Press, 1992.

49. World Health Organization. Global Status Report on noncommunicable diseases 2010. World Health Organization. 2011.

50. World Health Organization. From Burden to "Best Buys": Reducing the economic impact of non-communicable diseases in low- and middle -income countries. World Health Organization. 2011. http://www.who.int/nmh/publications/best_buys_summary.pdf (accessed September 27, 2011).

51. Seinfeld J, Beltran A, Morocho E. Background paper: Cost-benefit analysis of cancer care and control: The case of cervical and colorectal cancer in LMIC. GTF.CCC Working Paper and Background Note Series, No. 7, Harvard Global Equity Initiative, 2011.

52. Groot MT, Baltussen R, Uyl-de Groot CA, Anderson BO, Hortobágyi GN. Costs and health effects of breast cancer interventions in epidemiologically different regions of Africa, North America, and Asia. Breast Journal. 2006;12(1):81.

53. Ginsberg G, Edejer TT, Lauer JA, Sepulveda C. Screening, prevention and treatment of cervical cancer – A global and regional generalized cost-effectiveness analysis. Vaccine 2009; 27(43): 6060-6079.

54. Beaulieu N, Bloom D, Bloom R, et al., 2009.

55. Sepúlveda J, Bustreo F, Tapia R, et al. Improvement of child survival in Mexico: the diagonal approach. Lancet 2006; 368(9551): 2017-2027.

56. Frenk J. Bridging the divide: global lessons from evidence-based health policy in Mexico. Lancet 2006; 369(9539): 954-61.

57. Kirby T. Pulse oximeters breathe life into surgery in poorer nations. Lancet 2011; 377(9759): 17-18.

58. Anderson BO, Yip CH, Smith RA, Shyyan R, Sener SF, Eniu A, et al. Guideline implementation for breast healthcare in low income and middle income countries. Cancer. 2008; 113(S8):2221-43.

Much could be done

Part II

Chapter 4

HEALTH SYSTEM STRENGTHENING AND CANCER: A DIAGONAL RESPONSE TO THE CHALLENGE OF CHRONICITY

Felicia Marie Knaul, George Alleyne, Peter Piot, Rifat Atun, Julie R. Gralow, Claire Neal, Jaime Sepulveda, Julio Frenk

Key messages

- The classifications of disease by communicable/noncommunicable, acute/chronic or of-the-poor/of-the-rich detract from efforts to strengthen health systems in low and middle income countries (LMICs) to meet the challenges of chronic illness, as many communicable diseases are also chronic illnesses.

- Similarly, infectious origins of many cancers are increasingly recognized. Cancer, for example - a set of many diseases, several of which originate from infection or develop in patients with underlying disease of communicable origin - provides an example of the overlap between communicable and noncommunicable disease.

- Therefore, focusing on the chronic nature of many communicable and noncommunicable diseases (NCDs) (e.g. HIV/AIDS) provides a point of reference for transforming health systems originally designed to respond to acute illness to also provide a continuum of care for chronic illness.

- Strong health systems are essential to prevent and treat cancer effectively. At the same time, expanding cancer care and control (CCC) can strengthen health systems by producing synergies and opportunities that will benefit other chronic illnesses.

• A diagonal approach generates mutual reinforcement between CCC and health system strengthening to simultaneously address health system goals and deal with an explicit health priority.

• Health system innovations must encompass the six overlapping components of the CCC continuum by developing integrated programs for primary prevention, early detection, diagnosis, treatment, survivorship and long-term follow-up, and palliation.

4.i Introduction

Health systems in LMICs must be transformed in order to respond to the growing burden of cancer and other chronic illnesses. This requires rejecting the either-or, minimalist model of treating only specific, communicable diseases in favor of an "optimalist" approach, which seeks synergy among explicit health priorities to effectively respond to patient and population needs.

Investment in a systems approach to chronic diseases in LMICs is strategic.[1,2] Effective interventions exist to address the growing burden of chronic diseases in LMICs,[3] but the weakness of national health systems often prevents them from providing this care. Yet, discussions and studies on how to strengthen health systems in LMICs rarely consider chronic illness or specific diseases. Similarly, research and policy around specific diseases seldom include an analysis of the impact of disease specific investments on health systems or the ways in which to take better advantage of system-wide platforms.[4]

We propose a diagonal framework and analyze what this framework could mean in practice for health systems strengthening in LMICs, using cancer as a tracer condition for chronic diseases.[5,6] The first section discusses the implications for disease classification and health systems of changing disease patterns in LMICs. Next, we present the diagonal approach as a response to the resulting challenges faced by health systems. Finally, we outline the care control continuum and the opportunities to strengthen health systems using the case of cancer. The appendix to this chapter is a hypothetical case study describing the journey of a woman with breast cancer and her interactions with the Mexican health system, illustrating the opportunities to apply a diagonal approach.

4.ii The challenge of chronicity

The epidemiological transition, combined with new and more effective ways to prevent and treat disease, has transformed the experience of diseases such as HIV/AIDS and several types of cancer. Once considered death sentences, many are now chronic illnesses when treated appropriately.

Yet, neither conventional classifications of disease, nor approaches aimed at addressing the health needs of the poor, nor the priorities for health systems have moved at the same pace or in directions that follow the evolution of how patients actually live with these diseases. Although this is a distinction that no longer applies, health care providers and policy makers, especially in LMICs, continue to be taught to distinguish between so-called diseases of the rich (NCDs) and those of the poor (communicable diseases). Today, diseases previously considered "of the poor" are no longer the only diseases that plague people who live in poverty, just as diseases "of the rich" are no longer exclusive to this group.[7] Instead, a double and over-lapping burden of communicable and noncommunicable disease now afflicts the poor, especially in LMICs, with a mix of acute episodes and chronic conditions.

This transition has created new challenges to health in LMICs by combining the unfinished agenda of infections, malnutrition, and reproductive health problems with an emerging agenda of noncommunicable and chronic illness. Further, the unfinished and untouched agendas overlap. However, health systems have been slow to respond to these challenges that require well-integrated health systems, as opposed to systems that provide fragmented and episodic care for specific diseases at the expense of other conditions.[8,9]

Poverty intensifies the burden of illness and generates a vicious cycle: loss of health; lack of treatment; higher morbidity; lost income; deeper impoverishment; and reduced health.[10] Chronic diseases such as cancer inflict repeated financial onslaughts on families. As the Nobel Laureate and economist Amartya Sen warns "The poorest groups not only bear higher risks for NCDs but, once they develop an NCD, they also face higher health and economic impacts. The poor have less access to medical care, allowing NCDs to progress to advanced states resulting in higher levels of mortality and disability. Given their complexity and chronic character, medical expenditures for treatment of NCDs are a major cause for tipping households into poverty." [11]

Another outdated dichotomy, which classifies diseases as communicable or noncommunicable, refers to the transmission mechanism. Yet, patients are not confined to a single disease over a lifetime; they may suffer numerous communicable and noncommunicable diseases, often simultaneously or consecutively.

The distinctions between communicable and noncommunicable diseases, and between chronic and acute conditions, which need long-term or episodic care respectively, are increasingly blurred by scientific advances in both prevention and treatment, and in the knowledge of the origins of these diseases. Some communicable diseases are chronic while some NCDs are acute (Table 4.1). Several acute infections, only some of which are communicable, generate long-term sequelae. By contrast, some NCDs are characterized by acute exacerbations of underlying longer-term illnesses.

Risk factors add another layer of complexity to the simplistic communicable/noncommunicable taxonomy. Some behaviors, notably smoking, alcohol consumption, and unhealthy eating, increase the risk of cancer and other NCDs – behaviors which are increasingly considered to be "communicable" across groups, communities, and countries.[12]

Cancer, usually classified as an NCD, is in fact a set of diseases,[13] many of which are associated with an infection. Cancers associated with infection disproportionately affect poor populations. Cancers associated with infectious agents are responsible for almost 25% of cancer deaths in the developing world, and for only 6% in industrialized countries.[14] It is when primary prevention through vaccination, early detection, and treatment of certain infections fail that a disease becomes a cancer, and requires chronic care. Similarly, HIV/AIDS, a communicable disease, has become a chronic illness with an associated cancer – Kaposi sarcoma.[15] Further, several cancers are actually classified as acute, and the goal in many cancer cases is the cure and eradication of illness. Yet, the long-term nature of treatment and the issues of survivorship (see below) are chronic, and make cancer a chronic problem that requires an appropriate health system response.

Increased life expectancy means large cohorts of older populations in LMICs with multiple chronic diseases, with chronicity emerging as the defining characteristic of illness in both rich and poor countries. Hence, efforts to strengthen health systems in LMICs must address the growing burden of chronic illness.[16,17] Yet, most health systems were originally designed to respond to acute episodes of illness that led to either cure or death.[18,19] In the traditional "acute-repeat" model, chronic diseases are treated by health systems as a series of discrete, unrelated acute episodes rather than a set of interrelated events that progress over time – an approach that clearly fails to respond to the complexity of long duration, gradual progression diseases with multiple acute complications, multiple co-morbidities, and survivorship care.[20,21]

Table 4.1
Characterization of Disease by Chronicity and Association with Infection

Characterization of Disease by Chronicity and Association with Infection		
	Communicable or associated with infection	**Noncommunicable**
Chronic	Cancers associated with infection: • KS (human herpes virus 8) • Ano-genital and head and neck cancers (HPV) • hepatocellular carcinoma (hepatitis B and C) • Gastric cancer (H-pylori) • Bladder cancer (schistosomiasis) • Lymphoma (Epstein Barr Virus) • Tuberculosis (pulmonary disease) • HIV/AIDS Chronic sequelae of acute infections: • Physical disability (polio) • Chagas • Cardiomyopathy (Chagas' disease) • Rheumatic valvular disease (rheumatic fever. • Chronic kidney disease (streptococcus) • Brain disease (meningitis) • Blindness (measles)	Cancers: • Breast • Pancreas • Lung • Chronic leukemias • Prostate Cardiac and pulmonary: • Congestive heart failure • Hypertension • Diabetes • Chronic obstructive pulmonary disorder Other chronic disease with acute exacerbations: • Asthma • Mental health disorders
Acute	• Infectious diarrheal disease • Respiratory infections • Malaria	Cancers: • Acute myelogenous leukemia • Acute lymphoblastic leukemia Cardiac: • Acute myocardial infarction

Chronicity adds a new dimension and set of challenges to the financing and delivery of healthcare for a disease such as cancer. To the three standard dimensions for assessing coverage –who is covered, which services are covered, and with what degree of financial protection[22]– chronicity adds a fourth layer: for which parts of the continuum of care do patients have access. Coverage of one component of the continuum does not imply coverage of the disease or the needs of patients who live with the long-term consequences of the disease and treatment.

Even health systems in countries with innovative and comprehensive financing programs for cancer and other illness have failed to effectively deal with chronic conditions. Policy makers, particularly in LMICs, have few tools to guide their response to the long-term nature of chronic illness, both in general and to a specific disease like cancer. The few projects, policies, and tools that do exist, such as those developed by Partners in Health, integrate chronic care with a focus on endemic NCDs.[23] Further, the projects that do exist tend to be small scale and need to be piloted, evaluated, and scaled up if proven to be effective.[24-26]

In sum, there is an artificial division of diseases as acute/chronic, communicable/noncommunicable, or rich/poor. This diverts attention of policy makers from organizing health systems around the challenges represented by co-morbidity in individual patients, coexisting epidemiologic profiles in populations, and long-term rather than episodic care.

4.iii The diagonal approach to health system strengthening

A more appropriate model applies a diagonal approach. This concept was originally developed in Mexico in the late 1980s to deliver integrated health interventions against the most prevalent health problems there at the time (mostly infectious diseases in children). The diagonal approach was an effective way to respond to the old debate and false dilemma of vertical versus horizontal approaches and their claimed benefits. In short, the diagonal approach is a strategy where explicit health priorities become the drivers of change in a health system.[27]

The diagonal model makes optimal use of broad, systemic functions (e.g. health financing) and existing health system programs to respond to other health priorities (e.g. maternal, newborn and child health, HIV/AIDS, sexual and reproductive health). It adapts to the chronic and overlapping nature of diseases with a set of linked policies and interventions that target the care continuum, from prevention to palliation of specific diseases.

Rather than focusing on disease-specific vertical programs or on horizontal initiatives that address generic system constraints, such as limited resources, a diagonal approach identifies interactions and synergies, providing an opportunity to tackle disease-specific priorities while also addressing the gaps within a system.

By contrast, vertical programs focus on specific diseases, and often on only one aspect of care, such as prevention or early detection on a large scale, using a resource, information, and financing system that is managed separately from the rest of the health system and is frequently donor-driven. These disease-specific programs often do not interact with the larger health system.

Similarly, horizontal programming refers to resource sharing across disease and population groups. Often, it is part of an effort to strengthen health systems. Typically, such efforts address system-wide constraints, such as shortages of trained healthcare workers, lack of financial protection, or inadequate information systems. Evidence suggests that, in practice, few (if any) programs are purely vertical or horizontal.[28] Typically, vertical and horizontal programs are system-wide with little intent to adapt to specific diseases or the continuum of care and control required to meet the challenges of diseases such as cancer.

The integration of health system functions and disease-specific programs can create the types of interactions and synergies envisaged by the diagonal approach (Figure 4.1).[29,30] The vertical-only model typifies the disease-specific approach that has been criticized for being duplicative and wasteful, weakening fragile health systems as it fails to take advantage of system-wide financing and service delivery.[31-35] The horizontally integrated model is also lacking in practice, for it ignores the specialization that must be developed to treat specific diseases in each component of a health system. The purely horizontal model assumes an inappropriate "one-size-fits-all" approach. Even linkages between functions within disease-specific programs can be missed so that, for example, financing for cancer care may not align with service delivery. The most important limitation of this model is its failure to deal with the crucial policy goal of setting priorities.

Figure 4.1

Disease and Health System Functions
According to Types of Integration

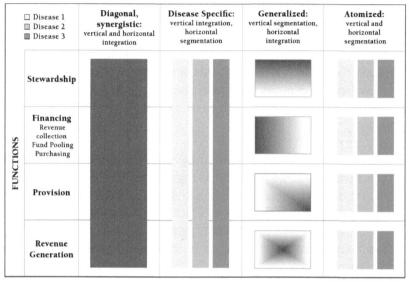

☐ Disease 1 ☐ Disease 2 ▥ Disease 3	**Diagonal, synergistic:** vertical and horizontal integration	**Disease Specific:** vertical integration, horizontal segmentation	**Generalized:** vertical segmentation, horizontal integration	**Atomized:** vertical and horizontal segmentation
Stewardship				
Financing Revenue collection Fund Pooling Purchasing				
Provision				
Revenue Generation				

FUNCTIONS

Source: Source: Adapted from Murray and Frenk; WHO Bulletin, 2000.

The diagonal approach provides a cross-cutting framework that empha-sizes: (i) interrelationships between diseases; (ii) requirements for targeted approaches that correspond to individual diseases and place specific demands on health systems; and (iii) ways to manage interrelationships between dis-eases across health systems, to improve coverage for many diseases and pop-ulation groups.

The diagonal approach proposes taking advantage of complimentary interventions and optimizing use of resources. Providing coverage for a specific intervention for one disease can promote expanded coverage for other diseases and population groups. For example, improving the regulatory framework for opioid use improves access for all patients who need pain control. Further, the diagonal approach requires new ways to analyze costs and benefits, since an investment in controlling or treating one disease can affect other diseases and improve overall cost-effectiveness. In addition, the diagonal approach encour-ages investment in public goods, and promotes coordinated and joint action across diseases.

The emphasis of a diagonal approach is on joint learning, collective action, and collaboration between the cancer community and other disease-specific groups to further the development of national and global public goods. This approach also applies to other NCDs and chronic communicable diseases like AIDS and TB, and is especially important because of the opportunities created by the 2010 United Nations General Assembly resolution on the prevention and control of NCDs.[36]

The literature specific to the diagonal approach is recent.[37-41] Evidence on the application of the diagonal approach is scant in spite of the potential efficiencies it offers.[42,43] One study demonstrates how vaccination and child health programs can be integrated with large-scale anti-poverty and maternal, newborn and child health initiatives to expand coverage within a broad-based program.[44]

Several authors propose approaches that are diagonal but not referred to as such. Extensive literature focuses on the integration of health services, including NCD prevention and management, into primary health care.[45,46] The Maximizing Positive Synergies Initiative, for example, identified the benefits and many opportunities to create mutually reinforcing links between disease-specific global initiatives and health system strengthening,[47] while highlighting the areas of greatest risk for drawing resources away from other programs, with suggestions for mitigating these risks. When broader needs and benefits have been identified as goals from the outset, disease-specific investments have contributed to health system strengthening and population health improvements as illustrated by Rwanda, Malawi, and Ghana, countries which have channeled HIV/AIDS investment into health systems strengthening.[48-50]

A main proposition of this paper —one that cuts across the chapters included in this volume— is that diagonal programs can be developed and successfully applied to cancer. This is illustrated through country cases that act as examples of how better prevention, early detection, treatment, survivorship, and palliation of cancer can strengthen health systems, reduce overall costs, and provide expanded access to prevention, treatment, and control of other diseases. Several examples of integrated approaches are provided below that are further developed in Chapters 6 through 10. Text Box 4.1 includes information on the experience of Rwanda.

Applications of the diagonal approach to cancer across the CCC continuum

✦ **Primary prevention – healthy lifestyles:**

- Tobacco control can help prevent certain cancers and reduce cardiovascular and respiratory diseases, and tuberculosis;
- Obesity prevention can reduce risk of several cancers as well as diabetes and cardiovascular disease;
- Hepatitis B vaccination can be integrated into existing immunization programs to prevent liver cancer;
- HPV vaccination can be promoted in adolescent, sexual and reproductive, and maternal, newborn and child health programs to prevent cervical cancer;
- Health promotion for the development of healthy lifestyles that allow for increased physical exercise and healthy eating that can reduce the risk of most NCDs.

✦ **Early detection – secondary prevention:**

- The integration of early detection programs for breast and cervical cancer into programs for women and health, anti-poverty, maternal, newborn and child health, sexual and reproductive health, and HIV/AIDS can broaden access to CCC.

✦ **Diagnostics and treatment:**

- Establishing the telecommunications needed for highly-qualified radiologists to review images, dermatologists to examine skin lesions, pathologists to review pathology, or oncologists to remote-monitor reactions to adjuvant chemotherapy administered by primary care physicians where no oncologists are physically present to improve access to CCC. Once these IT capabilities are in place, they can also be used to diagnose and treat other diseases and health conditions, as well as for training and capacity building.

✔ Treatment:

* Surgery is an important component of treatment for many cancers. Yet, pulse oximeters (Text Box 7.2), an element of safe surgery that should be part of any checklist, are absent from most operating theatres in LMICs.[51-53] Ensuring the availability of good quality pulse oximeters globally is the goal of project LIFEBOX. Success with this project will improve the effectiveness of surgery for cancer, as well as for other diseases and conditions.

* Establishing facilities in hospitals or primary care clinics to treat cancer patients, especially with chemotherapy, requires infection control because these patients have weakened immune systems. Stringent infection control procedures will benefit all patients by helping to reduce the incidence of infections acquired in health facilities.

✔ Survivorship:

* Cancer patients continue to be stigmatized. Patient advocacy can empower individuals and communities to significantly reduce the stigma associated with diseases like cancer, HIV/AIDS and tuberculosis, as well as stigma associated with gender and ethnicity. This will improve social cohesion and reduce the exclusion of marginalized populations.

* Pain control and palliation.

* Strengthening health systems and reducing price and other barriers to access to pain control medication is essential for cancer and many other diseases. It is also essential for being able to offer surgery.

Text Box 4.1
Rwanda: Partners In Health chronic care integration for endemic noncommunicable diseases[54]

Julia Lu, Gloria Sangiwa, Agnes Binagwaho

The Government of Rwanda considers health care a basic human right and its health care delivery system aims to serve all Rwandans, especially vulnerable populations. The country is aware of the emerging risk factors that accompany urbanization and has taken steps to expand access to integrated chronic care to address the emerging problem of NCDs. In partnership with Partners In Health (PIH), the Rwanda Ministry of Health began to shift NCD services in East Province from central referral centers to district hospitals. This move builds on a stable, decentralized health system and the framework Rwanda began in 2003 for HIV/AIDS diagnostic care and antiretroviral therapy. In this framework, complex holistic health interventions are integrated into basic health services.

The Rwanda strategy is a model for delivering services for chronic conditions in resource-poor settings. The process of building this integrated chronic care infrastructure involves incremental decentralization of services from referral centers to district hospitals, to health centers, to community health workers. As the services move away from the referral centers, services become increasingly simplified and more integrated with similar services. Simplified diagnostic techniques based on local epidemiology are used to place patients into broad categories of disease that correspond with appropriate clinical pathways. This allows for a more effective use of specialist time to evaluate patients to confirm diagnoses, and to assess needs. While the initiative is still evolving, some goals and outcomes have been identified:

- *Each PIH-supported public district hospital has an advanced chronic care clinic that is staffed by two or three nurses. The physician's role includes overseeing initial consultations, consulting on complex cases, and meeting regularly with nurse program leaders to discuss work plans, budget, and evaluation. Every one or two months, specialists from referral centers visit to confirm diagnoses and to provide ongoing training.*

- *Providing high-quality services at district hospitals can reduce transfers to referral centers. Management of more advanced conditions can be moved away from tertiary facilities by developing clinical program leaders at the district level. Uncomplicated chronic care is provided at sites closer to patient homes. Referral centers can focus on the services best delivered at the tertiary level, such as complex cases, specialized surgery, and chemotherapy.*

- *In settings with established and effective chronic care services, community-based screening may be a reasonable approach to increase case finding. Community health workers (CHW) provide the link between health facilities and patients, whether finding patients lost to follow-up or referring new cases.*

- *HIV/AIDS programs supported by PIH in Haiti and other countries have achieved exceptional patient retention and clinical outcomes. Building on the Rwandan CHW system comprised of three CHWs in each village, the Ministry of Health and PIH have customized this model in East Province to address HIV/AIDS and other advanced chronic conditions, such as heart failure, insulin-dependent diabetes, and malignancies. CHWs with additional training provide psychosocial support, administer medications, ensure adherence, and facilitate refills and clinic appointments through daily visits to patients.*

- *A chronic care team is designated to train and mentor health center clinicians in basic management of chronic conditions to provide better coordination of chronic care services and program leaders. Team members serve as trainers and mentors for health workers across the country.*

4.iv The cancer care control continuum and health system strengthening

A defining characteristic of cancer, and many other chronic diseases, is the need for a series of interventions along the care control continuum. The phases of this continuum, that are often overlapping, are: i) primary prevention, ii) secondary prevention or early detection, iii) diagnosis, iv) treatment, v) rehabilitation, long-term follow-up and survivorship care (Text Box 4.2), and vi) palliation and end-of-life care.[55]

Text Box 4.2
Survivorship

The term "survivorship" is gaining acceptance —despite its relatively recent introduction— as a description of long-term CCC for interventions that are not directly treatment related.[56] The term dates back to a 1985 article written by a physician living with cancer.[57] The concept of survivorship and its application to health systems has become increasingly important, especially in the US, where, for example, the National Cancer Institute (NCI) created an office in 1996, dedicated to this issue.[58,59]

The definition of survivorship has been evolving and will continue to do so as the standards and opportunities for care and for survival improve. While the term has been sometimes questioned and criticized as a US construct, this seems to be associated with the use of the word, 'survivor,' whereas there is general acceptance of 'survivorship'.

Cancer survivorship is usually defined as beginning at the moment of diagnosis and continuing throughout the lifetime of the patient. Survivorship also includes the family, friends, caregivers, and loved ones who share the cancer experience.[60]

The introduction of the concept and the opportunities to respond to the corresponding needs of patients has been belated. Even in high income countries, health systems are struggling to make up for lost opportunities to integrate these services and respond to the longer-term needs of people who live with cancer. The concept of survivorship, and hence the design of appropriate programs and policies, is just beginning to be been recognized in LMICs. It is largely unknown, possibly because a large proportion of patients die from the disease soon after diagnosis. As more people survive cancer, effective survivorship care can help reduce the burden of disease later in life. It will be important to integrate survivorship into efforts to build-up health systems in LMICs to respond to the immediate and long-term challenges of cancer.

Survivorship implies constant struggle with a disease, years of healthy life with treatment, and active patient involvement in care. It also suggests the long-term nature of the struggle for patients and caregivers. Survivorship is both medical and non-medical and includes access to schooling, employment, and insurance coverage. As a stage of care, it focuses on issues relating to stigma that go beyond the health care system and can affect families. Survivorship poses different concerns when applied to children and chronic illness.[61]

Greater access to CCC in LMICs, and, consequently, to cure and healthy life with disease, will make it increasingly important to incorporate survivorship as part of care. There are currently more than 28 million cancer survivors worldwide, and people now diagnosed with cancer are increasingly likely to survive at least five years.[62]

The most effective way to expand survivorship care in LMICs, especially given the long-term nature of the disease, is through a diagonal approach that involves the primary care network as well as community-based programs. This approach will also help to reduce stigma and discrimination.

An effective CCC continuum requires strengthening all health system functions –stewardship, financing, service provision, and resource generation– and all core components –health financing, governance, health workforce, health information, medical products and technologies, and health service delivery.[63-65] It also requires the engagement of multiple participants and stakeholders, including civil society patients, their families and communities.[66] Establishing effective delivery systems along the control care continuum necessarily involves a spectrum of care providers –from the expert patient and community health promoter, to the sub-specialty physician– in order to coordinate a combination of repeat-episodic and longer-term care.

Implementing effective primary and secondary prevention strategies presents additional challenges and opportunities. A life-cycle approach for prevention often begins with a healthy childhood. Further, awareness of prevention strategies needs to be integrated into all programs for women, especially programs focusing on sexual and reproductive health. Effective prevention strategies for all cancers include education (teaching children about healthy lifestyles and encouraging young women to know their bodies, for instance); appropriate fiscal policy such as taxing tobacco, food and beverages; environmental and occupational safety measures; antidiscrimination policies and legislation to combat social exclusion; and agricultural and food policies that control pesticide use and promote healthy eating.[67]

Underlying social determinants affect every stage of the CCC continuum.[68] Gender discrimination, limited access to education, unhealthy living conditions, social exclusion, lack of decent employment, and the dearth of social protection increase the risk of developing cancer. They also reduce the ability of individuals and communities to access care and live with the disease, both during and after treatment.

Figure 4.2

**Health System Functions by Components
of the CCC Continuum:**

Health System Functions	Stage of Chronic Disease Life Cycle/ Components CCC					
	Primary Prevention	Secondary prevention	Diagnosis	Treatment	Survivorship/ Rehabilitation	Palliation/ End-of-life care
Stewardship						
Financing						
Delivery						
Resource Generation						

The interactions between the CCC continuum and health systems function is complex (Figure 4.2). Each component of the CCC continuum requires specific stewardship, financing, delivery, and resource generation policies (vertical lines) usually differentiated by groups of cancers. Ideally, each function should be integrated with each of the six components, to ensure continuity and consistency (horizontal lines). While a comprehensive approach would be ideal, a phased approach will be needed because of resource and knowledge constraints.

The diagonal approach can be layered onto the health system function/care continuum matrix outlined in Figure 4.2. The policy maker must then consider how a horizontal, vertical disease–specific, or combination intervention can be designed and applied to address needs along the CCC continuum. A "litmus test" of how well a health system responds to a chronic illness such as cancer implies evaluating each health system function against each of the six elements of the CCC.[69]

4.v Conclusions

A well-functioning health system should address the comprehensive needs of its beneficiaries rather than dealing only with discrete episodes for specific diseases at the expense of others. We propose a diagonal approach to health systems strengthening to mobilize and invest resources more effectively and expand access to CCC and a response to other chronic conditions in LMICs.

The classifications of disease by communicable/noncommunicable, acute/chronic or of-the-poor/of-the-rich detract from efforts to strengthen health systems in LMICs to meet the challenges of chronic illness. Cancer, for example, is a set of many diseases, several of which originate from infection or develop in patients with underlying disease of communicable origin. This illustrates the overlap between communicable and noncommunicable diseases.

Health systems must be transformed to provide a continuum of care for chronic illness such as cancer. Health system innovations must encompass the overlapping components of the care control continuum by developing integrated programs for primary prevention, early detection, diagnosis, treatment, survivorship and long-term follow-up, and palliation. Focusing on the chronic nature of many communicable and NCDs (e.g. HIV/AIDS) provides a point of reference for refurbishing health systems that were originally designed to respond to acute illness.

A diagonal approach generates mutual reinforcement between vertical and horizontal interventions to simultaneously address health system goals and deal with specific diseases. In the case of cancer, strong health systems are essential. At the same time, expanding CCC can strengthen health systems by producing synergies and opportunities that will benefit other chronic illness.

The diagonal approach also helps address the issue of competing risk – the idea that saving a person from one disease increases the risk of incurring other diseases in the future. Applying diagonal thinking to health systems can transform zero-sum debates about what to deny poor patients with cancer into a search for opportunities that will strengthen health systems to address multiple conditions for all.[70]

APPENDIX 4.1

A HYPOTHETICAL CASE STUDY OF LATE DIAGNOSIS OF BREAST CANCER TURNED INTO LESSONS FOR IMPLEMENTING A DIAGONAL RESPONSE IN MEXICO

Background

Juanita's story is based on the experience and information from a patient at the Women's Hospital of Yautepec, Morelos, México, who was interviewed by Felicia Knaul in Spring, 2010. Her experience is one of late diagnosis, which caused her to require aggressive treatment and a much higher chance of future relapse. Juanita's story is a composite of the experiences of far too many women with breast cancer in LMICs – although with one huge difference: most of them cannot access financial support for treatment.

This hypothetical case study is derived from observation of a specific patient coupled with information from a specific hospital. The patient's journey is then traced using data on travel times and costs collected from primary sources.

The case is designed and developed to illustrate the importance of applying a diagonal approach that integrates strategies for cancer prevention, early detection, treatment and survivorship care into existing horizontal, population-based programs focused, for example, on alleviation of poverty, maternal and child health, sexual and reproductive health, and financial protection. It also highlights the challenges of guaranteeing financial protection for treatment, as well as the opportunities for innovating in the design of financing and delivery. This information complements the ideas presented in Chapters 6 and 8 of this volume.

The Mexican health system is one of the only, if not the only, health system in a developing region that offers universal financial protection to all citizens for several cancers, including breast cancer. As of January 2007, all Mexicans diagnosed with breast cancer are entitled to Seguro Popular, if they do not have another form of public social security. Further, the package is generous, including trastuzumub for HER2+ cancers and some support for reconstructive surgery.

Seguro Popular coverage is associated with a policy to guarantee quality. Coverage is only available through certified treatment centers that have demonstrated an ability to manage all aspects of breast cancer. These public centers are distributed throughout the country, but most are situated in the capital cities of larger states.

In this context, perhaps the best of any available to a breast cancer patient living in a developing country, consider Juanita's journey with breast cancer and the lessons it provides regarding health system strengthening. Her story also illustrates the opportunities for action and how these are being taken up in Mexico using a diagonal approach.

Background

Juanita comes from the small town of Tilancingo, population about 650, located 3 hours by bus from the district hospital in Yautepec, State of Morelos, in Mexico. From Tilancingo, it is 3.5 hours by bus to the nearest tertiary-level hospital with a full-range of cancer diagnosis and treatment services. Juanita arrived at the women's hospital in Yautepec with a 6 cm lump in her left breast and lymphedema in her left arm. Mammography and biopsy confirmed the obvious diagnosis of locally advanced Stage III breast cancer.

Juanita is 42 and has 4 children (ages 23, 15, 11, and 5), all of whom were born in the local primary-care clinic with a physician at hand, and breast-fed. Juanita works six days a week, cleaning one of the local beauty salons and earns close to the minimum wage if she gets tips –about $US 80, per month. Her job is not covered by social security, and she is not paid for the days that she does not work. Juanita finished primary school, is literate, and she reads magazines and short books– especially at the salon where she works.

Due to her low income and because she has young children, Juanita is a beneficiary of the social welfare program, *Oportunidades*, a conditional cash-transfer program that targets health, nutrition, and education. The program now covers 5.8 million poor households in Mexico, more than 22% of the population, and is available in almost all low income municipalities in Mexico.[71,72] As part of Oportunidades, for many years Juanita has attended monthly health promotion sessions at the local clinic. All of her children have an up-to-date health card, which is required to attend school and to participate in the Oportunidades program. Juanita has the women's health card, and hers has been regularly filled-out at the clinic. The card says that she does not need a mammogram – a term she is not familiar with, anyway – until age 50.[73]

The process of diagnosing Juanita's cancer

When she first realized she had the lump, nearly 2 years earlier, she went to see the physician at the primary health clinic who prescribed an antibiotic and sent Juanita home without a diagnosis or follow-up instructions. Mobile mammography vans had been to the town the previous year, but the test was offered only to women ages 50 and over. Younger women were encouraged to go to Cuernavaca, the state's capital, for routine testing or if they had particular concerns, but the trip meant losing a full day of work and so Juanita chose to not go.

As the lump grew, Juanita became more frightened – too frightened to act. A recent *Oportunidades* health promotion session at the clinic was devoted to the early detection of breast cancer, and she had read the section on breast cancer in the orientation manual.[74] The health promoter spoke about 'knowing your own body' and told the women that if they ever found a "bolita"–a small lump– they should ask for a clinical examination. The session gave Juanita courage, as the women were assured that the disease could be cured and that they had access to free treatment through the new insurance program, Seguro Popular.

Juanita asked to be examined and was referred to the district hospital. Unfortunately, what was a small lump when she first noticed it two years earlier had become a large mass encompassing much of her breast with obvious lymph node involvement in her armpit.

What could have been done better in detecting Juanita's breast cancer?

The health system failed to integrate early detection interventions into maternal and child health, sexual reproductive health, and anti-poverty programs. Early detection and prevention of cancer is not given sufficient emphasis in medical training programs. The physicians and nurses –mostly recent graduates doing a year of social service at the primary clinic– had received almost no training in breast cancer early detection.[75] Instead, the focus of primary caregivers was on infections and what are considered to be more common ailments. Further, they were taught that breast cancer is a disease of much older and wealthier women – a mistaken and outdated belief since breast cancer is now the second leading cause of death in young women in Mexico.

Although the Ministry of Health provided materials and some training about breast cancer, that training did not reach these clinics. As well, for similar reasons, until 2009 *Oportunidades* did not include breast cancer as one of the topics in the health promotion discussions, and no materials were made available to women. Finally, none of the local community organizations, several of which work to empower women, had any information on breast cancer. Although some civil society organizations do work on breast cancer, those organizations are mostly based in larger cities.

Developing Effective Responses Through Health System Innovations and Integration

Training about breast cancer for primary care health workers, including community promoters is underway.[76] *Oportunidades* now gives high priority to the topic of breast cancer in the manuals and guides provided to beneficiaries,[77] the age for free routine mammograms has been lowered to 40,[78] and NGOs are paying greater attention to increasing awareness of breast cancer and less attention to providing direct services because of the expanded coverage offered through Seguro Popular since 2007 (further information provided in Chapter 6 and 8). These concerted efforts will reduce the frequency of late detection of breast cancer and prevent many unnecessary deaths. Even so, two of every three Mexican women with breast cancer continue to be diagnosed at late-stages with advanced disease.[79,80]

Accessing Treatment

After diagnosis with Stage III breast cancer, Juanita found that she could not travel to Mexico City for treatment. Thus, the women's hospital in Yautepec, staffed by a surgical oncologist specializing in reproductive cancers, took over the case. With guidance from colleagues at the tertiary level, specialty hospital in Mexico City, where she had trained, the surgeon began administering chemotherapy to reduce the tumor size prior to surgery.

Yet, this presented a financial challenge for everyone involved. The hospital was not certified for treating breast cancer –because no clinical oncologist was available to work in the hospital. In the absence of full certification of capacity to treat breast cancer, care provided at the hospital could not be covered by the *Seguro Popular*.

If Juanita could have gone to Mexico City for treatment, she would have had all of her services covered. Unfortunately, the costs of the repeated transport for Juanita and for her daughter to accompany her were prohibitive. Further, travel for treatment meant an extra day of lost income for both mother and daughter. Worse, the trip was difficult because of the nausea from the chemotherapy, and Juanita worried about being so far away from her younger children.

To save Juanita the cost of seeking care in Mexico City, the hospital turned to a local NGO for support for the remaining 3-4 rounds of chemotherapy (MXN 15,000 =$US 1,200 per session, plus MXN 2,500 =$US 200 for the catheter), and Juanita searched for funds to pay for the drugs to control the symptoms (MXN 63 =$US 4-5) as well as the travel costs to the hospital in Yautepec.

Juanita's search for funds delayed treatment by another three weeks. While the support of the specialty center in Mexico City, the NGO, and the local hospital helped to solve the immediate challenges that Juanita faced, it placed an extra burden on everyone involved.

Further, Juanita is ER/PR and HER2+ and will benefit from tamoxifen (MXN 2,450 =$US 196 per year for 5 years) and ongoing infusions of herceptin. These drugs cannot be financed by the NGO (it costs approximately $US 2,000 per infusion, which is required every three weeks for up to one year).

The minimum overall costs for a patient like Juanita for one year, even if all drugs and services are covered by *Seguro Popular*, are significant: 30 trips to Mexico City or another urban center cost $US 25-30[1] per round-trip for each patient and caregiver, equaling a total of $US 1,500. By way of comparison, the minimum monthly wage in Mexico, which is higher than the average for about 50% of the workforce, is $US 146. A patient in treatment for breast cancer would probably be unable to work for about 1/3 of a year and so her annual income would be less than $US 1,200, if the patient were lucky enough to earn the equivalent of a minimum wage. This assumes that the patient and caregiver are able to stay at the hostel at the hospital, where costs are minimal. Otherwise, they must also pay for food and lodging. The costs of transport alone are likely to exceed the monthly income of a female-headed household if she is diagnosed with breast cancer and seeking treatment in Mexico City.

INNOVATIONS TO EXPAND ACCESS

Qualitative research demonstrated that Juanita's story repeated itself in many district hospitals throughout the country as patients sought care close to home. This research translated into a series of lessons and led to concrete steps to perfect what is now one of the very few national programs with universal coverage for a complete range of breast cancer treatments.[81]

With funding from the *Seguro Popular,* several states, such as Jalisco, are developing treatment sites at district hospitals located closer to patients. In addition to saving the patient the costs of transport, this strategy will reduce the strain on tertiary-level cancer centers, which often provide care that could be undertaken by a secondary-level hospital with appropriate supervision.

The patient is registered through the tertiary-level cancer center located in the capital city so that all treatment is covered through the *Seguro Popular.* Diagnosis, treatment design, surgery, radiation, and case management are undertaken at the specialty center – the National Cancer Institute, in Mexico City or one of the state-level cancer institutes. Case management is supervised by a clinical oncologist based at the tertiary hospital. This oncologist must authorize (by phone or e-mail) each drug infusion at the district hospital. Drugs are distributed to the district hospital through the tertiary center. Nurses and physicians at the district hospital receive special training from the specialty center with a particular focus on infusions, avoiding infection, and managing responses.

In Jalisco, where the project is being piloted, two secondary-level regional hospitals are involved *(Ciudad Guzmán and Tepatitán)*, and the anchor, tertiary-level center is the *Instituto Jaliscense de Cancerología*. Further, the *Instituto* is now offering home-based adjuvant therapy to patients living in Guadalajara.

In effect, this model turns the district hospital into a satellite of the specialty hospital and allows for the necessary certification of specific processes. This requires innovations in certification processes, funding, and supply chains – all of which are in process and will benefit not only breast cancer patients but also other cancer patients. These new sites are being designed for chemotherapy, but they will also eventually provide survivorship care.

This strategy has numerous benefits: it reduces overcrowding in specialty centers; offers the patient both specialty care and care closer to home; improves the overall capacity of the district hospitals, particularly in management of hygiene; and reduces costs for the patient and the health system. This strategy also has risks such as potentially overtaxing the local hospital staff. Thus, the project includes an imbedded qualitative evaluation component to help with scale-up to other states.

There are many challenges even at the pilot stage, particularly in patient monitoring, training local physicians, and guaranteeing that funds flow between different levels of the health system. Ongoing evaluation is making it possible to document solutions and improve the delivery model to work towards scale-up. Early results suggest that this is a model that could be generalized and applied in other, mostly middle income countries where specialty providers exist, but most are located in large urban centers.

The Mexico strategy is a hybrid of the models used by many hospitals in high income countries to provide care to a large catchment area. It draws on the models currently in use to improve access to care in resource-constrained countries that have no specialty oncologists, but in this case, the specialists are located in other areas of Mexico and do not have to be sourced internationally.

References

1. Samb B, Desai N, Nishtar S, et al. Prevention and management of chronic disease: a litmus test for health-systems strengthening in low -income and middle -income countries. *Lancet* 2010; 376(9754): 1785-97.

2. Beaglehole R, Horton R. Chronic diseases: global action must match global evidence. *Lancet* 2010; 376(9753): 1619-20.

3. World Health Organization. Global status report on noncommunicable diseases 2010. World Health Organization. 2011.

4. Samb B, Desai N, Nishtar S, et al., 2010.

5. Sepúlveda J, Bustreo F, Tapia R, et al. Improvement of child survival in Mexico: the diagonal approach. *Lancet* 2006; 368(9551): 2017-27.

6. Frenk J. Bridging the divide: global lessons from evidence-based health policy in Mexico. *Lancet* 2006; 369(9539): 954-61.

7. Ibid.

8. World Health Organization. Noncommunicable Diseases and Mental Health. Innovative care for chronic conditions: Global report. World Health Organization. 2002.

9. Farmer P, Frenk J, Knaul FM, et al. Expansion of cancer care and control in countries of low and middle income: a call to action. *Lancet* 2010; 376(9747): 1186-93.

10. World Health Organization. Global status report on noncommunicable diseases 2010. World Health Organization. 2011.

11. Alleyne G, Lloyd M, Atun R, Cooper Q. TIME TO ACT: The Global Emergency of Non-Communicable Diseases. Report on 'Health and Development: Held Back by Non-Communicable Diseases.' International Diabetes Federation; Union for International Cancer Care and Control; World Heart Federation. 2009. p. 1-20.

12. Mukherjee S. The emperor of all maladies: a biography of cancer. New York: Scribner, 2010.

13. Bukhman G. Ed. The PIH guide to chronic care integration for endemic non-communicable diseases. Partners in Health; Department of Global Health and Social Medicine, Harvard Medical School. 2011. http://www.pih.org/publications/entry/the-pih-guide-to-chronic-care-integration-for-endemic-ncd (accessed May 23, 2011).

14. Sloan FA, Gelband H. Cancer control opportunities in low- and middle income countries. Washington DC: National Academy Press. 2007.

15. Atun RA, Gurol-Urganci I, McKee M. Health systems and increased longevity in people with HIV and AIDS. *British Medical Journal* 2009; 339.

16. Allotey P, Reidpath D, Yasin S, Chan C, de-Graft A. Rethinking health-care systems: a focus on chronicity. *Lancet* 2010.

17. Samb B, Desai N, Nishtar S, et al., 2010.

18. Nolte E, McKee M. Eds. Caring for people with chronic conditions: a health systems perspective. European Observatory on Health Systems and Policy Series. McGraw Hill Open University Press. 2008.

19. World Health Organization. Noncommunicable Diseases and Mental Health. Innovative care for chronic conditions: Global report. World Health Organization. 2002.

20. World Health Organization. World Health Report 2010: World Health Organization. 2010.

21. World Health Organization. WHA 58.33: Sustainable health financing, universal coverage and social health insurance. World Health Assembly Resolution 58.33. 2005.

22. World Health Organization. World Health Report 2010. Health systems financing: the path to universal coverage. Geneva: World Health Organizations, 2010.

23. Bukhman G. Ed.. The PIH guide to chronic care integration for endemic non-communicable diseases. Partners in Health; Department of Global Health and Social Medicine, Harvard Medical School. 2011. http://www.pih.org/publications/entry/the-pih-guide-to-chronic-care-integration-for-endemic-ncd (accessed May 23, 2011).

24. Nolte E, McKee M (Eds.), 2008.

25. Coleman K, Austin B, Brach C, Wagner E. Evidence on the chronic care model in the new millennium. *Health Affairs* 2009; 28(1): 75-85.

26. World Health Organization. Noncommunicable Diseases and Mental Health. Innovative care for chronic conditions: Global report. World Health Organization. 2002.

27. Sepulveda J. Foreword. In Jamison DT, Breman JG, Measham AR et al (Eds.). Disease Control Priorities in Developing Countries, 2nd Edition. Washington, DC: World Bank. 2006.

28. Atun R, de Jongh T, Secci F, Ohiri K, Adeyi O. A systematic review of the evidence on integration of targeted health interventions into health systems. *Health Policy and Planning* 2010; 25: 1-14.

29. Frenk J. The new public health. *Annual Review of Public Health* 1993; 14(1): 469-90.

30. Murray C, Frenk J. A framework for assessing the performance of health systems. *Bulletin of the World Health Organization* 2000; 78(6): 717-31.

31. Samb B, Desai N, Nishtar S, et al., 2010.

32. Harries AD, Jahn A, Zachariah R, Enarson D. Adapting the DOTS framework for tuberculosis control to the Management of non-communicable disease in sub-Saharan Africa. *PLoS Medicine* 2008; 5: e124.

33. Committee on the U.S. Commitment to Global Health. The U.S. commitment to global health: Recommendations for the new administration. Institute of Medicine: National Academies Press. 2009.

34. Travis P, Bennett S, Haines A, Pang T, Bhutta Z, Hyder A, et al. Overcoming health-systems constraints to achieve the Millennium Development Goals. *Lancet* 2004; 364(9437): 900-6.

35. World Health Organization Maximizing Positive Synergies Collaborative Group. An assessment of interactions between global health initiatives and country health systems. *Lancet* 2009; 373(9681): 2137-69.

36. Alleyne G, Stuckler D, Alwan A. The hope and the promise of the UN Resolution on non-communicable diseases. *Globalization and Health* 2010; 6(15).

37. Frenk J. Bridging the divide: global lessons from evidence-based health policy in Mexico. *Lancet* 2006; 369(9539): 954-61.

38. Sepulveda J, Bustreo F, Tapia R, et al., 2006.

39. Ooms G, Van Damme W, Baker BK, Zeitz P, Schrecker T. The 'diagonal' approach to Global Fund financing: a cure for the broader malaise of health systems. *Global Health* 2008; 4(6): 1-7.

40. World Health Organization Maximizing Positive Synergies Collaborative Group. An assessment of interactions between global health initiatives and country health systems. *Lancet* 2009; 373(9681): 2137-69

41. Committee on the U.S. Commitment to Global Health. The U.S. commitment to global health: recommendations for the new administration. Institute of Medicine: National Academies Press 2009.

42. Atun R, de Jongh TE, Secci FV, Ohiri K, Adeyi O, Car J. Integration of priority population, health and nutrition interventions into health systems: systematic review. BMC Public Health, 2011, Vol:11

43. Tudor CL, van-Velthoven MH, Brusamento S, Atun R. Integrating prevention of mother-to-child HIV transmission (PMTCT) programmes with other health services for preventing HIV infection and improving HIV outcomes in developing countries. Cochrane Database Syst Rev, 2011

44. Sepulveda J, Bustreo F, Tapia R, et al., 2006.

45. World Health Organization. Noncommunicable Diseases and Mental Health. Innovative care for chronic conditions: Global report. World Health Organization. 2002.

46. World Health Organization. Global status report on noncommunicable diseases 2010. World Health Organization. 2011.

47. World Health Organization Maximizing Positive Synergies Collaborative Group. An assessment of interactions between global health initiatives and country health systems, *Lancet* 2009; 373(9681): 2137-69.

48. Price JE, Leslie JA, Welsh M, Binagwaho A. Integrating HIV clinical services into primary health care in Rwanda: a measure of quantitative effects. *AIDS Care* 2009; 21: 608–14.

49. Rasschaert F, Pirard M, Philips MP, Atun R et al, Positive spill-over effects of ART scale up on wider health systems development: evidence from Ethiopia and Malawi. *J Int AIDS Soc* 2011, 14(1)

50. Atn R, Pothapregada SK, Kwansah J, et al, Critical interactions between the Global Fund-supported HIV programs and the health system in Ghana, *JAIDS-J ACQ IMM DEF* 2011, 57: S72-S76

51. Kirby T. Pulse oximeters breathe life into surgery in poorer nations. *Lancet* 2011; 377(9759): 17-8.

52. Funk LM, Weiser TG, Berry WB, et al. Global operating theatre distribution and pulse oximetry supply: an estimation from reported data. *Lancet* 2010; 376(9746): 1055-61.

53. World Health Organization, Surgical Safety Checklist, Patient Safety: World Health Organization. 2009.

54. Bukhman G. Editor in Chief. The PIH guide to chronic care integration for endemic non-communicable diseases. Partners in Health; Department of Global Health and Social Medicine, Harvard Medical School, 2011. http://www.pih.org/publications/entry/the-pih-guide-to-chronic-care-integration-for-endemic-ncd (accessed May 23, 2011).

55. Adapted from Table 2.2 The Cancer Control Continuum. IOM. From Cancer Patient to Cancer Survivor: Lost in Transition. Washington DC: Institute of Medicine; 2005.

56. Based on: IOM. From Cancer Patient to Cancer Survivor: Lost in Transition. Washington DC: Institute of Medicine; 2005.

57. Mullan F. Seasons of survival: reflections of a physician with cancer. *New England Journal of Medicine* 1985; 313 (4): 270-273.

58. NCCS National Coalition for Cancer Survivorship. http://www.canceradvocacy.org (accessed March 31, 2011).

59. "DCCPS: OCS." Division of Cancer Control and Population Sciences – DCCPS. National Cancer Institute. http://dccps.nci.nih.gov/ ocs/ocs_factsheet.pdf (accessed March 31, 2011).

60. National Cancer Institute, Office of Cancer Survivorship. http://dccps.nci.nih.gov/ocs/definitions.html (accessed May 29, 2011).

61. Institute of Medicine. From Cancer Patient to Cancer Survivor: Lost in Transition. Washington DC: Institute of Medicine; 2005.

62. World Health Organization & International Agency for Research on Cancer.2008. World Cancer Report 2008. Boyle, Peter & Levin, Bernard (Eds.). France: Lyon. 2008.

63. World Health Organization, World Health Report 2000. World Health Organization. 2000.

64. Murray C, Frenk J, 2000.
65. World Health Organization. Monitoring the building blocks of health systems: a handbook of indicators and their measurement strategies. World Health Organization. 2010.
66. World Health Organization Maximizing Positive Synergies Collaborative Group 2009. An assessment of interactions between global health initiatives and country health systems. *Lancet* 2009; 373(9681): 2137-69.
67. Nugent R, Knaul F, Jamison D, et al. Fiscal policies for health promotion and disease prevention. Disease control priorities in developing countries. World Bank 2006(2nd Ed.): 211-23.
68. World Health Organization Commission on Social Determinants of Health. Closing the gap in a generation: health equity through action on the social determinants of health. 2008. WHO. http://whqlibdoc.who.int/publications/2008/9789241563703_eng.pdf (accessed May 21, 2011).
69. Samb B, Desai N, Nishtar S, et al., 2010.
70. Farmer P, Frenk J, Knaul FM, Shulman, et al. Expansion of cancer care and control in countries of low and middle income: a call to action. *Lancet* 2010; 376(9747): 1186-93.
71. Oportunidades: Indicadores de resultados. Gobierno Federal. 2011. http://www.oportunidades.gob.mx/Portal/wb/Web/indicadores_de_resultados (accessed May 21, 2011).
72. Frenk J. Bridging the divide: global lessons from evidence-based health policy in Mexico. *Lancet* 2006; 368(9539): 954-61.
73. Cartilla Nacional de Salud. Mujer de 20 a 59 años. Gobierno Federal. México, 2008.
74. Coordinación Nacional del Programa de Desarrollo Humano Oportunidades. Aprendemos Juntos a Vivir Mejor: Guía de orientación y capacitación para beneficiarios titulares beneficiarias del programa Oportunidades. México, DF: Coordinación Nacional del Programa de Desarrollo Humano Oportunidades, Secretaría de Desarrollo Social. 2010. http://www.oportunidades.gob.mx/Portal/work/sites/Web/resources/ ArchivoContent/1158/Libro%20Guia%20 Titulares%20Oportunidades%202010.pdf (accessed May 22, 2011).
75. Nigenda G, González-Robledo LM, Caballero M, Zarco A, González-Robledo MC. Proceso social del cáncer de mama. perspectiva de mujeres diagnosticadas, sus parejas y los prestadores de servicios de salud. Informe Final. Instituto Carso para la Salud-INSP, Cuernavaca, 2008.
76. Innovaciones en la prestación de servicios de detección temprana y tratamiento del cáncer de mama en México. Iniciativa inter-institucional Tómatelo a Pecho, A.C.-Comisión Nacional de Protección Social en Salud. México. 2011. http://www.tomateloapecho.org.mx/proyectos.html (accessed September 27, 2011).
77. Coordinación Nacional del Programa de Desarrollo Humano Oportunidades. Aprendemos Juntos a Vivir Mejor: Guía de orientación y capacitación para beneficiarios titulares beneficiarias del programa Oportunidades. México, DF: Coordinación Nacional del Programa de Desarrollo Humano Oportunidades, Secretaría de Desarrollo Social. 2010.
78. Norma Oficial Mexicana PROY-NOM-041-SSA2-2009, Para la prevención, diagnóstico, tratamiento, control y vigilancia epidemiológica del cáncer de mama. Mexico, 2010.
79. Knaul FM, Nigenda G, Lozano R, Langer A, Frenk J. Breast cancer in Mexico: a pressing priority. *Reproductive Health Matters* 2008; 16(32): 113-23.
80. Mohar A, Bargalló E, Ramírez T, Lara F, Beltran-Ortega A. Recursos disponibles para el tratamiento del cáncer de mama en México. *Salud Publica Mex* 2009; 51(2): 263-9.
81. Cancer de Mama: Tomatelo a Pecho. Proyectos Especificos: Innovaciones en la prestación de servicios de detección temprana y tratamiento del cáncer de mama en México. 2011. http://www.tomateloapecho.org.mx/proyectos.html (accessed October 4, 2011).

Chapter 5

CORE ELEMENTS FOR PROVISION OF CANCER CARE AND CONTROL IN LOW AND MIDDLE INCOME COUNTRIES

Julie R. Gralow, Eric Krakauer, Benjamin O. Anderson,
Andre Ilbawi, Peggy Porter, Mary Gospodarowicz,
Sarah Feldman, Carlos Rodríguez-Galindo, Lindsay Frazier,
Leslie Lehmann, Lawrence Shulman

Key messages

- Core elements of cancer care and control (CCC) must be decided within each country based on existing health resources and infrastructure, the burden of cancers, country-specific cancer risks, political and social conditions, and cultural beliefs and practices.

- Lack of information and education about cancer is a major barrier to effective CCC in developing countries, especially for the detection of cancers at earlier and more treatable stages.

- Education programs need to address cultural barriers to care, myths and misconceptions about cancer, and the stigma attached to cancer, and to increase awareness of what can be accomplished within existing health systems.

- Infectious agents cause almost 25% of cancers while modifiable risk factors, such as tobacco use, alcohol consumption, poor nutrition and physical inactivity, account for 9% of cancer deaths in low and middle income countries (LMICs). This makes both infectious agents and lifestyle factors obvious targets for CCC prevention programs.

- Diagnostic tests that are necessary for accurate diagnosis and treatment are essential, yet resources are lacking in most LMICs. Remote pathology (telepathology) is an alternative and can involve international partnerships.

- Surgical services are essential to cancer detection, diagnosis, staging, treatment, and palliation.

- Radiation therapy is an essential and proven cost-effective treatment in the cure and palliation of many cancers common in LMICs.

- Systemic therapy is an important component of cancer care, and anti-cancer drugs can substantially reduce recurrence and extend survival for many cancers.

- With proper training for healthcare personnel, chemotherapy can be safely prepared, administered, and monitored at district hospitals in LMICs without an on-site oncologist, as long as support is available from off-site specialists.

- Cancer patients and their families benefit from survivorship support to help them deal with the physical, psychological, and social side effects of the disease and its treatment.

- All patients have a basic right to pain relief and palliative care, which are essential elements of care that can improve patients' quality of life even when no disease-modifying treatment is available as well as reduce the discomfort of disease-modifying therapy.

5.i Introduction

Even with resource constraints, a well-conceived and well-managed national cancer care and control program can lower cancer incidence and deaths as well as improve the lives of cancer patients. The core elements of a comprehensive cancer program span the entire cancer continuum from prevention through long-term and palliative care. A national program should not only provide care, but should also incorporate education, metrics and data collection, and research.[1] In an ideal world, each of the core components would be accessible by the entire population at risk of or diagnosed with cancer, and would be uniquely adapted to local conditions and needs.

Unfortunately, scarce resources place limits on each of the core components of CCC and often force policy makers to make difficult decisions about how limited resources are either explicitly or implicitly invested in CCC. In these circumstances, it is critical to create service models and packages for prevention, early diagnosis, treatment, and palliation that will offer the greatest benefit to the population and provide a nucleus for further growth of CCC. The most effective interventions will have the greatest impact on CCC. The influx of global health funds from $5.6 billion in 1990 to $21.8 billion in 2007 was accompanied by the development of major global health initiatives such as the Global Fund and Global Alliance for Vaccines and Immunization (GAVI), which played central roles in mobilizing and channeling global health funds to address infectious diseases in LMICs.[2] Similar efforts are needed for improving outcomes with noncommunicable diseases (NCDs) in general and cancer in specific. Incidence and outcomes data available through cancer surveillance and monitoring programs can guide the development of appropriate national policies and help determine priorities for resource allocation.

While cancer programs in high income countries include at least some level of disease-modifying treatment for virtually all malignancies at all stages, treatment can be extremely complex, costly, and in some circumstances with limited oncologic benefit. Resource constraints and competing health priorities make this approach to cancer care inappropriate in low income countries. In those settings, cancer program design and implementation should use available health system resources as a foundation for more comprehensive care, targeting areas of cancer care where the greatest impact can be made.

To aid the decision-making process, this chapter outlines the fundamental elements of adequate CCC and the core components for basic, effective cancer control that can be applied even where resources are scarce. The appendix to this chapter includes a description of the core elements for care and control of a subset of specific cancers that can have the greatest impact on health in LMICs.

Text Box 5.1
Assumptions underlying analysis and recommendations regarding core elements of a CCC strategy for LMICs:

1. *Many cancers are preventable through infection control and lifestyle modifications.*

2. *An accurate cancer diagnosis is critical to determining an appropriate and successful treatment plan.*

3. *Many cancers are highly treatable with affordable interventions that result in the addition of many years of life:*

   a) *Denial of treatment for diseases that are highly curable or that can be controlled for many years is unacceptable;*

   b) *Treatment (or not) of more complex, less curable diseases requires evaluations specific to each country and available resources.*

4. *Palliation of pain and suffering from cancer is a basic human right and is therefore not subject to cost-benefit analysis.*

5. *Understanding the magnitude of the cancer burden and the potential impact of CCC interventions requires reliable data.*

Four principles can guide the design of cancer care models in LMICs from the outset and will result in saved lives and reduced suffering.

1. *Many of the cancers that pose the greatest health risk in LMICs are amenable to prevention, treatment, or palliation.*

2. *The majority of drugs used to treat cancers that are common in low-resource settings are off-patent and can be sourced at low prices.*

3. *Many elements of cancer prevention, screening, treatment, and palliation can be accomplished without specialized tertiary level providers or treatment centers.*

4. Palliation of pain and suffering from cancer should be a priority for all types of cancer.

These principles are applied throughout this report to identify innovative strategies for the financing, procurement, and delivery of drugs and services, for meticulous data collection and outcomes analysis, and for stewardship of CCC in LMICs. Our understanding of the causes and biology of cancer is undergoing rapid evolution and the development of new diagnostic tests, techniques, equipment, and drug treatment options makes it clear that the essential elements of CCC will evolve accordingly.

The framework proposed here is a starting point for the expansion of CCC in LMICs. These guidelines are meant to be general, as approaches will vary in different settings. This document is consensus-based, not a "meta-analysis" of existing and relatively weak scientific evidence. The field will likely evolve quickly as understanding of cancer in developing countries increases and knowledge of how best to deliver CCC in resource-constrained settings improves.

5.ii Core elements of CCC

The development of appropriate CCC strategies in LMICs must be country specific and will vary depending on disease-specific distribution and available healthcare economic resources. It should take into account the existing health system infrastructure, the frequency of different cancer types, country-specific cancer risks and exposures, political and social conditions, and cultural beliefs and practices. The goal should be the systematic and equitable implementation of evidence-based plans that make the best use of available resources. Even in resource-poor settings, cost-effective approaches, including the "best buys" identified by WHO, exist for each stage of the CCC continuum.[3] As one example, the Breast Health Global Initiative (BHGI) has developed a guideline model for stratifying resource-appropriate breast cancer services within each of the core elements for LMICs.[4]

Prevention, through promoting lifestyle change, reducing tobacco use and exposure to environmental risk is of the highest priority, and has been extensively reviewed in the literature. Cancer prevention offers the most cost-effective, long-term strategy for cancer control in adults and can include elements that are inexpensive and within the financial capability of lower income countries.[5] Investments in diagnosis and treatment will vary depending on the resource level of the country, but should include emphasis on early detection to increase the cure rate, as well as the development of standardized, evidence-based treatment guidelines. The newest technologies and drugs are usually expensive, but low-cost alternatives that are appropriate for use in LMICs frequently exist. For the lowest income countries, where most people present with late stage cancers, cure is uncommon, yet much can be done to offer palliative therapies and improve quality of life.

Establishing capacity for CCC in a country takes time and requires the commitment of financial and human resources. Some components of cancer control can be integrated into primary healthcare, while others require more specialized services. For some aspects of a cancer plan, cost-effectiveness or cost-benefit analysis may be used to rank priorities. Other aspects, such as palliative care, should receive priority because relief of pain and suffering is a basic human right. Building a cancer control program should start with high-impact interventions that are the most cost-effective and beneficial for the largest part of the population. For example, in a country with no existing cancer control plan, an initial focus on tobacco control, palliative care, and basic treatment for a few common cancers can provide early successes and establish a base for adding services. Once some cancer infrastructure exists and resources grow, incremental steps can be taken.[6]

Reliable data are needed to understand the cancer patterns and burden in each country and to track progress. Few LMICs have accurate, recent data about their cancer incidence or major risk factors. Global cancer estimates produced by the International Agency for Research on Cancer (IARC) are useful for setting initial priorities, but cannot be used to track progress or define priorities. Cancer registries that record incidence of cancer, stage, and outcomes over time in specific hospitals or defined geographic regions are important for understanding local cancer patterns. However, in many low income countries, people often die without medical care and/or without a diagnosis. Groups such as the Institute for Health Metrics and Evaluation (IHME) applied sophisticated statistical analytic approaches to estimate cancer statistics combining cancer registry data on mortality and incidence, vital registration, and verbal autopsy data for the period 1980-2010 to provide the most accurate estimates for breast and cervical cancers to date.[7] Nonetheless, collection of cause-specific mortality should be a long-term goal of every country. Where vital statistics systems are weak or nonexistent, data collection may begin in selected sites, rather than nationwide.

A commitment to CCC includes some investment in facilities, trained personnel, equipment, and drugs. An Institute of Medicine (IOM) 2007 report suggested that each LMIC consider supporting at least one specialized cancer center, even if capacity is limited.[8] Such a center need not be a freestanding facility, but could be a designated unit in a pre-existing hospital to maximize shared use of resources that are already part of the healthcare system. A cancer center of excellence can serve as the nexus for a national cancer program, and as an education and training facility, a central reference laboratory, and a site for the development of treatment guidelines and the conduct of locally relevant research. Additionally, such a center can be the focal point for partnerships at regional, national, and global levels, including twinning and partnering relationships with external cancer facilities.

Text Box 5.2
Jordan: Creating a regional center of excellence for cancer care as a focus for a national program on CCC [9]

Afsan Bhadelia, Imad Treish, Zaid Bitar,
Ruba Anastas, Mahmoud Sarhan

The King Hussein Cancer Center (KHCC) has progressed in only 15 years from being a weak institution offering little effective care to an internationally accredited hospital. Through its umbrella organization, the King Hussein Cancer Foundation, KHCC serves as a spearhead for improving access to CCC throughout Jordan, and, the Middle East. The foundation conducts ongoing fundraising, development and outreach activities to ensure sustainability of the center. These include meeting infrastructural and highly specialized human resource needs (reversing brain drain), as well as promoting collaborations and agreements to expand the center's regional and international network. It is through such parallel development activity that KHCC has generated the necessary resources to embrace the full spectrum and all facets of CCC:

prevention, early detection, diagnosis, treatment, palliative care, and survivorship.

KHCC is the only provider offering comprehensive, multi-disciplinary care in accordance with international standards, and, in 2006, was the first hospital in Jordan to receive international certification from The Joint Commission.[10] As of 2007, it also became the only hospital in the developing world to receive Joint Commission Disease or Condition-Specific Care Certification for oncology. Other certificates of distinction include those from the College of American Pathologists and the national Health Care Accreditation Council of Jordan.

Additionally, the center has been leading the palliative care initiative in the country, starting as a WHO demonstration project, and has a strong commitment to the use of morphine for pain management. The center administers 80% of the morphine used in all of Jordan. It serves as a regional model for palliative care.[11]

Innovations in delivery were part of these successes. These included shifting human resource responsibilities to nurses and community health workers to optimize delivery, investments in technological advancements to conduct teleoncology, and a commitment to regional and global partnership to help bridge the gap in care at other facilities. KHCC has adopted advanced nursing practices recommended in the Strong Model of Advanced Practice and has recruited clinical nurse coordinators who have made a significant impact on patient care. The empowerment of nurses and their expanded role in pediatric oncology teams has facilitated the provision of much-needed patient education, follow-up, and survivorship care.[12]

Furthermore, the institution organized an MOH-integrated national early detection and awareness program for breast cancer, the Jordan Breast Cancer Program, to combat the shortages of screening mammography and the cultural barriers that continue to challenge early detection.[13] The center is conducting direct, comprehensive training of health auxiliary workers and creating options for training through the medical education system at teaching hospitals. The objective is to train midwives, nurses, and health promoters to identiy risk factors, undertake breast clinical exams, and to promote early detection and referral of women for mammography. Further, two mobile mammography units have recently been acquired to strengthen screening efforts.

Since 1996, KHCC has had a successful twinning collaboration with St. Jude's International Outreach Program on pediatric oncology.[14,15] Other collaborating institutions include the Hospital for Sick Children in Toronto. Impressive results of teleconsult have demonstrated significant improvements in diagnosis and treatment, and have given KHCC medical staff the opportunity to engage with expert multidisciplinary teams and, together, to develop much more appropriate treatment regimens. KHCC has shown that highly specialized management of certain cancers (for instance retinoblastoma) can be successfully implemented in a developing country setting with collaborative twinning programs.[16,17]

Significant investments continue to be made in technology to provide better patient care. KHCC has been able to move to electronic record keeping, with previous records digitally archived to aid future research. Data is shared internationally with appropriate institutions and included in relevant databases: bone marrow data is reported to and exchanged with the international bone marrow registry, data on pediatric cancers is inputted into St. Jude's web-based database (POND-4Kids) for cancer registration, and a tissue bank to archive biospecimens is currently being established.

Efforts are underway to ensure that as many patients as possible receive top quality care closer to their homes and also to make it possible to rely less heavily on international support. KHCC is working to strengthen and improve the standard of care at other tertiary centers that provide cancer services by extending access to training and consult opportunities. It is currently working with one of two main teaching hospitals in the country to design and deliver more appropriate cancer treatment regimens and seeking to expand this type of collaboration with other providers. This infrastructure shifting process will strengthen various aspects of the health system, particularly the development of accredited facilities to improve service delivery. The Jordan Health Care Accreditation Council, launched in 2008, provides an opportunity to "piggyback" and upgrade standards at facilities other than KHCC through a focus on cancer care, and eventually to expand and integrate other illnesses. The Center has chosen not to remain "an island of highest quality care," but rather, led by its Foundation, to reach out to improve the quality of care at other centers in Jordan and in the region.

KHCC is also extending the scope of its work to include cancer policy development. The center participates in the government's National Cancer Control Strategy expert advisory group and is now an active participant in many international institutions and activities, including operating as a sister center of the MD Anderson Cancer Center, a WHO collaborating center, as well as partnerships with organizations such as the Union for International Cancer Control (UICC).

EDUCATION AND AWARENESS-BUILDING

Lack of information and education is a major barrier to CCC in the developing world. Educating the community, as well as healthcare professionals and governmental agencies, about cancer detection, diagnosis, and treatment is central to an effective national cancer program. Individuals need to understand that many cancers can be prevented through appropriate behavioral change, that effective treatments are available, and that cancer can often be cured. Knowledge- and awareness- building should reach all levels and participants, but especially policy makers and the healthcare community.

Population-based education is especially important in LMICs. Due to lack of education and information, patients tend to present late in the course of their disease, when the window for a curative intervention may have passed. In many developing countries, misconceptions about cancer, including the beliefs that cancer is incurable or contagious, may discourage people from seeking care. There is also fear that the disease will lead to ostracism from the community and family. Education to prevent stigma by the community for all patients and for specific groups, such as women, is important.[18] The personal interpretations of illness that guide health behavior vary across countries and cultures, and these can influence responses to prevention and screening campaigns, as well as the likelihood of initiating and complying with treatment and follow-up. Community education and outreach efforts must dispel common misconceptions in a manner that is culturally sensitive, unbiased, and easy to comprehend. Cancer outcomes cannot improve unless patients and the healthcare community understand the benefits of early detection and are willing to support timely diagnosis and treatment.

Ideally, cancer education should both draw from and strengthen local systems, rather than being externally imposed. Education is best accomplished when embedded into existing systems, such as the healthcare and education systems, as well as community, religious, and other social organizations. While there is widespread agreement that education and awareness are necessary, the barriers and most effective delivery methods have not been well studied. All individuals capable of delivering messages, including community health workers, volunteers, and expert patients, in addition to medical professionals, should be involved.[19-23] Indeed, advocacy by patients, a large source of cancer awareness and information in many developed nations, has not been used in resource-poor countries.[24,25] Access to the internet is essential to connect the emerging cancer program to the rest of the world, to transfer knowledge, and to provide mentoring and support with diagnostics and consultation.

PREVENTION AND RISK REDUCTION

While not applicable to all types of cancer, prevention offers the most cost-effective, long-term strategy to control cancer. Cancer prevention should be integrated into the primary healthcare system, where it can also help to prevent other diseases that share the same risk factors. As suggested in the discussion of facets of the cancer divide (Chapter 2), prevention and risk reduction strategies can be divided into two major categories: those that involve lifestyle alterations, and those that aim to control infectious disease. According to WHO estimates, more than 40% of cancer deaths worldwide are due to tobacco use, unhealthy diets, alcohol consumption, inactive lifestyles, and infection.[26]

The increase in cigarette smoking has made lung cancer the most common cause of cancer and cancer deaths in LMICs. Tobacco control represents the most significant and urgent intervention that will reduce the risk of developing many cancers, especially cancers of the lung, head and neck, and bladder. Countries can implement effective policies for reducing tobacco use, and they can do it inexpensively.[27] Many effective tobacco control interventions are legal or regulatory, including taxes and bans on advertising and promotion. An aggressive anti-tobacco program and adoption of the WHO Framework Convention on Tobacco Control is an essential element of any cancer prevention strategy.[28]

The potential impact of programs to modify other unhealthy lifestyle behaviors will vary according to the prevalence of each behavior. Cancers of the oral cavity, pharynx, larynx, esophagus, liver, and breast can be caused by heavy alcohol use, accounting for 5% of cancer deaths in LMICs, with the risk varying by cancer type. Diet, body weight, and physical activity levels are interrelated and act in complex ways to promote or reduce the risk of cancer. While the impact of these risk factors is far greater in high-resource countries, estimates suggest that these modifiable lifestyle factors account for 9% of cancer deaths in LMICs.[29]

Infectious agents are responsible for almost 25% of cancer deaths in the developing world, compared to only 6% in industrialized countries.[30] Due to the large burden of cancer from infectious agents (see Chapter 2), cancer prevention through vaccination or treatment of these infections should be a major focus of CCC in LMICs. Vaccines for the prevention of HPV (associated with cervical and head and neck cancer) and hepatitis B (hepatocellular cancer) are available. In areas endemic for liver cancer, hepatitis B virus immunization should be integrated with other childhood vaccination programs. Strategies to integrate HPV vaccination during childhood immunizations should also be considered.

Special measures to combat other infections associated with cancer are essential to a CCC program and need to be modified to fit the conditions in each country. For example, Kaposi sarcoma, among the most common cancers in sub-Saharan Africa, is strongly associated with HIV/AIDS infection; and most cases of gastric cancer –common in some parts of the developing world– are caused by the bacteria Helicobacter pylori.

SCREENING AND EARLY DETECTION

Early detection of cancer greatly increases the chances for successful treatment in most cancers and is fundamental to reducing cancer mortality. With few exceptions, early stage cancers are less lethal and more treatable than late stage cancers. Unfortunately, many patients in LMICs do not present for formal medical care until late in the course of their disease, if at all. Early detection involves two major components: screening of asymptomatic populations, and education about early signs and symptoms of cancer. Increased awareness of possible warning signs of cancer among physicians, nurses, and other healthcare providers as well as among the general public can have a great impact on the disease.[31] For any early detection program to be successful, both healthcare providers and the populations they serve need confidence that care will be available if cancers are diagnosed. Screening for early stages of cancer or precancerous states can reduce cancer death rates only if appropriate management is available when treatable conditions are detected.

Cancers for which screening is recommended in high income countries are breast, cervical, and colon. Breast cancer screening using mammography and cervical cancer screening using cytology screening methods, including Pap smears, are proven to reduce mortality. While many early detection screening techniques used in wealthier settings are not technically feasible or affordable for widespread use in other parts of the world, education of people and providers and targeted disease programs can improve early detection. Several studies seek to evaluate low-cost approaches to screening that can be used in low-resource settings.[32-35] For example, visual inspection with acetic acid may prove to be an effective screening method for cervical cancer. More studies that evaluate low-cost, alternative methods to mammography screening, such as clinical breast examination, community health worker training, and incorporation of simple checklists are needed.[36,37]

Screening a substantial portion of the population requires infrastructure and should only be undertaken when the following conditions are met: effectiveness has been demonstrated, resources (including personnel and equipment) are sufficient to cover nearly all of the target group, facilities exist for confirming diagnoses, treatment, and follow-up care of those with abnormal results, and prevalence of the disease is high enough to justify the effort and costs of screening.

DIAGNOSTICS AND STAGING

Diagnosis is an integral part of CCC, and an accurate diagnosis is the cornerstone of appropriate care. Diagnostic tests include physical examination, imaging, tissue sampling, laboratory, and pathology analysis. These techniques are also used during the course of treatment to monitor response and/or check for recurrence. With careful use of basic diagnostic resources, many patients can be assessed accurately and treated appropriately in LMICs.

Pathologic examination of cancer requires the technical skills to obtain a tumor sample, either through fine needle or body fluid aspiration for cytologic evaluation or a tissue biopsy for microscopic examination. High quality specimen processing is a critical component of CCC and is currently not available in many locations. Basic cancer pathology should include the capability for specimen fixation, embedding into paraffin, tissue slicing, and staining. Timely processing is important to ensure good quality (prolonged fixation degrades quality), and is critical for the care of the patient who must wait for pathological confirmation before beginning treatment.

Immunohistochemistry can be an important part of pathology testing, and many LMICs can obtain this relatively simple technology, at least in specialized regional centers. Testing for estrogen receptor in breast cancer should receive priority, as hormone therapy can significantly improve outcomes for patients with hormone receptor-expressing breast cancer. Testing breast cancer for HER2 will affect outcomes only if trastuzumab or other HER2-targeted therapies are available. Documenting the frequency of HER2-positive breast cancers in a country may ultimately affect decisions about coverage of trastuzumab. Some highly specialized cancer sub-classification techniques, such as flow cytometry evaluation in leukemia, are resource-intensive and not likely to be feasible at present in resource-limited settings.

Remote pathology, a system with on-site specimen preparation and histology by trained technicians and analysis by specialized pathologists in other countries, is an option for improving pathology preparation, histologic staining, and diagnosis until local pathologists can be trained as cancer diagnosticians.[38,39] This can be accomplished either by physical transportation of the slides to referral centers or by remote video reading, which can be done with a variety of affordable technologies. A remote system can provide access to specialized pathologists for difficult cases and can improve diagnostic quality overall. While remote pathology is an option to improve pathology diagnosis, it is not a substitute for developing in-country capacity in this area. A remote system of partnering with leading international centers for cancer treatment is, however, a good long-term investment as it also provides access to specialized pathologists for difficult cases and training and quality control.

Cancer staging varies by tumor type, but generally involves defining the size of the primary tumor, extension into regional lymph nodes, and spread to distant sites. Cancer staging requires imaging and laboratory evaluation, which may not be available in all settings. Despite this, important clinical decisions can often be made through a careful physical exam and history, basic laboratory investigations, and chest radiography and abdominal ultrasound. For many cancers, clinical stage may be assigned without extensive testing.

TREATMENT

The primary objectives of cancer treatment are cure, prolonging life, and improving the quality of life. An effective and efficient treatment program should be linked to screening and early detection, and follow evidence-based standards of care. Essential elements of cancer treatment include surgery, radiation therapy, systemic therapy (chemotherapy, hormonal therapy, and biological therapy), and supportive care. Some treatments require sophisticated technology and these treatments should be concentrated in relatively few places in a region to maximize efficiency and the use of resources.

Surgery is an essential part of cancer treatment.[40] For solid tumors, long-term survival usually depends on surgical removal of the primary tumor with adequate margins and evaluation of regional lymph nodes; however, in low income countries, where approximately 60-80% of cancer patients present with late- or end-stage disease, most cases are not amenable to definitive resection with intent to cure.[41,42] Even in cases of more advanced disease, surgical procedures are available to improve either duration or quality of life.

Selection of an appropriate surgical procedure varies with stage of disease, availability of cancer-related resources and services, and presence of local expertise. Therefore, one must establish pre-operatively which patients are at high risk for regional or distant disease. This can be accomplished with analysis of histopathology, staging studies, and/or diagnostic laparoscopy. Patients with local disease can often be cured with definitive surgical resection.

Even in the presence of regional or metastatic disease, procedural based interventions can improve the quality and duration of life. Palliative stents for dysphagia in patients with esophageal cancer have been used widely in sub-Saharan Africa with success.[43] Debulking and diverting surgeries are a critical adjunct to the care of those dying with cancer and can improve quality of life, reduce pain, and often increase life expectancy.

Surgical approach is also impacted by the availability of adjuvant therapies. For example, if radiation therapy is not available, localized breast cancers are best managed with mastectomy. If radiation therapy is available, however, then lumpectomy with radiation is a good alternative for patients with early stage disease.

Maturing cancer programs in which advancements in surgical therapy, medical oncology, and radiation oncology occur synchronously provide the optimal environment for progress in the care of patients afflicted with cancer. Outcomes can also be improved by addressing surgeon shortages, fostering surgical training models with expertise in cancer care, and strengthening critical services such as nursing and ancillary staff. To address these shortfalls, some have advocated for targeted training in cancer-specific interventions through partnering or twinning organizations.[44]

Each surgical program should undergo a process of continuous quality improvement targeted at adjusting surgical interventions to emerging technology, higher level of expertise, and increasing availability of adjuvant therapies. For example, the management of rectal cancer including the decision to perform total mesorectal excision depends on the expertise of the surgeon and the availability of chemotherapy and radiation therapy.

Ultimately, advancements in surgical care and referral networks augment existing surgery services as well as district and community level healthcare facilities. Laparoscopy and endoscopy can be introduced in a low-cost manner with significant clinical benefit and improved cost-effectiveness for the larger patient population and medical community. In addition, district and community care centers can help develop the infrastructure for referral systems. The role of surgery, which is currently directed mainly toward palliative procedures and diagnosis, should evolve with the cancer system into one based on intent to cure.

Radiation therapy is a component in the curative treatment plans for many cancers and is used in palliation and symptom relief for even more cancers.[45] Radiotherapy has limited medical uses in noncancerous conditions, and is overwhelmingly a cancer treatment modality. Radiation therapy is used in the treatment of most solid tumors, especially for those patients presenting with advanced disease, and is essential in the management of cancers of the cervix, head and neck, and lung.

Radiotherapy can be safely delivered in resource-constrained settings. Providing safe and effective radiation therapy requires an initial capital investment in radiotherapy equipment and specially designed space, as well as an investment in trained personnel and equipment maintenance. The professionals trained in radiation therapy are able to support other services such as diagnostic imaging and information technology. Cobalt machines or linear accelerators can deliver external beam radiation. Linear accelerators are favored but they require dependable access to electricity, which is not always available in developing countries. This makes cobalt machines, with replaceable cobalt sources, more appropriate initial equipment for many LMICs.

The requirements for medical and technical expertise is a constraint. A shortage of trained staff may limit the number of patients who can be treated, even if the equipment exists. Yet, the availability of modern information and communication technologies allows for long-distance mentorship and support for small radiotherapy programs in remote areas. Currently many radiotherapy professionals migrate from LMICs seeking careers in more developed countries. Investment in radiation services would attract them back to their native environment. New technologies more appropriate to low-resource settings are being developed by industry.

The requirements for developing a new radiotherapy program or facility must include meeting standards for safe and effective operation. In a program that can, and should, be expanded, the International Atomic Energy Agency (IAEA) provides radiotherapy to LMICs and supports monitoring and provision of radioactive sources. The IAEA has also developed a comprehensive guide for setting up radiotherapy services that include strengthened regulatory environments. The IAEA Program of Action for Cancer Treatment (PACT) fosters comprehensive cancer programs that include all aspects of cancer prevention, screening, therapies, and palliation.[46]

Currently, the availability of radiation therapy remains limited or nonexistent in many low income countries, or it may only be available at regional hospitals and inaccessible to many patients. Strategies such as short-course therapy should be explored to minimize the burden of travel for patients and to increase the number of patients who can be treated at a facility. One dose of radiotherapy is often enough to reduce pain for several months. Although these limitations present challenges in providing access to comprehensive cancer services, they are not unique to radiotherapy. Investment in comprehensive radiotherapy services together with surgery and chemotherapy is needed be building cancer centers that will be able to rationally direct the deployment of cancer care in LMICs.

Systemic therapy, an essential component of care for many cancers, aims to eradicate disease, prolong life, or alleviate symptoms. Some of the first successful cancer drug therapy regimens benefitted leukemia, lymphomas, testicular cancer, and childhood cancers.[47]

In some common cancers, including breast and colon, drugs can be used as an adjuvant modality in combination with surgery to reduce risk of recurrence and improve survival. Some cancers are relatively resistant to most systemic therapy, and patients with these cancers derive little benefit.

Systemic therapies fall into the categories of cytotoxic chemotherapy, hormonal therapy, and biologically targeted cancer therapies. The common routes of administration of cancer drug therapy are oral, intravenous, intramuscular, and topical. Depending on the route of administration and the need for monitoring, treatments can be given in a medical office or clinic, or must be given in a hospital. Periodic laboratory tests monitor for side effects. With proper training of personnel, chemotherapy can be safely prepared and administered at central and district hospitals, even in very poor countries (see Chapter 6).

Of particular importance to expanding access to CCC in LMICs is the fact that most of the essential anti-cancer drugs are off-patent and should be obtainable at reasonable cost (Table 1). The majority of the drugs listed in Table 1 are on complementary listings of the WHO Essential Drug List for 2011, with the provision that adequate resources and specialist oversight are available.

Table 5.1

Essential Anti-Neoplastic Agents
(for adult and pediatric cancers)

	Agent	Route of Administration	Patent Status	WHO Essential Drug List 2010
1	Anastrozole (or letrozole, exemestane)	oral	Off	no
2	asparaginase	parenteral	Off	yes
3	bleomycin	parenteral	Off	yes
4	carboplatin	parenteral	Off	yes
5	Cisplatin	parenteral	Off	no
6	cyclophosphamide	parenteral and oral	Off	yes
7	cytarabine	Parenteral and intrathecal	Off	yes
8	dacarbazine	parenteral	Off	yes
9	dactinomycin	parenteral	Off	yes
10	daunorubicin	parenteral	Off	yes
11	dexamethasone	oral	Off	yes
12	doxorubicin	parenteral	Off	yes
13	etoposide	parenteral and oral	Off	yes
14	fluorouracil (5-FU)	parenteral	Off	yes
15	hydroxyurea	oral	Off	yes
16	ifosfamide	parenteral	Off	yes
17	Imatinib	oral	On	no
18	Hydrocortisone	Parenteral, oral and intrathecal	Off	yes
19	leucovorin	parenteral and oral	Off	yes
20	melphalan	oral	Off	no
21	mercaptopurine	parenteral	Off	yes
22	mesna	parenteral and oral	Off	yes
23	methotrexate	Parenteral, oral, and intrathecal	Off	yes
24	paclitaxel	parenteral	Off	no
25	prednisone	oral	Off	yes
26	rituximab	parenteral	On	no
27	tamoxifen	oral	Off	yes
28	trastuzumab	parenteral	On	no
29	Tretinoin	oral	Off	no
30	Vinblastine	parenteral	Off	yes
31	Vincristine	parenteral	Off	yes

Cost is only one aspect of safe and effective use of systemic treatment. A supportive infrastructure is required to administer these drugs. Chemotherapy administration and management of side effects are complex and require standardized procedures, supportive care drugs, and significant training of nurses and medical staff. Clinical and laboratory monitoring during treatment is needed for safe administration of chemotherapy. Preparation and administration of chemotherapy and related drugs can be hazardous and so measures must be taken to protect healthcare workers. Chemotherapy and related medications should be administered in recommended doses, since any reduction can produce sub-therapeutic doses and poor outcomes, while still creating effort, expense, and toxicity for the patients. In addition, supratherapeutic doses can increase morbidity and mortality. A reliable drug supply must be available for optimal care and to minimize harmful treatment interruptions.

It is always preferable to have an on-site oncologist directing cancer care and, in particular, administering chemotherapy. Unfortunately, the global supply of oncologists is far from sufficient to provide care for all the world's cancer patients. Because of this shortage, it must be assumed that medical professionals who are not oncologists will deliver much of the care in order to treat more cancer patients worldwide. General physicians and nurses can administer treatment such as chemotherapy with the secure and readily available backup of off-site cancer specialists. Detailed policies, procedures, and training are required as well. Using resources this way should make it possible to treat a larger percentage of cancer patients in the many settings that lack specialty oncology services (Chapter 6).

Newer targeted biological therapies are drugs that block cancer's ability to grow, divide, repair, and communicate with other cells by interfering with specific molecules associated with cancer cells. About a dozen biologically targeted therapies are approved in at least one high income country, and many more are in clinical trials. Commonly used biological therapies include human epidermal growth factor receptor 2 (HER2)-targeted agents (trastuzumab and lapatinib) in breast cancer, imatinib for CML, rituximab in lymphoma, epidermal growth factor receptor (EGFR)-targeted therapies (erlotinib, gefitinib, cetuximab) for lung and colon cancer, and angiogenesis inhibitors targeting the vascular endothelial growth factor (VEGF) pathway (bevacizumab, sunitinib, sorafanib) in several cancer types. These agents can be highly effective with minimal side effects and are relatively easy to administer. Yet, because of the cost –in some cases as high as tens of thousands of dollars for a course of treatment– the use of many of these agents is not feasible at present in most low-resource settings. Some biological therapies, such as trastuzumab which is highly effective in a subset of breast cancers, are being included in universal benefit packages, as is the case in Mexico (see Chapter 8). However, strategies need to be developed to obtain these drugs at reduced cost for LMICs. There are examples, such as the Max Foundation partnership with Novartis for imatinib, of providing certain biologically targeted therapies at no cost in resource-poor settings.[48]

Many expensive yet effective biologic agents will be exiting from patent protection in coming years (e.g., rituximab, imatinib and trastuzumab). The creation of biosimilar pharmaceuticals –officially-approved generic versions of biological therapies following patent and exclusivity expiry– will help decrease the costs and increase availability of biological anti-cancer agents. Unlike the majority of pharmaceutical agents, biologics generally exhibit high molecular complexity, and can be very sensitive to differences in manufacturing processes which may impact efficacy. Additionally, differences in impurities and/or breakdown products may impact toxicity. This has created a concern that biosimilars might perform differently than the originally approved and tested biologic agent. Regulatory approval pathways for biologic drugs have been created in the European Union, and are undergoing development within the US. Healthcare systems in LMICs should continually re-evaluate what constitutes cost-effective healthcare based upon patent expirations and availability of generics and biosimilars.

Treatment of Side Effects and Supportive Care: The diagnosis and treatment of cancer can cause many physical and emotional side effects. Monitoring for infections and prompt antibiotic treatment of febrile neutropenia, a serious and potentially life-threatening side effect, is essential for any chemotherapy infusion center. Supportive and palliative care drugs are available to reduce many side effects, including low-cost anti-emetics and drugs that treat diarrhea and constipation. Oral complications, which can be lessened with good mouth care, are a common side effect of both chemotherapy and radiation. Some patients may suffer from post-operative morbidity such as lymphedema after mastectomy and other sequalae of their cancer treatment including loss of fertility, sexuality, concerns about body image, and/or early menopause. Psychosocial support is a critical component in the supportive care of cancer patients.

LONG-TERM FOLLOW-UP, REHABILITATION, AND SURVIVORSHIP CARE

Cancer survivorship care refers to care in the long-term, including interventions that are not directly treatment-related. At present, long-term survival following cancer diagnosis and treatment is not common in many LMICs, and a large proportion of cancer patients die soon after diagnosis. Greater access to cancer care and control in LMICs will result in more long-term cancer survivors, making it important to incorporate long-term follow-up and rehabilitation as part of a comprehensive cancer care and control program. The concept of cancer survivorship and its application to health systems has become increasingly recognized. Even in high income countries, health systems are struggling to integrate long-term follow-up, rehabilitation and survivorship services and respond to the longer-term needs of people with cancer. The concept of cancer survivorship and the design of appropriate programs and policies is just beginning in LMICs.

Anticipating that successful treatment will become more widely available, programs for survivorship care are needed to support patients for short- and long-term complications of their disease and treatment. Such follow-up should include screening for possible recurrence of the primary cancer or occurrence of secondary cancers, as well as monitoring and treating the physical and emotional side effects related to diagnosis and treatment. It is important to integrate survivorship into efforts to build-up health systems in LMICs to respond to the challenge of cancer. The most effective way to expand survivorship care in LMICs, especially given the long-term nature of the disease, is through a diagonal approach that involves the primary care network as well as community-based programs.[49] This approach will also help to reduce stigma and discrimination.

PALLIATIVE CARE

Palliative care is the assessment for and relief of suffering of any kind, physical, psychological, social or spiritual. Because suffering of all kinds is common among cancer patients, palliative care is an essential part of comprehensive cancer care.[50-52] In LMICs, the majority of cancer patients are in advanced stages of cancer when first seen by a medical professional. For most of them, pain relief and palliative care is the treatment option that offers the most benefit and the least burden. Relief of suffering through palliative care is a fundamental human right that is also inexpensive.

There is no contradiction between cancer treatment and palliative care. Chemotherapy and radiation therapy often relieve pain and other symptoms, and can be excellent palliatives. Conversely, good palliative care promotes adherence to cancer treatment and can both extend life and improve its quality.[53]

The diagnosis and treatment of cancer can itself cause physical and emotional side effects. Palliative care medicines, including low-cost anti-emetics and pain medications, can reduce the symptoms due to chemotherapy and other disease-modifying treatments. People with cancer, and those around them, also benefit from psychosocial support to cope with the physical, psychological, and social impacts of the disease. Psychosocial support should begin at diagnosis and continue through treatment and recovery, or death and bereavement. In LMICs, a wide range of healthcare workers and lay people can offer psychosocial support.

If possible, palliative care should be provided by a multidisciplinary team that should include at least one physician and nurse and the patient's family members or home caregiver. The team may also include one or more assistant physicians, clinical officers, social workers, pharmacists, spiritual counselors, community health workers, and volunteers.[54] This care can be provided at central, district, and community level care facilities and in patients' homes. The WHO has developed a strategy for integrating palliative care into healthcare systems.[55]

The International Association of Hospice and Palliative Care (IAHPC) has developed a list of essential medicines for palliative care.[56] At a minimum, all medicines on the essential medicine lists of both the IAHPC and the WHO should be available at any healthcare facility where cancer is treated. Yet access to oral, immediate release morphine, the most essential of palliative medicines, is severely limited in most LMICs because of overly restrictive or "imbalanced" national opioid policies and regulations. According to WHO guidelines, opioid policies and regulations should balance prevention of illicit opioid use with measures to assure accessibility of opioids for pain relief.[57] Experience has shown that overly restrictive opioid policies and prescription regulations can be changed quickly by working with ministries of health and by providing technical assistance and training in pain relief to public health officials, clinicians, patients, and the general public.[58]

RESEARCH

Development of a research agenda designed to address questions applicable to CCC in LMICs is not only essential to optimizing care and allocating resources effectively, but is also needed to demonstrate to governments and the public health community what can and cannot be accomplished in these settings. Further, more research is needed to identify potential differences in the presentation of disease across populations and responses to specific treatments that may differ across populations.[59] Research programs in LMICs can contribute evidence and knowledge to advance care and help patients worldwide.

Disease programs must be measured and monitored from their outset, prospectively, rather than retrospectively, with a primary goal of identifying the interventions that can improve cancer care most effectively, as well as those that do not. It should not be assumed that any given intervention or program is accomplishing the goal of better cancer care and improved patient outcome. Data must be accrued from the initiation of a program, monitored for quality, and made available. Health systems and implementation research is an important component of developing a CCC program in any LMIC and should be incorporated from the start –including baseline data– for greatest impact.

The prime research questions for LMICs differ from those of the developed world. High income countries test new therapies to determine which are most efficacious in ideal settings. In LMICs, the questions should revolve around what approaches will bring cancer care to the population and understanding disease differences in different population groups. Some possible topics for research include identifying elements needed to implement and/or scale-up effective cancer services, innovative treatment paradigms in resource-restricted settings, relative effectiveness of treatment prototypes for LMICs, and trends in incidence, stage distribution, and survival for cohorts of cancer patients. Research priorities and strategies for building evidence are also discussed in Chapter 9 of this book.

5.iii Categorization of "candidate cancers" amenable to care and control in LMICs

Many opportunities for prevention, diagnosis, treatment, and palliation of cancer can be applied in low-resource settings, especially for a subset of candidate cancers that are among the most significant challenges in LMICs. The identification of "candidate cancers" places particular emphasis on what can be done even in a setting with limited trained personnel and limited specialized oncology facilities. The Appendix outlines basic strategies for specific cancers. This is not meant to be a comprehensive list of diseases for inclusion in a national CCC plan, and it is assumed that disease prioritization will vary from country to country and across sites.

"Candidate cancers" can be grouped into four categories for care and control in LMICs: those most amenable to prevention and risk reduction; those for which cure can be significantly increased with early detection; those with high cure rates, based primarily on systemic therapy; and those for which substantial benefit in life extension or palliation can be gained with systemic therapy and supportive care (Table 2). It is important to note that several cancers fall into more than one category, particularly depending on stage at diagnosis. Further, pain control and palliative care can be provided to patients with any cancer.[60]

Table 5.2

Categorization of Cancers
Amenable to Care and Control in LMICs

Group 1:
Cancers amenable to prevention and risk reduction.
Examples:

- Lifestyle-related
- Tobacco and lung cancer, head and neck cancer, bladder cancer
- Alcohol and hepatocellular carcinoma
- Infection-related
- HPV and cervical cancer
- Hepatitis B and hepatocellular carcinoma
- H pylori and stomach cancer

Group 2:
Cancers amenable to curative approaches with early detection and treatment.
Examples:

- Cervical cancer
- Breast cancer
- Retinoblastoma
- Prostate cancer

Group 3:
Cancers amenable to curative approaches primarily based on systemic therapy.
Examples:

- Bukitt's lymphoma
- Hodgkin lymphoma
- Childhood Acute Lymphocytic Leukemia
- Non-Hodgkin lymphomas
- Wilm's Tumor

Group 4:
Cancers amenable to life extension and palliation with systemic therapy.
Examples:

- Kaposi sarcoma
- Chronic myelogenous leukemia

5.iv Conclusions

In the face of resource scarcity, packages of options need to be identified for countries at different levels of economic development. Two excellent examples of how to structure levels of care with different available resources are provided by the Breast Health Global Initiative guidelines for breast cancer and the adapted regimens for pediatric ALL.[61-66] In future work, this type of analysis and disease-specific recommendations are needed for other cancers, beginning with those of highest burden and those most amenable to prevention or treatment.

A full analysis based on Disability-Adjusted Life Years (DALYs) and cost-effectiveness should be given high priority in efforts to expand CCC in LMICs. The results of a more comprehensive analysis would be an invaluable guide to help policy makers in LMICs make more informed decisions about how to invest in CCC. The components of care that are outlined below can guide much more extensive analysis for all diseases.

APPENDIX 5.1

CATEGORIZATION OF "CANDIDATE CANCERS" AMENABLE TO CARE AND CONTROL IN LMICS

The core elements of cancer care and control required for a subset of cancers are described here.

Cervical cancer[67-71]

As discussed above, cervical cancer is common among women worldwide, particularly in developing countries. A large number of cervical cancer deaths are in young women, and the highest incidence rates are found in sub-Saharan Africa, Latin America and the Caribbean, and Southeast Asia. Cervical cancer fits into each of the four categories of care and control, with substantial opportunities for prevention, early detection, treatment and palliation in LMICs.

Nearly all cervical cancer is now known to be caused by HPV, and this has made possible prevention through vaccination. Even before HPV vaccination was developed, a dramatic decline in cervical cancer incidence and mortality was achieved in developed and several developing countries through the adoption of Pap smears to screen for precancerous lesions. Yet treatment for cervical cancer can be effective even at more advanced stages.

» **Prevention**

Cervical cancer is amenable to primary prevention through vaccination against HPV, which has been shown to substantially reduce the incidence of cervical cancer, and should be a major goal of healthcare systems in developing countries. The age at vaccination may depend on the specifics of the country involved. Approaches to reach the greatest number of girls, through schools or religious institutions, should be considered. In addition, research is required to determine what HPV subtypes are responsible for cervical cancer in different geographic areas and populations of patients, and to then develop appropriate strategies.

» **Early Detection**

Even if a successful vaccination program is initiated, it may not impact cervical cancer rates for 20-30 years. Furthermore, even in the best scenario, the vaccine can prevent only 70% of cervical cancer, so women will continue to develop cervical cancer, and cervical cancer screening will remain essential.

A variety of approaches can be taken for early detection of cervical cancer, and available resources will help to determine the specific program undertaken by a particular country or region. Pelvic exam and Pap smears are not likely to be practical in all parts of the world, as pelvic exams are time-consuming and Pap smears require trained personnel to both perform and interpret. By contrast, HPV DNA testing is a practical and easily performed technique that could be used in many developing countries. Ideally, it is performed as part of a pelvic examination, with a swab from the cervix. However, routine pelvic examinations on all women may not be achievable, and, as an alternative in these settings, the test may be self-performed using a vaginal swab.

» **Treatment**

Specific treatment approaches for women with positive HPV DNA testing will vary, depending on the resources available and local policies. One potential approach is that women with positive HPV DNA test results undergo visual inspection with acetic acid. Lesions limited to a small region of the cervix, with no visible evidence of cancer and no endocervical involvement may be treated with cryosurgery. Lesions which involve the endocervical canal, or have areas visibly suspicious for small cancers, should be treated with excision, either by LOOP, cone biopsy, or simple hysterectomy.

Women found to be suffering from advanced cancer involving more than the cervix should have a small, local biopsy which may be sent to distant pathology services with referral for radiation therapy wherever possible. Systemic therapy of metastatic cervical cancer has minimum benefit, at best.

» **Palliation**

Patients with advanced cervical cancer, beyond the scope of hysterectomy, should be treated with palliation, including radiation therapy where available. Systemic therapy of metastatic cervical cancer has minimum benefit, at best. Moderate or severe pain is common and should be treated aggressively with oral morphine or another opioid as per WHO guidelines on Cancer Pain Relief.[72] Other physical symptoms such as nausea, vomiting, or constipation, and psychological distress including adjustment disorder, anxiety disorders, and depression, should be treated just as aggressively. Inexpensive medicines for treating all common physical and psychological symptoms are included in the IAHPC List of Essential Medicines for Palliative Care.[54]

Breast Cancer[73-75]

Breast cancer accounts for nearly 25% of all cancers in women and has become the most common cancer in women in many developing nations. Survival rates for breast cancer are better than for many cancers, but with a significant divide between wealthier and poorer countries (Chapter 2). The incidence of breast cancer is rising globally, particularly where rates have historically been low.

» **Prevention**

Epidemiologic studies have implicated reproductive factors (including childbearing) and lifestyle factors (including obesity and inactivity) as increasing the incidence of breast cancer. Incorporation of healthy lifestyle recommendations into primary care will impact many chronic diseases, as well as breast cancer risk.

» **Early Detection**

Breast cancer is only curable when detected at an early stage; the earlier the stage, the more likely a cure. Increased awareness and screening are useful for secondary prevention. Education is a key component of any breast cancer program. Women must understand that breast cancer is curable if detected early and that this requires recognition of the early signs and routine breast examinations. Education can be integrated into programs such as maternal and child health.

Along with education, breast self-awareness and examination should be encouraged, and clinical breast examination by healthcare workers should become routine. Though the smallest cancers will not be detected in this manner, in many settings, this will still offer substantial opportunities for downstaging breast cancer diagnosis.

The role of mammography in developing countries remains controversial. In the most resource-poor settings, screening mammography is not feasible at present. In middle income countries, mammography is feasible, but only useful when given to asymptomatic women without palpable cancers. Detecting a large, palpable cancer by mammography is not a benefit of mammography, but rather a failure of overall breast care.

Implementation of screening mammography programs outside the context of a robust healthcare infrastructure has been of limited value. Mammography might be best employed when a breast care program already exists in a region, and women are well-educated and readily seek general and breast healthcare. In these settings, diagnostic mammography is likely already to have been developed, which is the first step in training radiologists for implementation of screening, whether that be in an opportunitistic (selective) or population-based setting.

Existing studies of combined breast health initiatives consider only the context of health systems where mammography is widely available. Interactions between mammography, routine care, clinical breast exams, and self-breast exams in other settings are less certain and deserve further study. Data from the US between 1950 and 1975, before the routine use of mammography, show a reduction in mortality/incidence ratios from 0.42 to 0.27, which can probably be attributed to improved breast cancer awareness, better healthcare infrastructure, and more routine physical examinations.[76]

» Diagnosis

Whether found through physical examination or through imaging, the ability to biopsy and accurately diagnose a breast lesion is essential. The diagnostic biopsy technique of choice is core needle biopsy, and ultrasound can help make this procedure more accurate. Some countries and regions implement fine-needle aspiration (FNA) for tissue sampling, due to lower cost and technical simplicity. However, the utility of FNA is limited by the availability of cytopathologists who can correctly interpret cytologic samples, and does not replace the need for histological evaluation of surgical specimens. The ability to perform stereotactic, mammographically-directed biopsy should be in place before the introduction of any mammography screening program.

Some nonpalpable abnormalities found on screening mammography can also be found through targeted ultrasound, although many cannot. Core needle biopsies can be taught to general physicians, nurses, and other medical personnel. The procedure is safe and it procures an adequate tissue sample for histology and for testing for estrogen receptors (ER) and HER2, both essential tests for determining the best therapy. In addition, guided core biopsy or fine needle aspirate can be performed on suspicious axillary lymph nodes to aid in staging. Biopsy specimens must be handled properly, placed in formalin immediately, and removed at the appropriate interval for further processing.

» Treatment

For patients who appear to have disease isolated to the breast and axilla, surgical removal of the tumor is crucial to potential cure. Successful surgical removal of the tumor can be accomplished either by mastectomy or by lumpectomy with negative surgical margins combined with breast radiation. In many locations, radiation facilities will not be available and mastectomy is the only sound option. Radiation therapy is an important component of breast cancer treatment as part of breast-conserving surgery, management of locally advanced disease, and in the palliation of locally advanced or metastatic disease.

Choice of primary systemic therapy will require the advice of an oncologist who may be off-site, and should reflect current recommendations. In general, hormone therapy consisting of tamoxifen and/or an aromatase inhibitor will be recommended for patients whose tumors are positive for ER. Chemotherapy is frequently recommended for tumors not expressing ER, and trastuzumab, if available, will be recommended for patients whose tumors over-express HER2.

» Survivorship

Breast cancer survivorship rates are high in high income countries and will grow in LMICs following improvements in early detection and treatment. In the US, 5-year survival following the diagnosis of invasive breast cancer is currently above 90%. The diagnosis and treatment of breast cancer can lead to long-term physical and emotional complications that include risk of recurrence, sexual dysfunction, fertility difficulties, ovarian failure, emotional distress, fatigue, cognitive problems, as well as side effects that may appear years after treatment. The implications are enormous for patients/ survivors, their families, caregivers, and the medical community. Post-treatment interventions can further improve breast cancer survivor outcomes. For instance, studies have shown that being overweight adversely affects survival for postmenopausal women with breast cancer, and that women who are more physically active are less likely to die from the disease than women who are inactive. Such considerations demonstrate the need for programs and services that provide long-term care and support to individuals and their families.

» **Palliation**

Patients with locally advanced or metastatic breast cancer generally cannot be cured even with the most intensive therapies available in developed countries. Patients can be palliated with hormone therapy if tumors express ER. Chemotherapy has a modest benefit for patients with metastatic disease, and trastuzumab can benefit patients whose tumors over-express HER2. Radiation therapy, where available, can also aid palliation of locally advanced or metastatic disease. Pain, upper extremity lymphedema, dyspnea, and depression are common symptoms of advanced breast cancer. All can be assessed and treated by generalist physicians with basic training in palliative care and with essential palliative medicines as described in the section on "Palliative Care" above.

Prostate Cancer[77-81]

Prostate cancer is a worldwide public health concern representing the second most commonly diagnosed cancer in men. Lifetime risk of developing prostate cancer in the U.S. is 16%, with a cause-specific mortality rate of 2.9%. Five-year survival correlates with spread of disease and is only 32% among those diagnosed with distant metastases. This critically alters outcomes in sub-Saharan Africa where almost two-thirds of patients have evidence of locally advanced or metastatic disease at presentation. Surveys have shown that there is a gap in awareness about prostate cancer. One study of native, urban Nigerians revealed only 21% had heard of prostate cancer; only 6% were aware of screening measures.

» Prevention

Because of the known hormone responsiveness of cancerous and noncancerous prostate cells, chemopreventive strategies have been actively pursued. The most extensive data come from 5-alpha reductase inhibitors, which have been shown to significantly decrease the incidence of prostate cancer. But, there is no trial demonstrating its impact on mortality, and its use has been limited by side effects and an indeterminate long-term clinical impact.

Non-modifiable risk factors include age (one of the strongest contributors), ethnicity and genetic factors, such as BRCA mutation carrier. Modifiable factors are thought to play a minor role and include a diet high in animal fat, history of prostatitis (often related to exposure to syphilis or gonorrhea), and exposure to Trichomonas vaginalis. Obesity has also been linked to prostate cancer aggressiveness.

» Early Detection

Screening using prostate specific antigen (PSA) testing in many high income countries has led to the diagnosis of prostate cancer in the asymptomatic patient. In areas where PSA testing is not available or used, it is detected either by digital rectal exam (DRE) or symptomatically. Community education should focus on symptoms of prostatism, which can represent a benign or malignant process and mandate clinical evaluation.

The role of screening serum PSA is widely debated in high, middle and low income countries. The positive and negative predictive values are 30% and 85% for PSA value greater and less than 4 ng/mL, respectively. Recent studies and guidelines in high income countries have raised concerns about the utility of PSA as a marker for clinically significant prostate cancer. Prostatic acid phosphatase was used historically as a screening tool and is a less expensive test. It fell out of favor due to poor specificity but is still employed in some low-income settings and is a predictor of response to therapy and recurrence. The clinical utility of DRE has also been questioned. Approximately 25-35% of tumors occur in other non-palpable parts of the gland, T1 cancers are not palpable, and its positive predictive value is only 15-29%. DRE also carries with it significant social stigma.

It is critical to note that most of these screening studies were performed in high income countries. In low-income countries, the mean duration from onset of symptoms to presentation extends greater than one year and is often associated with signs and symptoms of metastatic disease. Thus, the role of screening is less well understood, and it could increase detection and improve outcomes, particularly in high-risk groups.

» **Diagnosis**

Histologic diagnosis is recommended before proceeding with treatment given the high false negative rate and low sensitivity of screening modalities. This is usually performed by transrectal biopsy, which is a safe procedure, done in the office without sedation. It can be performed with ultrasound guidance or, if not available, with digital guidance. Sampling schemes have been devised to improve accuracy (eg., 14 core biopsies superior to 6) and can be more accurate when abnormal areas are identified on ultrasound. Fine needle aspiration is not considered sufficiently accurate to diagnose prostate cancer. Specimens should be labeled according to the position sampled to ensure precise localization and capacity to repeat biopsy.

» **Treatment**

When early stage, clinically localized prostate cancer is detected, often with screening PSA, several standard management options exist including radical prostatectomy, definitive radiotherapy (external beam and/or brachytherapy), or active surveillance. Locally advanced prostate cancer is managed successfully with hormone therapy and radiotherapy with long term survival expected in a large proportion of patients. Androgen deprivation therapy (ADT) is a very effective systemic treatment for metastatic disease.

» **Survivorship**

Similar to breast cancer, survival rates are high in high income countries (>90%) but historically lower in low-income countries (10-40%). A survey of urologists in Nigeria found that most cases of prostate cancer present late and the major obstacle to improvement in outcomes is poor health education. To that end, major screening and education initiatives are being organized across the world with increased government funding and survivors of prostate cancer assuming prominent roles.

» **Palliation**

Androgen deprivation therapy (ADT) is the optimal treatment for men with metastatic prostate cancer. Bilateral orchiectomy, which is commonly employed in low-income settings, is a very effective androgen deprivation method, associated with effective palliation of bone pain and other disease-related symptoms. Few alternatives to ADT are available at low costs. The prognosis of metastatic disease is particularly poor in low-income countries where it carries a 64% mortality rate in 2 years usually due to the late presentation of disease. The endocrine side effects and psychological impact of androgen withdrawal due to orchiectomy are not clinically insignificant and act as a major disincentive for men pursuing treatment. Chemotherapy offers limited benefit for patients who have progression of disease on ADT – castrate-resistant prostate cancer. More successful disease-specific palliative interventions are needed. Bone pain due to metastatic disease is common in advanced prostate cancer. Essential treatment modalities include non-steroidal anti-inflammatory drugs (NSAIDs) and opioids. Monthly bisphosphonate therapy also can help to control pain as well as reduce the risk of pathologic fractures.

Retinoblastoma[82-85]

Retinoblastoma is the most frequent neoplasm of the eye in childhood and the third most common intraocular malignancy in all ages, following uveal melanoma and metastatic carcinoma. An estimated 8,000 children develop retinoblastoma each year worldwide. However, the retinoblastoma burden is unequally distributed, with higher numbers and higher incidence of metastatic and recurrent disease in low and low middle income countries.

Retinoblastoma represents 2.5% to 4% of all pediatric cancers, but 11% of cancers in the first year of life. The average age-adjusted incidence rate of retinoblastoma in the US and Europe is 2-5/10^6 children (approximately 1 in 14,000-18,000 live births). However, it appears to be higher (6-10/10^6 children) in Africa, India, and among children of Native American descent in the North American continent. Whether these geographic variations are due to ethnic or socioeconomic factors is not well known. However, even in industrialized countries, an increased incidence of retinoblastoma is associated with poverty and low levels of maternal education, suggesting a role for environment.

Retinoblastoma presents in two distinct clinical forms: 1) Bilateral or multifocal, hereditary (25% of cases), characterized by the presence of germline mutations of the RB1 gene. Multifocal retinoblastoma may be inherited from an affected survivor (25%) or be the result of a new germline mutation (75%); and 2) Unilateral retinoblastoma (75%), almost always non-hereditary.

» **Prevention**

As with many pediatric cancers, retinoblastoma is not amenable to primary prevention. However, identification of the hereditary forms and proper counseling of these patients and their families can guide appropriate screening and limit the incidence and burden of retinoblastoma on those families.

» **Early detection**

The successful management of retinoblastoma depends on the ability to detect the disease while it is still intraocular. Disease stage correlates with delay in diagnosis; growth and invasion occur as a sequence of events, and extra retinal extension occurs only when the tumor has reached large intraocular dimensions. Although retinoblastoma is curable when diagnosed early and treated appropriately, the prognosis is dismal when early diagnosis and treatment are lacking. In high income countries, retinoblastoma typically presents intraocular, but in LMICs, 60-90% of children present with extraocular disease. For these reasons, early diagnosis initiatives are essential. In developing countries, retinoblastoma educational and public awareness campaigns have been shown to increase referrals, decrease rates of advanced disease, and improve outcomes.

» **Treatment**

Treatment of retinoblastoma aims to save life and preserve useful vision, and needs to be individualized. Factors that need to be considered include unilaterality or bilaterality of the disease, potential for vision, and intraocular and extraocular staging. In high income countries, more than 90% of children with retinoblastoma present with intraocular disease, and clinical and research programs in retinoblastoma aim to develop treatments that improve ocular salvage and preserve vision. While enucleation is commonly performed for patients with advanced intraocular unilateral disease, more conservative approaches are followed for children with bilateral and early unilateral disease. This is often accomplished with systemic chemotherapy and intensive focal treatments that include laser thermotherapy and cryotherapy. Orbital radiation therapy is used when those methods fail. These are sophisticated treatments that usually require referral of patients to specialized treatment centers.

Countries with more limited resources present a radically different picture: patients present late and with extremely advanced disease, usually extraocular and metastatic, where the chances of cure are low. For patients presenting with orbital disease, the use of chemotherapy, surgery (enucleation), and radiation therapy may offer possibility of cure. However, patients presenting with metastatic disease, typically to the brain, bone, and bone marrow, are not curable with standard therapies, although patients without brain and leptomeningeal disease may benefit from intensive chemotherapy and consolidation with high-dose chemotherapy and autologous stem cell rescue, only available in high -income countries.

» Survivorship

Visual impairment and integration into school and society are constant challenges for retinoblastoma survivors and so survivorship programs must coordinate with programs for the visually disabled. More importantly, survivors of bilateral or hereditary disease have an increased risk of developing second malignancies. The cumulative incidence of a second cancer is between 30% and 40%. This risk is particularly high in patients who received radiation therapy. The most common second tumor is osteosarcoma, both inside and outside the radiation field, and soft tissue sarcomas and melanomas are next in frequency. Patients with hereditary retinoblastoma are also at risk of developing epithelial cancers, frequently lung cancer, later in life.

» Palliation

Children presenting with advanced extraocular retinoblastoma are not curable, so measures to decrease suffering and improve the quality of life should be maximized. Low dose, oral chemotherapy and radiation therapy may help to control symptoms.

Burkitt Lymphoma[86]

Burkitt lymphoma (BL) is a malignant disease endemic in sub-Saharan Africa, primarily in the malaria belts. It is associated with Epstein-Barr virus (EBV), though the biology of this association is poorly understood.

» **Diagnosis**

BL tends to occur in children and frequently presents with submandibular lymphadenopathy. As it progresses, it results in extrusion of the teeth of the lower jaw. Diagnosis is established from a lymph node biopsy.

» **Treatment**

Burkitt lymphoma is a disease amenable to curative approaches primarily based on systemic therapy. The drugs used to treat BL are inexpensive, readily available on the world market, and relatively easily administered. Systemic chemotherapy comprised of cyclophosphamide and vincristine is highly curative in the majority of patients. These drugs are well-tolerated with a low treatment-related complication rate. Given that the disease affects children and young adults and has a high cure rate, the potential number of years of life saved is very high, making BL a prime candidate cancer to target in low-resource settings.

Hodgkin Lymphoma[87]

Hodgkin lymphoma is a highly curable disease of uncertain etiology. It occurs most often in young adults – those between the ages of 17 and 35– and effective treatment has the potential to save many years of life.

» **Diagnosis**

Diagnosis of Hodgkin lymphoma is established by incisional or core biopsy. Involved lymph nodes in the neck or supraclavicular regions can often be accessed for biopsy. For patients with mediastinal involvement only, tissue can be obtained by CT guided percutaneous biopsy or thoracotomy. Both of these procedures require considerable expertise and technical support. Diagnosis can often be made on H&E sections, with the classic Reed Sternberg cells identified. Immunohistochemistry (IHC) studies can, in some circumstances, be helpful, but usually are not needed. Staging imaging, in particular CT scans, can help delineate the extent of disease, and can be useful for following the course of disease during treatment.

» **Treatment**

Hodgkin lymphoma is amenable to curative approaches, primarily those based on systemic therapy. The mainstay of treatment is chemotherapy and the most commonly used regimen is ABVD – doxorubicin, bleomycin, vinblastine, and dacarbazine. Radiation is very effective in Hodgkin lymphoma and is often used as an adjunct therapy in areas of bulk disease or to decrease the amount of chemotherapy needed. However, where radiation is not available, many patients may be cured with chemotherapy alone.

Kaposi Sarcoma[88]

Kaposi sarcoma (KS) is an HIV/AIDS associated disease, which some speculate has become the most common cancer in some regions, including sub-Saharan Africa. Left untreated, it is progressive and life-threatening, but treatment can lead to substantial prolongation and improved quality of life. For KS to be effectively treated, the HIV/AIDS infection must be treated with anti-retroviral agents and be in good control. If the HIV/AIDS infection is not in good control, then treating the KS is not likely to be fruitful.

» **Diagnosis**

KS often presents as an easily diagnosed, subcutaneous disease, though there can be visceral involvement as well.

» **Treatment**

Systemic chemotherapy can control, but usually not cure the disease. Control, though, often provides substantial prolongation and improvement in quality of life. A number of chemotherapy regimens are used in the treatment of KS. Because of cost and availability, bleomycin and vinblastine have been used exclusively or for patients with less advanced disease in many resource-poor settings, reserving taxanes for patients with more extensive and life-threatening disease.

» **Palliation**

Typical symptoms include painful oral and skin lesions and lymphedema, but dyspnea and gastro-intestinal symptoms also can be present depending on the location of lesions. The skin lesions and lymphedema also are disfiguring and mark the patient, rightly or wrongly, as HIV-positive. Palliative care should be combined with systemic chemotherapy if possible and include relief of pain and other symptoms, and psychosocial supports.

Chronic Myelogenous Leukemia[89]

Chronic Myelogenous Leukemia (CML) is amenable to life extension and palliation with systemic therapy. The etiology is unknown.

» **Diagnosis**

The disease is confirmed by molecular testing for the t(9;22) translocation and the bcr-able fusion gene. This testing is not readily available in most developing countries, but can be performed on peripheral blood at regional centers in many developed countries.

» **Treatment**

Agents, such as imatinib can be highly effective for many patients with CML, and can provide prolonged clinical and cytogenetic remissions with substantial prolongation of life and reduction or complete resolution of symptoms.

Imatinib, and similar agents, are relatively well-tolerated oral agents, but a high degree of patient compliance is required for effective treatment and patients must be followed closely.

Imatinib can often be secured, free-of-charge, from the Max Foundation, with confirmation of the presence of the bcr-abl translocation.[90] This is one of several examples of drugs, diagnostic tests, and vaccines that have been donated, or are being donated, through foundations or companies.

References

1. World Health Organization. National cancer control programmes: policies and managerial guidelines. 2nd Ed. Geneva, Switzerland: World Health Organization. 2002.

2. Ravishankar N, Gubbins P, Cooley RJ, Leach-Kemon K, Michaud CM, Jamison DT, Murray CJL. Financing of global health: tracking development assistance for health from 1990 to 2007. *Lancet* 2009; 373: 2113-24, 2009.

3. World Health Organization. Global status report on noncommunicable diseases 2010. Geneva, Switzerland: World Health Organization. 2011.

4. Anderson BO, Yip CH, Smith RA, et al. Guideline implementation for breast healthcare in low-income and middle-income countries: overview of the Breast Health Global Initiative Global Summit 2007. *Cancer* 2008; 113(Suppl 8):2221-43.

5. WHO. Global status report on noncommunicable diseases 2010.

6. Bridges JFP, Anderson BO, Buzaid AC, et al. Identifying important breast cancer control strategies in Asia, Latin America and the Middle East/North Africa. *BMC Health Services Research* 2011; 11(227).

7. Forouzanfar MH, Foreman KJ, Delossantos AM, et al. Breast and cervical cancer in 187 countries between 1980 and 2010: a systematic analysis. *Lancet* 2011; 378: 1461-84.

8. Sloan FA, Gelband H (Eds.). Cancer control opportunities in low-and middle -income countries. Washington DC: National Academy Press, 2007.

9. King Hussein Cancer Foundation and Center. Annual Report. King Hussein Cancer Foundation and Center. 2011. http://www.khcc.jo/showcontent.aspx?ContentId=265 (accessed October 11, 2011).

10. The Joint Commission. About the Joint Commission. The Joint Commission, 2012. http://www.jointcommission.org/about_us/about_the_joint_commission_main.aspx (accessed October 16, 2011)

11. Stjernsward J, Ferris FD, Khleif SN, et al. Jordan Palliative Care Initiative: A WHO Demonstration Project. *Journal of Pain and Symptom Management* 2007; 33(5):628-33.

12. Al-Qudimat MR, Day S, Almomani T, Odeh D, Qaddoumi I. Clinical Nurse Coordinators: a new generation of high specialized oncology nursing in Jordan. *J Pediatr Hematol Oncol* 2009; 31:38-41.

13. Jordan Breast Cancer Program. Goals and Objectives. Jordan Breast Cancer Program, 2011. http://www.jbcp.jo/node/6 (accessed May 16, 2011).

14. St. Jude Children's Research Hospital. International Partners Sites. St. Jude Children's Research Hospital. 2011. http://www.stjude.org/stjude/v/index.jsp?vgnextoid=9e566f9523e70110VgnVCM1000001e0215acRCRD&vgnext channel=48a9f8f281901110VgnVCM1000001e0215acRCRD (accessed May 16, 2011).

15. Qaddoumi I, Mansour A, Musharbash A, et al. Impact of telemedicine on pediatric neuro-oncology in a developing country: the Jordanian-Canadian experience. *Pediatric Blood & Cancer* 2007; 48(1):39-43.

16. Qaddoumi I, Nawaiseh I, Mehyar M, et al. Team management, twinning, and telemedicine in retinoblastoma: A 3 tier approach implemented in the first eye salvage program in Jordan. *Pediatric Blood & Cancer* 2008; 51(2):241-4.

17. Hazin R, Qaddoumi I. Teleoncology: current and future applications for improving cancer care globally. *Lancet Oncol* 2010; 11(2):204-10.

18. LIVESTRONG. Cancer stigma and silence around the world: A LIVESTRONG Report. Austin, TX, 2010.

19. Harries AD, Zachariah R, Tayler Smith K, et al. Keeping health facilities safe: one way of strengthening the interaction between disease specific programmes and health systems. *Tropical Medicine & International Health* 2010; 15(12): 1407-12.

20. Hermann K, Van Damme W, Pariyo GW, et al. Community health workers for ART in sub-Saharan Africa: learning from experience–capitalizing on new opportunities. *Human Resources for Health* 2009; 7(1):1-11.

21. Kober K, Van Damme W. Expert patients and AIDS care: A literature review on expert patient programmes in high -income countries, and an exploration of their relevance for HIV/AIDS care in low -income countries with severe human resource shortages. Berlin and Antwerp: Department of Public Health, Institute of Tropical Medicine, 2006.

22. Assefa Y, Van Damme W, Hermann K. Human resource aspects of antiretroviral treatment delivery models: current practices and recommendations. *Current Opinion in HIV and AIDS* 2010; 5(1):78-82.

23. Lehmann U, Van Damme W, Barten F, Sanders D. Task shifting: the answer to the human resources crisis in Africa? *Human Resources for Health* 2009; 7(1):12-4.

24. Azenha G, Bass LP, Caleffi M, et al. The role of breast cancer civil society in different resource settings. *Breast (Edinburgh, Scotland)* 2011; 20(2):S81-S7.

25. Durstine A, Leitman E. Building a Latin American cancer patient advocacy movement; Latin American cancer NGO regional overview. *Salud Pública de México* 2009; 51(2):316-22.

26. World Health Organization. Global status report on noncommunicable diseases 2010. Geneva, Switzerland: World Health Organization, 2011.

27. Sloan FA, Gelband H (Eds.), 2007.

28. FIX THIS http://www.who.int/fctc/en/ (accessed October 11, 2011).

29. Murray CJL, Lopez AD (Eds.). The Global Burden of Disease: A comprehensive assessment of mortality and disability from diseases, injuries and risk factors in 1990 and projected to 2020. Cambridge, MA: Harvard University Press on behalf of the World Health Organization and the World Bank, 1996.

30. Sloan FA, Gelband H (Eds.), 2007.

31. Institute of Medicine (IOM). Ensuring quality cancer care through the oncology workforce: Sustaining care in the 21st century: Workshop summary. Washington, DC: The National Academies Press, 2009.

32. McAdam M, Sakita J, Tarivonda L, Pang J, Frazer I, Masucci M. Evaluation of a cervical cancer screening program nased on HPV testing and LLETZ excision in a low rsource setting. *PLoS ONE* 2010; 5(10):e13266.

33. Valencia-Mendoza A, Sánchez-González G, Bautista-Arredondo S, Torres-Mejía G, Bertozzi SM. Cost-effectiveness of breast cancer screening policies in Mexico. *Salud Pública de México* 2009; 51(2):s296-s304.

34. Goldie S, Gaffikin L, Goldhaber-Fiebert J, et al. Cost-effectiveness of cervical-cancer screening in five developing countries. *The New England Journal of Medicine* 2005; 353(20):2158.

35. Quentin W, Adu Sarkodie Y, Terris Prestholt F, Legood R, Opoku BK, Mayaud P. Costs of cervical cancer screening and treatment using visual inspection with acetic acid (VIA) and cryotherapy in Ghana: the importance of scale. *Tropical Medicine & International Health* 2011; 16(3):379-89.

36. Haynes AB, Weiser TG, Berry WR, et al. A surgical safety checklist to reduce morbidity and mortality in a global population. *New England Journal of Medicine* 2009; 360(5):491-9.

37. Conley DM, Singer SJ, Edmondson L, Berry WR, Gawande AA. Effective surgical safety checklist implementation. *Journal of the American College of Surgeons* 2011:1-7.

38. Carlson J, Lyon E, Walton D, et al. Partners in pathology: a collaborative model to bring pathology to resource poor settings. *The American Journal of Surgical Pathology* 2010; 34(1):118-23.

39. American Joint Commission on Cancer (AJCC) in Edge SB, Byrd DR, Compton CC, et al (Eds.) AJCC Cancer Staging Manual. 7th ed. New York: Springer, 2010.

40. Mukherjee S. The emperor of all maladies: a biography of cancer. New York: Scribner, 2010.

41. Sankaranarayanan R, Boffetta P. Research on cancer prevention, detection and management in low- and medium-income countries. *Ann Oncol.* 2010; 21(10):1935-43.

42. MacGrath, I. Cancer in Low and Middle Income Countries. Health G20 eBook edition 1, 2010. http://healthg20.com/. (accessed March 23, 2012).

43. Thumbs A, Borgstein E, Vigna L, et al. Self-expanding metal stents (SEMS) for patients with advanced esophageal cancer in Malawi: an effective palliative treatment. *J Surg Oncol.* 2012; 105(4):410-4.

44. Elit LM, Rosen B, Jimenez W, et al. International Community of Practice Committee of the Society of Gynecologic Oncology of Canada. Teaching cervical cancer surgery in low- or middle- resource countries. *Int J Gynecol Cancer* 2010; 20(9):1604-8.

45. International Atomic Energy Agency. Setting Up a Radiotherapy Programme: Clinical, Medical Physics, Radiation Protection, and Safety Aspects. International Atomic Energy Agency, 2008.

46. International Atomic Energy Agency. Documents on Cancer Control and Treatment. International Atomic Energy Agency. 2011. http://cancer.iaea.org/documents.asp#content (accessed October 11, 2011).

47. Mukherjee S, 2010.

48. The Max Foundation. Homepage. Home Page. 2011 http://www.themaxfoundation.org/ (accessed October 1, 2011).

49. Institute of Medicine. Implementing Cancer Survivorship Care Planning. National Academies Press, Washington, D.C., 2007.

50. Teunissen SCCM, Wesker W, Kruitwagen C, et al. Symptom prevalence in patients with incurable cancer: a systematic review. *J Pain Symptom Manage* 2007; 34:94-104.

51. Krakauer EL. Just palliative care: responding responsibly to the suffering of the poor. *J Pain Symptom Manage* 2008;36:505-12.

52. Black F, Brown S, Ennals D, Diego Harris J, LeBaron V, Love R. INCTR Palliative Care Handbook. International Network on Cancer Treatment and Research, 2008. http://inctr-palliative-care-handbook.wikidot.com/ (accessed October 1, 2011)

53. Temel JS, Greer JA, Muzikansky A, et al. Early palliative care for patients with metastatic non-small-cell lung cancer. *N Engl J Med* 2010; 363:33-742.

54. Stjernswärd J, Foley KM, Ferris FD. The public health strategy for palliative care. *J Pain Symptom Manage* 2007; 33:486-93.

55. World Health Organization. Palliative Care. World Health Organization, 2011. (http://www.who.int/cancer/palliative/en/ (accessed October 1, 2011).

56. De Lima I, Krakauer EL, Lorenz K, et al. Ensuring palliative medicine availability: the development of the IAHPC list of essential medicines for palliative care. *Journal of Pain and Symptom Management* 2007; 33:521-6.

57. World Health Organization. Ensuring Balance in National Policies on Controlled Substances: Guidelines for Availability and Accessibility of Controlled Medicines. Geneva: WHO Press, 2011.

58. Bosnjak S, Maurer MA, Ryan KM, et al. Improving the availability and accessibility of opioids for the treatment of pain: the International Pain Policy Fellowship. *Support Care Cancer* 2011; 19:1237-47.

59. Love RR. Defining a global research agenda for breast cancer. *Cancer* 2008; 113 (Suppl 8): 2366-71.

60. Sloan FA, Gelband H (Eds.), 2007.

61. Anderson BO, Cazap E. Breast Health Global Initiative outline for program development in Latin America. *Salud Pública de México* 2009; 51(2):S309-S15.

62. Anderson BO, Cazap E, El Saghir NS, et al. Optimisation of breast cancer management in low-resource and middle-resource countries: executive summary of the Breast Health Global Initiative consensus, 2010. *Lancet Oncology* 2011; 12(4):387-98.

63. El Saghir NS, Adebamowo CA, Anderson BO, et al. Breast cancer management in low resource countries (LRCs): Consensus statement from the Breast Health Global Initiative. *Breast (Edinburgh, Scotland)* 2011; 20(2):s3-s11.

64. Harford JB, Otero IV, Anderson BO, et al. Problem solving for breast health care delivery in low and middle resource countries (LMCs): consensus statement from the Breast Health Global Initiative. *The Breast* 2011; 20:S20-S9.

65. Anderson BO, Yip CH, Smith RA, et al., 2008.

66. Hunger SP, Sung L. Treatment strategies and regimens of graduated intensity for childhood acute lymphoblastic leukemia in low -income countries: a proposal. *Pediatric Blood and Cancer* 2009; 52(5):559-65.

67. IARC. Cervix Cancer Screening. IARC Handbook of Cancer Prevention, Volume 10. Lyon: IARC, 2005.

68. PATH, Child Health and Development Centre, and the Uganda National Expanded Program on Immunization. HPV Vaccination in Latin America: Lessons learned from a pilot program in Peru. Seattle: PATH, 2011.

69. WHO, IARC, PAHO, ACCP, FIGO. Comprehensive Cervical Cancer Control: A guide to essential practice. Geneva: WHO, 2006

70. Blumenthal PD, Lauterbach M, Sellors JW, Sankaranarayanan R. Training for cervical cancer prevention programs in low-resource settings: Focus on visual inspection with acetic and cryotherapy. *International Journal of Gynecology & Obstetrics* 2005; 89: S30-S7.

71. Alliance for Cervical Cancer Prevention. Planning and Implementing Cervical Cancer Prevention and Control Programs. A Manual for Managers. Seattle: ACCP, 2004.

72. World Health Organization. Cancer Pain Relief, 2nd Edition. Geneva: WHO, 1996.

73. El Saghir NS, Adebamowo CA, Anderson BO, et al., 2011.

74. Breast Health Global Initiative. Homepage, 2011. http://portal.bhgi.org/Pages/Default.aspx (accessed October 1, 2011).

75. Olov HA, Hunter D, Trichopoulos D. Textbook of Cancer Epidemiology. New York: Oxford University Press. 2008.

76. Shulman LN, Willett W, Sievers A, Knaul FM. Breast cancer in developing countries: opportunities for improved survival. *Journal of Oncology* 2010; 2010:1-6.

77. Ajape AA, Babata A, Abiola OO. Knowledge of prostate cancer screening among native African urban population in Nigeria. *Nig Q J Hosp Med* 2009; 19(3):145-7.

78. Coleman MP, Quaresma M, Berrino F, et al; CONCORD Working Group. Cancer survival in five continents: a worldwide population-based study (CONCORD). *Lancet Oncol* 2008; 9(8):730-56.

79. Coley CM, Barry MJ, Fleming C, Mulley AG. Early detection of prostate cancer. Part I: Prior probability and effectiveness of tests. *Ann Intern Med* 1997; 126(5):394-406.

80. Ajape AA, Mustapha K, Lawal IO, Mbibu HN. Survey of urologists on clients' demand for screening for prostate cancer in Nigeria. *Niger J Clin Pract* 2011; 14(2):151-3.

81. Olapade-Olaopa EO, Obamuyide HA, Yisa GT. Management of advanced prostate cancer in Africa. *Can J Urol* 2008; 15(1):3890-8.

82. Rodriguez-Galindo C, Wilson MW, Chantada G, et al. Retinoblastoma: one world, one vision. *Pediatrics* 2008; 122: e763-70.

83. Wilimas JA, Wilson MW, Haik BG, et al. Development of retinoblastoma programs in Central America. *Pediatric Blood and Cancer* 2009; 53:42-6.

84. Chantada GL, Qaddoumi I, Canturk S, et al. Strategies to manage retinoblastoma in developing countries. *Pediatric Blood Cancer* 2011; 56:341-8.

85. Olov HA, Hunter D, Trichopoulos D, 2008.

86. Ibid.

87. Ibid.

88. Ibid.

89. Ibid.

90. The Max Foundation. Homepage. The Max Foundation, 2011 http://www.themaxfoundation.org/ (accessed October 1, 2011).

Much can be done

Part **III**

Chapter 6

INNOVATIVE DELIVERY OF CANCER CARE AND CONTROL IN LOW-RESOURCE SCENARIOS

Felicia Marie Knaul, Afsan Bhadelia, Rashid Bashshur, Amanda J. Berger, Agnes Binagwaho, Erin Blackstock, Amy Judd, Ana Langer, Doug Pyle, Mounica Vallurupalli, Julie R. Gralow

Key messages

- Cancer can and is being treated by using innovative delivery strategies where specialized cancer services are not locally available. Actual experiences provide lessons for countries at all income levels.

- Several aspects of cancer care and control (CCC) can be integrated into a number of programs with broad population coverage, such as maternal and child health, sexual and reproductive health, HIV/AIDS, and social welfare/anti-poverty programs.

- Non-specialist human resources and primary and secondary levels of care can be used to deliver several components of CCC. This can help to alleviate the shortage of specialists for those services.

- The potential and capacity of non-specialist health personnel and limited infrastructure can be increased through the use of information and communications technology and telemedicine, and through formal and informal operational links with specialized clinical centers around the world. This can reduce barriers to access that many patients face, and at the same time contain costs.

- Training and capacity building are essential to reduce the shortage of specialized personnel and oncologists, especially in the long run.

- Initiatives by medical centers in high income countries to partner with treatment centers and oncology associations in low and middle income countries (LMICs) are flourishing. This approach could be expanded into global, virtual treatment networks to increase access to specialty services for adults and children in LMICs, and also to provide training and exchanges that will boost human resource capacity.

- Free access to information and knowledge for patients and providers can enhance CCC in LMICs.

- Identifying and evaluating the interventions in LMICs that make use of task and infrastructure shifting could benefit the health systems of countries, at all levels of income.

- Low and middle income countries should establish, at the national or sub-regional level, where relevant and feasible, a comprehensive cancer center of excellence to serve as a focal point for CCC.

- A database of existing programs and lessons learned, both positive and negative, should be established and disseminated globally. Existing programs should be evaluated for scale-up potential, and those results also must be shared broadly.

6.i Introduction

Low and middle income countries face a severe shortage of health care workers and an acute shortage of clinicians trained in oncology.[1-5] In Honduras, for example, fewer than 20 oncologists are available for a country with a population of 8 million, and in Ethiopia, 4 oncologists care for more than 80 million people.[6,7] Similar shortages exist in other specialty services, such as pathology. In addition, access is limited to tertiary centers where diagnosis, surgery, and specific treatments, such as radiation therapy, are available.

All things considered, closing the cancer divide can begin immediately, even in the most resource-constrained environments. Experience is demonstrating that early detection and treatment of many cancers is possible, despite a lack of specialty services and specialized human resources.

The gap between need and available human and physical resources must be filled both by building new capacity and by expanding existing capacity through the use of innovative and complementary delivery mechanisms. In the long run, the supply of local specialists (oncologists and others) and specialty centers must be increased to provide many of the essential core elements of cancer care (Chapter 5).

At the same time, strategies must be found to reduce, if not eliminate, barriers of distance by deploying innovative delivery models that have not been sufficiently exploited for CCC. Closing the cancer divide also requires harnessing existing programs that are not commonly used to meet the challenge of cancer. These include programs for anti-poverty/social welfare, women's empowerment, sexual and reproductive health, HIV/AIDS, and maternal and child health. Appropriate mechanisms must be identified, evaluated, adapted, and disseminated so these programs can be expanded.

The first part of this chapter reviews relevant literature and the models for harnessing platforms using a diagonal approach. These models optimize the use of human and physical resources at the primary and secondary levels, and apply information and communication technology to bridge time and distance barriers to care. The second part includes a review of a number of projects and programs currently underway in several LMICs, some of which have strong links to institutions in high income countries. Each of these projects applies innovative delivery methodologies to expand access to CCC in LMICs and provides important lessons and opportunities for expansion.

6.ii Innovations in delivery

The Task Force focuses on three broad categories or types of health system delivery innovations that can expand access to CCC: infrastructure or spatial shifting to use existing delivery systems that are not usually used for CCC, optimal tasking; and the use of information and communication technology to facilitate both tasks. These innovations provide opportunities for more effective use of scarce human and physical resources.

HARNESSING PLATFORMS AND SYSTEM-WIDE INTERVENTIONS

A particularly important aspect of innovative delivery in CCC is the use of existing programs, some of which are designed for a) specific diseases (HIV/AIDS), population groups and conditions (maternal and child health, sexual and reproductive health), or b) social development objectives (anti-poverty or the empowerment of women). The development of systems utilizing existing programs can be especially important when a cancer is related to a specific group, such as children, or women and reproductive health. In addition, many existing programs often already have broad coverage and community acceptance.[8,9]

Further, elements of each component of the CCC continuum for several cancers can be integrated into existing programs. For example, early detection of breast and cervical cancer, and preventative risk factors such as smoking and obesity, can be integrated into women and health, sexual and reproductive health, and maternal and child health programs, and the health components of anti-poverty initiatives.[10] Such integration can promote the best possible use of care providers within a health system, especially when they are enabled to perform their functions aided by the tools of information and communication technology, and telemedicine. Common platforms should allow the provision of care using a life course perspective, taking into account all ailments across a woman's life cycle, including and beyond reproduction.[11,12]

The potential of cancer-specific innovations in delivery may be enhanced by interventions that are not strictly disease-specific and more horizontal in application. Some of these interventions are system-wide and others are specific to a given area of health care. Examples of a system-wide intervention would be the introduction of health insurance that covers rural areas or health professional certification to establish standards of quality.

OPTIMAL TASKING

The notion that all care must be provided by highly specialized clinicians must be challenged.[13] For instance, the assumption that non-specialty care or care from qualified but not specialized health staff is somehow inferior is not valid. Indeed, while access to specialty care, and certainly to oncologists, is essential, specialty care can be complemented by non-specialty care in several ways to enhance capacity.

The companion assumption that no care is better than some care also is counterproductive. Non-specialty car or care performed by health workers who are not physicians does not necessarily result in poor outcomes, especially when such care is rendered under supervision and by those with appropriate training. Indeed, in some settings that are bound by geography, resource constraints, or culture the use of trained, non-medical staff may be the only feasible option for the foreseeable future.

In the case of CCC in LMICs, as well as care for other chronic illnesses, some emerging tasks are necessary (for example, long-term survivorship care for patients who have undergone chemotherapy and breast clinical exams). For this reason, we use the term "optimal tasking" to accommodate such needs. The prevailing literature refers to "task shifting" as the decentralization, delegation, or substitution of services, and the reorganization of the health workforce from highly trained and/ or specialized health workers to existing or newly trained health workers who have lesser training and limited qualifications.[14,15] Whereas, "task sharing" refers to the combination of tasks among health workers with various levels of training to enhance the effectiveness of certain aspects of care, using existing skill sets within the health workforce.[16] Optimal tasking encompasses both of these strategies.

Experiences that are well documented in the literature for other diseases or more general care settings (Text Box 6.1) provide some lessons and replicable strategies for introducing and scaling-up CCC in low-resource settings, in ways that strengthen national health systems. These strategies rely on organizing and deploying available and new human, physical, technological, and information resources to support health systems.

Text Box 6.1
Optimal tasking: A partial review of the literature

Community health workers, expert patients, and clinical officers are examples of less skilled health workers who can be used to deliver care and follow-up. This has been well documented in the literature, and below are some examples:

Community Health Workers

The benefits of including community members in primary health care teams have been recognized for several decades.[17] The HIV/AIDS crisis generated impetus for incorporating community health workers (CHWs) in care delivery in LMICs, and that has provided important lessons for CCC. The HIV/AIDS programs demonstrate that complex drug regimens can be managed at the community level by CHWs,[18-21] with the desirable side effects of creating expanded demand and an ensuing reduction in stigma.[22] Bangladesh Rehabilitation Assistance Committee (BRAC) CHWs, for example, have been responsible for detecting about half of TB cases, and under their supervision, treatment compliance compares favorably to other programs.[23] The cost of the government program that does not use CHWs is 50% higher.[24]

Evidence for including CHWs in the delivery of noncommunicable disease (NCD) care and control is limited. In the US, CHWs have helped reduce disparities in management of hypertension and in cardiovascular health promotion.[25,26] One cluster randomized trial from Pakistan shows that family-based home health education from lay health workers, coupled with education of general practitioners, can help control blood pressure among hypertensive patients.[27] A randomized controlled intervention with the Hispanic population on the US-Mexico border showed that CHW intervention was associated with a 35% difference in re-screening.[28,29]

Expert Patients

Task shifting also involves the delegation of some clearly delineated tasks to newly created types of health workers, and the use of expert patients is a particularly promising innovative option.[30,31] People living with HIV/AIDS are being trained in several expert patient programs to enhance the capacity of health workers.[32] These expert patients can impart firsthand knowledge of what it means to live with the disease, which is an important step in strengthening health systems. In high income countries, expert patient programs in cancer are well known. Further, volunteer groups and civil society organizations often make use of this model – particularly for breast cancer.

Clinical Officers

There are examples of successfully training teams of health professionals to undertake complex tasks, often in primary- or rudimentary, secondary-level centers. In some parts of Africa, clinical officers or medical assistants provide the majority of care, and in many countries, they outnumber the doctors. Results from 25 sub-Saharan countries with non-physician clinicians who undertake varied tasks (from basic diagnosis and medical *treatment to c-sections, ophthalmology, and anesthesia) showed that the costs and duration of training were low and that rural placement was successful.[33,34] An economic evaluation showed that major obstetric surgery by surgically trained assistant medical officers in Mozambique was 3.5 times cheaper than surgeons or OBGYNs. In Swaziland, nurse-led primary care was more effective than hospital care for antiretroviral therapy (ART).[35] There is some evidence of success in emergency obstetric care in Senegal and Malawi, and in surgery in Mozambique.[36,37] Challenges include resistance from senior health professionals, lack of systemic support for teams, and insufficient financial remuneration and motivation.[38,38]*

Based on experience in management of other diseases, especially HIV/AIDS, several aspects of CCC can be delegated to non-specialist or less specialized medical professionals. There are ways to engage expert patients, health promoters (sometimes called acompañateurs or community health workers), clinical health assistants, nurses, and physicians working in primary- and secondary-level care facilities to provide more and better access to CCC, including the provision of some treatment. Broader use of this strategy has been proposed to respond to the crisis in access to services.[40]

Several tools can facilitate optimal tasking. For example, the surgical checklist is a particularly appealing tool because it is being used for procedures such as childbirth. Lives are being saved with such low-cost interventions that do not require new or sophisticated infrastructure.[41-44] Checklists are potentially applicable to all health care providers and the entire CCC continuum. Some of them could be used by patients themselves, and some could be embodied in health cards so women can promote their own health and that of their children.[45]

Task shifting has been well-demonstrated, particularly with regards to community health workers and task substitution among health professionals.[46] Overall, a strategy of task redistribution can generate improved access and coverage of similar quality, at a comparable or lower cost.[47-49] Still, community health workers require focused tasks, adequate and stable remuneration, general and disease-specific training, supervision, involvement of the communities in which they work, and effective integration and team work with other health professionals, especially physicians and nurses at the primary level of care.[50-53]

Integrating CHWs and their programs into national health systems is a challenge.[54,55] Several successful integrated programs have been developed in different parts of the world.[56-58] A review of their experiences demonstrates the importance of stewardship from national governments in developing CHW and other optimal tasking programs. Governments need to establish enabling regulatory frameworks, stable and long-term program funding, support for formal training, and support for all stakeholders.[59,60]

INFRASTRUCTURE SHIFTING AND USE OF INFORMATION AND COMMUNICATION TECHNOLOGY

Infrastructure shifting has been less studied than task shifting. It includes bringing care closer to the patient, removing geographical barriers to care, reducing opportunity costs for the patient, and providing cost-containment for the health system.

In the case of CCC, task shifting specifically refers to undertaking particular care components in primary- and secondary-level, less specialized facilities. This care is often assumed to require either tertiary-level or specialty cancer centers.

Telemedicine technology embodies the electronic acquisition, processing, dissemination, storage, retrieval, and exchange of information to promote health. Telemedicine systems have demonstrated the capacity to improve access to all levels of care (primary, secondary, and tertiary) for a wide range of conditions (including heart and cerebrovascular disease, diabetes, cancer, psychiatric disorders, and trauma) and services such as radiology, pathology, and rehabilitation to promote patient-centered care at a lower cost and in local environments. This technology also can enhance efficiency in clinical decision-making, prescription ordering, and mentoring, increase effectiveness of chronic disease management in both long-term care facilities and in the home, and promote individual self-care and adoption of a healthy lifestyle.[61]

Telemedicine refers to all systems for delivering personal health services that substitute electronic communications and information for in-person contact between patients and providers; communication among providers; and, patient or provider contact with sources of information, decision-making, and support systems.[62] It is, in fact, a modality of care that challenges the traditional dependence on physical presence for health promotion and care delivery.

The widespread availability of cell or mobile phones throughout LMICs can facilitate access to CCC in many ways. Patients can be provided with educational and resource information for awareness-building, self-management and the promotion of screening and follow-up. Primary health care workers can be reached easily when needed, and they can use their phones to send images and information directly from the field.

In areas where no specialists are available, spatial shifting can allow highly trained health workers from other countries to deliver CCC remotely, often through twinning programs or collaboration. Information and communication technology facilitates resource and infrastructure shifting by providing a fast and relatively inexpensive way to gain access to the expertise of specialists and sub-specialists without moving the patient. This allows for diagnosis and treatment by on-site less specialized medical personnel and in less complex health care units. Management and supervision of adjuvant therapy, for example, can take place at a distance from the clinical oncologist if information and communication is used in real time. Teleoncology can be used to overcome a variety of other CCC shortages through telepathology and teleradiology. These areas of work have advanced in high income countries and now include standards and guidelines that can be adapted for LMICs. The call for telepathology may be misinterpreted as diverting efforts from strengthening in-country capacity to provide pathology services,[63] but should in fact be seen as an opportunity to provide interim and long-term support while countries invest in training and equipment to delivery safe and effective pathology and laboratory services.[64] A two-pronged approach to improving in-country diagnosis, along with the use of collaborative models of consult with regional and global counterparts would expedite progress in this area, increasing accuracy in diagnosis and maximizing opportunities for expanding CCC.[65]

At the opposite end of the spectrum, as treatment becomes increasingly individualized, spatial shifting becomes ever more necessary - even in high income settings and for wealthy populations (see Case 6). Care that used to be constrained by national boundaries now can be more efficiently –and sometimes only– provided by specialists in distant places.

Telecommunications can also be used for training and capacity-building. At the primary level, training for a range of primary care personnel can be enhanced by distance learning through structured courses. In Mexico, for example, health promoters, nurses, physicians, and outreach workers are being trained about breast cancer early detection through the National Institute of Public Health. Too, professionals, especially those at the specialty and sub-specialty levels, can use telecommunications for mentoring, collaboration, and networking, similar to the work being done at St. Jude (see Case 4).

Information and communication also provides the opportunity to give both providers and patients increased access to information required for decision-making and awareness-building. Still, financial barriers exist because much of this information is not available free of charge. This emphasizes the need to provide access to databases for institutions and users in developing countries, as well as to promote public digital libraries and open-access publishing.[66] Cure4Kids is an example of a successful effort to share and provide expanded access to core information for providers, patients, and families (see Case 4).

Applications of information and communication and telemedicine in cancer also can strengthen health systems and contribute to health reform efforts through the adoption of innovations that can be used at the population level. The use of personal electronic health records is but one example.[67]

Some authors have suggested teleoncology as a means for reducing disparities in outcomes and access between LMICs and high income countries.[68-70] One study highlights significant results of the St. Jude Cure4Kids international twinning (see Case 4), but also cites examples from India, Cambodia, Solomon Islands, Brazil, and Jordan, as well as the efforts in high income countries to reach underserved populations. The same study highlights the opportunities for teleoncology to link resource-rich and resource-poor settings, support clinical research, and improve palliation and survivorship care.[71] The Cambodia pilot program suggests that simple communication technologies can improve cancer care, even in impoverished communities, as the demand for acute care decreased when patients sought care earlier and showed better adherence to treatment regimes.[72]

Text Box 6.2
Breast and cervical cancer:
examples of innovative delivery

Building on a base of public health programs and with links to a comprehensive cancer center preferably located in-country, human and physical resources can be maximized to expand access to CCC. These delivery innovations can also free-up core resources that then can be applied to much-needed, cancer-specific facilities such as radiotherapy.

The examples below focus, for the most part, on cancers specific to women where actions can – but typically do not - build on the extensive networks of sexual and reproductive health, and maternal and child health programs that operate in most LMICs.

Prevention – healthy lifestyles:

• Integrating health promotion activities including tobacco control and healthy lifestyles into anti-poverty and social welfare programs.

• Promoting HPV vaccination through adolescent, sexual and reproductive, and maternal and child health programs.

Early detection – secondary prevention:

• Integrating early detection programs for breast and cervical cancer into anti-poverty, maternal and child health, sexual and reproductive health, and HIV/AIDS programs.

• Training expert patients, community health workers, nurses, and primary care physicians to provide early diagnosis, especially for high-risk women.

Diagnosis:

• Using telemedicine to expand capacity for breast imaging by linking specialists and specialty centers to primary and secondary providers of health care for diagnosis and training.

• Strengthening pathology processing facilities, where they exist, by using telemedicine for pathology consultation.

Treatment:

• Training primary and secondary care providers and facilities to safely provide some chemotherapy and adjuvant therapy with a strong link *to specialists and specialty centers, reducing costs for patients, the need for young women to leave children for long periods, and the demand placed on tertiary facilities.*

Survivorship:

- *Training expert patients, community health workers, nurses, and primary care physicians to provide long-term emotional support, guidance in symptom management, and patient navigation, including knowledge of rights and health care benefits.*

Pain control and palliation:

- *Putting systems in place to enable the safe and effective management of pain medications at the primary and secondary care levels, including administering drugs through simple presentations.*

6.iii Case studies of CCC delivery innovations

Having identified a host of possible delivery innovations, the Task Force studied examples of projects and programs underway in LMICs. Some of these are described in this volume. Formal evaluation of innovative delivery models in LMICs is non-existent, which makes it necessary to rely on descriptions of pilot projects in countries of different income levels,with different cancers as "proof-of-concept". The selection of projects described below is not exhaustive. There is great need for a database of programs and an archive of lessons learned, including through review of models to expand access in high income countries.

CASE 1
PIH-DFCI-BWH PARTNERSHIP
INNOVATIVE DELIVERY STRATEGIES FOR CANCER CARE
IN RURAL RWANDA, MALAWI, AND HAITI

*Luke Messac, Megan McLaughlin, Kelly Bogaert, Jarred Mcateer,
David Shulman, Amy Sievers, Sara Stulac, Amy Judd*

Drawing on the experience of Partners in Health (PIH) in developing successful care delivery systems in resource-limited settings, along with the expertise of the Dana-Farber Cancer Institute (DFCI) and the Brigham and Women's Hospital (BWH), this collaborative model has delivered high quality cancer care at PIH sites in Haiti, Malawi, and Rwanda without the physical presence of an oncologist. The PIH-DFCIBWH cancer program was developed within the context of existing PIH programs, in a horizontal, rather than vertical, manner – an example of the diagonal approach to health systems strengthening (Chapter 4). The partnership has also developed specific disease-based protocols to set guidelines for care at all the sites, and to help guide research and planning to improve care and outcomes in the future.

The programs take advantage of PIH's proven success in treating complex infectious diseases such as HIV/AIDS and tuberculosis, and have integrated cancer care into these existing services. PIH has expanded their accompagnateur model and other supportive services offered to cancer patients. Trained community health workers –a key component of the success of PIH programs in infectious disease– provide care, social and psychological support, and serve as a link to patients in settings where distances can be far and transportation, nonexistent. The community health workers not only provide companionship during treatment and palliation, but they also provide supportive care for side effects (hydration, antiemetics, analgesics) through home visits, accompaniment during clinic visits, and close contact with the hospital, which guarantees that no patient is lost during follow-up. The care model is holistic; community health workers ensure that patients have a supportive economic and social environment including food, housing, means of transportation, and family support.

Task shifting –where on-site primary-level clinicians with additional training provide care with the back-up support of specialists– has been a cornerstone of the cancer care delivery model. An important component is the use of information and communication technology to link clinicians in the field with off-site oncologists. In Rwanda, online forums facilitate consultations with specialists. A pediatric hematologist/oncologist at Dartmouth and a clinical advisory group at DFCI provide pro bono expert consultation. Once a diagnosis is confirmed by pathology, DFCI oncologists provide advice on the selection of a chemotherapy protocol and supportive medications via an online forum within the Global Health Delivery Online System, which was designed to aid the sharing of knowledge and collaboration between international and US physicians. An online patient database provides information on the cases for the US-based specialists and tracks patient outcomes for monitoring and evaluation.

Pathology is one area where linkages have been especially important. As discussed in Chapter 5, pathology is vital to ensuring the appropriate diagnosis and treatment, but is often neither available nor affordable in LMICs. In 2003, PIH and BWH began a project that allows clinicians in the field in PIH clinics to have access to pathology interpretative services.[73] They established a safe transport system for specimens between the field and the pathology department at BWH. Two pathology residents from BWH and two medical residents from PIH were trained to do individual follow-up with health care workers in the field to guarantee the proper handling and safety of specimens. The pathology department provided free pathology services. Over five years, 131 patients received biopsies, and 102 were definitively diagnosed. BWH provided pathology analysis of tumor tissues free-of-charge. The partnership has developed models for in-country-based sample preparation and electronic transmission.

In Haiti, with support from DFCI, PIH has provided chemotherapy and has performed hysterectomies, lumpectomies, and other oncologic surgeries at their location in the village of Cange, on Haiti's Central Plateau. A DFCI surgical oncologist travels regularly to Haiti to perform breast surgery, and Boston-based surgical oncologists have also performed surgeries for cancer patients in Haiti. Patients requiring radiation therapy are referred to the Oncology Center of Santiago, in the Dominican Republic. In 2012, PIH reported 19 patients under chemotherapy and an additional 20-30 patients needing treatment.

The PIH oncology team is developing posters and handouts in Haitian Creole with instructions for performing breast self-exams. These are to be available at health facilities and mobile clinics in the catchment area. Also, CHWs are to be trained to perform breast exams and teach patients about breast cancer during home visits. Additionally, PIH has begun distribution of scarves and educational information to women who have begun chemotherapy as part of an effort to protect patient dignity and provide a form of social support.

In Malawi, where the adult HIV/AIDS prevalence rate is 14%, hospital clinicians regularly encounter Kaposi sarcoma. When PIH first began working in Malawi, the organization hired hundreds of community health workers and tripled both the hospital staff and the voluntary counseling and testing (VCT) counselors to extend HIV/AIDS testing and treatment across several districts.

Screening for Kaposi sarcoma was incorporated into the protocols at the VCT clinics. Now, any person who tests HIV-positive receives a physical examination for Kaposi sarcoma lesions and symptoms of pulmonary and gastrointestinal Kaposi sarcoma during baseline clinical assessment. In February 2008, PIH opened a clinic for Kaposi sarcoma, and since then has treated more than 80 patients with chemotherapy. Because all but two of the patients were HIV-positive, follow-up could be incorporated into regular patient visits to HIV/AIDS clinics as well as daily accompagnateur visits to the patients' home.

In Rwanda, adult and pediatric patients are logged into an online cancer database and followed. On-site physician and nurse teams at the PIH district hospitals administer chemotherapy to a select number of patients with curable cancers, with DFCI oncologists providing clinical advice. This program has proven complementary to national, MOH-defined initiatives such as the formulation of a national cancer plan, a countrywide cervical cancer prevention program (the first such program in Africa), a new national palliative care project, and the development of a population-based national cancer registry. Most notably, in 2012, Rwanda revolutionized CCC in the country with the launch of the Butaro Cancer Center of Excellence, a comprehensive specialized facility providing the full range of care from screening, diagnosis, chemotherapy and surgery to palliative care, social work services and socioeconomic support programming.[74]

Several key lessons that could be applied to other institutional collaborations and different resource-constrained settings have emerged from the PIH-DFCI-BWH partnership:

- Task shifting for cancer care, utilizing training, and back-up from specialists can be implemented safely and effectively;

- Implementation requires flexibility and creativity– the models for prevention, screening, diagnosis, and treatment vary across countries and socio-economic environments;

- Cancer care is easier to sustain when incorporated into existing primary and chronic care programs, including programs for infectious disease;

- Resources should be used for palliation to reduce human suffering as well as for prevention and treatment;

- Operational research on factors affecting the successful adaptation of cancer care delivery models to local circumstances can help to identify delivery strategies that can be applied in other settings.

The PIH-DFCI-BWH partnership shows how inputs from high income countries can build capacity for cancer care delivery in resource-limited settings, through international collaborations in training and sharing of technical expertise. It also illustrates how international collaborations can help to spur national CCC programs, and how these can be layered onto existing disease-specific initiatives and primary care systems by applying the diagonal approach to build more sustainable health systems. However, these programs require ongoing evaluation, adaptation, and support for scale-up and sustainability. National governments will need to adapt programs like the PIH-DFCI-BWH partnership to promote a good fit with national cancer plans and eventually guarantee sustainable funding.

CASE 2
UCI / HUTCHINSON CENTER CANCER ALLIANCE
A COLLABORATION BETWEEN THE FRED HUTCHINSON CANCER RESEARCH CENTER AND THE UGANDA CANCER INSTITUTE

Corey Casper, Erica Sessle, Warren Phipps, Jessica Yager,
Lawrence Corey, Jackson Orem

To conduct the most efficient and impactful cancer service interventions and research in infection-related cancers, scientists from the Fred Hutchinson Cancer Research Center (FHCRC) in Seattle partnered with the Uganda Cancer Institute (UCI) in Kampala in 2004 to form the UCI / Hutchinson Center Cancer Alliance. The main focus of the work was infection-associated cancers, but it has been expanded to include other cancers of public health importance in both resource-rich and resource-poor settings.

The program has three core components: research, capacity-building, and care delivery. This combination was considered necessary to achieve the programmatic goal of reducing the mortality from infection-associated cancers in diverse settings around the globe. Over the first five years, substantial progress was made in each area.

Research projects are aimed at elucidating the fundamental questions that need to be answered to provide comprehensive cancer prevention and treatment for infection-related malignancies. Examples include examining the interaction between host and infectious oncogen to identify biomarkers that would predict the development of cancer or prognosticate the response to treatment, evaluating new medication strategies for preventing cancer among persons thought to be at high risk, developing less toxic, inexpensive and effective therapy for infection-related cancers aimed at the infectious pathogen, and developing preventative cancer vaccines. Importantly, each of the methods under evaluation would lead to prevention and treatment strategies that could be used in both resource-rich and resource-poor settings. More than a dozen research projects are under way at the research clinic, with work to date clarifying the pathogenesis, diagnosis, and treatment of two common cancers in sub-Saharan Africa – Kaposi sarcoma and lymphoma. Other projects seek to understand predictors of survival from non-infection associated cancers such as breast and prostate cancer, as well as the role of nutrition and care delivery models focusing on adherence to care to improve cancer outcomes.

A central mission of this program is to provide training activities to build the human capacity for cancer care and research in resource-limited regions. The training program has expanded the capacity to treat cancer in Uganda several fold. By 2012 ten Ugandan physicians had been trained in cancer care through a 13-month fellowship at FHCRC, in a program that provides the foundations of cancer care tailored to settings with few resources. In addition, more than 120 Ugandans and Americans in a variety of disciplines – including pharmacy, nursing care, infectious disease medicine, epidemiology, laboratory sciences, research coordination, regulatory management, and program administration – have trained with the program.

A unique aspect of this program is the development of a cancer treatment facility model for low-resource regions that would allow for the efficient and impactful delivery of care. Working with an international team of architects, the program is building a cancer clinic, training center, and laboratories in Kampala as a collaboration between a clinical and research cancer center in the US, the FHCRC, and a local cancer institute in Uganda, the UCI.

CASE 3
EXPANDING ACCESS TO GYNECOLOGICAL CCC
IN PERU THROUGH AN MOH-PATH COLLABORATION

Vivien Tsu

Peru has had a National Plan for the Prevention of Gynecological Cancer since 1998. The plan included cervical and breast cancer screening, but numerous problems in implementing screening services led the Ministry of Health to partner with the Pan American Health Organization (PAHO) and PATH through the TATI (acronym for the Spanish term, tamizaje y tratamiento inmediato) demonstration project in 2000. Limited screening services were centered primarily in Lima, the capital, which has hampered access in rural areas. Recent government prioritization of five high-burden cancers, including breast and cervical cancer, has resulted in a significant increase in the availability of funds to expand early detection, treatment, and care services. These new resources were accompanied by heightened interest in finding workable models for expanding coverage to low-resource sections of the country and led to the introduction of the Community-based Program for Breast Health.

The TATI program focused on three aspects of delivery: 1) community information and education; 2) screening services; and 3) diagnostic and/or treatment services, with the goal of screening 80% of women between the ages of 25 and 49 years in the region of San Martin, over a period of three years.[72] Teams of midwives and a primary care physician based in 30 primary health centers were trained to screen using visual inspection with acetic acid (VIA), triage those who were VIA-positive using a low-power magnification device (visual inspection with acetic acid magnified or VIAM), and treat using cryotherapy.[73] A total of 35 primary care physicians and 48 midwives received training for screening and treatment.[74] Although the project did not meet the 80% coverage target, it did reach more than 30% of the eligible women in just three years and over half of those reached had never been screened before.[75] The project demonstrated that successful cervical cancer screening programs are feasible where resources are limited.

Following up the TATI project, PATH worked with Peru's National Cancer Institute (INEN) and Jhpiego to establish a regional Technical Excellence Center for training master trainers in VIA, cryotherapy, community outreach and other essential elements of cervical cancer prevention. With validated competency-based curricula, the center has now certified master trainers not only within Peru but also from other countries in the region, including Colombia and Bolivia.

In partnership with PATH, the Breast Health Global Initiative, the Union for International Cancer Control, and the Norwegian Cancer Society, INEN initiated a Community-based Program for Breast Health in 2011. Working with a new regional cancer center in the northern part of the country, (IREN Norte) in Trujillo –an example of infrastructure shifting– the program is piloting screening and initial diagnostic evaluation of breast cancer in a rural community and evaluating the potential for national scale-up with the prospective development of other regional centers. Trujillo has had a cancer registry that predates these new efforts, providing an opportunity to analyze impact through down- staging. The work on breast cancer is building on previous efforts on cervical cancer.

Essential to the project is the training of nurses and midwives, primary caregivers at health centers and health posts, to conduct clinical breast exams. Patients with suspected masses are referred to the local hospital for evaluation by physicians trained to use ultrasound, where ultrasound is available, and fine needle aspiration (FNA) biopsy. Biopsies are sent to a cytologist at IREN Norte for interpretation. Oncologists at IREN Norte are being trained as master trainers for FNA so they can train and supervise physicians at community hospitals. Women with a diagnosis of cancer are referred to IREN Norte for treatment. The project plans to train district-level physicians to administer follow-up management after treatment. This approach ensures that a woman stays within the community for as much of the process as possible. At the same time, she has access to quality specialty care.

Community outreach and modification of the health information system are other parts of this collaborative pilot project. New tracking variables are being identified in the existing health information system to determine the number of women in the target age group who receive CBE, how many are referred, how many FNAs are conducted and their results, and the number of women referred to IREN who comply. A comparison of screening rates and diagnostic follow-up in the pilot area with those of neighboring districts where training has not yet been provided will be conducted. The lessons learned will provide evidence to help INEN shape its strategy on early detection services and diagnostic follow-up and treatment.

CASE 4
TWINNING IN PEDIATRIC ONCOLOGY
MODELS FOR THE INNOVATIVE USE OF INFORMATION AND
COMMUNICATION TECHNOLOGY TO BRIDGE DISTANCE

Felicia Marie Knaul, Afsan Bhadelia,
Carlos Rodríguez-Galindo, Lindsay Frazier

St. Jude International Outreach Program (IOP) seeks to improve the survival rate of children with cancer globally, but particularly in developing regions where outcomes are extremely poor. The IOP was established with the belief that pediatric oncology care is both appropriate and feasible in developing countries.[75] The program is primarily funded by an allocation of approximately one percent of the hospital's annual budget.

IOP currently collaborates with 19 partner medical institutions in 14 developing countries to help develop local pediatric cancer centers.[76] It is estimated that by 2010, more than 17,000 patients in developing countries were treated in the IOP affiliated programs.[77] The IOP strategy involves assessing local needs, identifying an appropriate model for action, implementing services accordingly, and monitoring outcomes.[78] The cornerstone of the IOP approach is twinning. The IOP promotes a mentorship model between centers of excellence in pediatric oncology in developed countries with centers in developing countries. The St. Jude IOP employs targeted education and training of key personnel at mentee institutions to transfer the knowledge needed to lead the twinning program.[79] Ongoing distance learning and continuing medical education is offered through teleconference and web technology. Weekly, bi-weekly, or monthly webconferences for consultations on complex cases between the mentor and mentee centers ensure real time and continuous access to specialist and expert care, while providing a forum for continuing education and program-building. There is also an opportunity for intensive training at St. Jude through the International Visitors Program, a fellowship for health care professionals from LMICs.[80] Twinning activities have been shown to reduce abandonment of treatment, relapse, and mortality from the toxic effects of treatment.[81] Further, this model has important and potentially replicable, built-in elements that guarantee programmatic and financial sustainability.

While St. Jude's is the most evaluated and extensive of the existing programs in pediatric cancer, other hospitals are becoming active. Rwanda, for example, has a system of teleconsult between the Clinical Director of PIH Rwanda, a pediatrician, and a pediatric oncologist at Dartmouth Medical School. The specialist provides advice on both the diagnosis and treatment plan, including chemotherapy, radiation, and supportive care. Counterparts communicate by email, sharing pathology reports and photographs of the radiological images, which are then reviewed by a pathologist and radiologist at Dartmouth.

One particularly innovative project unique to St. Jude is Cure4Kids. This is a free, open source e-library with educational materials (e-textbooks, journals, and a repository of cases and related content presented thorough its Oncopedia, which is reviewed by an international editorial board), training resources (online seminars and courses), and opportunities for interactive knowledge exchange (discussion boards) between pediatric oncologists and health professionals worldwide through a secure information-sharing interface. Informatics infrastructure support for development of secure hospital-based databases and data sharing, as well as web communication tools for ongoing exchange, are offered by the web collaboration. More than 200 regional and international groups gather regularly through web-based meetings to discuss complex cases. Cure4Kids reaches 17,000 health care professionals across 169 countries. The website provides both a public and private interface for interaction and has earned numerous awards, including Best Medical Website from the Web Marketing Association and the Strategic e-HealthCare Leadership Award. Cure4Kids provides an exemplary model of a global public good with broad access and far-reaching effects, and one that could, and should, be replicated for all cancers.

CASE 5
INTERNATIONAL TRAINING AND EXCHANGES
AMERICAN SOCIETY OF CLINICAL ONCOLOGY

Doug Pyle

To begin to address the gap between need and human resources, specialist training in LMICs needs to be supported and expanded, but, at the same time, capacity needs to be further increased by extending oncology training to other members of the medical team, when appropriate. To be successful, these efforts need to be made in a systematic, sustained way, and in the context of local clinical settings where needs are understood and training can be put into practice.

With these challenges and goals in mind, the American Society of Clinical Oncology (ASCO) partnered in 2008 with Health Volunteers Overseas (HVO), an international medical education organization, to create a program to pair ASCO's member oncologists with colleagues from medical centers in LMICs that serve as national cancer referral hospitals. This "International Cancer Corps" aims to exchange medical expertise, develop training programs, and build long-term, supportive relationships between ASCO, these essential medical institutions, and the clinicians who practice there.

The program is a fortuitous marriage of expertise. For the past two decades, HVO has worked to increase health care access in LMICs through clinical training and education programs in child health, primary care, trauma and rehabilitation, essential surgical care, oral health, infectious disease, nursing education, and burn management. Active in more than 40 hospitals in 25 countries, HVO-affiliated medical volunteers train, mentor, and provide crucial professional support to health care providers. With more than 30,000 members in more than 100 countries, ASCO is able to draw on extensive oncologic and regional expertise to implement cancer programs in LMICs.

The first International Cancer Corps (ICC) sites are Honduras, Vietnam, and Ethiopia, selected from among those hospitals where HVO has experience implementing programs in other specialties, the size of the cancer patient population, and the nature of the overall need and potential for ASCO impact. Efforts are underway to add two sites in 2013, for a total of five active sites.

Once a site is selected, ASCO and HVO appoint an ASCO member volunteer with prior experience in the country or region to conduct a two-week site assessment at the hospital. On the basis of this assessment, and working closely with these partners, the International Cancer Corps establishes a set of program objectives. Care is taken to set objectives that fall within the scope of clinical training, can be achieved within several years, and lead to sustainable change.

For example, the Honduras ICC site is located at three hospitals in the Honduran capital city of Tegucigalpa: the Hospital Escuela ("Teaching Hospital"), Hospital San Felipe, and Cancer Center Emma Callejas. Objectives for Honduras were defined in the areas of pathology, palliative care, gynecological cancers, pediatric hematology-oncology, and oncology training curricula. The program began accepting volunteers in January 2010, and in its first two years, 21 volunteers have conducted 38 visits. Each volunteer had specific expertise that matched the goals of the program.

Though too early to assess the long term clinical impact of the program, it is clear that the engagement of both the volunteers and the local clinicians is strong. A critical factor for the program will be to ensure effective volunteer-to-volunteer communication so that each volunteer builds on the work of other volunteers. Another factor is the creation of volunteer-partner project teams to focus on specific objectives, such as developing curriculum materials, so that progress is not solely dependent on volunteer site visits. These are project management issues that ICC partner Health Volunteers Overseas is familiar with, based on 20 years of experience administering similar programs in other medical specialties, and that expertise is crucial. The ICC program also provides opportunities for collaboration with other international organizations and agencies in the cancer field, such as the Oncology Nursing Society and the Society for Gynecological Oncologists.

6.iv Conclusions

This analysis of existing initiatives and available literature provides evidence that supports harnessing platforms, optimal tasking, and infrastructure shifting using information and communication technology, and telemedicine to facilitate access to CCC in LMICs. Synergistic health system platforms and programs can effectively incorporate elements of CCC. Several examples such as programs for reproductive, maternal and child health, social welfare, and anti-poverty demonstrate this potential. A systematic identification of opportunities is necessary further develop, evaluate and scale-up successful models. The most obvious areas are prevention of risk factors, early detection and screening, some aspects of treatment including chemotherapy, adherence to treatment, and some aspects of long-term survivorship care including community reintegration, pain relief, and palliation.

Several lessons can be surmised in terms of mapping of delivery innovations, closer understanding of these innovations in practice, implications for scale-up, and developing a path to comprehensive care.

First, a database of existing CCC programs, technologies, and lessons learned needs to be developed, financed, and institutionalized to make the evidence easily accessible for translation into policy and programming. This invaluable information can be shared globally through a clearinghouse based at WHO or IARC, or it could be managed through a multi-stakeholder partnership that engages key global actors.

Second, a new cadre of non-specialized health care workers can be trained to diagnose and provide core treatment where appropriate, especially for the candidate cancers identified in Chapter 5, and in areas and communities where no specialized cancer care is available. This does not substitute for trained oncologists and specialists, but can make their services more accessible to many. Further, the expanded use of communications technology and telemedicine can be critical in providing access to diagnosis and specialized care in remote areas through partnerships and linkages with distant oncology specialists. This technology can also be used to share diagnostic information, data and knowledge, and for training and continuing education.

Third, while each of the specific projects described in this volume offer encouraging examples, a major concern is scale-up. Existing programs and projects are small-scale, often depend on individuals or specific institutions, have precarious budgets, and require evaluation. Lessons learned from implementation research on innovative CCC programs and experiences globally should be adapted and incorporated into large-scale programs to increase access, improve quality, and bring care closer to home and community. Tertiary treatment centers, cancer institutes, and bilateral donors should consider establishing dedicated funds to support the expansion and solidification of promising pilot programs and to establish new initiatives. Alternative innovative and complimentary delivery mechanisms can also be identified, evaluated, and scaled up to close the gap between need and available resource capacity.

Finally, the development of a comprehensive cancer center at the national or subregional level should be a key objective of any and all cancer planning. The establishment and institutionalization of a central body for CCC can significantly improve cancer outcomes.[76]

It is evident that while innovations in delivery can expand access for many patients, these innovations are not a panacea. More is needed in order to respond to the challenge of expanding access to CCC in LMICs. Diagnostic services, drugs, surgery, and radiotherapy are essential, but often missing in many parts of the world. In the absence of some services and specialists, certain cancers can only be palliated and patients receive only survivorship support. Other innovations to begin to address these needs are discussed later in this volume.

References

1.   Frenk J, Chen L, Bhutta ZA, et al. Health professionals for a new century: transforming education to strengthen health systems in an interdependent world. *Lancet* 2010; 76(9756):1923-58.

2.   Chen L, Evans T, Anand S, et al. Human resources for health: overcoming the crisis. *Lancet* 2004; 364(9449):1984-90.

3.   World Health Organization. The world health report 2006: working together for health. Geneva, Switzerland: World Health Organization; 2006.

4.   Ferlay J, Shin H, Bray F, Forman D, Mathers C, Parkin D. GLOBOCAN 2008: cancer incidence and mortality worldwide. *International Journal of Cancer* 2010 ;127(12):2893-917.

5.   Joint Learning Initiative, Global Equity Initiative. Human resources for health: overcoming the crisis. The President and Fellows of Harvard College 2004. http://www.who.int/hrh/documents/JLi_hrh_report.pdf (accessed October 4, 2011).

6.   American Society of Clinical Oncology/Health Volunteers Overseas International Cancer Corps Needs Assessment Reports on Honduras. 2008.

7.   American Society of Clinical Oncology/Health Volunteers Overseas International Cancer Corps Needs Assessment Reports on Ethiopia. 2010.

8.   Knaul F, Bustreo F, Ha E, Langer A. Breast cancer: why link early detection to reproductive health interventions in developing countries? *Salud Pública de México* 2009; 51(2):220-7.

9.   Forouzanfar MH, Forman KJ, Delossantos AM, et al. Breast and cervical cancer in 187 countries between 1980 and 2010: a systematic analysis. *Lancet* 2011: Epub ahead of print. http://www.thelancet.com/journals/lancet/article/PIIS0140-6736(11)61351-2/fulltext (accessed October 1, 2011).

10.   Knaul F, Bustreo F, Ha E, et al., 2009.

11.   Bustreo F, Knaul FM, Bhadelia A et al. Women's health beyond reproduction: meeting the challenges. WHO Bulletin 2012; 90(7): 477-556.

12.   Knaul FK, Bhadelia A, Gralow J, Arreola-Ornelas H, Langer A, Frenk J. Meeting the challenge of breast and cervical cancer in low- and middle-income countries. *International Journal of Gynecology and Obstetrics* 2012; Forthcoming.

13.   Hongoro C, McPake B. How to bridge the gap in human resources for health. *Lancet* 2004; 64(9443):1451-6.

14.   World Health Organization. Task shifting: rational redistribution of tasks among health workforce teams: global recommendations and guidelines: World Health Organization PEPFAR UNAIDS; 2008.

15.   Janse van Rensburg-Bonthuyzen E, Engelbrecht M, Steyn F, Jacobs N, Schneider H, van Rensburg D. Resources and infrastructure for the delivery of antiretroviral therapy at primary health care facilities in the Free State Province, South Africa. *Sahara Journal* 2008; 5(3):106-12.

16.   Shumbusho F, van Griensven J, Lowrance D, et al. Task shifting for scale-up of HIV care: Evaluation of nurse-centered antiretroviral treatment at rural health centers in Rwanda. *PLoS Med* 2009; 6:1-12.

17.   Love MB, Gardner K, Legion V. Community health workers: who they are and what they do. Health *Education & Behavior* 1997; 24(4): 510-21.

18.   Koenig S, Leandre F, Farmer P. Scaling-up HIV treatment programmes in resource-limited settings: the rural Haiti experience. *AIDS* 2004; 18(3): 21-5.

19.   Mukherjee JS, Ivers L, Leandre F, Farmer P, Behforouz H. Antiretroviral therapy in resource-poor settings. Decreasing barriers to access and promoting adherence. *Journal of Acquired Immune Deficiency Syndromes* 2006; 43 (1): 123-6.

20.   Callaghan M, Ford N, Schenider H. A systematic review of task-shifting for HIV treatment and care in Africa. *Human Resources for Health* 2010; 8: 1-9.

21.   Lehmann U, Van Damme W, Barten F, Sanders D. Task shifting: the answer to the human resources crisis in Africa? *Human Resources for Health*. 2009; 7(1):12-4.

22.   Koenig S, Leandre F, Farmer P, 2004.

23.   Chowdhury AMR, Chowdhury S, Islam MN, Islam A, Vaughan JP. Control of tuberculosis by community health workers in Bangladesh. *Lancet* 1997; 350(9072):169-72.

24.   Islam MA, Wakai S, Ishikawa N, Chowdhury AM, Vaughan JP. Cost-effectiveness of community health workers in tuberculosis control in Bangladesh. *Bulletin of the World Health Organization* 2002;80:445–50.

25.   Brownstein JN, Bone LR, Dennison CR, Hill MN, Kim MT, Levine DM. Community health workers as interventionists in the prevention and control of heart disease and stroke. *American Journal of Preventive Medicine* 2005; 29: 128-33.

26.   Kim S, Koniak-Griffin D, Flaskerud JH, Guarnero PA. The impact of lay health advisors on cardiovascular health promotion: using a community-based participatory approach. *Journal of Cardiovascular Nursing* 2004; 19(3):192-9.

27.   Jafar TH, Levey A, Jafary F, et al. Ethnic subgroup differences in hypertension in Pakistan. *Journal of Hypertension* 2003;21: 905-12.

28.   Hunter JB, de Zapien JG, Papenfuss M, Fernandez ML, Meister J, Giuliano AR. The impact of a promotora on increasing routine chronic disease prevention among women aged 40 and older at the US-Mexico border. *Health Education & Behavior* 2004; 31:18 -28.

29. Earp JAL, Viadro CI, Vincus AA, et al. Lay health advisors: a strategy for getting the word out about breast cancer. *Health Education & Behavior* 1997; 24(4):432-49.

30. Lehmann U, Van Damme W, Barten F, et al., 2009.

31. World Health Organization. Treat, Train, Retain The AIDS and health workforce plan. Report on the Consultation on AIDS and Human Resources for Health Geneva, Switzerland: World Health Organization. 2006:1-80.

32. Samb B, Desai N, Nishtar S, et al. Prevention and management of chronic disease: a litmus test for health-systems strengthening in low -income and middle -income countries. *Lancet* 2010; 376(9754):1785-97.

33. Mullan F, Frehywot S. Non-physician clinicians in 47 sub-Saharan African countries. *Lancet* 2008; 370(9605):2158-63.

34. Hongoro C, McPake B, 2004.

35. Humphreys C, Wright J, Walley J, et al. Nurse led, primary care based antiretroviral treatment versus hospital care: a controlled prospective study in Swaziland. *BMC Health Services Research* 2010; 10(1):229.

36. Cumbi A, Pereira C, Malalane R, et al. Major surgery delegation to mid-level health practitioners in Mozambique: health professionals' perceptions. *Human Resources for Health* 2007; 5(1):1-9.

37. Chilopora G, Pereira C, Kamwendo F, Chimbiri A, Malunga E, Bergstrom S. Postoperative outcome of caesarean sections and other major emergency obstetric surgery by clinical officers and medical officers in Malawi. *Human Resources for Health* 2007; 5(17): doi: 10.1186/1478-4491-5-17 .

38. Richard F, Witter S, De Brouwere V. Innovative approaches to reducing financial barriers to obstetric care in low -income countries. *American Journal of Public Health* 2010; 100(10):1845-52.

39. Dovlo D. Using mid-level cadres as substitutes for internationally mobile health professionals in Africa. A desk review. *Human Resources for Health* 2004; 2(1):1-12.

40. Samb B, Desai N, Nishtar S, et al., 2010.

41. Brennan TA, Gawande A, Thomas E, Studdert D. Accidental deaths, saved lives, and improved quality. *New England Journal of Medicine* 2005; 353(13):1405-09.

42. Conley DM, Singer SJ, Edmondson L, Berry WR, Gawande A. Effective Surgical Safety Checklist Implementation. *Journal of the American College of Surgeons* 2011;212(5):873-9.

43. Haynes AB, Weiser TG, Berry WR, et al. A surgical safety checklist to reduce morbidity and mortality in a global population. *New England Journal of Medicine* 2009;360(5):491-9.

44. Weiser TG, Haynes AB, Lashoher A, et al. Perspectives in quality: designing the WHO Surgical Safety Checklist. *International Journal for Quality in Health Care* 2010;22(5):365-70.

45. Cartilla Nacional de Salud. Mujer de 20 a 59 años. Gobierno Federal. México, 2008.

46. Definition if needed: Witmer, in Hunter et al: community members who work almost exclusively in community settings and who serve as connectors between health care consumers and providers to promote health among groups that have traditionally lacked access to adequate care.

47. Lewin S, Munabi-Babigumira S, Glenton C, et al. Lay health workers in primary and community health care for maternal and child health and the management of infectious diseases. *The Cochrane Collaboration* 2010; 3:1-209.

48. Laurant M, Reeves D, Hermens R, Braspenning J, Grol R, Sibbald B. Substitution of doctors by nurses in primary care (Review). *Cochrane Database of Systematic Reviews* 2009; 1-39.

49. World Health Organization, UNICEF. Management of sick children by community health workers: intervention models and programme examples. World Health Organization. 2006. http://whqlibdoc.who.int/publications/2006/9789280639858_eng.pdf (accessed October 4, 2011).

50. Haines A, Sanders D, Lehmann U, et al. Achieving child survival goals: potential contribution of community health workers. *Lancet* 2007; 369(9579): 2121-31.

51. World Health Organization, Global Health Workforce Alliance. Scaling up, Saving Lives. World Health Organization. 2008. http://www.who.int/workforcealliance/knowledge/resources/scalingup/en/index.html (accessed October 4, 2011).

52. Callaghan M, Ford N, Schenider H, 2010.

53. Doherty TM, Coetzee M. Community health workers and professional nurses: defining the roles and understanding the relationships. *Public Health Nursing* 2005; 22: 360-5.

54. Berman P, Gwatkin D, Burger S. Community -based health workers: Head start of false start towards health for all? *Social Science and Medicine* 1987; 25(5):443-59.

55. Bhutta Z, Lassi Z, Pariyo G, Huicho L. Global experience of community health workers for delivery of health related Millennium Development Goals: a systematic review, country case studies, and recommendations for integration into national health systems. Geneva, Switzerland: Global Health Workforce Alliance, 2010.

56. Ahmed SM. Taking healthcare where the community is: the story of the Shasthya Sebikas of BRAC in Bangladesh. *BRAC University Journal* 2008; V: 29-45.

57. Frenk J, Chen L, Bhutta ZA, et al., 2010.

58. World Health Organization, Global Health Workforce Alliance. Scaling up, Saving Lives. World Health Organization. 2008. http://www.who.int/workforcealliance/knowledge/resources/scalingup/en/index.html (accessed October 4, 2011).

59. Lewin S, Munabi-Babigumira S, Glenton C, et al., 2010.

60. World Health Organization, UNICEF. Management of sick children by community health workers: intervention models and programme examples. World Health Organization. 2006. http://whqlibdoc.who.int/publications/2006/9789280639858_eng.pdf (accessed October 4, 2011).

61. Bashshur RL, Shannon GW. National Telemedicine Initiatives: Essential to Healthcare Reform. *Telemedicine and e-Health* 2009; 15(6): 600-10.

62. Bashshur R, Shannon G, Krupinski E, Grigsby J. The Taxonomy of Telemedicine. *Telemedicine and e-Health* 2011; 17(6):484-94.

63. Roberts DJ, Wilson ML, Nelson AM et al. The good news about cancer in developing countries – pathology answers the call. *Lancet* 2012; 379(9817): 712.

64. Knaul FM, Shulman LN, Gralow J et al. Improving pathology for better cancer care and control in countries of low and middle income. *Lancet* 2012; 379(9831): 2052.

65. Knaul et al 2012.

66. Harold Varmus. The art and politics of science. New York, NY: WW Norton & Company. 2009.

67. Bashshur RL, Shannon GW. National Telemedicine Initiatives: Essential to Healthcare Reform. *Telemedicine and e-Health* 2009; 15(6):600-10.

68. Maserat E. Information communication technology: new approach for rural cancer improvement. *Asian Pacific Journal of Cancer Prevention* 2008; 9:811-4.

69. Qaddoumi I, Mansour A, Musharbash A, Drake J, Swaidan M, Tihan T, et al. Impact of telemedicine on pediatric neuro-oncology in a developing country: the Jordanian-Canadian experience. *Pediatric Blood and Cancer* 2007; 48(1):39-43.

70. Hazin R, Qaddoumi I. Teleoncology: current and future applications for improving cancer care globally. *Lancet Oncology* 2010;1 1(2):204-10.

71. Ibid.

72. Kvedar J., Heinzelmann Pj., Jacques G. Cancer diagnosis and telemedicine: a case study from Cambodia. *Annals of Oncology* 2006; 17(18 Suppl): viii 37-viii42

73. Carlson J, Lyon E, Walton D, et al. Partners in Pathology: A Collaborative Model to Bring Pathology to Resource Poor Settings. *American Journal of Surgical Pathology.* 2010; 34(1):118-23.

74. Partners in Health. Revolutionary Cancer Care in Rwanda. PIH News, July 18, 2012. http://www.pih.org/news/entry/revolutionary-cancer-care-in-rwanda/ (accessed on August 3, 2012).

75. Robles SC, Ferreccio C, Tsu V, et al. Assessing participation of women in cervical cancer screening program in Peru. Revista Panamerica de Salud Publica 2009: 25(3): 189-95.

76. Sloan FA, Gelband H (Eds.). Cancer control opportunities in low- and middle -income countries. Washington, DC: Institute of Medicine of the National Academies, National Academies Press, 2007.

Chapter 7

ACCESS TO AFFORDABLE MEDICINES, VACCINES, AND HEALTH TECHNOLOGIES

Niranjan Konduri, Jonathan Quick, Julie R. Gralow,
Massoud Samiei, Philip Castle, Ramiro Guerrero

Key messages

- Access to cancer medicines, vaccines, and technologies is unacceptably poor for most people living in low and middle income countries (LMICs). Reasons for this include high cost, inadequate funding, poor availability, and weak support services. The human papillomavirus (HPV) vaccine for cervical cancer is just being introduced in many countries and coverage with hepatitis B vaccine for liver cancer remains below target. Two-thirds of the medicines needed for the ten most common cancers in LMICs are unavailable and/or unaffordable in many of these countries. By one report, just 5% of those afflicted with cancer in Africa receive needed chemotherapy. And as few as 25% of people in LMICs have access to needed radiotherapy.

- **Three vital levers are required to expand access to cancer medicines, vaccines, and health technologies:** expanded domestic and international financial resources, political will, and a health-systems approach. Within this approach, management of medicines, vaccines, and health technologies must link wise selection, vigorous price optimization to ensure sustained response, reliable procurement, assured quality, engagement of key stakeholders, action to address barriers to palliation and pain control, and innovation.

- **The cost of curative or life-extending cancer medicines varies considerably among cancers.** Costs range from less than US$ 300 per patient for cervical cancer, Kaposi sarcoma (the most common AIDS-related cancer) and Burkitt lymphoma (a primarily childhood cancer endemic in Africa) to an average of roughly US$ 5,500 for breast cancer, and over US$ 25,000 per year for lifelong treatment of chronic myelogenous leukemia. The most costly chemotherapy regimens include on-patent agents.

- **Despite the variability in individual treatment costs, increasing global access to cancer treatment is more affordable than many believe.** The annual estimated global cost of unmet needs for medicines for four selected cancers varies from roughly US$ 21 million for cervical cancer to US$ 4.3 billion for breast cancer. That US$ 4.3 billion translates to an estimated US$ 341 million for Latin America and the Caribbean, US$ 550 million for Africa, and just over US$ 1.7 billion for Asia.

- **Nine out of ten cancer medicines most needed for LMICs are off-patent generics,** many of which are available for under US$ 100 per course of treatment, and nearly all are available for under US$ 1,000. Yet world market prices for the same product vary four-fold or more between low and high prices.

- **A wide range of screening, diagnostic, surgical, and radiotherapy capabilities are necessary** for effective detection, care, and treatment of cancer. National and international efforts must be accelerated to develop resource-appropriate strategies, technologies, capacity building, information exchange, standardization, procurement, and other needed support in these areas.

- **Quality assurance and safety monitoring must go hand-in-hand with efforts to increase access to and optimize the price** of novel and generic medicines. Strategies to eliminate or minimize policy, regulatory, and administrative barriers for palliative care are exigent to reduce unnecessary pain and suffering.

- **Multilateral agencies, the international community, and the private sector should expand current efforts to increase access to cancer vaccines,** reduce non-price barriers to palliation and pain control, develop new bioavailable oral chemotherapy, and create "frugal innovations" such as low-cost radiation therapy and other technologies for resource-poor settings.

7.i Challenges in affordable access to cancer medicines, vaccines, and technologies

High cost and poor availability of cancer treatment are significant barriers to access in many LMICs.

High cost and poor availability of cancer treatment are significant barriers to access in many LMICs. In the Philippines, the expenditure for cervical cancer treatment is more than double the average annual income.[1] In Pakistan, which zwith chemotherapy and associated transfusion requirements is US$ 20,000.[2] In Rwanda, with over 75% of the population living on US$ 1.25 a day, the average cost of treating AIDS-related Kaposi's sarcoma is US$ 278.[3] Meeting this need would constitute a significant addition to the budget of any ministry of health. In most LMICs, patient out of pocket payments cover from 50% to 90% of the cost of medicines,[4] including those for chronic conditions.[5] Control of pain and suffering is hampered less by the cost of oral liquid morphine for medical use, which can be less than US$ 3 per week, than by legal and administrative barriers. Despite the Government of Kenya's negotiated cost of 35,000 Kenya shillings ($400) for a week of radiotherapy services at a local private hospital, the cost is too high for most Kenyans relative to their ability to pay.[6]

Cancer medicines remain unaffordable in sub-Saharan Africa,[7,8] India,[9] Latin America,[10] and middle income countries such as Egypt[11] and Morocco.[12] Poor availability of chronic disease medications is pervasive in the public sectors of these countries.[13] The final cost to the patient can be higher if the medicine is subject to import duties and taxes, and if procurement is inefficient. Too often, patients are reduced to receiving substandard or interrupted treatment regimens or to abandoning treatment altogether because of unaffordability and unavailability, which decreases their odds of survival.[14] Given that 5% of cancer patients in Africa receive chemotherapy,[15] even after late diagnosis, complementary health system-related components need to be addressed to ensure availability, accessibility, quality, and rational use, including efforts to provide low cost cancer medicines.

Too often, patients are reduced to receiving substandard or interrupted treatment regimens or abandoning treatment because of unaffordability and unavailability, thereby decreasing the odds of survival.

If we are to meet the 2008 World Cancer Declaration's seventh target to "Improve access to diagnosis, treatment, rehabilitation and palliative care and reduce the global cancer burden by 2020," a number of global initiatives must be put into place swiftly. This chapter discusses several feasible options and addresses key challenges that need to be overcome to ensure widespread access to cancer medicines, vaccines, and health technologies in LMICs.

As discussed in previous chapters, the processes that guarantee accessibility to medicines, vaccines, and technologies for cancer care and control (CCC) can be understood within the framework of the diagonal approach. Improving access to cancer medicines, vaccines, and technologies can help strengthen health systems to support other disease priorities and basic healthcare for populations. Medicines that can be allocated to support specific, vertical programs and interventions in many cases are used to treat or manage the symptoms of more than one disease. Palliative care is a prime example. In the case of cancer, many chemotherapy agents are highly specific to a single disease and radiation therapy is used primarily for cancer. Still, the process of establishing access that includes, for example, a guarantee that a site meets the norms of hygiene and safety to manage both care delivery and waste disposal is part of strengthening health systems overall. Efforts to consolidate purchasing medicines, vaccines, and health technologies strengthen markets and potentially improve conditions for both purchasers and suppliers.[16] Finally, applying frugal innovations and searching for options for public-private mixes in provision can reverberate throughout a health system and improve access to many medicines and services.[17]

Strengthening the core functions of health systems will facilitate better access to medicines, vaccines, and technologies for improved CCC. Improving access to medicines is an important challenge in LMICs that involves all health system functions, including stewardship.[18] Medicines constitute a major source of health expenditure for national government. For families that lack financial protection in health, medicines may need to be paid for out of pocket, which can lead to impoverishment (Chapter 8).[19]

7.ii Systems approach to affordable access to quality pharmaceuticals and health technologies

Widespread availability and use of medicines, vaccines, and health technologies for cancer requires three vital levers: financial resources, political will, and a health systems approach to address the pressing priority of cancer in LMICs. Only with these three levers in place is it possible to achieve steady increases in the availability of essential and affordable quality cancer care and treatment.

Cancer is the most variable and arguably the most complex noncommunicable disease with respect to prevention, early detection, diagnosis, treatment, and palliation. In addition, the cost per patient treated and capital investment along the continuum from early detection to palliation are highly variable. Expanding access to affordable medicines, vaccines, and technologies for cancer will require a pharmaceutical systems approach. Such an approach includes international standard treatment guidelines (STGs); a list of essential medicines, vaccines, and technologies for cancer; medicine price information and price reduction strategies; reliable national, regional, and global procurement mechanisms; effective quality assurance; engagement with manufacturers; and action to address non-price barriers to palliation and pain control (Figure 7.1). This approach, which is based on experience with medicines, vaccines, and health technologies for AIDS, tuberculosis (TB), childhood illness, and other primary care needs, would also apply to all chronic noncommunicable diseases (NCDs).

An integrated systems approach for affordable access to pharmaceuticals and health technologies considers all critical success factors from the current situation of cancer care and control in LMICs to large scale availability of affordable medicines, vaccines, and health technologies.

An integra ted systems approach for affordable access to pharmaceuticals and health technologies considers all critical success factors from the current situation of CCC in LMICs to large-scale availability of affordable medicines, vaccines, and health technologies. Several elements are described elsewhere in this volume, including the core elements of CCC (Chapter 5) and innovative financing mechanisms (Chapter 8), which have an important influence on procurement options.

Figure 7.1

Pharmaceutical Systems Approach

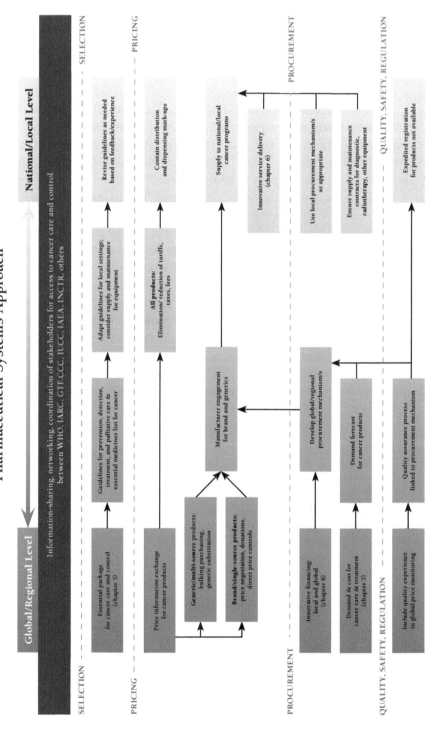

7.iii Medicines and vaccines for CCC

Prevention, early detection, diagnosis, treatment, and palliation depend on a variety of pharmaceutical products and health technologies. Pharmaceutical products for cancer include chemotherapeutic agents, hormones, a wide range of ancillary and palliative care medicines, and, currently, two vaccines. Health technologies for CCC range from simple diagnostics such as pathology services to sophisticated radiation therapy facilities. Informed and sometimes difficult choices must be made concerning what to include and what not to include in emerging national cancer programs. Proceeding with one element when the other crucial components are not in place may result in expensive treatment failures.

TREATMENT GUIDELINES AND ESSENTIAL MEDICINES LISTS FOR CANCER

Several decades of global health experience have demonstrated the value of evidence-based prevention, care, and treatment guidelines developed by the WHO and other recognized international bodies from which national and local guidelines can be adapted. Such STGs and essential medicines lists (EMLs) have become a cornerstone for increasing access, improving use, reducing cost, and increasing quality for medicines and vaccines in public health programs.[20] Especially in low income countries, national stakeholders depend on WHO recommendations to develop treatment strategies or change existing approaches.[21,22] At the same time, developing such guidelines is often an interactive national-to-global, then global-to-national process in which, as in the case of HIV/AIDS treatment, pioneering national or local programs work out individual standard approaches that then inform an international process.[23]

There is growing consensus on the need to develop resource-appropriate treatment strategies for major cancers.

There is growing consensus on the need to develop resource-appropriate treatment strategies for major cancers.[24-26] The Union for International Cancer Control (UICC) called on the international community to "develop a comprehensive global strategy to facilitate cancer drug access worldwide," beginning with WHO's EML for cancer.[27] A number of institutions are actively involved in developing such strategies. A prime example is the Breast Health Global Initiative's comprehensive treatment protocols for settings with various levels of resources,[28] which served as a template for cancers other than breast cancer.[29] Additionally, the National Comprehensive Cancer Network is another example of an institution that has developed a number of de facto clinical practice guidelines for use by healthcare providers and patients.[30]

If essential medicines for cancer are listed in a country's National Essential Medicines List and linked to STGs, selection and procurement become easier and can contribute to lower prices.

If essential medicines for cancer are listed in a country's National EML and linked to STGs, selection and procurement become easier and can contribute to lower prices. For example, antihypertensive medicines were found to be cheaper in the public sector when listed in a national EML.[31] Due to the varying burden and types of cancers, resource-poor countries need to be able to make decisions based on cost-benefit analysis to distinguish between essential cancer medicines for their programs and high-cost medicines for limited use.[32] In addition, chemotherapeutic agents included in WHO's 2011 EML for childhood cancer[33] are not unique to children and are commonly used in the treatment of adult cancer. Therefore, national programs must implement the same policies and procedures used in the procurement of medicines for adult cancer to procure medicines for childhood cancer.

Some countries have used STGs to help decrease costs. For example, STGs in Mexico recommended generic antineoplastic medicines whose quality conforms to international standards at a cost savings of 60%.[34] For acute lymphoblastic leukemia, India's STG lists the most cost-effective medicines in their generic form and institutes low-dose protocols for lung cancer; this has reduced the cost of gemcitabine by 66%.[35,36] However, in most resource-poor settings, evidence-based treatment guidelines are needed for a wide range of cancers. WHO's standardized public health approach for antiretroviral therapy (ART) facilitated rational selection and procurement of antiretrovirals (ARVs) through well known and diverse global, regional, and central mechanisms. Likewise, national STGs for TB and malaria have compelled national authorities to link the standardized treatment with their NEMLs, resulting in progressively lower prices of medicines and health commodities in the last decade. WHO treatment guidelines help shape demand and create incentives for manufacturers to respond to changing market needs as notably seen for HIV/AIDS-related medicines when funding dramatically increased.[37]

In summary, international guidelines for cancer prevention, detection, treatment, and palliative care in LMICs should be developed and the range of cancer agents in the WHO model list of essential medicines and vaccines should be expanded. This effort should be spearheaded by the UICC, International Network for Cancer Treatment and Research, American Society of Clinical Oncology, European Society of Medical Oncology, Sociedad Latinoamericana y del Caribe de Oncología, and others working closely with the WHO.

WHO treatment guidelines help shape demand and create incentives for manufacturers to respond to changing market needs as notably seen for HIV/AIDS-related medicines when funding dramatically increased.

VACCINES FOR CANCER PREVENTION

As prices continue to fall and the number of prequalified manufacturers increases, vaccines such as the human papillomavirus (HPV) vaccine for cervical cancer and the hepatitis B vaccine for liver cancer will be an increasingly important element in comprehensive cancer programs.

Currently, these are the only cancer prevention vaccines available (Table 7.1). Funding support from the Global Alliance for Vaccines and Immunizations (GAVI) provided impetus for low income countries to include hepatitis B as part of their immunization programs, which in turn led five manufacturers to attain WHO prequalification in the last decade (Table 7.1). This, in addition to the dramatic price reduction of hepatitis B vaccine from a 1982 launch price of over US$ 100 to US$ 0.18 a dose, has enabled developing countries to dramatically increase vaccination rates (Figure 7.2).

Table 7.1

Vaccines for Cancer Prevention – Potential Impact, Current Coverage, Financing, Pricing, and WHO prequalification

	Hepatitis B	Human Papillomavirus (HPV)
Cancer prevented	Liver cancer – 749,744 new cases[38] every year, of which roughly 80% are preventable with immunization.[39]	Cervical cancer – 530,232 new cases[38] every year, of which roughly 70% are preventable with immunization.[40]
Coverage	68 % coverage in developing countries.[41]	• 33 countries – national programs; • 20 countries – pilot programs.[42]
Financing	National governments; bilateral donors; GAVI; UN agencies.	National governments; ongoing manufacturer-led donation programs.
Price reduction	• Reduction since launch: 99%. • Launch price (1982): > US$ 100.00/3 doses. • Price when introduced in national immunization programs (1993): US$ 2.00. • Current price (2011): US$ 0.18/dose. • Vaccine cost per full immunization (3 doses): US$ 0.54.	• Reduction since launch: 96%. • Launch price (2006): > $ US$ 120.00/single-dose. • Price when first introduced into US national immunization program (2007): US$ 97.00/dose. • Current price (2011): US$ 5.00/dose (GAVI differential pricing – see text). • Vaccine cost per full immunization (3 doses): US$ 15.00.
WHO prequalification	9 manufacturers from 6 countries for 30 different dosages in vials/ampoules.	2 manufacturers from 2 countries for 2 dosages in vials.
Year of prequalification	1987, 1996, 2001, 2002, 2004, 2006, 2008	2009

Likewise, the differential pricing of US$ 5 per dose of HPV vaccine offered by the originator company to GAVI could avert hundreds of thousands of unnecessary deaths due to cervical cancer that occur mostly in low income countries.[44] Further price reduction of the HPV vaccine to under US$ 2 may double the impact in lives saved. For public health programs in middle income countries that are not eligible for GAVI support, attractive tiered pricing should be offered by manufacturers. The history of immunization over the last half-century, and especially the last two decades, is encouraging. It suggests that price reductions of 80% to more than 90% from initial vaccine launch prices can be expected over time. Current academic partnerships with developing country manufacturers show promise in the provision of quality-assured HPV vaccines at lower cost.[45] HPV vaccines have demonstrated to be highly efficacious, safe, and well tolerated, but there is continuing discussion in the public health and cancer control communities regarding the priority of HPV vaccines in routine vaccination.[46] We recommend an integrated program of HPV vaccination and cervical cancer screening.[47] HPV vaccination prevents new HPV infections, but it does not treat pre-existing HPV infections and related conditions (i.e., pre-cancerous lesions). The median time from HPV infection to the development of invasive cancer is on the order of 25 years.[48] Thus, even if universal HPV vaccination were implemented today, millions of women would remain at risk in the absence of screening and treatment for secondary prevention before the effects of HPV vaccination are fully realized.[49]

The history of immunization over the last half century, and especially the last two decades is encouraging; particularly price reductions of 80% to more than 90% from initial vaccine launch prices can be expected over time.

Figure 7.2

Global Price Changes in Monovalent Hepatitis B Vaccine (1993-2005)

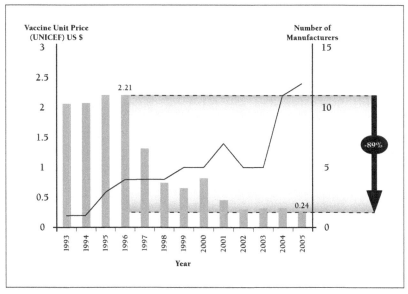

Source: Cunningham G. Public market response to public health needs. Presentation at the International Vaccine Technology Workshop hosted by the World Health Organization (WHO) and the U.S. Department of Health, and Human Services (HHS). Hyderabad, India; Sep 18, 2010. http://www.globalhealth.gov/global-healthtopics/communicable-diseases/influenza/vaccine-workshops/september2010/20100918.html (accessed Feb 1, 2012) based on UNICEF Supply Division; GAVI Annual Report 2008; team analysis.

7.iv Health technologies for cancer detection, diagnosis, and treatment

The core elements for provision of CCC in LMICs outlined in Chapter 5 include a wide range of essential health technologies, from biopsy devices to radiotherapy machines to surgical equipment. Previous research suggests that histopathology, conventional radiology, ultrasonography, and basic endoscopy are the minimum health technologies for cancer management programs.[50]

A lack of histopathology is a key barrier in much the same way that culturing multidrug-resistant TB has been. International cooperation in providing access, perhaps through telemedicine techniques, may become imperative. Despite low income countries having poor diagnostic capacity for cancer, initiatives by international cancer community members demonstrates that it is possible to build capacity for diagnosis in low resource settings. The Breast Health Global Initiative identified several components that, at a minimum, require investments for pathology services to be effectively used for correct diagnosis and cancer staging.[51] Partners in Health demonstrated a collaborative model for implementing pathology services in challenging situations and building local capacity where possible.[52] In Central America, a regional flow cytometry for diagnosis of acute leukemia was established by connecting the equipment to the cytometry laboratory at St. Jude Children's Research Hospital in the United States, where all the cases were reviewed. This provided quality control while increasing capacity and improving training at the same time.[53]

Despite low income countries having poor diagnostic capacity for cancer, initiatives by international cancer community members demonstrates that it is possible to build capacity for diagnosis in low resource settings.

Recent advances in low-cost cervical cancer screening methods, such as visual inspection with acetic acid and promising lower-cost molecular tests for HPV, as an alternative to conventional screening methods demonstrate that developing feasible interventions for resource-limited settings is possible with the right partnerships. Ongoing efforts by WHO's Global Initiative for Emergency and Essential Surgical Care are addressing needs for CCC programs by making available guidelines and training materials. This effort must be augmented through surgical capacity building and mobilization to increase sharing of expertise and experience in well-resourced institutions in LMICs. Given the challenges that limit the scale-up of laboratory services in the clinical management of HIV/AIDS, TB, and malaria, the Maputo Declaration (2008) called for a comprehensive strategy to strengthen laboratory systems with the vision of a unified system to support diseases of public health importance.[54] This mandate presents an excellent opportunity to develop appropriate strategies to strengthen laboratory support systems for cancer detection, diagnosis, and treatment. The establishment of the African Society for Laboratory Medicine (ASLM) and launch of the *African Journal of Laboratory Medicine* are encouraging developments.[55,56] The international cancer community must build on the momentum established by key stakeholder groups to strengthen laboratory systems across a spectrum of cancers.[57]

ACCESS TO RADIOTHERAPY SERVICES

Because of the late stage of presentation of cancer in many low income countries, there is an urgent need to expand access to affordable radiotherapy machines and services. The International Atomic Energy Agency (IAEA) has taken the lead to expand access to radiotherapy services which have led to a 30% increase in the number of machines in the last 10 years.[58] However, such machines are not readily available in many LMICs, in addition to the paucity of qualified personnel to operate them.[59] Despite being home to 85% of the world's population, LMICs only maintain approximately 40% of the world's radiotherapy facilities, leaving only about 25% of cancer patients in LMICs with access to radiotherapy treatment.[60]

This inequity goes even further when comparing the availability of radiotherapy services across regions. This can been be shown by the fact that Europe maintains 17 times as many radiotherapy units as are available in Africa, or that Latin America and the Caribbean contain just one-third of the number of machines available in North America (Figure 7.3).[61] One example of low availability of radiotherapy is in Uganda, where only one radiotherapy service is available to treat the country's annual 30,000 cancer case burden. To service a fraction of these patients in need of radiotherapy, this single machine would need to treat at least 15,000 people a year, a number that is 30 times the annual number of patients a radiotherapy unit can handle.[62] The over-reliance on just one unit can also cause prolonged wait times for receiving treatment and affect the timing between the administration of radiation doses, which can seriously compromise clinical outcomes and treatment effectiveness.[63] The lack of available radiotherapy

Figure 7.3

Access to Radiotherapy

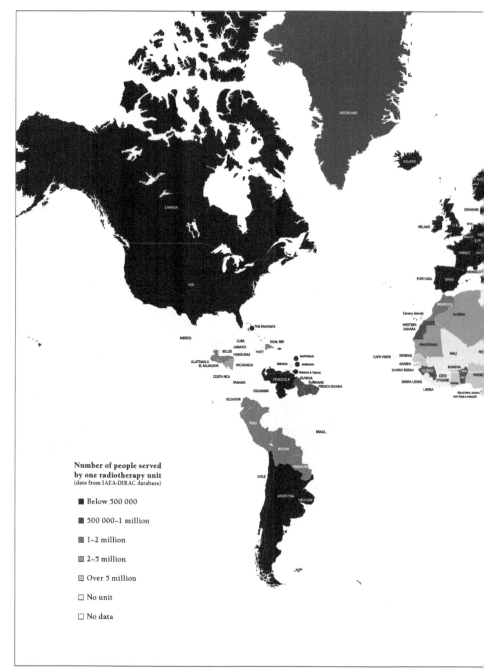

Number of people served by one radiotherapy unit
(data from IAEA-DIRAC database)

- ■ Below 500 000
- ■ 500 000–1 million
- ■ 1–2 million
- ▨ 2–5 million
- ▨ Over 5 million
- ☐ No unit
- ☐ No data

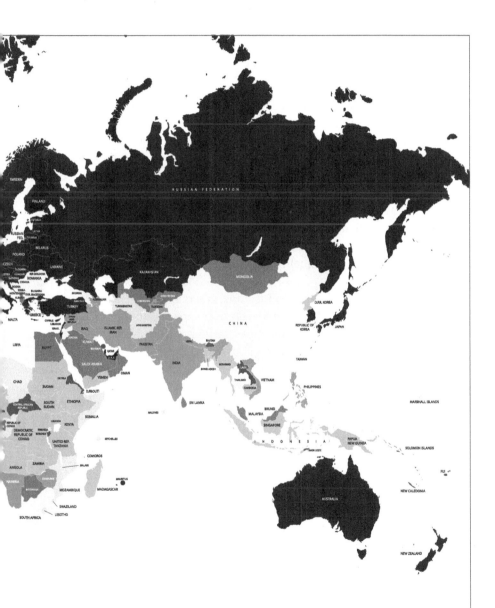

Radiotherapy programmes offered by the IAEA are an essential part of the treatment of cancer.
There is a shortfall of over 5000 radiotherapymachines in developing countries.
IAEA's PACT builds partnerships to fight the global cancer epidemic.

greatly reduces the number of patients that can actually receive treatment, and makes receiving treatment an unattainable option for many cancer patients in Uganda. The situation is not much better in most African countries. Only Egypt, with 85% coverage of cancer patients needing radiotherapy, Libya with over 100% coverage, Morocco with 89% coverage, and South Africa with 100% coverage have acceptable situations[1] - Libya also has adequate number of machines, as can be seen in Figure 7.3. However, not all the machines available are utilized due to a shortage of cancer professionals.

When governments bear a portion of cancer treatment costs, that burden is directly based on procuring and maintaining radiotherapy equipment, maintaining facilities, and paying staff. With some radiotherapy packages selling for as much as US$ 4 million, and with building costs for a radiotherapy treatment room ranging from US$ 40,000 to US$ 1 million, many countries are deterred by the capital costs associated with starting a national radiotherapy service.[64] In addition to these initial costs are auxiliary costs for source replacement (for Co-60 units) and quality assurance that are required over time. Yet, despite these expenses, the administration of radiotherapy, when evaluated per fraction throughout the lifetime of a machine, is actually a relatively economical procedure. Even after factoring in all levels of cost related to the procurement, maintenance, and operation of a machine, estimates from 2004 place the cost per fraction for a cobalt machine at a median of US$ 4.87 and for linear accelerators at a median of US$ 11.02, which, compared to chemotherapy costs that can reach over US$ 600 per treatment, are comparatively inexpensive.[65]

Cost is not the only challenge to establishing a radiotherapy service, particularly in the selection and procurement of equipment. For LMICs, the radiotherapy manufacturer from which the government is purchasing a unit is generally located far from the purchasing country, most commonly in Europe or North America. Besides the additional transportation costs associated with this, other issues arise in terms of unit maintenance, particularly the length and extent of a unit's warranty. If a unit's warranty is not sufficient, countries that are already operating with limited resources could be confronted with the issues of replacing the radioactive source inside of the unit or needing to bring in maintenance workers from Europe or North America, at high cost, to repair a broken unit. Often, if the warranty has expired or does not cover the costs, a cancer center may be forced to leave a machine non-operational due to insufficient funds to support maintenance and upkeep or source replacement. Due to the technology present in cobalt units (radioactive materials), transport is complicated and costly. Often special authorization and licensing is required from other countries in transit, unless the supplier is able to use international routes and direct transport means.[66]

Albania's radiotherapy program is an example of the difficulties that can arise from insufficient maintenance support. Having purchased one of their radiotherapy units from a North American manufacturer, the country cannot afford the manufacturer's annual maintenance program, which would be the equivalent of US$ 110,000 annually or US$ 2.2 million over the course of a cobalt machine's 20-year average life-span.[67] Unfortunately, one of the country's three machines now requires a source replacement, which, priced at US$ 150,000, may take some time to acquire, leaving Albania's nearly 8,000 cancer patients to receive treatment on only two machines.[67] To overcome problems of maintenance and support, all acquired equipment must come with a maintenance contract with a company located close to where the radiotherapy unit will be housed. For areas that do not have immediate access to a radiotherapy producer, local staff should be trained to maintain a radiotherapy unit, which would help to drive down the costs associated with long-distance travel between a user and a producer.

In recognition of the reality that radiotherapy resources are negligible in some areas and non-existent in others, the IAEA's Program of Action for Cancer Therapy (PACT) embarked on a new approach to help LMICs acquire radiotherapy capabilities through an initiative called the Advisory Group on increasing access to Radiotherapy Technology (AGaRT) in LMICs. Deemed "frugal innovation" by some, AGaRT was first conceptualized in 2009 as a way to bring together radiotherapy manufacturers, regional experts, and international organizations from around the world to find affordable, suitable, and sustainable solutions to address the shortage of radiotherapy machines in LMICs. To support the long-term sustainability of radiotherapy units, the IAEA's AGaRT encourages the provisions for "whole of life" support packages from radiotherapy suppliers that will ensure affordable functionality for the entire life cycle of a unit. This will include evolution in the contracting of radiotherapy units, the repatriation and re-supply of radioactive sources, the development of regional expertise for radiotherapy unit repairs in low-resource settings, and financial planning that might make the initial procurement of equipment more expensive, but that has the potential to reduce aggregate costs over time.

Viral load and CD4 count, machines for monitoring HIV treatment were once unavailable in resource-poor settings, but are now accessible despite numerous obstacles, such as weak infrastructure and limited human capacity. With the availability of unprecedented international funding sources, systems and procedures are gradually being built to support clinical decision-making and to improve patient care for HIV/AIDS.[68,69] Even so, development of appropriate infrastructure and human resources to provide radiotherapy is costly and will take time in many low income countries. The IAEA's AGaRT approach of encouraging manufacturers to simplify the design of machines along with a guaranteed market leading to competitive prices shows much promise.

The IAEA's AGaRT approach of encouraging manufacturers to simplify the design of machines along with a guaranteed market leading to competitive prices shows much promise

ACCESS TO PATHOLOGY SERVICES

Pathology plays a necessary role in clinical objective decision-making in most of modern medicine and healthcare delivery, and is critical to cancer prevention, control, and care efforts. A profound shortage of pathology services exists in most LMICs because of an equally profound lack of trained personnel, facilities, and equipment and supplies. Short-term solutions to address immediate needs and long-terms solutions to create self-sustainable programs are required.

SHORT-TERM SOLUTIONS

The pathology laboratory. The physical laboratory space and equipment, often inadequate and/or in disrepair, must be a top priority, "No glass, no diagnosis." Assuming an adequate laboratory space is available, the basic pathology equipment, which include grossing station with sink and ventilation, tissue processor, embedding unit, microtome and water bath, drying oven, stainer, coverslipper, clinical grade microscopes, transcription and reporting system plus immunostainer, special histochemical stainer, miscellaneous refrigerator freezers, instruments, and furniture, costs approximately US$ 500,000. Annual laboratory expenses, including supplies and maintenance, may be another US$ 100,000 for start-up and another US$ 50,000 per annum, depending on what diagnostics are offered (i.e., antibodies for immunohistochemistry add significantly to reagent costs). Supply chain for laboratory reagents and equipment maintenance must be available. Novel strategies such as microfinance to establish supply and maintenance companies might be employed to address any gaps.

Histotechnologists. To complement the development of a functional laboratory, histotechnologists and laboratory technicians must be trained to gross, process, and prepare tissues. In the United States, histotechnologist training programs typically take 1-2 years to complete. As histotechnology is art as well as science, a practicum is necessary to complete the training. Ideally, technical schools providing a histotechnologist curriculum would utilize the same equipment for tissue handling, processing, and preparation in training as used in the pathology laboratory to make the skills completely transferrable. To address immediate needs, focused, intensive trainings of available laboratory or medical personnel on basic specimen handling and preparation might be used while waiting for fully trained histotechnologists to be trained.

Telepathology. Telepathology can be used effectively as a stopgap for LMICs that lack pathology services.[70,71] Telepathology can be used for education (virtual libraries), consultation, and, with proper legal protection (indemnification), primary diagnosis. Primary diagnosis requires the exchange of much larger data files because the whole slide must be captured digitally, which means a T-1 fiber-optic connection must be used. If a T-1 connection is not available, satellite linkage must be used, and this costs approximately US$ 250,000 in the first year, which includes equipment, satellite uplink, and information management system including a virtual microscopy to permit the remote evaluation. Annual costs for maintaining a satellite uplink, once it is established, are approximately US$ 100,000 although costs continue to decline.

Volunteer pathologists. Volunteer pathologists have been an effective resource for providing short-term in-country focused trainings, consultative services, and primary diagnosis. For example, Pathologists Overseas, a 501c3 organization of volunteer pathologists, has been providing these types of services for 20 years.[72] Loan repayment programs for young, board-certified pathologists to do volunteer in-country service for a year or two in exchange for forgiveness of medical school debts could be used to increase the number of volunteers.

Fine needle aspiration cytology. (FNAC). Fine needle aspiration (FNA), the technique of drawing a sample of cells from externally visible or palpable lumps using a simple hypodermic needle and syringe, can be used to create cytology slides (FNAC) that can potentially serve as substitute diagnostic material for a standard biopsy. Ultrasound, when available, can be used to help guide FNA as needed. FNA/FNAC can be used in a wide-range of applications, including the diagnosis of neoplastic (e.g., breast, thyroid, and lymph node tumors) versus non-neoplastic (e.g., infections causing tumor-like benign lesions) disease.[73]

Combined with different stains, FNA/FNAC can be used to diagnose the infectious agent, to determine the origins of a tumor that has metastasized for prognosis (e.g., breast cancer), and in clinical decision-making for targeted therapy (e.g., Herceptin for HER2+ breast cancer)[73] demonstrated the diagnostic utility of FNAC in LMICs. Because community health workers might possibly be trained to perform FNA, prepare the slide, stain the slides, and perhaps even render preliminary diagnoses, diagnostic services could be expanded to cover more remote regions for earlier detection (downstaging) of tumors, even if these methods are not as accurate as the current but unavailable state-of-the-art methods, such as mammography. A number of reports have confirmed the diagnostic utility of FNAC in LMICs.[74-79]

LONG-TERM SOLUTIONS

There is only one long-term viable and sustainable solution for overcoming the gaps in pathology personnel-development of in-country education and training programs in the major teaching hospitals in LMICs. The teaching faculty would at first be composed mostly of volunteer, foreign pathologists until a critical mass of in-country pathologists has been trained.

Sustainability remains a major challenge to providing pathology services in the absence of infrastructure and demand, which are needed to retain pathologists in country. One of the main concerns regarding the development of a pathology program in LMICs is "brain drain,"[80] the exodus of trained in-country pathologists because of greater financial opportunities in private practice or in better positions in other countries. Without commitments from hospitals, universities, and/or ministries of health to provide competitive salaries and support to pathologist, no incentive exists for pathologists to stay. As noted by Fleming et al. from the Royal College of Pathologists, "Establishment of a durable culture of laboratory medicine cannot happen without a stable national infrastructure and political will to establish and fund it."[81]

7.v Pricing, procurement, quality, and regulation

Ensuring affordable access to quality cancer medicines, vaccines, and health technologies depends not only on wise selection, but also on price reduction and procurement strategies appropriate to each type of product. As noted in Chapter 8, innovative approaches to reliable financing are especially important for achieving the best long-term availability and prices for medicines. This includes optimizing the use of both push and pull mechanisms.[82]

PRICE REDUCTION STRATEGIES FOR CANCER MEDICINES AND VACCINES

The final price paid for a specific medicine or vaccine by government health services, nongovernmental organizations, private healthcare providers, or individual patients varies widely from country to country and from source to source within countries. Price differences of two- to five-fold or more are not uncommon. At the same time, dramatic price reductions are possible through such measures as informed public policy, regulation, efficient procurement systems, advocacy, competition, and corporate social responsibility. Therefore, achieving the best prices requires a multi-strategy approach.[83]

Transparent information on prices and sources of essential cancer medicines is vital for price reduction, program planning, forecasting, procurement management, and supply system performance monitoring. Transparency in price information for ARVs through initiatives by Médecins Sans Frontières and WHO's Global Price Reporting Mechanism contributed to informed purchasing decisions for HIV/AIDS programs. Likewise, the Global Fund to Fight AIDS, Tuberculosis and Malaria (Global Fund) requires that principal recipients submit prices paid for a range of procured medicines for HIV/AIDS, TB, and malaria which are then publicly posted through its Price and Quality Reporting System with country and region specific analyses. The WHO's Western Pacific Region has made available actual procurement prices of essential medicines from 19 participating countries.[84] The 2010 World Health Report states that if countries want to eliminate inefficient spending on medicines, data from international reference prices such as the Management Sciences for Health's (MSH) International Drug Price Indicator Guide, help procurement officers in negotiations.[85]

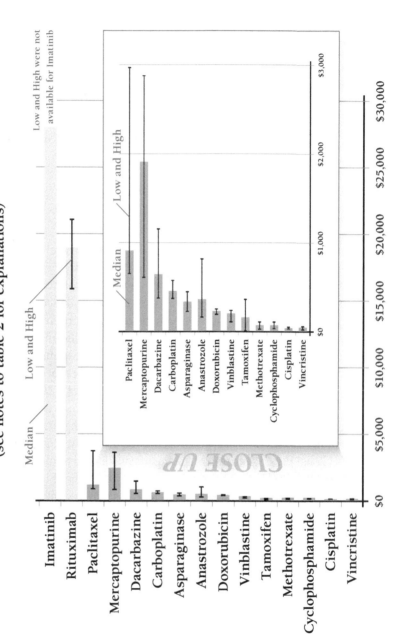

Figure 7.4

Median (bar), Low and High (bracket) World Market Institutional Purchase Prices for Selecting Essential Medicines for Cancer in Low and Middle Income Countries (see notes to table 2 for explanations)

Table 7.2

Indicative Chemotherapy and Hormone Therapy Costs for Selected Essential Medicines for Cancer in Low and Middle Income Countries[86]

Agent*	Patent Status	WHO EML (2011)		Indicative cost per treatment (US$)**			High/Low ratio
		Adult	Children	Low	Median	High	
Anastrozole	x			$172	$368	$824	4.8
Asparaginase	x	√	√	$233	$344	$455	2.0
Carboplatin	x	√		$380	$470	$581	1.5
Cisplatin	x			$38	$49	$60	1.6
Cyclophosphamide	x	√	√	$44	$81	$119	2.7
Dacarbazine	x	√		$382	$653	$1,159	3.0
Doxorubicin	x	√	√	$199	$238	$264	1.3
Imatinib***	On				$28,300		
Mercaptopurine	x	√	√	$614	$1,917	$2,877	4.7
Methotrexate	x	√	√	$37	$78	$116	3.1
Paclitaxel	x	√		$658	$914	$2,968	4.5
Rituximab****	On			$16,031	$18,609	$21,186	1.3
Tamoxifen	x	√		$16	$164	$372	22.7
Vinblastine	x	√	√	$114	$212	$247	2.2
Vincristine	x	√	√	$26	$56	$65	2.5

   * Estimated costs for anastrozole, imatinib and tamoxifen is per year; costs can vary depending on length of treatment course; each chemotherapeutic agent.

  ** Cancer Medicine Prices in low and middle-income countries. Management Sciences for Health, Harvard Global Equity Initiative, Global Task Force on Expanded Access to Cancer Care and Control in Developing Countries, and LIVESTRONG (2011). (http://www.msh.org/resource-center/publications/upload/2011-10-29-cancer-medicine-prices.pdf). Treatment regimen calculations by David Shulman and Gene Bukhman, Partners in Health.

  *** Sold by Novartis as Gleevec or Glivec.

  **** Monoclonal antibody sold under trade names including Rituxan and MabThera. Currently co-marketed by Biogen Idec and Genentech in the US; by Roche in Canada (under the trade name Rituximab) and the European Union; by Chugai Pharmaceuticals and Zenyaku Kogyo in Japan; and by Dr. Reddy's Laboratories from India.

Access to competitive prices for vaccines remains a challenge for countries graduating from GAVI support, as well as other LMICs. In response, WHO launched the Vaccine Product, Price and Procurement Project (V3P) to increase the availability of key data and information, particularly to assist countries in making informed and evidence-based decisions on sustainable vaccine introduction.[87]

Transparent information on prices and sources of essential cancer medi-
cines is vital for price reduction, program planning, forecasting, pro-
curement management, and supply system performance monitoring.

Global and regional medicine pricing surveys have been conducted for other chronic diseases, including palliative cancer care, but no comprehensive surveys have been performed for cancer.[88,89] Using available world market prices and illustrative treatment regimens described in Chapter 5 for treatable cancers common in LMICs, indicative chemotherapy and hormone therapy costs were estimated for 15 selected essential medicines (Figure 7.4, Table 7.2).

This analysis shows a more than four-fold difference between the lowest and highest prices for 4 of the 15 products, and a more than ten-fold difference for one product. It also shows tremendous variation in the per treatment costs for medicines alone, ranging from less than US$ 100 for cyclophosphamide, used to treat Burkitt lymphoma, to more than US$ 28,000 for imatinib, used in chronic myelogenous leukemia. Such variations are associated with differences in price information, supply source, purchase volume, patent status, timing of patent expiration, among other factors. Unfortunately, such variations in the price of medicines for chronic diseases, including palliative cancer care, are not uncommon.[87,88]

The actual final cost to the patient will be great when higher distribution margins, dispensing fees, import duties and taxes, and common supply system inefficiencies are considered. Therefore, national governments must do their utmost to reduce or eliminate substantial taxes, tariffs, and customs duties on imported cancer medicines. The WHO Commission on Intellectual Property Rights, Innovation and Public Health recommended that countries wanting to improve affordability of medicines should eliminate such costs.[90] Even if a policy on tariff elimination or reduction is in place, policy implementation must be monitored to ensure seamless access. Despite elimination of an import tax (12%) and a general sales tax (19%) for a range of cancer medicines by the Government of Peru, the savings were not passed on to consumers because of poor monitoring of their policy's implementation.[91] Finally, reliable demand estimates for essential cancer medicines are needed to guide procurement operations and facilitate pooled procurement, prepare manufacturers to meet demand, and inform policy makers. Despite system-wide constraints, it is possible to estimate demand in a dynamic marketplace with progressive improvement in data quality.

STRATEGIES FOR GENERIC/MULTISOURCE PRODUCTS

Competition among qualified suppliers is the single most effective mechanism to achieve the lowest price for generic/multisource medicines and vaccines.[93,94] For the public sector, nongovernmental organizations, and private institutions the most effective way to tap the full power of generic competition is through one of the procurement mechanisms described later in this chapter, with careful attention to selection of generic medicine suppliers whose products meet national and international quality standards and who also have an established record of reliable, timely delivery.

Figure 7.5

Reducing the Price of AIDS Treatment by 99% Through a "Leap Frog of Differential Pricing and Competition"

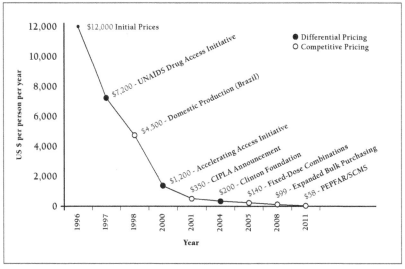

Source: Data Sources: For years 1996, 1998, 2004, 2008, 2011 – Quick J and Konduri N. For years 1997, 2000, 2001, 2005 Schwartländer B, Grubb I, Perriëns J. The 10-year struggle to provide antiretroviral treatment to people with HIV in the developing world. Lancet 2006; 368:541-6.

The power of generic competition and price negotiation was seen in the remarkable decrease in the price of medicines for HIV/AIDS in the early 2000s resulting from a "leap-frog" of negotiation and competition.

In Brazil, generic competition alone has led to an almost 90% reduction for certain cancer medicines.[95] The power of generic competition and price negotiation was seen in the remarkable decrease in the price of medicines for HIV/AIDS in the early 2000s resulting from a "leap-frog" of negotiation and competition. Beginning with a US$ 12,000 per year market price, the annual per person cost of ART was reduced over a four-year period to roughly US$ 7,200 (UNAIDS negotiation), then US$ 4,500 (generic competition in Brazil), then US$ 1,200 (voluntary reduction/negotiation through the Accelerated Access Initiative [AAI]), then US$ 350 (generic competition, initially from India), and finally to US$ 200 (negotiation by the Clinton HIV/AIDS Initiative) (Figure 7.5).[96] Producers of both finished products and active pharmaceutical ingredients (API) in LMICs, such as in China and India, should engage in developing innovative models for using real-time consumption and demand forecast information to ease the shortages of critical off-patent chemotherapeutic agents in the developed world and reduce prices in LMICs.

STRATEGIES FOR ON-PATENT/SINGLE-SOURCE PRODUCTS

Among the on-patent medicines used in the treatments outlined in Chapter 5 are imatinib (Gleevec or Glivec) used in treating chronic myelogenous leukemia and certain other cancers, and two monoclonal antibodies, trastuzumab (Herceptin) for breast cancer and rituximab (Rituxan, MabThera) for lymphomas and leukemias. The cost of such products typically runs in the tens of thousands of dollars per treatment or per year when chronic treatment is required – which is prohibitively expensive for LMICs.

Price reduction for on-patent/single-source products requires active engagement with the research-based pharmaceutical industry.

Price reduction for on-patent/single-source products requires active engagement with the research-based pharmaceutical industry. Effective price reduction strategies include price negotiation, differential pricing by producers, sustained donation programs ("zero price" e.g., ivermectin for river blindness; imatinib for chronic myeloid leukemia),[97] and voluntary and compulsory licensing in line with the flexibilities afforded by the Trade-Related Aspects of

Intellectual Property Rights (TRIPS) Agreement (Table 7.3). Price reduction strategies must be implemented in appropriate territories where feasible, and taking into account impacts elsewhere.

Table 7.3

Price Reduction Strategies for Medicines

Category of medicine	Price reduction strategies and factors
All medicines	• Price information. • Reduced duties, taxes, tariffs, import fees. • Reliable financing.
Generic medicines (off-patent/multi-source) • 26/29 GTF.CCC "essential package" cancer agents. • 30 on WHO essential medicines list (EML)	• Sources and prices information. • Bulk purchasing. • Reliable quality assurance/ prequalification. • Generic substitution legislation.
Brand medicines (on-patent/single source) • 3/29 GTF.CCC "essential package" cancer agents. • None on WHO EML.	• Differential pricing. • Donations. • Voluntary licensing (licensed competition). • Compulsory licensing. • Direct price controls.

Source: Quick J. Medicine pricing: What's happening? And where do we go from here? Presentation at the second Conference on Strategies for Enhancing Access to Medicines, Dar es Salaam, United Republic of Tanzania; December 2003. Available at: http://www.msh.org/seam/conference2003/index.cfm?action=agenda&area=agenda&day=2 (accessed Feb 6, 2012).

Differential pricing was most notably used in the 2001 Accelerating Access Initiative (AAI) created by five research-based pharmaceutical companies. The AAI had an impact on decreasing the price of triple therapy at a time when it was still unaffordable for +LMICs. However, generic competition, a massive increase in financing, and expanding market volume also played important roles in the eventual 99% reduction in prices.[98] Still, there are many challenges yet to be overcome for implementing differential pricing or tiered pricing that were largely confined to ARVs, vaccines, and contraceptives. A critical analysis discovered significant shortcomings associated with differential pricing.[99] The study found that tiered prices are generally higher than those achieved by competition. In many developing countries, resources are stretched so tight that affordability can only be approached by obtaining medicines at or near the cost of production. The United Kingdom-based Industry Government Forum on Access to Medicines made a number of recommendations for donors and industry representatives to work together to (1) prevent physical arbitrage by securing distribution channels; (2) strengthen pro-poor distribution channels by assuring low prices in the public sector and charging higher price in the private sector; (3) explore high-volume, low-margin models: and (4) promote pharmacoeconomic assessment based on local health context and minimize reference pricing.[100]

A clearly defined market for cancer medicines with robust demand will be needed for successful implementation of differential pricing, which happens on a case-by-case basis. Donation programs should follow established guidelines and address local needs. Even then only a limited number of patients may benefit.[101,102]

Voluntary licensing, where originator companies specify terms and conditions, can significantly increase access to life-saving treatments, but it does not necessarily result in affordable prices.[103] One reason is that voluntary licenses are commonly issued on an exclusive basis for individual markets – essentially a licensed monopoly. Multiple licenses are more likely to achieve price-lowering licensed competition. Generic manufacturers that are awarded voluntary licenses face market restrictions, such as high royalty rates and restrictions on sourcing APIs while struggling to achieve economies of scale. The high cost of APIs, which is an estimated 50% of the ex-works price of ARVs, and expensive bioequivalence tests (US$ 50,000) per product to achieve WHO prequalification, creates disincentives for potential manufacturers from low income countries.[104] A South African generic firm was able to successfully take advantage of a voluntary license despite competition from dominant producers because of a favorable national policy climate. To date, voluntary licensing arrangements for cancer medicines have yet to emerge.[105]

Compulsory licensing may be a useful negotiating tool under very specific circumstances, but is likely to achieve substantial price reductions only with a high volume market and multiple licenses to stimulate competition. Although the use of compulsory licenses has been widely advocated by many as a populist measure, only middle income countries, such as Brazil and Thailand have had some success in implementation. The only country to have issued a compulsory license for cancer medicines (docetaxel, erlotinib, imatinib, and letrozole) was Thailand. Developing countries may be reluctant to implement compulsory licenses because they fear political backlash. The situation for generics producers in India became more difficult after the country amended its Patents Act in 2005 to comply with the TRIPS.[106] Experience from Canada (as an exporting nation) and Rwanda (as an importing nation) exposed many shortcomings with TRIPS flexibilities, while the Canadian firm spent four years navigating the process for a one-time shipment of seven million doses.[107-109] Given the "widespread misunderstanding" in the application of compulsory licensing, a number of structural and administrative obstacles need to be overcome when using TRIPS flexibilities as described elsewhere.[110]

Evidence from sub-Saharan African countries makes a strong case for legal and technical expertise to enhance administrative structures and increase political engagement for compulsory licensing to be feasible, including employment of TRIPS flexibilities.[104,111] A country's patent legislation also must be amended and adapted so TRIPS flexibilities can be easily implemented along with robust policy instruments.[112] For example, in the Philippines, the president enacted measures to curb ever-greening of patents by brand-name manufacturers and approved a code for parallel imports of cheaper medicines, which helped provide quick access to cardiovascular medicines.[113] Given India's strong capacity to manufacture pharmaceutical products, a local manufacturer was awarded a compulsory license for sorafenib, prescribed for treating kidney and liver cancer. This manufacturer expects to produce sorafenib locally with a monthly cost of US$ 175, compared to the patent holding manufacturer charging a monthly cost of US$ 5,500, promising eventual access and availability to over 100,000 Indian patients suffering from both forms of the disease.[114] Cancer medicines that are being manufactured under a compulsory license must, however, adhere to internationally accepted quality standards. Otherwise, poor quality products can undermine treatment programs and affect patient outcomes.

Compulsory licensing remains an option to potentially reduce prices and increase access to cancer medicines, provided there is political will and sustained pressure from civil society coupled with the capacity to implement the policy. According to WHO's Director General Dr. Margaret Chan, *"Countries unskilled in trade negotiations fear they will be tricked or duped. Countries seeking to use the flexibilities under TRIPS fear they will be punished by trade sanctions imposed in retaliation. Countries fear that pharmaceutical companies will use unfair tactics, really, every trick in the book, to reduce competition from lower-priced generics."* [115] It is therefore not surprising to find that efforts to issue a compulsory license for a pharmaceutical product have largely occurred in upper middle income countries.[116] The collaboration of the World Trade Organization and the World Intellectual Property Organization with WHO to jointly consider policies for medicines pricing, procurement, and intellectual property from a public health perspective is a positive step.[117,118]

Text Box 7.1
**Working towards affordable pricing for HPV vaccines
for developing countries: The role of GAVI Alliance**

*Aurélia Nguyen, S. Deblina Datta, Nina Schwalbe,
Diane Summers, Geoff Adlide*

In April 2009, WHO recommended that national immunization programs include routine HPV vaccination, with the specific provision that cervical cancer or other HPV-related disease prevention measures should be a public health priority.[119] WHO advised that the vaccine should be part of a comprehensive approach to cervical cancer prevention and control including education, screening, diagnosis, and treatment. Yet, price has remained a major barrier. Merck licensed its HPV vaccine in the US in 2006. The vaccine requires three doses and the private market price was US$ 120 per dose. In 2007, the price available to the US public market was US$ 97 per dose,[120] making it the most expensive publicly funded vaccine at the time. GlaxoSmithKline's (GSK) first license for its three-dose HPV vaccine was obtained in 2007, and prices, initially in line with Merck's, then rapidly decreased. For example, GSK announced in late 2008 a 60% price reduction in the Philippines to approximately US$ 48 per dose.[121] In South Africa, a 36% price decrease brought the price to US$ 44 per dose.[122]

Overall, the reported prices of HPV vaccine varied widely from 2007 to 2011. In industrialized countries prices ranged from US$ 100 to US$ 233 per dose and from US$ 30 to US$ 100 per dose in developing countries and were mainly available to the private sector.[123] Both Merck and GSK obtained WHO pre-qualification in 2009, which opened the door for purchase by UN organizations. The price offered to the Pan American Health Organization (PAHO) Revolving Fund decreased from US$ 32 per dose in January 2010 to US$ 14 per dose in April 2011 for the GSK vaccine.[124] The Merck vaccine was offered to PAHO within the same price range.

Another milestone in vaccine prices was achieved in 2011. In response to a call by GAVI Alliance for Vaccines and Immunisation to accelerate the introduction of new vaccines in developing countries, Merck offered to provide its HPV vaccine at US$ 5 per dose to GAVI-eligible countries.[125,126] Merck's announcement marked the first-ever public offer of a price for HPV vaccines for low income countries.

The work to achieve these results began in October 2008 when the GAVI Alliance Board prioritized support for HPV vaccines. However, due to financial constraints at the time, the GAVI Alliance was not able to provide immediate support. GAVI worked with manufacturers on strategies to lower prices, encouraging them to announce an indicative price for HPV vaccine for GAVI-eligible countries. Such information is needed to help countries decide if the vaccine will be a cost-effective and appropriate public health intervention.

In the short term, GAVI is working with the two existing manufacturers to further increase the affordability of the vaccines. GAVI also has been meeting with new suppliers to explore the possibilities of push-funding mechanisms and procurement strategies, such as advanced purchase agreements and longer term awards for reducing prices. Such strategies would leverage GAVI's ability to pool procurement for volumes over longer time periods, allowing manufacturers to forego some level of margin in exchange for certainty of demand.[127]

In November 2011, the GAVI Alliance Board took the first steps towards the introduction of HPV vaccines in the developing world. Eligible countries with demonstrated ability to successfully deliver HPV vaccines can apply for national introduction support. Countries lacking experience can apply for support to conduct demonstration projects in order to "learn by doing."

The breakthroughs of 2011 —a lowering of vaccine prices and the GAVI Board's decision to support HPV vaccines in eligible countries— constitute major steps towards helping to prevent the deaths of hundreds of thousands of women in LMICs every year and meeting the expressed demand of developing countries for the vaccine as part of their immunization programs.

Procurement options

Successful global, regional, and national procurement organizations –whose establishment requires substantial investments of time, expertise, and money– provide viable options for procurement of cancer medicines, vaccines, and health technologies. The Interagency Pharmaceutical Coordination Group (made up of representatives from WHO, the World Bank, the United Nations Children's Fund (UNICEF), and the United Nations Population Fund) in 1999 issued an "Operational Guidelines for Good Pharmaceutical Procurement," which outlined several strategic objectives: procure the most cost-effective drugs in the right quantities; select reliable suppliers of high-quality products; ensure timely delivery; and achieve the lowest possible total cost.[128]

Competently managed pooled procurement systems generally offer the best opportunity to achieve these objectives for any large-scale health system. Pooled procurement can be effectively implemented and managed at sub-national levels (in large countries with competitive markets) and at national levels (any national health system with centralized contracting mechanisms is effectively operating a pooled procurement system). The key requirements for successfully operating a pooled procurement system are well understood and have been described in the Interagency Guidelines, as well as in publications such as *Managing Drug Supply*.[20]

Lower income countries often do not have sufficient market size or local access to high quality, competitive supply sources, and in many cases, the public health systems lack existing local capacity to implement and sustain an effective in-house pooled procurement system for priority medicines and vaccines. In response, a variety of regional- and global-level pooled procurement mechanisms and a number of nonprofit international procurement agencies were established in the later part of the 20th century, often financed by significant investment from donors and international agencies).

At the global level, there are programs that offer "integrated local to global" procurement and supply chain systems (such as UNICEF and the US Government's Supply Chain Management System) that help participating countries improve their local supply chain systems and play a strong role in forecasting and demand aggregation. In addition, programs such as the Global Fund's Voluntary Pooled Procurement function as a more traditional procurement agent, responding to orders placed by participating countries. Table 7.4 illustrates several prominent global procurement programs currently in operation along with some established international procurement agents serving low income countries.

Table 7.4

Examples of Global, Regional and National Procurement Mechanisms

Mechanisms	Name of Program/Procurement Agent	Products
Donor-supported global procurement agent	Stop TB/Global Drug Facility (GDF) http://www.stoptb.org/gdf/	First-line and second-line TB medicines, diagnostics, and health commodities.
	Global Fund's Voluntary Pooled Procurement Program http://www.theglobalfund.org/enprocurement/vpp/	ARVs, artemisinin-based combination therapies (ACTs), essential medicines, laboratory and other health commodities, insecticide-treated bed nets.
	Asthma Drug Facility http://www.globaladf.org/	Four inhaled asthma medicines.
Global-to-local integrated supply chain	USAID's Supply Chain Management System (Partnership for Supply Chain Management) http://scms.pfscm.org/scms	ARVs, diagnostics, and health commodities.
	UNICEF www.unicef.org/supply/index_procurement_services.html	Essential medicines, vaccines, and health commodities for children.
Nonprofit procurement agencies	Action Medeor, ECHO, IDA Foundation, IMRES, Mission Pharma, Orbipharma, Trimed.	Essential medicines and other health commodities; in some cases health-related equipment.
Regional and National		
Managed by WHO (central contracting model)	PAHO Expanded Program on Immunizations (EPI) Revolving Fund http://www.paho.org/english /hvp/hvi/revol_fund.htm	Vaccines and immunization supplies.
	PAHO Strategic Fund http://new.paho.org/hq/ index.php?option=com_ content&task =blogcategory&id=1159&Itemid=588)	Medicines and Commodities for HIV/AIDS and Malaria, planning to incorporate some anti-cancer medicines.
Self-managed (group purchasing program)	Gulf Cooperation Council	Vaccines, medicines and health commodities.
	African Association of Generic Essential Drugs Purchasing Centers www.acame.org	Essential medicines and health commodities.
	Pharmaceutical Procurement Service – Organization of Eastern Caribbean States http://www.oecs.org/pps	Medicines and health commodities (includes some anti-cancer medicines).

Countries able to procure essential medicines on their own have had substantial success resulting in strengthened national and regional procurement systems. Pooled procurement achieves the best prices and availability when it concentrates purchase volumes, is linked to reliable and prompt payment, provides reasonably accurate forecasting, and maintains a procurement schedule that reduces shipping and storage costs (Text Box 7.1). National, regional, or global pooled procurement influences market dynamics, makes procurement more efficient, and pushes market power towards purchasers rather than suppliers (Text Box 7.2).

National, regional, or global pooled procurement influences market dynamics, makes procurement more efficient, and pushes market power towards purchasers rather than suppliers.

At the local level, a pooled procurement system in Delhi, India, provided a 30% savings to the local government as well as more than 80% availability of essential medicines at health facilities.[129] Using ocean and land transport, instead of air transport, to deliver ARVs contributes to price reductions by saving as much as 85% of freight costs.[130] Successful global and regional pooled procurement is invariably linked to reliable financing. For national supply systems, reliable financing and good governance are arguably the two pivotal determinants of national pharmaceutical system performance.

Although the regional and global level pooled procurement systems (such as the IDA Foundation and Imres) are not currently focused on procurement of cancer-related commodities, it is possible that at least some of these mechanisms could be expanded to address cancer requirements (several nonprofit international procurement agents already offer selected, generically available cancer medications). Building a new procurement and supply organization exclusively for cancer agents, or even more broadly for all non communicable diseases, should be avoided, given the time, expertise, and money required to build a reliable, efficient, and high turnover procurement organization. Instead, the focus must be on working through existing mechanisms and agents such as those listed in Table 7.4.

Text Box 7.2
Partnership and pooled procurement for
a life-saving health technology[131]

Surgery is an essential element of treatment for certain cancers, such as breast cancer, cervical cancer, and head and neck cancer. In sub-Saharan Africa, nearly 70% of operating theaters do not have oxygen monitors (pulse oximeters), which could save thousands of lives through safer surgery and anesthesia. Depending on the type of oximeter and supply source, the typical cost of a model designed for the operating theater is about US$ 2,000-3,000 in developing countries while in the United States, the same equipment can be purchased for US$ 1,000. A partnership of the World Federation of Societies of Anaesthesiologists, Association of Anaesthetists of Great Britain and Ireland, and Harvard School of Public Health established the LifeBox project (www.lifebox.org) as a pooled procurement mechanism for pulse oximeters. The partnership also provided educational materials and helped launch the concept with health professionals. Manufacturers were engaged early on about the potential market in resource-poor settings and the desired characteristics for such devices, which included battery operation, affordability, reliability, durability, and minimal or no maintenance. Subsequently, WHO hosted a consultative meeting with a wide range of stakeholders, including manufacturers, to discuss procurement and distribution options as well as training models for widespread introduction of pulse oximetry. After a competitive tender, one manufacturer was selected to provide oximeters for a low cost of US$ 250, including delivery charges. Hospitals in Ethiopia, Ghana, India, Kenya, Liberia, Uganda, and the Philippines have ordered pulse oximeters and Smile Train has ordered 2,000 devices. The LifeBox experience demonstrates that professional advocacy and early engagement with manufacturers can create a solid market with robust demand for essential health technologies.

QUALITY, SAFETY, AND REGULATION

Measures to assure medicine and vaccine quality and monitor safety must go hand-in-hand with efforts to reduce price.

Measures to assure medicine and vaccine quality and to monitor safety must go hand-in-hand with efforts to reduce price. Medicine quality cannot be sacrificed for the sake of lower prices, given the implications of substandard products for treatment efficacy. The long-term aim would be for all countries to have national regulatory authorities with the capacity to ensure the quality of all medicines coming into or manufactured within the country. Unfortunately, evidence on antibiotics, ARVs, antimalarials, and other essential medicines demonstrates considerable variation in the quality of producers and products in many low income markets.[132]

As one response to this situation, WHO has established a prequalification program for a growing number of products for high burden diseases, including HIV/AIDS, malaria, and TB. As seen earlier in Table 7.1, prequalified manufacturers for hepatitis B and HPV vaccines paved the way for a global marketplace with concomitant support from GAVI for implementation. In a survey of medicine quality for ARVs and antimalarial products sampled at central locations from six African countries, WHO prequalification had a favorable effect as shown by the low failure rate in quality tests.[133,134] Another study on TB medicine quality confirmed that all WHO prequalified and Stop TB Partnership/Global Drug Facility supplied products complied with specifications.[135] The WHO prequalification program, which greatly helped increase access to quality-assured products for high-burden diseases, could therefore be expanded to include essential cancer medicines and agents for palliative care which can help countries procure products from reliable suppliers.

The US Food and Drug Administration's tentative approval process facilitated the widespread use of quality-assured generics in countries supported by the US President's Emergency Plan for AIDS Relief (PEPFAR).[93] The Global Fund has helped to strengthen quality assurance for HIV/AIDS, TB, and malaria products, and public posting of quality test results have helped countries make decisions on the sources of quality-assured medicines.[136] However, for medicines not obtained from vertically funded programs, both substandard and counterfeit products can be risky,[137] which means that strengthened capacity for national governments to monitor and regulate product quality is especially important.[138]

The Global Fund has helped to strengthen quality assurance for AIDS, TB, and malaria products; and public posting of quality test results have helped countries make decisions on the sources of medicines of assured-quality.

While global efforts are being made for the provision of low cost cancer medicines, persistent weaknesses in pharmaceutical management at the country level must be simultaneously addressed with appropriate mechanisms to ensure their safe handling, rational use, and safety monitoring. Research from high income countries documented substantial contamination in drug preparation areas (75%) and drug administration areas (65%) in cancer hospitals.[139] Poor handling of chemotherapeutic agents can be hazardous, especially in low income countries with inadequate infrastructure, policies, and procedures to minimize occupational exposure.[140] In addition, policies and procedures must be in place for safe disposal of expired chemotherapeutic agents and radioactive waste to ensure that these items are appropriately managed and eliminated and to minimize risks of environmental contamination.[141]

NON-PRICE BARRIERS TO PALLIATION AND PAIN CONTROL

No one with cancer should die in pain simply because of where they live. Yet, there is a stunning access gap in morphine consumption, and high income countries with much smaller populations are consuming 90% of the morphine. About 5.5 million terminal cancer patients do not have access to controlled medicines. Strategies to eliminate or minimize policy, regulatory, and administrative barriers for palliative care are exigent to reduce unnecessary pain and suffering. If we are to eliminate this gap, governments must take the lead with national laws and policies that draw on existing international guidelines and best practices to first ensure seamless access to opioid analgesics for those in need.

Each country's formulary list must be revised to contain at minimum the various morphine formulations and codeine that are part of WHO's EML.

The access gap can only be closed through a well-documented, multi-pronged approach.[141] Each country's formulary list must be revised to contain at minimum the various morphine formulations and codeine that are part of WHO's EML.[143] Administrative barriers such as weak forecasting due to poor demand, supply management, insecure storage, and lengthy authorization processes must be addressed to ensure consistent availability and accessibility of opioid analgesics, including mechanisms for decentralization. Efficient forecasting is crucial as international conventions regulated by the International Narcotics Control Board require annual forecasts before these controlled substances can be shipped. Evidence from resource-poor settings shows that this is possible if strong government support is combined with balanced measures to effectively regulate the opioid supply chain.[144]

Innovative financing strategies through existing programs, such as PEPFAR and the Global Fund, and additional funding subsidies will be required. Also, more work must be done to ensure that currently allocated donor funds are fully utilized for increased access to pain relief.[145] Health workers need to be adequately trained in pain management and in the administration of correct and safe dosages. Through increased availability of oral morphine, home-based care can be effectively delivered, thus reducing costs to the family and health system.

The high cost of fentanyl patches (costing 30 times that of modified release forms)[146] needs to be reduced to make this alternative available and to reduce barriers in administration. Local production of morphine, where feasible, can substantially increase access to pain relief as seen in Jordan and Uganda.[147,148] Indeed, effective pain treatment is arguably a human right, and national governments and international organizations must work together to meet their obligation of breaking barriers.[149]

Indeed, effective pain treatment is arguably a human right and governments and international governments must work together to meet their obligation of breaking barriers.

7.vi Treatment affordability and unmet need for cancer medicines

Estimating the total cost of the unmet need for cancer medicines is a key factor in developing a global plan of action for closing the cancer divide. It enables cancer alliances such as the Global Task Force on Expanded Access to Cancer Care and Control in Developing Countries (GTF.CCC), the UICC, the International Network for Cancer Treatment and Research, and others to work with pharmaceutical companies, price information services, current and potential supply organizations, and other stakeholders to develop strategies for increasing access through reduced prices, efficient procurement, and other strategies outlined earlier in this chapter.

Text Box 7.3
Estimating the global unmet need for cancer medicines: Hodgkin lymphoma, cervical cancer, childhood acute lymphoblastic leukemia, and breast cancer

Ramiro Guerrero, Jaime Andrés Giraldo,
Héctor Arreola-Ornelas, Felicia Marie Knaul

Robust estimation of the potential demand and global unmet need for medicines is a necessary first step to plan the financing and overcome the obstacles to developing successful schemes for the pooled procurement and negotiation of prices for cancer medicines and to shape market dynamics. Sound estimates are also essential for developing national cancer plans and programs, and for developing annual health sector budgets, especially for CCC.

Estimates of potential demand and unmet need are highly dependent on good quality national data of current and future needs. In practice, this implies knowing the number of prevalent cases. In addition, it is necessary to estimate the number of incident cases and make projections of how these numbers may evolve over time. For most cancers, the preferred drug regimen depends on a precise diagnosis and, in some

Table 7.5

Estimated Chemotherapy Costs for Selected Cancers in LMICs[*],[**],[***]

Disease	Patient type assumed (a)	Medicines cost per patient (US$) (average) (b)	HIV/AIDS Related (c)	Epidemiological context and role of chemotherapy in treatment
Cervical (average across several stages)	Adult woman	121	Yes	Most common cancer in women worldwide, particularly in developing countries. Cryosurgery is reserved for lesions with no visible evidence of cancer. Areas visible with cancer, should be treated with excision either by loop, cone biopsy or hysterectomy.
Kaposi Sarcoma (bleomycin+ vincristine)	Adult	245	Yes	Most common HIV/AIDS related cancer, endemic in Africa. Chemotherapy offers substantial palliation. Effective chemotherapy depends on concomitant control of HIV infection. This regimen provides effective low-cost treatment for patients with less advanced disease. Retreatment required for recurrences.
Burkitt	Child ~8 y.o.	109		Primarily a childhood cancer, endemic in Africa. Treated with systemic chemotherapy, which can be highly curative early and complete treatment.
Childhood Sarcomas	Child ~12 y.o.	$1,055		Inexpensive chemotherapeutic regimen is available, but without surgery it is not curable.
Hodgkin Lymphoma	Adult	1,328		Mostly occurs in young adults aged 17 to 35 years. Highly curable disease based on systemic therapy. Radiation, if available, is used as adjunct therapy to decrease usage of chemotherapy.
Acute Lymphocytic Leukemia (ALL)	Child ~12 y.o.	2,458		Most common in children. Highly curable with chemotherapy alone.
Kaposi Sarcoma (paclitaxel)	Adult	$2,588	Yes	Most common AIDS related cancer, endemic in Africa. If HIV is not under control then treatment may not be effective. This regimen is reserved for patients with more extensive and life-threatening disease.
Breast Cancer (weighted average across several stages)	Adult woman	$5,466		In many countries the most common women's cancer and worldwide accounts for 1/4 of all cancers in women. Surgical removal of tumor is key. With systemic chemotherapy and hormone, treatment can be curative in early stage and often life-prolong in later stages. Radiation can be important, depending on clinical setting.
Diffuse Large B-Cell Lymphoma	Adult	$18,982		Diffuse large B-cell lymphoma (DLBCL) is the most common form of non-Hodgkin lymphoma in high income countries and one of several common AID-related cancers. DLBCL can advance very quickly and usually requires immediate treatment. A combination of chemotherapies and the monoclonal antibody rituximab can lead to a cure in a large number of cases.
Chronic Myelogenous Leukemia (CML)	Adult	$28,300		Once an incurable disease, CML can now be controlled with imatinib for a longer time. Also affects older people. With oral, continuous life-long therapy, lifespan is extended

* See Body Surface Area Calculations, www.halls.md/body-surface-area/bsa.htm

** Cancer Medicine Prices in low and middle-income countries. Management Sciences for Health, Harvard Global Equity Initiative. Global Task Force on Expanded Access to Cancer Care and Control in Developing Countries, and LIVESTRONG (2011). (http://www.msh.org/resource-center/publications/upload/2011-10-29-cancer-medicine-prices.pdf). Treatment price calculations based on work by David Shulman and Gene Bukhman, Partners in Health.

cases, staging. The latter can be particularly important, as the stage at diagnosis often determines the type and quantity of recommended medications, as well as other treatments and therapies. Early detection usually implies a lesser quantity of medicines and, especially in terms of potential years of life that can be saved, is always the best option.[150]

Estimating potential volumes of demand and unmet need for services and medicines is not a onetime exercise. Rather it should be continuously and regularly updated as new and better sources of information become available, coverage of services expands, and new options for treatment are developed. A background document for this report "Estimation of global potential demand of cancer drugs" proposes basic methods for these estimates.[151]

As a first approximation, the total annual cost of covering chemo- and adjuvant therapy is estimated by multiplying the cost of drug regimens for specific cancers (Table 7.5) by the number of incident cases, based on data from Globocan (2008),[152] for a select group of cancers (Table 7.6A). This provides an estimate of the total cost of treatment for all cases identified in a given year for a specific cancer.

A key quantity for the purposes of improving prices and procurement is the unmet need for cancer services and drugs. Unmet need can be conceived as the incident cases in a given period that are not being treated, multiplied by the quantities of services and drugs that are required to treat these cases. For this report, untreated cases are estimated by subtracting estimates of current coverage from the incidence figures for each country. Current coverage is inferred based on the ratio of mortality to incidence (an approximation of case fatality), as well as taking into account information from medical sources on the survival ratios with and without treatment. Applying a specific level of prices or costs of inputs yields the monetary value of the services that would be required for expanding coverage (Table 7.6B).[153]

The incidence data have several limitations as they are based on projections for many countries where cancer registries are lacking, especially in LMICs (chapter 9). Further, it is not possible to differentiate certain types of cancers. In the case of childhood leukemia, for example, it is not possible to separately identify acute lymphoblastic leukemia cases from other types of leukemia. Hence, for the calculations used to estimate costs, 75% of leukemia in children is assumed to be acute lymphoblastic leukemia. This is a rough assumption, and variance by region and by country is likely.

It is noteworthy that for several cancers, the total cost of covering the chemotherapeutic treatment regimens for all unmet needs, and even for all incident cases, is relatively low. This is largely because most of the medicines are off-patent.

However, these estimates refer only to chemotherapies and do not include diagnostics or other aspects of treatment, such as surgery and radiation therapy. One estimate for the National Institute of Social Security of Mexico showed that in the case of breast cancer, drugs account for about 50% of the overall cost of CCC.[154]

For acute lymphoblastic leukemia for all children 0-14, the total cost of unmet need for chemotherapy for one year of incident cases is US$ 6 million for Africa, US$ 8 million for Latin America and the Caribbean, and US$ 38 million for the LMICs of Asia. The total cost of meeting unmet need in LMICs is US$ 52 million. Further, even the cost of treating all incident cases is just US$ 149 million for all LMICs.

For cervical cancer, the costs of unmet need for medicines are US$ 5 million, US$ 2 million, and US$ 12 million, for Africa, Latin America and the Caribbean, and the LMICs of Asia respectively. For all LMICs, the figure is US$ 20 million and for all incident cases is US$ 48 million. For Hodgkin lymphomas, the total cost of unmet need for LMICS is US$ 35 million, compared to US$ 63 million for all incident cases.

The cost of drugs for treating breast cancer is much higher, largely driven by the effective yet costly drug traztuzumab that is used in a subset of cases (20% of breast cancer cases are assumed to be HER2+ and can benefit from traztuzumab). Further, the doses of drugs used and their costs are also highly sensitive to the stage of diagnosis. These calculations also take into account two scenarios: (1) only 10% of cases are detected in early stages, and (2) 60% of cases are detected in early stages. These scenarios are based on existing data from LMICs and high income countries.[155-157] Without HER2+ treatment and with only 10% of cases detected in early stages, the cost of drugs required to satisfy unmet need for all LMICs is just over US$ 700 million. For incident cases, the cost is estimated to be more than US$ 2 billion. If 60% of cases are *detected early, the figures go down by approximately 40%. With HER2+ treatment, at current prices, the costs increase more than six-fold to US$ 4.5 billion for unmet need and more than US$ 13 billion for all incident cases. Again, early detection saves lives and implies a lower volume of drugs needed and a reduction of approximately 30% in costs. Thus, in the case of breast cancer securing better prices for HER2+ treatment is very important, but promoting early detection is equally important for reducing costs as well as for improving outcomes.*

An analysis of the global economic burden of NCDs diseases suggests wide variation among cancers in the average cost of treatment, ranging from more than US$ 30,000 for some leukemias to less than US$ 1,500 for cervical cancer.[158] The major drivers of treatment costs are chemotherapy, radiation therapy, surgery-related hospitalization, and, in some cancers, high-cost diagnostic procedures. An analysis of breast cancer treatment in Mexico found that the average cost breakdown across all stages was 52% for chemotherapy (86% of which was for medicines), 16% for surgery, and 11% for radiation. For treatment in Nigeria for a very different cancer, Burkitt lymphoma, the cost breakdown was 63% for medicines, 19% for hospitalization, and 12% for laboratory testing. Where radiation is required and available, the reported cost per patient for breast cancer varies widely, from US$ 6,465 in North America to US$ 323 in Africa and US$ 173 in Asia, as do hospitalization and other costs association with surgical treatment.[159]

For the many cancers for which chemotherapy plays the sole or a major role in treatment, it will generally account for the largest share of total treatment costs.

Table 7.6A

Cost of Covering Chemotherapy Therapy for One Year of Incident Cases for Hodgkin Lymphoma, Childhood Acute Lymphoblastic Leukemia, and Cervical and Breast Cancer 2010 Prices (US$ millions)

Region	Hodgkin lymphoma	Acute Lymphoblastic* Leukemia (Children 0-14)	Cervix (females)	Breast (females)			
				With HER2+ treatment		Without HER2+ treatment	
				10% early detection	60% early detection	10% early detection	60% early detection
World	94	223	54	23,379	16,764	3,606	2,195
High Income Countries	31	74	5	10,310	7,393	1,590	968
Low and Middle Income Countries	63	149	48	13,069	9,371	2,016	1,227
Africa	11	17	8	1,570	1,126	242	147
Latin-American and the Caribbean	8	29	7	1,933	1,386	298	181
Asia (excluding high income countries)	34	63	30	7,568	5,427	1,167	710

*   These figures assume that 75% of all leukemias in 0-14 year olds are acute lymphoblastic leukemia. Globocan 2008 incidence data do not specify type of leukemia.
Source: Author calculations based on Table 7.3, Globocan 2008 and Guerrero et al. (2011). Estimation of global potential demand of cancer drugs. (http://gtfccc.harvard.edu/icb/icb.do?keyword=k69586&pageid=icb.page420088).

Table 7.6B

Cost of Covering Chemotherapy Therapy for Unmet Needs for Hodgkin Lymphoma, Childhood Acute Lymphoblastic Leukemia, and Cervical and Breast Cancer, 2010 Prices (US$ millions)

Region	Hodgkin lymphoma	Acute Lymphoblastic Leukemia (Children 0-14)	Cervix (females)	Breast (females)			
				With HER2+ treatment		Without HER2+ treatment	
				10% early detection	60% early detection	10% early detection	60% early detection
World	39	58	21	6,005	4,306	926	564
High Income Countries	4	5	1	1,460	1,047	225	137
Low and Middle Income Countries	35	52	20	4,544	3,259	701	427
Africa	9	6	5	768	550	118	72
Latin-American and the Caribbean	3	8	2	476	341	73	45
Asia (excluding high income countries)	19	38	12	2,424	1,738	374	228

*   These figures assume that 75% of all leukemias in 0-14 year olds are acute lymphoblastic leukemia. Globocan 2008 incidence data do not specify type of leukemia.

Source: Author calculations based on Table 7.3, Globocan 2008 and Guerrero et al., (2011). Estimation of global potential demand of cancer drugs. (http://gtfccc.harvard.edu/icb/icb.do?keyword=k69586&pageid=icb.page420088).

For many cancers where chemotherapy plays the sole or a major role in treatment, it usually accounts for the largest share of total treatment costs. A full curative course of chemotherapy may require a period of weeks to months to complete. Only for a few cancers, such as chronic myelogenous leukemia (CML); is continuous life-long treatment required. However, average chemotherapy costs vary widely (Table 7.5), from less than US$ 300 for cervical cancer, Kaposi sarcoma (the most common HIV/AIDS-related cancer), and Burkit's lymphoma (a primarily childhood cancer endemic in Africa), to an average of roughly US$ 5,500 across all stages of breast cancer, to an annual cost of over US$ 35,000 for CML. As indicated by individual drug prices (Table 7.2), the most costly chemotherapy involves the newest on-patent agents such as trastuzumab (Herceptin) for HER2+ cases, imatinib (Gleevec/Glivec) for CML, and rituximab (Rituxan/MabThera) for diffuse large B-cell lymphoma.

As noted earlier, a substantial gap in access to cancer treatment exists in most LMICs. Text Box 7.3 presents an estimate of the annual cost of unmet needs for chemotherapy medicines for four common cancers that suggests that the cost of increasing access to chemotherapy may be more affordable than many have suggested. Among these cancers, the annual global cost of cancer medicines varies from roughly US$ 21 million for cervical cancer to US$ 4.3 billion for a breast cancer scenario that assumes 20% HER2+ and 60% early detection. For breast cancer, the unmet need with this scenario is estimated at US$ 341 million for Latin America and the Caribbean, US$ 550 million for Africa, and just over US$ 1.7 billion for Asia.

The high cost of unmet need for medicines for breast cancer is primarily a reflection of the high incidence of breast cancer worldwide and the high cost of current trastuzumab treatment for HER2+ breast cancer. The impact of HER2+ breast cancer treatment is reflected in the alternative scenarios presented in Text Box 7.3.

7.vii Engaging the private sector

ACCESS TO EXISTING MEDICINES, VACCINES, AND TECHNOLOGIES

The international cancer community, WHO, and other partners must strategically engage with pharmaceutical and health technology manufacturers –brand and generic, north and south– for widespread access to cancer medicines, vaccines, and health technologies. The decline in prices seen for ARVs beginning in the early 2000s would not have happened without the engagement of the pharmaceutical manufacturers with UNAIDS, WHO, and the European Commission, along with pressure from activists.[95] The HIV/AIDS experience represented a paradigm shift as the research-based pharmaceutical industry modified its business model in a high-volume market. The international cancer community can provide stewardship by engaging both patent-holding multinational pharmaceutical firms and generic manufacturers from the developing world. Through engagement with manufacturers built on the advance market commitment model, the pneumococcal vaccine was introduced for US$ 3.50 a dose – a 90% price reduction.[160]

The HIV/AIDS experience demonstrated a paradigm shift for the research-based pharmaceutical industry to modify their business model in a high-volume market.

Though South-South collaboration is encouraged by donor governments and international organizations, such entities initiated only 17 of 279 reported South-South collaborations among research institutes and manufacturing firms in Africa, Asia, and Latin America actively working together to produce pharmaceutical products for shared health priorities. For example, Cuba's Center of Molecular Immunology in partnership with 20 developing countries and 7 developed countries is spearheading clinical trials for nimotuzumab (already approved for head and neck cancers) to treat other cancers of epithelial origin, thus bypassing large pharmaceutical companies.[161,162] This suggests that through such arrangements, the international cancer community can promote the development and supply of health technologies that are appropriate for resource-limited settings. For instance, manufacturers and regulatory agencies in Brazil and Cuba, with encouragement from WHO, responded to the need for a large scale supply of meningitis A vaccine to combat the outbreak in Africa. Similarly, PEPFAR engaged a private medical diagnostic company to strengthen laboratory capacity for managing TB and HIV/AIDS diagnosis in eight African countries.[163] Transfer of technology has been an important element in increasing production of medicines for multidrug-resistant TB in the South.[164] While the intended purpose of technology transfer initiatives differ widely between profit and nonprofit entities, notwithstanding their challenges, NGOs or foundations with a public interest must step in to promote access to cancer medicines and health technologies.[165]

Given their strong manufacturing capacity and ability to commercialize affordable health products, countries like Brazil, China, India, and Mexico have the opportunity to serve the world as they prepare to manufacture generic products for cancer.[166] For example, there are manufacturers of cobalt and LINAC radiotherapy equipment from China, India, Argentina, and for some equipment, and also from Brazil. The IAEA, WHO, and the Industry (International Electrotechnical Commission) set strict quality and safety standards that all manufacturers must meet. The developing country manufacturers have had difficulties in getting licenses for this reason and also in competing with western companies to supply radiotherapy machines to other developing countries. However, there have been encouraging developments. Argentina, China and India have successfully placed low-cost quality cobalts and LINACs on the market, often at half the market price. The IAEA's PACT has received three donations of Bhabhatron-II cobalt from India for transfer to Vietnam, Sri Lanka, and Namibia.[167] Several African countries are now considering purchasing the Indian and Chinese equipment. Venezuela bought over 30 radiotherapy machines from Argentina. Through the AGaRT initiative, these examples demonstrate that there is hope to further develop the health technology market in LMICs while ensuring the highest quality, reliability, and safety standards.

PRODUCT INNOVATION

Targeted innovations in cancer medicines, vaccines, and related health technologies for resource-poor settings are urgently needed.

Targeted innovations in cancer medicines, vaccines, and related health technologies for resource-poor settings are urgently needed. With ultrasound and mammography machines running in the tens of thousands of dollars and radiotherapy equipment running in the millions, appropriate lower cost radiotherapy technology that can function effectively with unstable electricity is urgently needed as are other cancer-related health technologies that can function in resource-limited settings. The IAEA has challenged manufacturers not only to reduce the cost of radiotherapy machines from US$ 3 million to US$ 1 million, but also to provide simpler designs that integrate all essential radiotherapy technology with high quality and safety and are feasible in resource-limited settings. Termed "frugal innovation," such efforts are essential for scaling up cancer detection, diagnosis, and treatment (Text Box 7.4).[168]

In response to WHO's call for innovative health technologies for 19 global health concerns, cancer received the second-highest number of applications (26) from interested manufacturers wanting to commercialize resource-appropriate, lower cost health technologies.[169] Further, the First Global Forum on Medical Devices optimistically concluded that manufacturers are showing their willingness to develop or adapt health technologies for global health purposes.[170] Costs for mammography, radiotherapy, and ultrasound machines do not have to be insurmountable. Using the frugal innovation approach, opportunities to design machines suitable for resource-poor settings exist. However, there is an absolute need to ensure appropriate quality and patient safety of lower cost devices, along with the requisite regulatory approvals, quality-assurance mechanisms, post-market vigilance, innovations in healthcare delivery models, and options for health system capacity building.[171]

Costs for mammography, radiotherapy and ultrasound machines do not have to be insurmountable. Using the frugal innovation approach, there are opportunities to design machines suitable for resource-poor settings.

Text Box 7.4
"Frugal Innovation" for high-cost technologies

Manufacturers are increasingly changing their business models based on "frugal innovation" or "reverse innovation" with the goal of mass producing lower cost health technologies that are appropriate for resource-poor settings. For example, continuous positive air pressure machines (CPAP) save the lives of premature babies. The high price tag of US$ 4,500 coupled with expensive consumables and disposable tubes costing US$ 300 make CPAP too expensive to stem the high rate of newborn death in Vietnam. An innovative scheme called Breath of Life in collaboration with a local manufacturer developed locally appropriate technology that can work despite unstable electricity, using inexpensive consumables and reusable silicone pipes. At an attractive price of US$ 2,200, this locally developed health technology saved the lives of 40,000 babies.[172]

Similarly, General Electric (GE) developed a hand-held electrocardiogram (ECG) costing US$ 800 (compared to US$ 2,000) that work on batteries, has only four buttons, and is equipped with a portable printing machine.[173] With the cost of US$ 1 per patient, this portable ECG machine is expected to help prevent the 5 million deaths due to cardiovascular disease in India. Likewise, GE pioneered the development and commercialization of high performance abdominal ultrasound imaging capabilities at much lower cost than earlier generation products for routine liver cancer screening in China.[174]

Turning to medicines, a wider range of oral chemotherapy would reduce the need for patients to travel hundreds of miles to a metropolitan area to receive prolonged infusions, saving both time and transportation costs. The design of effective treatment regimens utilizing oral therapies, where feasible, eliminates costs for in-patient care with the potential to alleviate staffing shortages and ensure that a greater number of patients are treated.[175] Using existing off-patent products for the treatment of AIDS-related lymphoma, oral chemotherapy demonstrated reasonable efficacy and safety.[176] Analysis of oral products under development shows that some of them overcome the concerns of efficacy and bioavailability relative to infusions.[177] Targeted chemotherapeutic agents that specifically attack malignant cells and minimize toxicity are greatly needed for improved quality of care. Evidence from South Africa highlights the need for cheaper liposomal drugs, which have a comparative advantage in efficacy and tolerability for the management of AIDS-associated Kaposi sarcoma.[178]

Analysis of available data indicates that promising cancer products receive the highest research investment, when compared to other NCDs, by nonprofit agencies and the research-based pharmaceutical industry.[179] For new products that are expected to be commercialized, prior engagement with product developers is necessary for rapid availability of products for predominant cancers in LMICs. Fast-track approval of expanded indications for existing oral therapies that minimize toxicity must be given priority. Product development partnerships (PDPs) have been fairly successful in licensing products to combat major infectious diseases, with funding leveraged from various streams.[180] In the context of health technologies for cancer, developing, manufacturing, and commercializing resource-appropriate technologies will require a paradigm shift to speed up access to LMICs. At the 2010 Berlin World Health Summit, PDPs called on governments for increased funding, building on Germany's announced intent to deliver more global health aid through such mechanisms.[181]

7.viii Conclusions and recommendations

National cancer control programs in LMICs must work systematically to adapt global guidelines for national cancer prevention, detection, treatment, and palliation programs; strengthen procurement and distribution systems; ensure regulation of quality and safety; and pursue other critical actions such as controlling distribution mark-ups and eliminating tariffs on cancer medicines. International guidelines for cancer prevention, detection, diagnosis, treatment, and palliative care in LMICs should be developed and the range of cancer agents in the WHO model list of essential medicines and vaccines should be expanded. This effort should be spear-headed by the Union for International Cancer Control, International Network for Cancer Treatment and Research, American Society of Clinical Oncology, European Society of Medical Oncology, Sociedad Latinoamericana y del Caribe de Oncología, and others, working closely with WHO.

Access to existing, proven diagnostic technologies must be improved through novel programs such as breast cancer detection and cervical cancer screening and prevention programs. Such programs can have immediate impact on cancer outcomes and provide the necessary healthcare infrastructure to address a wider spectrum of healthcare needs in LMICs. Accurate detection and diagnosis is essential in the delivery of cancer prevention, control and management, and care. Transparent web-based exchange of information on prices and sources of cancer medicines, vaccines, and selected technologies, such as that provided by the MSH-WHO International Drug Price Indicator Guide, should be expanded to include demand forecast information that can be widely disseminated and actively used by cancer program planners and procurement agencies. Observed price reductions of more than 90% for HPV and hepatitis B vaccines and 99% for ARVs also should be possible for some chemotherapy agents and diagnostics. Competitive pooled procurement by reliable global, regional, or national procurement and supply organizations should be used to ensure uninterrupted supply, optimal price, assured quality, and reliable service support. Such efforts should specifically address access to the essential health technologies so urgently needed for cancer diagnosis and treatment in LMICs.

For off-patent chemotherapeutic agents, producers of both finished products and APIs in LMICs, such as China and India, should develop innovative models for using real-time consumption and demand forecast information to ease the shortages of critical off-patent chemotherapeutic agents in the developed world and reduce prices in LMICs. For on-patent cancer agents, for which world market prices can be prohibitively expensive at US$ 28,000 or more per patient, increased access should be pursued through differential pricing by companies, negotiation with companies, sustained targeted donations and work with global, regional, and national procurement agencies to expand their range of cancer agents as need and demand grow. Compulsory and voluntary licensing can be useful tools under very specific circumstances, but alone rarely achieve large-scale price reduction.

National cancer care efforts must ensure access to radiotherapy and surgery, which remain essential modalities for treatment and palliation of prevalent cancers. The international community should support efforts by the International Atomic Energy Agency's Program of Action for Cancer Therapy, Union for International Cancer Control, International Agency for Research on Cancer, International Network for Cancer Treatment and Research, cancer institutions and the private sector to scale up comprehensive cancer control planning and resource mobilization in LMICs. Surgical services include surgeons and surgical staff qualified in cancer care, safe anaesthesia, and reliable pre- and post-operative care.

Efforts must be accelerated to develop appropriate, affordable, easily-maintained, and user-friendly technologies essential for screening, diagnosis, radiotherapy, and other technology-dependent elements of a comprehensive cancer program. "Frugal innovations" championed by multilateral organization such as the IAEA and WHO, and private companies such as Medtronic and General Electric Healthcare Systems are vital for CCC to reach the currently under-served. Cancer detection, diagnosis, treatment, and palliation should be made more accessible and affordable through diagnostic tests, medications, and radiotherapy that can be easily delivered in remote settings, reducing the cost of key components, especially through strategies described in this chapter and in Chapter 6 on innovative delivery.

References

1. Domingo EJ, Dy Echo AV. Epidemiology, prevention and treatment of cervical cancer in the Philippines. *J Gynecol Oncol* 2009; 20: 11-6.

2. Aziz Z. Across generations: cancer treatment in developing countries. *J Clin Oncol* 2008; 26:4990-91

3. Shulman D, Bukhman G. Partners in Health, Rwanda. Personal Communication. March 9, 2011.

4. Quick J. Essential medicines twenty-five years on: closing the access gap. *Health Policy Plan* 2003; 18: 1-3.

5. Kanavos P, Das P, Durairaj V, Laing R, Abegunde DO. *Options for financing and optimizing medicines in resource-poor countries.* Background Paper 34: World Health Report, 2010. Geneva: World Health Organization (WHO), 2010.

6. Department of Research, Government of Kenya. Policy Brief on the Situational Analysis of Cancer in Kenya. Prepared for the Departmental Committee on Health. Available at the Parliament of the Republic of Kenya website http://www.parliament.go.ke/index.php?option=com_docman&Itemid=&task=doc_download&gid=637 (accessed Jan. 26, 2012).

7. Orem J, Wabinga H. The roles of national cancer research institutions in evolving a comprehensive cancer control program in a developing country: experience from Uganda. *Oncology* 2009; 77: 272-80.

8. Meremikwu MM, Ehiri JE, Nkanga DG, Udoh EE, Ikpatt OF, Alaje EO. Socioeconomic constraints to effective management of Burkitt's lymphoma in south-eastern Nigeria. *Trop Med Int Health* 2005. 10: 92-8.

9. Cancer Patients Aid Association India. Cancer drugs-Pricing and Patents: September 2010. India: Department of Industrial Policy and Promotion, Ministry of Commerce and Industry, Government of India, 2010. http://dipp.nic.in/ipr-feedback/Feedback_01_CL_10September2010.pdf (accessed Feb. 2, 2012).

10. Howard SC, Marinoni M, Castillo L, et al. MISPHO Consortium Writing Committee. Improving outcomes for children with cancer in low-income countries in Latin America: a report on the recent meetings of the Monza International School of Pediatric Hematology/Oncology (MISPHO)-Part I. *Pediatr Blood Cancer* 2007; 48: 364–9.

11. El-Zawahry HM, Zeeneldin AA, Samra MA, et al. Cost and outcome of treatment of adults with acute myeloid leukemia at the National Cancer Institute-Egypt. *J Egypt Natl Canc Inst* 2007; 19: 106-13.

12. Boutayeb S, Boutayeb A, Ahbeddou N, et al. Estimation of the cost of treatment by chemotherapy for early breast cancer in Morocco. *Cost Eff Resour Alloc* 2010; 8: 16.

13. Mendis S, Fukino K, Cameron A, et al. The availability and affordability of selected essential medicines for chronic diseases in six low- and middle-income countries. *Bull World Health Organ* 2007; 85: 279–88.

14. Ekenze SO, Ekwunife H, Eze BI, Ikefuna A, Amah CC, Emodi IJ. The burden of pediatric malignant solid tumors in a developing country. *J Trop Pediatr* 2010; 56: 111-4.

15. Wairagala W. Working to improve access to palliative care in Africa. *Lancet Oncol* 2010; 11: 227-8.

16. HAI Global. Universal Access to Medicines for Non-Communicable Diseases: Within our Grasp but Out-of-Reach. Briefing note for delegates to the NCD High Level Meeting, September 2011. [http://www.haiweb.org/12092011/NCDSummitpaper13Sept2011.pdf]

17. Cameron A, Roubous I, Ewen M, et al. Differences in the availability of medicines for chronic and acute conditions in the public and private sectors of developing countries. *Bulletin of the World Health Organization* 2011, 89(6):279-87.

18. Carrin G, Mathauer I, Xu K, Evans DB. Universal coverage of health services: tailoring its implementation. *Bulletin of the World Health Organization*, 2008, 86(11):857-63.

19. Knaul FM, Arreola-Ornelas H, Mendez-Carniado O, et al. Evidence is good for your health system: policy reform to remedy catastrophic and impoverishing health spending in Mexico. *Lancet* 2006;368(9549):1828-41

20. Management Sciences for Health. 2011. MDS-3: Managing Access to Medicines and other Health Technologies. Arlington, VA: Management Sciences for Health.

21. Wells WA, Konduri N, Chen C, et al. Tuberculosis regimen change in high-burden countries. *Int J Tuberc Lung Dis* 2010; 14: 1538-47.

22. Beck EJ, Vitoria M, Mandalia S, Crowley S, Gilks CF, Souteyrand Y. National adult antiretroviral therapy guidelines in resource-limited countries: concordance with 2003 WHO guidelines? *AIDS* 2006; 20: 1497-502.

23. WHO. Scaling up antiretroviral therapy in resource-limited settings: guidelines for a public health approach. Geneva: WHO, 2002.

24. Sloan FA, Gelband H, eds. Cancer control opportunities in low- and middle-income countries. Washington, DC: Institute of Medicine of the National Academies, National Academies Press, 2007.

25. UICC World Cancer Declaration. http://uicc.org/declaration/world-cancer-declaration (accessed Feb. 2, 2012).

26. Kerr DJ, Midgley R. Can we treat cancer for a dollar a day? Guidelines for low-income countries. *N Engl J Med* 2010; 363: 801-3.

27. Union for International Cancer Control (UICC). Access to Cancer Drugs: A UICC Position Paper (Revision 2008/2009). Geneva: UICC, 2009. http://www.uicc.org/resources/access-cancer-drugs-uicc-position-paper-revision-200809 (accessed Feb. 2, 2011).

28. Eniu A, Carlson RW, El Saghir NS, Bines J, et al. Breast Health Global Initiative Treatment Panel. Guideline implementation for breast healthcare in low- and middle-income countries: treatment resource allocation. *Cancer* 2008; 113 (suppl 8): 2269-81.

29. Collingridge D. Delivering consensus from the Asian Oncology Summit 2009. *Lancet Oncol* 2009; 10: 1029-30.
30. National Comprehensive Cancer Network (NCCN). About Us. http://www.nccn.org/about/default.asp (accessed Feb 9, 2012).
31. Twagirumukiza M, Annemans L, Kips JG, Bienvenu E, Van Bortel LM. Prices of antihypertensive medicines in sub-Saharan Africa and alignment to WHO's model list of essential medicines. *Trop Med Int Health* 2010; 15: 350-61.
32. Network (The Newsletter of the International Network for Cancer Treatment and Research [INCTR]). Annual meeting special issue (Replaces Winter and Spring Issues 2007). Annual meeting panel A: WHO Drug Essential Drug List. INCTR 2007;7:10. http://www.inctr.org/fileadmin/user_upload/inctr-admin/Network%20Magazine/Vol%207%20No%202%20Winter%20Spring%202007LR2.pdf (accessed Feb. 2, 2012).
33. WHO. Model List of Essential Medicines for Children. Third Edition. Geneva: World Health Organization 2011.
34. Network (The Newsletter of the International Network for Cancer Treatment and Research [INCTR]). Winter 2007-2008. REPORT: Childhood Cancer in a Developing Nation: The Impact of a National Program. INCTR 2007; 7: 9-10. http://www.inctr.org/fileadmin/user_upload/inctr-admin/Network%20Magazine/Vol%207%20No%204%20Winter%202007%202008LLR.pdf (accessed Feb. 2, 2012).
35. Network (The Newsletter of the International Network for Cancer Treatment and Research [INCTR]). Winter 2002-2003. Profiles in Cancer Medicine: Standardizing Cancer Treatment. INCTR 2003; 3: 20. http://www.inctr.org/fileadmin/user_upload/inctr-admin/Network%20Magazine/Vol%203%20No%203%20-%20Winter%202002-2003LLR.pdf (accessed Feb. 2, 2012).
36. Sharma DC. Boost to cancer care in India. *Lancet Oncol* 2005; 6: 835-7.
37. Gilks CF, Crowley S, Ekpini R, et al. The WHO public-health approach to antiretroviral treatment against HIV in resource-limited settings. *Lancet* 2006; 368: 505-10.
38. Ferlay J, Shin HR, Bray F, Forman D, Mathers C, Parkin DM. GLOBOCAN 2008: cancer incidence and mortality worldwide. Lyon: International Agency for Research on Cancer, 2010.
39. Hepatitis B Foundation http://www.hepb.org/professionals/hepb_and_liver_cancer.htm
40. PATH. Progress in preventing cervical cancer: Updated evidence on vaccination and screening. Outlook 2010, 27(2). http://www.path.org/publications/files/RH_outlook_27_2.pdf (accessed Feb. 2, 2012).
41. GAVI. Press Release; 4 Feb, 2010. Increasing access to vaccines will reduce the global burden of cancer. http://www.gavialliance.org/library/news/statements/2010/increasing-access-to-vaccines-will-reduce-the-global-burden-of-cancer/ (accessed Feb. 2, 2012).
42. Scott Wittet, Senior Communications Officer, PATH Cervical Cancer Project. Personal Communication, Jan 27, 2012.
43. WHO. Filterable search for prequalified vaccines with product details. http://www.who.int/immunization_standards/vaccine_quality/PQ_vaccine_list_en/en/index.html (accessed Feb. 2, 2012).
44. GAVI. Press Release; 6 June, 2011. GAVI welcomes lower prices for life-saving vaccines. http://www.gavialliance.org/library/news/press-releases/2011/gavi-welcomes-lower-prices-for-life-saving-vaccines/ (accessed Feb 2, 2012).
45. Crager SE, Guillen E, Price M. University contributions to the HPV vaccine and implications for access to vaccines in developing countries: addressing materials and know-how in university technology transfer policy. *Am J Law Med* 2009; 35: 253-79.
46. Lu B, Kumar A, Castellsagué X, Giuliano AR. Efficacy and safety of prophylactic vaccines against cervical HPV infection and diseases among women: a systematic review & meta-analysis. *BMC Infect Dis* 2011; 11:13.
47. Schiffman M, Castle PE. The promise of global cervical cancer prevention. *N Engl J Med* 2005; 353:2101-4
48. Schiffman M, Castle PE, Jeronimo J, Rodríguez AC, Wacholder S. Human papillomavirus and cervical cancer. *Lancet* 2007; 370:890-907
49. Gage JC, Castle PE. Preventing cervical cancer globally by acting locally: If not now, when. *J Natl Cancer Inst* 2010; 102:1524-7
50. Sankaranarayanan R, Boffetta P. Research on cancer prevention, detection and management in low- and medium-income countries. *Ann Oncol* 2010; 21: 1935-43.
51. Masood S, Vass L, Ibarra JA Jr, et al. Breast Health Global Initiative Pathology Focus Group. Breast pathology guideline implementation in low- and middle-income countries. *Cancer* 2008; 113 (suppl 8): 2297-304.
52. Carlson JW, Lyon E, Walton D, et al. Partners in pathology: a collaborative model to bring pathology to resource poor settings. *Am J Surg Pathol* 2010; 34: 118-23.
53. Howard SC, Campana D, Coustan-Smith E, et al. Development of a regional flow cytometry center for diagnosis of childhood leukemia in Central America. *Leukemia* 2005; 19:323-5.
54. World Health Organization. *The Maputo Declaration on Strengthening of Laboratory Systems*. Maputo, Mozambique: World Health Organization, 2008. http://www.who.int/diagnostics_laboratory/Maputo-Declaration_2008.pdf (Feb 2, 2012).
55. African Society for Laboratory Medicine (ASLM) http://www.afslm.org/. African Journal of Laboratory Medicine. http://www.afslm.org/journal/.
56. *African Journal of Laboratory Medicine* http://www.afslm.org/journal/ (accessed Oct. 11, 2011).

57. Nkengasong JN, Nsubuga P, Nwanyanwu O, et al. Laboratory systems and services are critical in global health: time to end the neglect? *Am J Clin Pathol* 2010; 134: 368-73.

58. Sitas F, Parkin DM, Chirenje M, Stein L, Abratt R, Wabinga H. Part II: Cancer in Indigenous Africans-causes and control. *Lancet Oncol* 2008; 9: 786-95.

59. Barton MB, Frommer M, Shafiq J. Role of radiotherapy in cancer control in low-income and middle-income countries. *Lancet Oncol* 2006; 7: 584-95.

60. International Atomic Energy Agency (IAEA). Inequity in cancer care: a global perspective. Vienna, Austria; IAEA. 2011.

61. Ibid.

62. Ibid.

63. Ibid.

64. Van Der Giessen PH, Alert J, Badri C et al. Multinational assessment of some operational costs of teletherapy. *Radiother Oncol.* 2004 Jun; 71(3):347-55.

65. Ibid.

66. Ibid.

67. IAEA. *imPACT Review Report 2011.* Submitted to Albanian Ministry of Health, PACT Programme Office, 2011.

68. Abimiku AG. Building laboratory infrastructure to support scale-up of HIV/AIDS treatment, care, and prevention: in-country experience. *Am J Clin Pathol* 2009; 131: 875-86.

69. Spira T, Lindegren ML, Ferris R, Habiyambere V, Ellerbrock T. WHO/PEPFAR collaboration to prepare an operations manual for HIV prevention, care, and treatment at primary health centers in high-prevalence, resource-constrained settings: defining laboratory services. *Am J Clin Pathol* 2009; 131: 887-94.

70. Hitchcock CL. The future of telepathology for the developing world. *Arch Pathol Lab Med* 2011; 135:211-4.

71. Pagni F, Bono F, Di BC, Faravelli A, Cappellini A. Virtual surgical pathology in underdeveloped countries: The Zambia Project. *Arch Pathol Lab Med* 2011; 135:215-9.

72. Hoenecke H, Lee V, Roy I. Pathologists overseas: coordinating volunteer pathology services for 19 years. *Arch Pathol Lab Med* 2011; 135:173-8.

73. DeMay, R.M. The Art & Science of Cytopathology. 2nd ed. Chicago: ASCP Press, 2012.

74. Ahmed HG, Ali AS, Almobarak AO. Utility of fine-needle aspiration as a diagnostic technique in breast lumps. *Diagn Cytopathol* 2009; 37:881-4.

75. Guggisberg K, Okorie C, Khalil M. Cytopathology including fine-needle aspiration in sub-Saharan Africa: a Cameroon experience. *Arch Pathol Lab Med* 2011; 135:200-6.

76. Michelow P, Dezube BJ, Pantanowitz L. Fine needle aspiration of salivary gland masses in HIV-infected patients. *Diagn Cytopathol* 2011.

77. Michelow P, Dezube BJ, Pantanowitz L. Fine needle aspiration of breast masses in HIV-infected patients: results from a large series. *Cancer Cytopathol* 2010; 118:218-24.

78. Mueller JS, Schultenover S, Simpson J, Ely K, Netterville J. Value of rapid assessment cytology in the surgical management of head and neck tumors in a Nigerian mission hospital. *Head Neck* 2008; 30:1083-5.

79. Taye AA, Gemechu T. Fine needle aspiration cytology of breast lesions: a clinicocytologic review of 1211 cases. *Ethiop Med J* 1998; 36:219-25.

80. Benediktsson H. Pathology against the odds. *Arch Pathol Lab Med* 2011; 135:171-2.

81. Fleming KA, Howat AJ, Lucas S, Prentice A. Pathology in resource-poor healthcare systems. *Bulletin Royal Coll Pathol* 2010; 152:182-6.

82. Fisk NM, Atun R. Market failure and the poverty of new drugs in maternal health. *PLoS Med* 2008; 5(1): e22.

83. Management Sciences for Health. 2011. Pharmaceutical Pricing: Theory and Practices. In Managing Drug Supply, 3rd ed. Arlington, VA: Management Sciences for Health.

84. World Health Organization. Western Pacific Region. Price Information Exchange for Selected Medicines in the Western Pacific Region. http://www.piemeds.com/page/About (accessed Feb 9, 2012).

85. World Health Organization. The world health report- Health systems financing: The path to universal coverage. Geneva: World Health Organization, 2010; 59-84.

86. Based on Essential Package of Cancer Services and Drugs for Low and Middle Income Countries, chapter 5

87. Kaddar, M. New project to provide lower-middle and middle-income countries with up-to-date product, price and procurement information. Geneva: World Health Organization, 2011. Global Immunization News, August 2011. http://www.who.int/immunization/GIN_August_2011.pdf#page=3: (accessed Feb. 2, 2012).

88. Gelders S, Ewen M, Noguchi N, Laing R. *Price availability and affordability: An international comparison of chronic disease medicines.* Background report prepared for the WHO Planning Meeting on the Global Initiative for Treatment of Chronic Diseases held in Cairo in December 2005. Cairo: World Health Organization Regional Office for the Eastern Mediterranean, 2006. http://www.haiweb.org/medicineprices/08092008/EDB068final.pdf (accessed Feb 2, 2012).

89. Cameron A, Ewen M, Ross-Degnan D, Ball D, Laing R. Medicine prices, availability, and affordability in 36 developing and middle-income countries: a secondary analysis. *Lancet* 2009; 373: 240-49.

90. Olcay M, Laing R. Pharmaceutical Tariffs: What Is Their Effect on Prices, Protection of Local Industry and Revenue Generation? Study prepared for The Commission on Intellectual Property Rights, Innovation and Public Health. Geneva: WHO, 2005. http://www.who.int/intellectualproperty/studies/TariffsOnEssentialMedicines.pdf (accessed Feb. 2, 2012).

91. Alcalde GV, Ubillús RC, Palacín JS, Serna ZJP. Evaluación de los potenciales efectos sobre acceso a medicamentos del tratado de libre comercio que se negocia con los Estados Unidos de América. Lima, Peru: Ministerio de la Salude de Peru, 2005. http://www.bvsde.paho.org/bvsacd/cd65/MINSA-TLC-salud.pdf (accessed Feb 8, 2012).

92. Galárraga O, O'Brien ME, Gutiérrez JP, et al. Forecast of demand for antiretroviral drugs in low and middle-income countries: 2007-2008. AIDS 2007; 4 (suppl 21): S97-103.

93. Waning B, Diedrichsen E, Moon S. A lifeline to treatment: the role of Indian generic manufacturers in supplying antiretroviral medicines to developing countries. Int AIDS Soc 2010; 13: 35.

94. Holmes CB, Coggin W, Jamieson D, et al. Use of generic antiretroviral agents and cost savings in PEPFAR treatment programs. JAMA 2010; 304: 313-20.

95. Schwartsmann G, Picon PD. When drugs are worth more than gold! Lancet Oncol 2007; 8: 1049-50.

96. Schwartländer B, Grubb I, Perriëns J. The 10-year struggle to provide antiretroviral treatment to people with HIV in the developing world. Lancet 2006; 368: 541-46.

97. Kanavos P, Vandoros S, Garcia-Gonzalez P. Benefits of global partnerships to facilitate access to medicines in developing countries: a multi-country analysis of patients and patient outcomes in GIPAP. Global Health 2009; 5: 19.

98. The Global Fund. Making A Difference: Global Fund Results Report 2011. Geneva: The Global Fund, 2011.

99. Moon S, Jambert E, Childs M, von Schoen-Angerer T. A win-win solution? A critical analysis of tiered pricing to improve access to medicines in developing countries. Global Health 2011;7(1):39

100. Yadav, P. Differential pricing of pharmaceuticals: Review of current knowledge, new findings and ideas for action. UK Department for International Development (DFID), 2010. http://www.dfid.gov.uk/Documents/publications1/prd/diff-pcing-pharma.pdf (accessed Feb 2, 2012).

101. Bero L, Carson B, Moller H, Hill S. To give is better than to receive: compliance with WHO guidelines for drug donations during 2000-2008. Bull World Health Organ 2010; 88: 922-9.

102. Brower V. Drugs are scarce as mix of programs aims to ease access. J Natl Cancer Inst 2009; 101: 1304-6.

103. Amin T. Voluntary licensing practices in the pharmaceutical sector: Anan acceptable solution to improving access to affordable medicines? Oxfam GB, 2007. http://www.i-mak.org/storage/Oxfam%20-%20Voluntary%20Licensing%20Research%20IMAK%20Website.pdf (accessed Feb 2, 2012).

104. Osewe PL, Nkrumah YK, Sackey EK. Improving access to HIV/AIDS medicines in Africa: trade-related aspects of intellectual property rights flexibilities. Washington, DC: World Bank, 2008.

105. Singh K. Natco may seek compulsory license for Bayer's cancer drug. The Economic Times. January 24, 2011. http://economictimes.indiatimes.com/news/news-by-industry/healthcare/biotech/pharmaceuticals/natco-may-seek-compulsory-licence-for-bayers-cancer-drug/articleshow/7350869.cms (accessed Feb. 2, 2012).

106. 't Hoen EFM. The Global Politics of Pharmaceutical Monopoly Power: drug patents, access, innovation and the application of the World Trade Organization Doha Declaration on TRIPS and Public Health. Diemen, The Netherlands: AMB Publishers, 2009. http://www.soros.org/initiatives/health/focus/access/articles_publications/publications/aem_20090312 (accessed Feb. 2, 2012).

107. Weber A, Mills L. A one-time-only combination: emergency medicine exports under Canada's access to medicines regime. Health Hum Rights 2010; 12: 109-22.

108. Babovic S, Wasan KM. Impact of the trade-related aspects of intellectual property rights (TRIPS) agreement on India as a supplier of generic antiretrovirals. J Pharm Sci 2010; 100: 816-21.

109. Lybecker KM, Fowler E. Compulsory licensing in Canada and Thailand: comparing regimes to ensure legitimate use of the WTO rules. J Law Med Ethics 2009; 37: 222-39.

110. Smith RD, Correa C, Oh C. Trade, TRIPS, and pharmaceuticals. Lancet 2009; 373: 684-91.

111. Adusei, P. Exploiting Patent Regulatory "Flexibilities" to Promote Access to Antiretroviral Medicines in Sub-Saharan Africa. The Journal of World Intellectual Property 2011; 14: 1-20. DOI: 10.1111/j.1747-1796.2010.00407.x.

112. Eimer T, Lutz S. Developmental states, civil society, and public health: patent regulation for HIV/AIDS pharmaceuticals in India and Brazil. Regulation and Governance 2010; 4: 135-53. DOI: 10.1111/j.1748-5991.2010.01074.x.

113. Rathod S. Ever-greening: a status check in selected countries. Journal of Generic Medicines. 2010; 7: 227-42. DOI: 10.1057/jgm.2010.14.

114. New York Times. India orders Bayer to license a patented drug. March 12, 2012. http://www.nytimes.com/2012/03/13/business/global/india-overrules-bayer-allowing-generic-drug.html (accessed March 15, 2012).

115. Chan M. "Access to Medicines: lessons from procurement practices." Opening remarks at a joint technical symposium by WHO, WIPO and WTO, Geneva; July 16, 2010. http://www.who.int/dg/speeches/2010/access_medicines_20100716/en/index.html (accessed Feb 2, 2012).

116. Beall R, Kuhn R. Trends in compulsory licensing of pharmaceuticals since the Doha declaration: a database analysis. PLoS Med. 2012 ;9(1):e1001154.

117. Access to Medicines: Pricing and Procurement Practices. A joint technical symposium by WHO, WIPO and WTO, Geneva, 2010. http://www.who.int/phi/phi_symposium/en/index.html (accessed Feb 2, 2012).

118. Access to Medicines, Patent Information and Freedom to Operate. A joint technical symposium by WHO, WIPO and WTO, Geneva, 2011. http://www.who.int/phi/access_medicines_feb2011/en/index.html (accessed Feb 2, 2012).

119. World Health Organization. Human papillomavirus vaccines WHO Position Paper. WHO Weekly epidemiological record 10 April 2009: No .15, 2009, 84 117-132. http://www.who.int/wer/2009/wer8415.pdf (accessed August 9, 2011).

120. IAVI, PATH. HPV Vaccine Adoption in Developing Countries: Cost and Financing Issues. December 2007. http://screening.iarc.fr/doc/IAVI_PATH_HPV_financing.pdf (accessed Feb. 2, 2012).

121. GSK press release. GlaxoSmithKline cervical cancer vaccine now accessible to more Filipinas. 28 November 2008. http://www.gsk.com.ph/CervarixAccessible.html (accessed Feb. 2, 2012).

122. Cervical Cancer Action. GSK Announces South African Price for HPV Vaccine. 2 December 2008. http://www.cervicalcanceraction.org/news/news-detail.php?id=30 (accessed Feb. 2, 2012).

123. Politi C, Kaddar M. Briefing note HPV vaccine: supply, demand, price and financing for low and middle income countries - preliminary analysis. WHO: December 2009.

124. PAHO. Financing for HPV Vaccines: America's Experience with New Vaccines. 2011. http://www.technet21.org/index.php/documents/view-document/1098-financing-for-hpv-vaccines-americas-experience-with-new-vaccines.html (Accessed Feb. 2, 2012).

125. Merck press release. Merck Commends GAVI Alliance on Continued Efforts to Improve Access. 05 June 2011. http://www.merck.com/newsroom/news-release-archive/corporate-responsibility/2011_0605.html (Accessed Feb 2, 2012)

126. GAVI press release. GAVI welcomes lower prices for life-saving vaccines. 06 June 2011. http://www.gavialliance.org/library/news/press-releases/2011/gavi-welcomes-lower-prices-for-life-saving-vaccines/ (accessed Feb. 2, 2012).

127. Nguyen A, Furrer E, Schwalbe N and GAVI Alliance. Market shaping: strategic considerations for a healthy vaccine marketplace. GAVI Alliance: Paper 6b. June 2011.

128. Chaudhury RR, Parameswar R, Gupta U, Sharma S, Tekur U, Bapna JS. Quality medicines for the poor: experience of the Delhi programme on rational use of drugs. Health Policy Plan 2005; 20: 124-36.

129. Partnership for Supply Chain Management. Supply Lines. http://scmsweb.pfscm.org/scms/resources/newsletter (accessed Feb. 2, 2012).

130. Atul Gawande; Iain Wilson personal communication. March 11, 2011.

131. Caudron J-M, Ford N, Henkens M, Macé C, Kiddle-Monroe R, Pinel J. Substandard medicines in resource-poor settings: a problem that can no longer be ignored. J Tropical Medicine & International Health, 2008, 13(8): 1062–72.

132. WHO. Survey of the quality of antiretroviral medicines circulating in selected African countries. Geneva: WHO, 2007. http://apps.who.int/prequal/info_general/documents/ARV_survey.pdf (accessed Feb. 2, 2012).

133. WHO. Survey of the quality of selected antimalarial medicines circulating in six countries of sub-Saharan Africa, 2011. http://www.who.int/medicines/publications/WHO_QAMSA_report.pdf (accessed Feb. 2, 2012).

134. WHO/Europe. Survey of the quality of anti-tuberculosis medicines circulating in selected countries of Eastern Europe and NIS, WHO/Europe workshop, Copenhagen, 17-18 June 2010. Copenhagen: WHO 2010. http://www.euro.who.int/__data/assets/pdf_file/0020/118055/Survey_quality_antiTBdrugs.pdf (accessed Feb.2, 2012).

135. The Global Fund. List of products and corresponding batch numbers tested on behalf of the Global Fund (updated 10 Feb 2011). Geneva, The Global Fund .http://www.theglobalfund.org/en/procurement/pqr/ (accessed Feb 2, 2012).

136. Bate R, Coticelli P, Tren R, Attaran A. Antimalarial drug quality in the most severely malarious parts of Africa - a six country study. PLoS One 2008; 3: e2132.

137. Vijaykadga S, Cholpol S, Sitthimongkol S, et al. Strengthening of national capacity in implementation of antimalarial drug quality assurance in Thailand. Southeast Asian J Trop Med Public Health 2006; 37 (suppl 3): 5-10.

138. Connor TH, Anderson RW, Sessink PJ, Broadfield L, Power LA. Surface contamination with antineoplastic agents in six cancer treatment centers in Canada and the United States. Am J Health Syst Pharm 1999; 56: 1427-32.

139. Elshamy K, El-Hadidi M, El-Roby M, Fouda M. Health hazards among oncology nurses exposed to chemotherapy drugs. African Journal of Haematology and Oncology 2010; 1: 70.

140. WHO. Wastes from health care activities. Fact sheet number 253 (November 2007). http://www.who.int/mediacentre/factsheets/fs253/en/ (accessed Feb 2, 2012)

141. WHO. Ensuring balance in national policies on controlled substances: Guidance for availability and accessibility of controlled medicines. Geneva: WHO, 2011.

142. Cherny NI, Baselga J, de Conno F, Radbruch L. Formulary availability and regulatory barriers to accessibility of opioids for cancer pain in Europe: a report from the ESMO/EAPC Opioid Policy Initiative. Ann Oncol 2010; 21: 615-26.

143. Logie DE, Harding R. An evaluation of a morphine public health programme for cancer and AIDS pain relief in Sub-Saharan Africa. BMC Public Health 2005; 5: 82.

144. Human Rights Watch. Needless Pain: Government failure to provide palliative care for children in Kenya. Chapter 6: International donors' lack of attention to palliative care. United States: Human Rights Watch, 2010.

145. Dehghan R, Ramakrishnan J, Ahmed N, Harding R. The use of morphine to control pain in advanced cancer: an investigation of clinical usage in Bangladesh. *Palliat Med* 2010; 24: 707-14.

146. Crane K. Cancer in the developing world: palliative care gains ground in developing countries. *J Natl Cancer Inst* 2010; 102: 1613-35.

147. O'Brien M. Director, Global Access to Pain Relief Initiative, Union for International Cancer Control (UICC). Personal Communication. March 22, 2011.

148. Lohman D, Schleifer R, Amon JJ. Access to pain treatment as a human right. *BMC Med* 2010; 8: 8.

149. Knaul FM, Arreola-Ornelas H, Velázquez E, Dorantes J, Méndez O, Ávila-Burgos L. El costo de la atención médica del cáncer mamario: el caso del Instituto Mexicano del Seguro Social. *Salud Pública de México* 2009; 51(suppl 2:): S286-95.

150. Ramiro Guerrero, Jaime Andrés Giraldo, Héctor Arreola-Ornelas, Felicia Marie Knaul (2011). Estimation of global potential demand of cancer drugs. Background paper. Harvard Global Equity Initiative and Global Task Force on Expanded Access to Cancer Care and Control in Developing Countries. (http://gtfccc.harvard.edu/icb/icb.do?keyword=k69586&pageid=icb.page420088)

151. Globocan, 2008.

152. Guerrero R, Giraldo JA, Arreola-Ornelas H, Knaul FM. Estimation of global potential demand of cancer drugs. Background paper. Boston: Harvard Global Equity Initiative and Global Task Force on Expanded Access to Cancer Care and Control in Developing Countries, 2011. http://gtfccc.harvard.edu/icb/icb.do?keyword=k69586&pageid=icb.page420088 (accessed on October 11, 2011).

153. Knaul FM, Arreola-Ornelas H, Velazquez E, et al., 2009.

154. Shulman LN, Willett W, Sievers A, Knaul FM. Breast cancer in developing countries: opportunities for improved survival. *Journal of Oncology* 2010; 2010: 595167.

155. Knaul FM, Arreola-Ornelas H, Velazquez E, et al., 2009.

156. American Cancer Society. Breast cancer facts and figures. 2009-2010. http://www.cancer.org/Research/CancerFactsFigures/BreastCancerFactsFigures/index (accessed Octoboer 11, 2011)

157. Author calculations from data presented in: Bloom, D.E., Cafiero, E.T., Jané-Llopis, E., et al. (2011). The Global Economic Burden of Non-communicable Diseases. Geneva: World Economic Forum.

158. Groot MT, Baltussen R, Uyl-de Groot CA, Anderson BO, Hortobágyi GN. Costs and health effects of breast cancer interventions in epidemiologically different regions of Africa, North America, and Asia. *Breast Journal* 2006; 12(1):81.

159. Kmietowicz Z. Developing countries roll out pneumococcal vaccine thanks to novel funding scheme. *BMJ* 2010; 341: c7230.

160. Thorsteinsdóttir H, Melon CC, Ray M, et al. South-South entrepreneurial collaboration in health biotech. *Nat Biotechnol* 2010; 28: 407-16.

161. Sáenz TW, Thorsteinsdóttir H, de Souza MC. Cuba and Brazil: an important example of South-South collaboration in health biotechnology. *MEDICC Rev* 2010; 12: 32-5.

162. The US President's Emergency Plan for AIDS Relief: BD and PEPFAR collaborate to strengthen laboratory systems in fight against HIV/AIDS and TB. http://2006-2009.pepfar.gov/press/94440.htm (accessed Feb 2, 2012).

163. International Federation of Pharmaceutical Manufacturers and Associations (IFPMA). Technology transfer: a collaborative approach to improve global health. The research-based pharmaceutical industry experience. International Federation of Pharmaceutical Manufacturers and Associations (IFPMA) 2011. http://www.ifpma.org/fileadmin/content/Events/Pharma_Forums/9_March_2011/IFPMA_Forum_Highlights_Tech_Transfer_09March2011.pdf (accessed Feb 2, 2012).

164. World Health Organization. Pharmaceutical production and related technology transfer: landscape report. Geneva: World Health Organization, 2011.

165. Jayaraman K. India's Cipla sets sights on Avastin, Herceptin and Enbrel. *Nat Biotechnol* 2010; 28: 883-4.

166. International Atomic Energy Agency. India Renews Commitment to Fighting Cancer Through IAEA. 25 November, 2011. http://www.iaea.org/newscenter/news/2011/indiacommitment.html (accessed Feb 2, 2012)

167. Wood J. Old problems fresh solutions: Indonesia's new health regime. A report from the Economist Intelligence Unit, 2010. http://graphics.eiu.com/upload/GE_Indonesia_main_Sep21_WEB_FINAL.pdf (accessed April 1, 2011).

168. WHO. Innovative Technologies That Address Global Health Concerns. Outcome of the Call – Global Initiative on Health Technologies. Geneva: WHO, 2010.

169. World Health Organization. Landscape analysis of barriers to developing or adapting technologies for global health purposes. Global Initiative on Health Technologies. Department of Essential Health Technologies. Geneva: World Health Organization, 2010.

170. Riband H. Vice-President, Legal and External Affairs, Medtronic International. Personal communication, Mar 14, 2011.

171. Wood J, 2010.

172. The Economist. Frugal healing - Inexpensive Asian innovation will transform the market for medical devices. The Economist Newspaper Limited, 2011.

173. Ishrak O. Former President and CEO, General Electric Healthcare Systems. CEO of Medtronic International. Personal communication, March 28, 2011.

174. Lingwood RJ, Boyle P, Milburn A, et al. The challenge of cancer control in Africa. *Nat Rev Cancer* 2008; 8: 398-403.

175. Mwanda WO, Orem J, Fu P, et al. Dose-modified oral chemotherapy in the treatment of AIDS-related non-Hodgkin's lymphoma in East Africa. *J Clin Oncol* 2009; 27: 3480-8.

176. Findlay M, von Minckwitz G, Wardley A. Effective oral chemotherapy for breast cancer: pillars of strength. *Ann Oncol* 2008; 19: 212-22.

177. Chu KM, Mahlangeni G, Swannet S, Ford NP, Boulle A, Van Cutsem G. AIDS-associated Kaposi's sarcoma is linked to advanced disease and high mortality in a primary care HIV programme in South Africa. *J Int AIDS Soc* 2010; 13:23.

178. WHO. Research and Development Coordination and Financing Report of the Expert Working Group. Geneva: WHO, 2010.
http://www.who.int/phi/documents/ewg_report/en/index.html (accessed Feb. 2, 2012).

179. International AIDS Vaccine Initiative. Innovative Product Development Partnerships: Advancing Global Health and Economic Development Goals, Policy Brief 26. International AIDS Vaccine Initiative, 2010. http://www.iavi.org/Lists/IAVIPublications/attachments/eb7b4247-6816-4094-9f54-9f2f2b99e95a/IAVI_Innovative_Product_Development_Partnerships_2010_ENG.pdf (accessed Feb 2, 2012).

180. Kondro W. "The best or the worst" end up in product development partnerships. *CMAJ* 2010; 182: E761-2.

Chapter 8

INNOVATIVE FINANCING: LOCAL AND GLOBAL OPPORTUNITIES

Rifat Atun, Felicia Marie Knaul

Key messages

GLOBAL

* International donor support for cancer and noncommunicable diseases in low and middle income countries has been far too limited compared to their burden and the funding provided for communicable diseases.

* Innovative global and domestic health system financing are two potential sources of new funding that need to be explored to meet the growing burden of cancer, other noncommunicable diseases (NCDs), and chronic illness, especially in the face of declining global development financing.

* Innovative financing refers to non-traditional approaches to external donor financing for health. The Global Alliance for Vaccines and Immunisation (GAVI) and the Global Fund to Fight AIDS, Tuberculosis and Malaria (the Global Fund) are examples of innovative financing mechanisms which have successfully channeled external funding to low and middle income countries (LMICs) to address HIV/AIDS, malaria, tuberculosis, and vaccine preventable diseases in children. The experiences of these innovative financing mechanisms provide platforms and lessons for financing cancer care and control (CCC) in LMICs.

* New initiatives can provide models and platforms for strengthening international partnerships and catalyzing innovative financing for cancer and other NCDs. The UN Secretary General's Every Woman Every Child strategy provides a commitment-based model that could be adopted to increase funding for cancer control. The strategy also provides opportunities for incorporating cancer into programs for women and children. The Pink Ribbon Red Ribbon is another promising initiative that links cancer to HIV/AIDS platforms.

* Newer international innovative financing initiatives beyond GAVI, Global Fund, and UNITAID have yielded very limited additional funding; they are unlikely to be options for expanding resources for CCC or other NCDs in the near future.

DOMESTIC

* Domestic sources fund almost all health expenditure in middle income countries and more than half of the health expenditure in most of the world's poorest countries.

* Out-of-pocket spending by families, which accounts for more than half of total health expenditure in many LMICs, is associated with catastrophic spending that drives families into poverty. This is especially true for chronic illness such as cancer.

* Many middle income and some low income countries have introduced health financing reforms to offer population-wide financial protection to reduce reliance of citizens on out-of-pocket spending. Several of the reforms include cancer and this constitutes a significant investment of resources that provides an opportunity to offer more effective CCC.

* Countries that have adopted guaranteed health benefits packages as part of universal entitlement programs are addressing the challenge of financing catastrophic chronic diseases, such as cancer, that can impoverish patients and their families.

* Domestic financing of CCC needs to balance prevention, early detection and treatment to ensure financial protection is most effectively targeted to reduce mortality and morbidity. Investing in treatment is made much less effective if prevention and early detection are underfunded.

8.i. Introduction

Since 2000, development assistance for health for low and middle income countries has effectively targeted HIV/AIDS, tuberculosis, and malaria, with notable increases since 2008 for maternal, newborn, and child health programs.[1,2] Noncommunicable diseases, including cancer, received the least amount of funding, accounting for only 0.5% of total development assistance for health in 2008.[3]

Globally, funding for cancer is heavily skewed to high income countries. Though cancer in LMICs accounts for 80% of the global cancer burden, only 5% or less of global health spending is for cancer in LMICs.[4]

Projections show that by 2030, NCDs will cause 74% of mortality and 64% of morbidity in LMICs.[5] The dearth of funding for NCDs and cancer is inexcusable, given the increasing burden and rising number of deaths they cause in LMICs.

Rapidly increasing burden of NCDs and the declining development assistance for health (DAH) requires new and innovative domestic and global sources of funding. While several middle income countries have effectively mobilized domestic resources, no innovative global financing mechanisms specifically target NCDs and cancer.

This chapter discusses innovative financing mechanisms for health. It is divided into two main parts, the first global and the second domestic. Each section ends with lessons learned from current innovative financing experience and offer specific conclusions that can be of global relevance.

The global analysis is based on the value chain approach that conceptualizes innovative financing holistically as resource mobilization, pooling financial resources, and channeling new funds to countries.[6] Case studies of approaches that have reached a global scale are used to explore how lessons learned can be applied to financing the burden of NCDs and cancer in LMICs.

This chapter also includes an analysis of several innovative approaches to financing health that have been implemented in LMICs. Case studies from China, Colombia, the Dominican Republic, India, Mexico, Peru, Rwanda, and Taiwan are discussed and synthesized in the second part of the chapter to arrive at overall recommendations for improving domestic financing to better meet the challenge of cancer and other chronic illness.

8.ii Innovative global financing

8.ii.1 THE ODA LANDSCAPE

Following the large increases seen between 2002 and 2009, overall DAH flattened in 2010 and 2011. This decrease was largely due to the economic problems faced by donor countries. Considerable increases in external financing for global health from traditional bilateral donors, the European Commission, and emerging economies, is unlikely to materialize until 2015.[1]

The Millennium Declaration at the United Nations General Assembly Special Session in 2000 galvanized donors to increase their financial investments to support efforts aimed at controlling HIV/AIDS, tuberculosis, malaria, vaccine preventable diseases in children, and much less convincingly, conditions affecting the health of pregnant women and neonates.[7-10]

Official development assistance (ODA) for population and reproductive health increased from $6.5 billion in 2002 to between $17 and $26 billion in 2009 (both in constant 2008 $US).[11] Private citizens through taxes, corporations through donations, and foundations have funded an increasingly large share of DAH, rising to 27% in 2007.[12]

The Global Fund to fight AIDS, Tuberculosis, and Malaria and GAVI, new institutions that apply innovative financing mechanisms, have driven the significant increase in development assistance for health. The focus of these institutions includes vaccine preventable childhood diseases and maternal health in the case of GAVI and tuberculosis, malaria, maternal and child health, and, most importantly, HIV/AIDS in the case of the Global Fund. HIV/AIDS also benefits significantly from the US President's Emergency Program for AIDS Relief (PEPFAR), a program funded from bilateral sources.[13]

By contrast, the total contribution from innovative revenue-raising sources to global ODA has been low between 2000 and 2009. Excluding local currency bonds issued by the multilateral development banks and aid extended by emerging donors, the total is a relatively modest amount of $6.3 billion from 2000 through 2008. Global solidarity levies, such as those placed on airline tickets, accounted for only about $1 billion. Further, the total raised through other innovative efforts and pooling with private donors was only $3.7 billion.

Financing for noncommunicable diseases[14] and cancer in LMICs –despite an increase in real terms from $238 million in 2004 to $686 million in 2008– pales in significance when compared to the funding for communicable diseases. In 2004, NCD and cancer funding in LMICs was a mere 1.3% of total communicable disease funding. In 2007, this share was 2.3%. From 2004 to 2008, the estimated donor funding for cancer was a paltry $60 million. Bilateral and multilateral agencies provided one half of the total $2 billion in accumulated donor funding for NCDs and cancer between 2004 and 2008, with the remaining amount funded by private for-profit and private non-profit organizations – especially the Wellcome Trust UK, which provided $458 million.[15]

8.ii.2 INNOVATION ALONG THE FINANCING VALUE CHAIN[16]

The term "innovative financing" gained prominence in 2002, following the International Conference on Financing for Development that led to the development of the Monterrey Consensus.[17] Innovative financing focuses on non-traditional, catalytic approaches to external donor financing for health. It encompasses many aspects of financing, from identifying additional funding to more effective use of funds.[18]

An expanded definition of innovative financing considers the financing value chain.[16] This financing value chain includes: nontraditional approaches to resource mobilization to supplement official contributions; innovative ways of pooling resources; channeling resources to other countries; new incentives for delivery and allocation at the country and program levels; and implementation of programs through contracting, financing, and oversight. The expanded definition encompasses funding from both private not-for-profit foundations and the for-profit private sector.

Resource mobilization in the expanded innovative financing framework involves gathering funds for health from various sources beyond the traditional donors. Innovative approaches to pooling involve combining funds at the global level through financing mechanisms from traditional and "novel" sources, such as the private sector, philanthropic agencies, innovative financing instruments, and funding from countries that are not part of the Development Assistance Committee of the OECD. New approach to channeling funds in the new innovative financing framework differs from traditional approaches because it emphasizes country ownership, in line with the Paris Principles of Aid Effectiveness,[19] involving an inclusive process for developing proposals or national plans with participation of a wide range of stakeholders, involving civil society and the private sector in establishing health priorities. Innovative financing approaches to channeling finances involve mechanisms that use performance-based funding principles. Innovations in resource allocation encourage recipient countries to develop their own programs, aligned with national and strategic health plans.

Innovative resource allocation can be used to create incentives to promote funding for areas that private markets will not serve, or to scale-up successful interventions. Financial guarantees and recognition of corporate social responsibility are examples of these incentives, which can be categorized as push mechanisms that offer supply-side incentives, or pull mechanisms that rely on demand creation or signaling for new health products and uptake of implementation.[20]

8.ii.3 HARNESSING THE MOST EFFECTIVE PLATFORMS

The results of innovative global financing efforts have been highly uneven. In spite of the many possible approaches to innovative development financing, only three major health-related innovative mechanisms have reached global scale: GAVI, the Global Fund, and UNITAID. These mechanisms have mostly addressed vaccine-preventable childhood diseases (GAVI), HIV/AIDS, tuberculosis, and malaria (the Global Fund and UNITAID) by investing in medicines, vaccines, diagnostics, preventative interventions, and health systems strengthening.[21-23] The Global Fund, GAVI, and the President's Emergency Plan for AIDS Relief (PEPFAR) have helped to create pull mechanisms for HIV/AIDS, tuberculosis, and malaria medicines, diagnostics, and for vaccine development.

OECD has singled out GAVI and the Global Fund as two important innovative financing mechanisms, and distinguishes them from new resource generation schemes such as air-ticket levy, International Finance Facility for Immunisation (IFFIm), and (PRODUCT)RED. Unlike initiatives that focus mainly on raising funds for health, the Global Fund and GAVI are innovative integrated financing mechanisms because they span the essential functions of resource mobilization, pooling, channeling, and allocation.[24]

GAVI, the Global Fund, and UNITAID have introduced innovations in their resource mobilization and resource allocation mechanisms. For example, GAVI is largely funded through IFFIm, which raises funds by issuing bonds in the capital markets and converts the long-term government pledges into immediate available cash resources, effectively front-loading the financing. The Advance Market Commitment (AMC) for pneumococcal disease also supports GAVI financing through a long-term pledge that provides new incentives to pharmaceutical companies to develop products. The Global Fund receives contributions from private companies, such as Chevron and Takeda, and private philanthropic foundations, such as the Bill and Melinda Gates Foundation. It also receives funds from innovative resource mobilization approaches such as (PRODUCT)RED, a brand licensed to partner companies such as Nike, American

Express, GAP, Starbucks, and Apple Inc. which give a percentage of the profits associated with their products that carry the (PRODUCT)RED logo to raise awareness and funds to address HIV/AIDS in Africa.[25] The Global Fund has also used debt swaps to make domestic resources available for the approved Global Fund programs through the Debt2Health initiative. The latter requires participating creditor and debtor countries, which are also grant recipients from the Global Fund, to agree to a three-party accord. Through this accord, creditors forgo repayment of a portion of their claims on the condition that the beneficiary country invests an agreed-upon counterpart amount in health through Global Fund-supported programs.

The two major, innovative resource mobilization mechanisms are the Global Fund and GAVI, both of which have been predominantly supported by donor governments. As of February 2011, the $17.9 billion in pledges from the public sector represented 95% of total pledges to mid-2012 to the Global Fund, with the $950 million from the private sector contributing the remaining 5%. The Bill & Melinda Gates Foundation accounted for most of the remaining $950 million. Since its launch in 2006, (PRODUCT)RED has generated $160 million. Financing from Debt2Health has amounted to around $120 million.

Total funds received by GAVI between 2000 and 2010 summed to $5.2 billion. Of this, 39% came from donor governments and the European Commission, 24% from private contributions, 36% from IFFIm to GAVI Fund Affiliate transfers, and 1% from AMC funds. Atun et al[16] provide a more detailed discussion of innovative financing of the Global Fund and GAVI.

UNITAID has committed more than $500 million in 80 primarily low income recipient countries. In partnership with the Clinton Foundation, UNITAID has successfully achieved a reduction in the price of second-line AIDS treatments, ranging from 25% to 50%, depending on the country's income level, and a 40% reduction in the price of pediatric antiretroviral drug treatments.

The independent, not-for-profit Millennium Foundation was established to forge a partnership with the travel industry in countries that have not adopted the UNITAID airline levy. The foundation created the MASSIVEGOOD donation program to enable voluntary contributions by ordinary citizens at the point-of-sale. To establish the Millennium Foundation, UNITAID provided an initial grant of $22.3 million. However, MASSIVEGOOD had not been able to raise significant funding realizing by mid 2011 only in the region of $200,000 from their leisure program, matching funds, and donations from their corporate program, leading the Millennium Foundation to end the initiative.

More recently, efforts to mobilize new funds for reproductive, maternal, newborn, and child health (RMNCH) have been promising.[26] In the UN General Assembly's 66th Session in 2011, at the special first anniversary High-Level

Meeting of Every Woman Every Child, the UN Secretary-General announced more than 100 new commitments to the UN's Global Strategy for Women's and Children's Health from domestic sources, private foundations, multilateral organizations, the UN, the private sector, and professional associations. The pledges by these institutions total an unprecedented amount of more than $40 billion, including "game-changing" multi-stakeholder endeavors that involve private sector partners.

The momentum created by these pledges offers an important opportunity for applying a diagonal approach in global financing innovations. Linking interventions for cancer and NCDs to those for RMNCH will enable greater synergies from investments made and better protect women and children against health risks, not just at childbirth and during the early years of life (Chapter 6), but also throughout their life cycles.

This apparent success of efforts to secure large pledges from diverse sources to finance the implementation of the RMNCH strategy, Every Woman Every Child, offers a model for cancer.[27] By utilizing the considerable investments countries have already made for CCC as a platform (see domestic financing section below), the cancer movement could encourage key stakeholders to co-invest and leverage these investments, not by establishing a new global fund, but by better engaging the cancer movement and mobilizing additional domestic and international resources for CCC in LMICs. Actions to expand funding should draw on a broad range of stakeholders, especially those groups involved in resource mobilization and investment for other NCDs.

Another promising innovative resource mobilization and service delivery initiative is the Pink Ribbon Red Ribbon partnership, designed to leverage public and private investments to combat cervical and breast cancer in sub-Saharan Africa and Latin America.[28] The initiative, led by the George W. Bush Institute, PEPFAR, Susan G. Komen for the Cure, and UNAIDS with an initial commitment of $75 million across five years, aims to improve the linkage between CCC and HIV/AIDS through a diagonal investment and service delivery approach. The initiative seeks to expand the availability of cervical cancer screening and treatment —especially for high-risk HIV-positive women— and to promote breast cancer education by leveraging existing HIV/ AIDS platforms and PEPFAR investments, and by drawing on the lessons learned from the, significant scale-up of HIV/AIDS services.

8.ii.4 Global innovative financing: Conclusions

The analysis of investment patterns for global health suggests that to date, international sources have provided limited additional funds for innovative financing, especially for cancer and NCDs. While funding from new sources has played an increasingly important role in development assistance for health, official contributions from bilateral sources have continued to be the major source of international financing. The contributions from the private sector and innovative financing appear to be relatively small and uneven, yet play an important role in reducing country dependence on official contributions.

Instead, what has worked in innovative financing in global health is the emergence of viable innovative, integrated financing mechanisms, such as the Global Fund and GAVI, which have effectively pooled and channeled investment of donor funds at a global scale, to achieve results. These innovative, integrated financing mechanisms can provide effective platforms for expanding access to CCC, especially by linking and leveraging investments from new initiatives, such as the Pink Ribbon Red Ribbon and RMNCH platforms, which offer opportunities to expand programs for cancer and other NCDs.

Several important lessons emerge from innovative global health financing efforts to mobilize and channel external resources for CCC:

1. It appears unlikely in the near term that significant amounts of new monies will be available from innovative revenue-raising sources. Traditional donor and domestic funding will likely continue to predominate.

2. Innovative integrated financing mechanisms that have worked at the global scale for disease- and population-specific initiatives, such as the Global Fund and GAVI, could be utilized to create synergies for CCC, especially because the Global Fund will have to continue to invest in health systems to manage HIV/AIDS as a chronic illness.[29-32] RMNCH is an example where such synergies have been achieved. Significant growth in financing since 2006 has come not from targeted investments, but through cross-investments largely driven by GAVI and the Global Fund.[33] Thus, investments in HIV/AIDS are providing clear benefits for the health of women and children.[34] These two innovative integrated financing mechanisms have been able to channel large amounts of funding to LMICs to strengthen health systems.[35]

3. Initial start-up costs for new innovative financing mechanisms can be very high, far outweighing investments or returns achieved (for example, MASSIVEGOOD spent more than $11 million to start up the

initiative, with relatively small amounts of money raised). Rather than creating new agencies to fund CCC, the existing innovative financing mechanisms should be used to pool and invest new monies.

4. New financing commitments for RMNCH announced at the 66th UN General Assembly and the Pink Ribbon Red Ribbon initiative on cancer and HIV/AIDS provide additional opportunities for engagement and for channeling new funds.

5. New RMNCH platforms that have succeeded in mobilizing additional resources, as well as global support and coordination, provide good models for broad-based international partnerships for cancer and NCDs. A similar platform should be developed to bring together stakeholders and highlight existing investments in CCC.

Further, mobilization and investment of any new international funding for CCC in LMICs should be guided by the following principles:

i. *Additionality:* New funding should be in addition to existing international and domestic investments for CCC.

ii. *Subsidiarity:* Resources from the international donor community should be subsidiary in the sense that they are supplementary to local alternatives when these have been exhausted, and are used in ways that do not diminish local efforts.

iii. *Non-duplicative:* New funding should be channeled through existing innovative global financing mechanisms to reduce transaction costs, minimize start-up costs, and create synergies by leveraging investments for both disease control and health system strengthening.

iv. *Stability:* Funding should be predictable and stable over time.

v. *System-wide synergy:* Targeted investments should create synergies across diseases or population groups. These investments also should make the best possible use of existing mechanisms and institutions in ways that serve multiple health needs, increase coordination, and avoid duplication of efforts. The allocation of resources should avoid crowding out other important priorities. This means investments should favor programs and projects that also benefit other health problems, following the diagonal approach.

vi. *Continuity:* Investments should focus not only on scaling-up interventions, but also on protecting gains and providing sustainability.

vii. *Relevance:* Local relevance should be guaranteed through comprehensive cancer plans.

8.iii Innovative domestic financing: Effective and equitable options[1]

8.iii.1 THE DOMESTIC FINANCING LANDSCAPE

Much of the financing for CCC is and will continue to be domestically sourced. Thus, a great deal of innovation in CCC financing will involve reorganizing domestic finance to focus on equity and efficiency. Still, even in countries where global financing is relatively small, these additional external investments can play an important catalytic role in driving policy change and innovation in care delivery.

Domestic sources of financing account for a substantial share of total health expenditure (THE), especially in middle income countries where external financing is 1% of THE, or less. Even in low income countries, WHO estimates that in 2008, external sources covered, on average, 16.4% of total health expenditure in LMICs. With the important exception of the poorest and most aid-dependent countries –Malawi, Tanzania, and Mozambique– even countries as poor as Ethiopia, Niger, and Haiti rely on domestic funding for more than half of total health expenditure.[36]

Domestic finance of health and disease management is primarily of two types: (1) private, out-of-pocket and at point of service by families; and (2) public spending, social protection, or insurance schemes. The first type is regressive, a source of inefficiency and can cause impoverishment. The second, is an effective and equitable way of organizing health system financing. Out-of-pocket spending by families, which accounts for more than 50% of total health expenditure in many LMICs, is the least equitable and most inefficient means of financing a health system.[37-40]

While acute care costs even for simple ailments can push an already poor family much deeper into poverty, the repeating and ongoing costs of a chronic illness are even more devastating. Recent research in India demonstrates the substantial financial vulnerability of households to NCDs, especially to cancer. The share of out-of-pocket health expenditure devoted to NCDs increased from one-third to almost 50% in a decade. Further, the cost of a single stay for cancer or heart disease in a public hospital is the equivalent of 40 to 50% of annual per capita income.[41] In South Asia, the probability of incurring catastrophic health expenditure from hospitalization is 160% higher for cancer, and 30% higher for cardiovascular disease, than hospitalization for a communicable disease.[42,43]

1. The authors acknowledge the contributions of Yoko Akachi for this section.

One of the most insidious aspects of this vicious illness-impoverishment cycle is that for many cancer patients the out-of-pocket spending is wasted, as it does nothing to improve health. First, the cancer is often detected late, and so the best and only useful investment is for pain control and palliation. Second, a substantial proportion of what is spent by patients is not effective because they receive low-quality, poor, or inappropriate care. Third, care is often coupled with prohibitive transportation costs and investments of time. These difficulties are more likely to occur with a disease like cancer, where primary-level physicians are ill prepared for early detection and diagnosis, and care often requires travel and ongoing treatment.

Universal health coverage is at the center of many health system reforms. For a health system to achieve universal coverage, inclusion of both beneficiaries (population) and benefits (interventions or diseases) must be taken into account.[44] The composition and depth of the package of covered services is a key determinant, and a shallow package, even if it covers a large proportion of the population, is unlikely to offer protection from financial catastrophe and financial barriers to accessing care. The inclusion of interventions for cancer and many NCDs in the package poses a specific set of challenges due to the chronic nature of illness and the importance of considering all facets of the CCC continuum (Chapter 4).

A number of countries have achieved, or are near to achieving, universal financial coverage through public insurance and pre-payment using domestic funding sources. Some countries have established universal entitlements to key services as guaranteed benefits packages. These innovations directly address the challenge of financially catastrophic and chronic illnesses, such as cancer. This coverage can include prevention and early detection of some cancers as well as partial support for tertiary-level care.

The experiences of several LMICs that have implemented universal health insurance and other innovations to provide financial protection for cancer are described below. The recommendations synthesize the lessons learned about the financing of cancer care through those experiences.

In the Latin American and Caribbean region (LAC), social insurance and health reform have been ongoing for more than a decade. The analysis below includes several countries and provides some basis for comparison. Some reforms have been relatively well documented, both in initial and in later phases (Colombia, Chile, Mexico), while others are very recent or have not yet been evaluated (Peru, Dominican Republic). These health financing reform efforts have built on each other and have much in common, such as the separation of funds for public and catastrophic expenditures, the development of contributory and subsidized plans for different population groups, the challenges of incorporating and financing the informal sector, and building on basic services associated with social welfare programs. Each of these reforms is facing the challenge of including chronic, catastrophic illness such as cancer in the package for both rich and poor population groups. In each of the LAC countries, cancer is a tracer disease that marks the depth of the package.

8.iii.2 INNOVATIVE FINANCING COUNTRY CASES

CASE 1: MEXICO

Felicia Marie Knaul, Salomón Chertorivski Woldenberg,
Héctor Arreola-Ornelas

The Mexican health system employed innovative financing mechanisms to respond to the health challenges posed by epidemiological transition and poverty.[45] The health reform of 2003 and the *Seguro Popular de Salud* (SPS) initiative have been internationally recognized.[46,47] The reform was launched in 2004 and was designed to achieve universal financial protection in health through public insurance coverage, and by expanding supply and improving the quality of services. The reform innovations concentrated first on the poorest segments of the population, taking into account the complex health backlog of poverty and the impact of chronic and noncommunicable disease.[48-52]

Until 2003, the Mexican health system was based on a segmented model. Formal sector workers and their families had been able to access pooled, prepayment options for decades through public social security programs. The packages officially offered by the social security institutions were virtually unlimited, yet in reality their use was limited by long waiting times and lack of quality. At the same time, half of the population –approximately 50 million people, who are mostly poor, non-salaried workers, and rural residents– relied on coverage through the Ministry of Health, based on a residual budget, with a restricted package of covered services, low per capita investment in health, and limited access. Approximately half of total health expenditure was out-of-pocket and concentrated among the uninsured and an estimated 2 to 4 million families –mostly poor– faced catastrophic and impoverishing health expenditures each year.[53,54]

All Mexicans who do not have access to social security are eligible for SPS. Seguro Popular coverage began with the poorest segments of the population and steadily expanded with the goal of attaining universal coverage by 2012. In 2012 Mexico achieved a major milestone: coverage reached over 52 million people who were previously uninsured and the budgetary allocation for universal coverage was achieved.[55,56] Funding is primarily federal, with contributions from states, and a small segment from sliding scale pre-payment by households (which is zero for all families living in poverty).[57,58]

The SPS applies a diagonal approach to health insurance.[54] Horizontal, population-based coverage is provided for all public and community health services. A package of essential health services is managed at the state-level for all those enrolled with SPS. Catastrophic illnesses are aggregated into the national Fund for Protection against Catastrophic Expenses (FPCE), which offers accelerated vertical coverage– anyone diagnosed with a covered disease is eligible for SPS, and a complete range of treatment services is included. In the case of breast cancer, for example, the fund covers medications and interventions such as trastuzumab and partial breast reconstruction that often cannot be included in less comprehensive packages. Further, as of 2006 all children under five are covered for a wide range of health needs, supplementing both the package of basic services and the FPCE through a horizontal approach entitled Insurance for a New Generation.[59]

Parallel to the extension of population coverage, the package of interventions and covered diseases has expanded to include a wider range of personal health services at the primary, secondary, and tertiary levels of care. Similarly, the FPCE has expanded to cover additional diseases. By the end of 2010, the package of personal health services covered 275 interventions, and the FPCE covered 49 interventions for eight disease groups.[60-62] Among the first diseases to be covered in the FPCE in 2004-05 were cervical cancer, HIV/AIDS and ALL in children.[63,64] All childhood cancers were added in 2006, breast cancer in 2007, and testicular and prostate cancer and non-Hodgkin lymphoma in 2011. Although the fund and number of covered diseases and interventions have increased continually and substantially –even in the face of economic crisis– an ongoing challenge is to expand to cover the diseases that are not yet covered, including several cancers.[65]

Rigorous evaluation processes have been underway since the SPS was established, and the results are encouraging. Overall, the incidence of catastrophic spending has decreased by more than 20% among those enrolled in Seguro Popular, as has overall out-of-pocket spending, especially among the poorest households.[66,67]

Evidence on specific covered diseases is also positive. One study showed that hypertensive adults insured through Seguro Popular had a significantly higher probability of obtaining effective treatment, and that this was associated with a greater supply of health professionals.[68] Between 2006 and 2009, coverage of new cancer cases of cancer in children through Seguro Popular increased from 3% to 55% and 36-month survival rates reached 50% for ALL and 75% for Hodgkin lymphoma, although with significant variance by region indicated the need to strengthen service provision and capacity. Abandonment of treatment was approximately 6% and substantially lower than in other countries of the Latin America region.[69] Results for breast cancer are preliminary yet suggestive of important gains in access to care and improving the financial situations of families. By 2010, Seguro Popular was financing treatment for more than 17,000 women.[70] In 2005, approximately 30% of the 600 women diagnosed with breast cancer at the National Institute of Cancer of Mexico abandoned treatment within a year, compared to less than 1% of 900 women in 2010.[71]

The combination of horizontal coverage of personal health services with a catastrophic fund makes it possible to offer financial protection for chronic-catastrophic illness such as cancer, as well as investing in prevention, early detection, and survivorship care. The six stages of the CCC continuum can and should be fully integrated into the health insurance system to maximize the benefits to patients and the value of the significant investments in treatment. Barriers remain particularly around early detection in the case of breast cancer. Further, survivorship introduces a new set of challenges and of patient needs that will have to be integrated into the health system.

CASE 2: COLOMBIA

Ramiro Guerrero, Ana María Amaris

In the early nineties, Colombia adopted a universal social health insurance system and introduced a mandatory benefits package.[72-77] Implementation has been gradual, and universal coverage is expected in 2011.[78] Overall, enrollment has protected households against catastrophic expenditures, and improvements in access and utilization of health services, particularly among the poor, have been documented.[79]

Colombia has a contributory plan for workers and employers in the formal sector, and a subsidized one for the informal sector, the unemployed and the poor. The average per capita rate in 2009 was $US 182 per year in the contributory plan, and $US 105 in the subsidized plan.[80] Multiple competing insurers, who receive established risk adjusted per capita payments, deliver the legally approved package of services. The subsidized plan has a smaller benefits package, but the Colombian government is committed to equalizing the two plans by 2014.

This financing reform has been implemented in the context of a growing NCD and cancer epidemic. Prior to the financing reform, most services for catastrophic illnesses were paid out-of-pocket in both public and private facilities. When the content of the insurance package was first defined in 1994, coverage was mandated for a series of basic interventions. Cancer was classified as a catastrophic disease along with HIV/AIDS, chronic renal failure, transplants, genetic disorders, and severe trauma. In 1995, some coverage for high-cost catastrophic diseases like cancer was also included in the basic plan for the subsidized system.

Coverage of catastrophic illness has expanded gradually. For cancer, surgery, chemotherapy, radiotherapy, and some drugs (such as tamoxifen and paclitaxel) have been included in the insurance package. In 2000, screening interventions were included for breast, cervical, prostate, and colorectal cancers. Radiotherapy treatment with linear accelerators was included in the package for both plans in 2002, while mammography and breast biopsies were included for both regimes since 2012.[81]

Still, important exclusions remain, which make coverage of treatment less effective, for instance, certain higher-cost drugs, such as trastuzumab, are excluded from both packages. Geographical disparities and barriers in access to prevention and care also persist.[82] More than 77.8% of breast cancer patients are diagnosed when breast cancer has reached advanced stages.[83]

In the courts, patients often successfully challenge the denial of services and drugs, even those that are not included in the package. The number of such legal claims has grown explosively, as have costs fueled by the resulting inefficient, ad hoc procurement and payment methods.[84] In this context, substantial amounts of resources are devoted to very expensive drugs that are given to patients who sue, often after late diagnosis, when treatment is not very effective. Meanwhile, prevention and detection remain underfunded.

In 2007, the government mandated the creation of a high-cost sub-account to pool and redistribute risk for catastrophic conditions across the entire population. This was a response to a fiscal crisis in the system generated by the concentration of catastrophic patients in the main public insurer. Based on a successful pilot of the sub-account for chronic renal failure, several cancers are being added. These would include cervical, breast, stomach, colorectal, prostate, acute lymphoid leukemia, acute myeloid leukemia, Hodgkin and non-Hodgkin lymphomas, along with epilepsy, rheumatoid arthritis, and HIV/AIDS.

CASE 3: THE DOMINICAN REPUBLIC

Magdalena Rathe

The Dominican Republic began implementation of extensive health financial reform in 2007.[85-89] Prior to the reform, cancer patients – and many others who required complex and specialized services for NCDs – severely lacked financial protection. Most specialized services were (and still are) provided by two not-for-profit oncological hospitals where the most comprehensive cancer care in the country is available, as well as private facilities serving mainly high income groups. The public hospitals offered only basic services to low income patients in early stages of their disease. Most insurance plans provided limited coverage for cancer, and only minor support and subsidized care was available otherwise from civil society organizations and not-for-profit hospitals, respectively, forcing patients into out-of-pocket spending.

The financial reform created a compulsory, publicly financed health insurance scheme– the Seguro Familiar de Salud (SFS). The scheme was designed to cover the entire population over a ten-year period. Similar in design to the Colombian reform, the SFS has both contributory and subsidized components. The contributory portion is financed with employer and employee contributions while the subsidized portion is financed by the federal government. As of early 2011, 45% of the population was covered by the scheme – 25% within the contributory plan and 20% within the subsidized plan. A third regime, aimed at covering informal workers through a combination of individual and federal government contributions is under discussion.

The SFS covers an explicit and comprehensive package of community and personal health goods and services. There is one single benefit package, although cost and quality differ given that the subsidized population may only have access to services at the public facilities, which provide lower quality because they lack adequate resources and frequently confront governance issues. Rationing in the traditional public sector facilities is, therefore, implicit. The difference of prices among the subsidized and contributory package is due to the still widely used supply side financing mechanism of the public facilities.

Cancer and other NCDs were not a priority in public health plans until recently, despite their high and increasing burden. However, with the reform, cancer was included in the benefit's package. When services do not exist in the public sector, the SFS pays for them in private institutions for the subsidized plan, such as the not-for-profit private oncological hospitals, most of whose patients are insured either by the subsidized or contributory plans.

The fund covers one million Dominican pesos per person ($28,000 at 2010 exchange rates) per year, with a 20% co-payment, for diagnosis, treatment, and palliative care for a specific set of diseases. In addition to adult and pediatric cancers, the fund lists several other conditions including heart disease, dialysis and joint replacement. Cancer coverage includes diagnostic procedures, surgery, hospitalization, chemotherapy, radiotherapy and other procedures, up to the limit of catastrophic coverage. An additional $2,500 (with 30% co-payment) per year is available for cancer drugs on a specified list, beyond other outpatient prescription drugs, including new drugs such as trastuzumab for positive HER2 breast cancer. The package includes screening services for several cancers, such as Pap smear and mammography, integrated within preventative women's health programming. However, this is not always feasible due to insufficient resources available to public providers.

The health system now offers comprehensive financial protection for treatment of all cancers and has a fund to cover catastrophic illnesses with some similarities in design to the Mexican Seguro Popular, but some important differences, too. The Dominican package is broad, which forces the introduction of implicit rationing measures. Further, these funds are not separated from the basic package, which is likely to result in financial unsustainability for the rest of the health system. Specific to cancer, the existing rationing mechanism by intervention jeopardizes the comprehensiveness of treatment for the patients.

The implementation of the reform represented a major breakthrough in financial protection for Dominicans living with cancer. Yet, the reform is new and not well documented, lacking studies on its long term sustainability. The lack of a population based cancer registry will make it difficult to evaluate the implications of new policies.

CASE 4: PERU[90]

Janice Seinfeld

In 2009, the Peruvian government passed the Universal Health Insurance Law,[2] which established mandatory membership in a health insurance plan for the entire population. This law offers opportunities to incorporate cancer into the new universal health insurance system.

Drawing on reforms in Colombia and Mexico, and similar in some ways to the Dominican Republic, the new plan established three programs: the contributory, the semi-contributory, and the subsidized which is for the population that lives in poverty. The law sets out a package of conditions, interventions, and services that will be covered in all institutions administering health insurance funds. In relation to cancer, the law covers the diagnosis of cancer of the cervix, breast, colon, stomach, and prostate, but covers treatment only for cervical cancer. The package does not cover prevention or health promotion, which severely limits the possibilities of applying cost-effective health insurance strategies.

Because high-cost treatments are not included in the Essential Health Insurance Plan[3] (Plan Esencial de Aseguramiento en Salud), additional coverage of $3200 for a list of specific conditions has been provided for those affiliated with the subsidized plan.

In addition to the issue of funding for cancer, there are problems of capacity and limited information. Supply is fragmented and provided through a combination of public and private sectors. Cancer drugs are expensive and typically marketed by monopolistic suppliers. Few medical oncologists and health personnel for prevention and early detection are available. In 2010, training was initiated through a special budget line with the National Institute of Neoplastic Diseases, aiming to increase capacity in the public sector. With the implementation of the law, additional mechanisms for strengthening supply will be developed. Strengthening MOH capacity for stewardship in CCC is a key element. Such stewardship is needed to counterbalance and work with leading oncology groups in a multi-stakeholder effort.

CASE 5: RWANDA

Agnes Binagwaho, Afsan Bhadelia

Several countries in Africa have introduced community-based health insurance. Rwanda provides a model of rapid scale-up and near-universal coverage.[91] The country-wide plan has been made more effective by strong government stewardship, which includes the coordination of external and donor aid, and the introduction of a performance-based pay program.[92-94]

Over the last decade, based on a strong commitment to providing universal health coverage, the Government of Rwanda (GoR) has undertaken extensive health care reforms and adopted innovative health care financing mechanisms. The share of GDP spent on health went from 4% in 2000 and 2002, to 6.6% in 2003,[95] and from 1998 to 2007, the annual budget share allocated to health increased from 2.5 % to 10%.[96,97]

The Mutual Health Insurance (MHI or mutuelles de santé) is the largest insurance plan and is dedicated to serving poorer households. In 1996, after the genocide, MHI was reintroduced to mitigate out-of-pocket catastrophic health expenditure and to increase health service utilization. A national policy to scale-up the mutuelles was initiated in 2004.[98] In 2008, a law on MHI was put in place to make health insurance compulsory with a goal of reaching universal coverage by 2012. Current enrollment is near 91% of the population. Increased utilization of modern healthcare services and reduced catastrophic expenditure on health is further evidence of the success of the insurance plan.[99-101]

Sources of funding include annual household user fees or premiums stratified by household revenue, with 25% (the very poor) paying nothing, approximately 71% (those with middle income) paying 3,000 Rwandan francs and about 4% (those with higher income) paying 7,000 Rwandan francs per person per year. These premiums are combined with government and donor subsidies. Payments are collected by the sections of mutuelles and the funds are kept at the section level, with 45% transferred to the district pooling funds and 10% to the national pooling fund. The district pooling fund covers all care conducted within the district outside of the section catchment areas and the national pooling fund covers care conducted outside of the district catchment areas. A flat rate co-payment of $0.40 per visit at the health center level, and 10% of costs at the hospital level, also apply.[102]

Even that financial contribution seems onerous for many households. Premium subsidies are provided for 25% of the vulnerable, and membership fees are waived for them. Initially, this included genocide survivors and people living with HIV/AIDS (PLWHAs), though PLWHAs now pay according to their revenue stratification.[103] Through a five-year grant provided by the Global Fund, mutuelle membership fees for almost one million poor and orphans, as well as PLWHAs, has been covered. The social insurance program for the formal sector, the Military Medical Insurance, the central government, international partners and private insurers contribute to the national solidarity fund.[104,105]

There are three complimentary packages: primary health services at the health center, services at the district level, and tertiary-level services at national referral teaching hospitals and the psychiatric hospital. Health care centers serve as the key point for managing referrals, which are required for care at the district and tertiary levels.[106]

The expansion of the insurance plan is limited by availability of human resources, medical diagnostics, and treatment facilities. Although the MHI system seeks to provide a baseline financial infrastructure for more comprehensive care for chronic diseases, its depth is limited by insufficient specialized services.

Reviews of the mutuelle program highlight several lessons learned: the importance of broad dialogue and stakeholder inclusion; subsidies for the poorest are required even though they increase the pressure on the public budget, with external and NGO funding as the stopgap; monitoring and evaluation with feedback to policy makers, is essential; and, the political and economic spillovers have stimulated household and community empowerment, providing a base for other programs for poverty reduction and lending.[107]

The Government of Rwanda considers cancer, along with other NCDs, as a priority. The CCC package is being expanded starting with cervical cancer vaccination through the National Strategic Plan for the Prevention, Control, and Mitigation of Cancer affecting Women.[108] Further, the government of Rwanda is seeking to integrate CCC into existing service systems using an integrated approach, beginning with women's cancer, which can be integrated into existing maternal and child health, and sexual and reproductive health programs and services, as well as cancers associated with HIV/AIDS.

CASE 6: TAIWAN[109]

Tsung-Mei Cheng

For over a quarter century, cancer has been the leading cause of death in Taiwan. In response to this challenge, Taiwan's government has in recent years intensified efforts for both cancer prevention and treatment. Specific targets are breast, cervical, colon, lung, and oral cancers, which account for more than 50% of cancer mortality.[110,111] Taiwan's National Health Insurance (NHI), which offers universal access to health and medical services, and financial protection for both prevention and treatment, has made it possible to implement this policy initiative.

In March of 1995, Taiwan established the single-payer National Health Insurance program (NHI) with comprehensive benefits. With the new program 41% (8.6 million) of Taiwan's previously uninsured population, most of them children under 14 and the elderly over 65, became eligible for health insurance coverage.[112] The NHI enrolled over 90% of the population at the end of the first year of implementation, and since the mid-2000s, the NHI has covered over 99% of Taiwan's population of 23 million.[113]

For many years, Taiwan's total annual national health spending has remained at or below 6.2% of GDP, rising to 6.9% in 2010, in part because of the global financial crisis, which affected Taiwan's economy while health expenditure remained largely unchanged. At 6.9% of GDP, Taiwan's health spending remains at the low-cost end of rich OECD countries.[114] Annual growth rate of Taiwan's national health spending has been between 3% and 5%.[115]

The NHI accounts for 50.2% of total national health spending in 2010.[116] The NHI benefit package is comprehensive and uniform across beneficiaries, and includes outpatient- and inpatient care, drugs, dental care, traditional Chinese medicine, day care for the mentally ill, home nursing care, palliative care, and dialysis.

The NHI is a pay-as-you-go premium-based social insurance program. As a single payer, the government sets the fees for all services and drugs covered by the NHI. The NHI's premium rate, which for several years remained at 4.55% of wage and salary, increased to 5.17% in 2010.[117, 118] Even this premium rate is low compared to the contributions required in most OECD countries. For certain population groups, such as low income households, the government subsidizes 100% of the NHI premium.

Payment for NHI covered benefits, including cancer treatment, is predominantly fee-for-service (FFS) for outpatient care, and both FFS and diagnosis-related group (DRGs) for inpatient care. Taiwan's NHI also has a pay-for-performance (P4P) program for five diseases, including breast cancer.[119] The breast cancer P4P program is based on input, process, and outcome measures, and participation is voluntary.

In 2003, Taiwan implemented the bill passed by parliament on cancer prevention and treatment. The five-year plan (2005-2009) developed following the passing of this bill provides comprehensive guidelines and programs for cancer education for the public, cost-effective cancer screening for the four major cancers mentioned above, and improved quality of cancer care to reduce both cancer incidence and mortality.

Despite the five-year plan on cancer prevention and treatment, no comprehensive cancer-screening programs existed in Taiwan before 2009. As of 2009, the screening rate for breast cancer was a low 5-10% of women, and screening rates for oral and lung cancers also were inadequate.[120] One notable exception was the government screening programs for cervical cancer, which resulted in reducing mortality from cervical cancer by half between 1995-2005 with a reduction of 37% in the overall prevalence of invasive cervical cancer between 1999-2003.[121]

Inadequate preventive measures, including a lack of designated funding for a broader screening program, which caused delays in implementing nationwide screening programs, led to missed opportunities for early diagnosis and treatment.[122] In 2009, recognizing Taiwan's significant lag in overall five-year cancer survival compared to high health spending countries like the US, Germany, and Switzerland, and the inadequate screening due to lack of a comprehensive cancer screening program as the main causes of this lag, Taiwan's minister of health at the time, Dr. Yeh Ching-Chuan, announced that her was making available "a special sum from the tobacco tax revenue solely for screening three major cancers in Taiwan: colon, oral and breast." [123] As Taiwan has a high prevalence of liver cancer, the government made liver cancer screening available for carriers of Hepatitis B and C viruses beginning in 2010.

The objective of the nation-wide cancer screening program is to reduce breast cancer mortality by half within ten years, as Taiwan achieved for cervical cancer earlier.

Funding for cancer screening programs comes from the cigarette tax revenue, aptly called "Tobacco Products Health and Welfare Contribution." In January of 2009, Taiwan's parliament passed a bill that doubled the cigarette tax from NT$ 10 per pack to NT$ 20 per pack, raising the cost per package from NT$ 55 to NT$ 70.[124] Tobacco tax is viewed as a 'sin tax' by Taiwan's public and raising it has met with little political resistance.

Revenue from the Tobacco Products Health and Welfare Contribution (tobacco tax) is put into the special Tobacco Prevention and Health Promotion Fund and spent on tobacco cessation and health promotion programs, including government cancer prevention measures. According to government statistics, 6% of the total 2011 budget of the Tobacco Prevention and Health Promotion Fund is designated for cancer screening and management, and 3% for tobacco use prevention.[125]

Of particular significance of the policy response to the cancer challenge is the earmarking of funding for specific cancer prevention measures. This strategy prevents underinvestment in cancer prevention and early detection which comes from relying on a general health insurance fund to cover cancer care but not necessarily screening, an unfortunate reality in many health insurance systems.

Taiwan's residents access screening services at any hospital or clinic that have contracted with the government to provide screening services. Providers are paid on a FFS basis by the government.

In summary, while overall cancer incidence rate in Taiwan has been increasing due to population ageing, life style changes and obesity, the rate shows a downward trend if ageing is removed.[126] Mortality from all cancers also shows overall improvements. These encouraging trends in both cancer incidence and mortality rates may be the results of intensified efforts by Taiwan's government for population-wide cancer prevention through cost-effective screening programs supported by earmarked funding and related preventive and treatment measures.

CASE 7: CHINA
COVERING ACUTE LYMPHOCYTIC LEUKEMIA IN CHILDREN[127]

Jing Ma

Childhood leukemia is a catastrophic disease that threatens both patients and their families. Annually, an estimated 16,000 to 20,000 cases are diagnosed in China. About 75 to 80% are acute lymphocytic leukemia (ALL) or acute promyelocytic leukemia (APL).

The 5-year survival rate of ALL is 75 to 80%, and the five-year survival rate for APL has reached 90% with accurate diagnosis and proper treatment in major hospitals. Yet, only about 8% of patients – about 1,200 to 1,500 children–receive formal diagnosis and systematic treatment. The rest of the children and their families abandon treatment because of financial difficulties or because they lack access to major hospitals and can only seek treatment in local hospitals that have limited capacity for proper diagnosis and treatment. Some children and their families do not seek treatment at all because they are unaware that these cancers could be curable.

To address this devastating situation, especially for families living in the rural areas, Premiere Wen Jiabao, in his 2010 government report, proposed pilot programs to provide health care coverage for certain types of childhood leukemia and congenital heart defects, and to increase the health care coverage of catastrophic diseases for rural areas. In response, the ministry of health and ministry of civil affairs, together, issued "Suggestions for experiments on health-care coverage for major childhood diseases in rural areas of China."

Beginning in 2010, China's ministry of health started a series of programs across the country to expand medical coverage for childhood ALL, APL, and congenital heart defects. Programs on health care coverage for major childhood diseases have been implemented in several rural areas in Sichuan, China. Led by the provincial health department and in collaboration with the department of civil affairs, two counties (Zhongjiang and Fushun) have been linked to several major hospitals in Sichuan for treatment of ALL/APL and four types of congenital heart defects, when the young patients are identified. Local village doctors will be trained to recognize early symptoms of ALL/APL, patient medical records will be established, and the social health insurance and medical costs will be closely monitored.

With support from the "xin nong he" (rural health insurance) and the medical aid systems, 90% of the total cost of treatment is covered for children up to 14 years of age. The estimated medical cost is 80,000 RMB for low-risk ALL,

120,000 RMB for intermediate-risk ALL, and 25,000 RMB for congenital heart defects. An effective treatment guideline for ALL with relatively low cost has been established at the Shanghai Xinhua Children's Medical Center through an expert committee of the ministry of health.

The programs offering financial protection for these two major childhood diseases, especially with their focus on rural areas, have the potential to catalyze and guide broader national programs, and pave the path for future medical insurance in China.

CASE 8: INDIA
AROGYASRI COMMUNITY HEALTH INSURANCE SCHEME AND
RASHTRIYA SWASTHYA BIMA YOJANA

Maja Pleic, Suneeta Krishnan

Recognizing that poor families were borrowing money and selling assets in order to pay for health services, the Indian state of Andhra Pradesh launched the Arogyasri Community Health Insurance Scheme in 2007.[128,129] The scheme is a public-private partnership between the State of Andhra Pradesh, the insurer Arogyasri Health Care Trust, and public and private hospitals. Arogyasri aims to improve access to health services for the poor by providing financial protection against high medical expenses for families below the poverty line.[130] It covers the full costs of 330 health services/ conditions related to a list of diseases considered "catastrophic," including cancers (such as head and neck, gastrointestinal, gynecological, breast, skin, and lung, among others) and several other NCDs. Arogyasri also covers screening and outpatient consultations at the primary-level. The state government pays the premiums while the insurer pays the healthcare provider directly so that beneficiaries have an entirely cashless experience at the point of service. While the scheme covers a broad range of major diseases and a large segment of the population (nearly 80% of the population of Andhra Pradesh, 20 million households living below the poverty line), families with conditions that are not covered still lack financial protection.[131]

The Rashtriya Swasthya Bima Yojana (RSBY) is a national health insurance program launched in 2008, with the aim of providing, by 2012, financial protection in health for all households below the poverty line, across India.[132] The program, a public-private partnership that involves central and state governments, and public and private insurance companies and hospitals, covers health services for any disease or ailment that requires hospitalization, with a cap of Rs 30 000 ($650) per year, per family. Also included in the package is basic support for transportation costs. While there is an annual registration fee of Rs 30 ($0.65), which is paid by families, the premium is paid by central and state governments through general taxes.[133] Registered beneficiaries can access hospitals across the country with a smartcard so that they pay nothing at the point of service.

Both of these insurance programs are publicly funded via general taxes, with either no contributions or minimal registration fees paid by the beneficiaries. Further analysis is needed to determine whether the poorest families, particularly in rural areas, are being reached, and whether they are financially sustainable in the long run.

In relation, instituted by the Planning Commission of India, the 2011 report of the High-Level Expert Group on Universal Coverage for India provides recommendations on future research and opportunities to expand existing schemes to ensure financial protection of India's most vulnerable populations.[134]

8.iii.3 Domestic innovative financing: Conclusions

The cases of innovative financial reform that enable inclusion of cancer in essential health services or in insurance packages offer several important lessons for LMICs. These can provide valuable insight on harnessing equitable and effective domestic CCC financing.

1. The financial barriers faced by families can lead to impoverishment, and many families will spend out-of-pocket, utilizing all family assets and jeopardizing future stability, often for ineffective treatments. Social protection in health based on pre-payment and pooling helps to resolve this problem.

2. CCC can be integrated into broader health insurance initiatives. Experience from the several LMICs analyzed in this report suggests a suitable set of prevention, early detection, treatment, and care interventions that can be effectively integrated into basic service packages covered by insurance. These interventions can be financed from general revenues that cover the overall insurance program or through specific levies.

3. Establishing entitlements around a guaranteed benefits package that includes cancer leads to improved access. People become aware of their rights and make them effective.

4. The benefits package has to be guaranteed with permanent revenue sources and capacity-building to ensure effective coverage. Low effective coverage –particularly of early detection– is common even in countries with relatively complete treatment coverage in the benefits package. This compromises final outcomes.[135]

5. Improvements in the delivery model are not achieved automatically by the mere existence of the package. Resources need to be increased with expanded training and incentives for providers in order to emphasize preventive activities and achieve better outcomes.

6. Not being able to set limits to the list of services and drugs that are publicly funded compromises both financial sustainability and equity. Resources that could save more lives if allocated to early detection can be diverted to costly treatments that offer fewer health benefits. Although the package of covered services and treatments can and should grow over time, new benefits need to be underpinned by strong evidence of their comparative effectiveness, and with sufficient funding to treat all the persons that need them. If funding for a given service or drug is only sufficient to cover part of the population, equity is compromised.

7. Separate funds for personal versus catastrophic health services should be established.

8. Although insurance covers treatment costs, families face many other financial and non-financial barriers that need to be overcome including transportation costs, care-giving for the patient and other family members, and stigma.

9. Effective financing considers the entire CCC continuum to avoid overspending on very costly, difficult, complex and painful treatments that often do not significantly extend healthy life and could have been avoided with effective prevention or early detection.

10. A strong evidence base, including the results of rigorous evaluation, is key to developing innovative financing mechanisms overall and to implementing, and continually upgrading, CCC financing and programs.

References

1. Institute for Health Metrics and Evaluation. Financing Global Health 2010: Development assistance and country spending in economic uncertainty. Seattle, WA: Institute for Health Metrics and Evaluation, 2010. http://www.healthmetricsandevaluation.org/publications/policy-report/financing-global-health-2010-development-assistance-and-countryspending-economic-uncertaint (accessed October 3, 2011).

2. Pitt C, Greco G, Powell-Jackson T, Mills A. Countdown to 2015: assessment of official development assistance to maternal, newborn, and child health, 2003–08. Lancet 2010; 376:1485-1496.

3. Institute for Health Metrics and Evaluation, 2010. http://www.healthmetricsandevaluation.org/publications/policy-report/financing-global-health-2010-development-assistance-and-countryspending-economic-uncertaint (accessed October 3, 2011).

4. Farmer P, Frenk J, Knaul FM, et al. Expansion of cancer care and control in countries of low and middle income: a call to action. Lancet. 2010;376:1186-93.

5. World Health Organization. The global burden of disease: 2004 update. Geneva, Switzerland: World Health Organization, 2008. http://www.who.int/healthinfo/global_burden_disease/2004_report_update/en/index.html (accessed October 3, 2011).

6. Porter ME. Competitive advantage: creating and sustaining superior performance. New York, NY: The Free Press. 1985.

7. United Nations General Assembly. Resolution adopted by the General Assembly. 55/2 United Nations Millennium Declaration. 18 September 2000.

8. Fisk NM, Atun R. Systematic analysis of research underfunding in maternal and perinatal health. British *Journal of Obstetrics & Gynaecology.* 2009; 116: 347-56.

9. Fisk NM, Atun R. Market failure and the poverty of new drugs in maternal health. PLoS Medicine. 2008; 5(1): e22.

10. Fisk NM, McKee M, Atun R. Relative and absolute addressability of global disease burden in maternal and perinatal health by investment in R&D. Tropical Medicine and International Health 2011; April 7.

11. Kates J, Wexler A, Lief E, Seegobin V. Donor funding for health in low and middle income countries, 2001-2008. Washington, DC: Kaiser Family Foundation, 2010. 2010.

12. Institute for Health Metrics and Evaluation, 2010.

13. Ibid.

14. Nugent RA, Feigl AB. Where have all the donors gone? Scarce donor funding for non-communicable diseases. Centre for Global Development. Working Paper 2008. 2010. Washington D.C., U.S.A.

15. Ibid.

16. For a more detailed analysis on innovative financing that draws on the above framework see Atun R, Knaul FM, Akachi Y, Frenk J. Innovative financing for health: what is truly innovative? Mimeo.

17. United Nations. Monterrey Consensus of the International Conference on Financing for Development. 2002.

    http://www.un.org/esa/ffd/monterrey/MonterreyConsensus.pdf (accessed October 3, 2011).

18. Girishankar N. Innovating development finance: from financing sources to financial solutions. The World Bank. Policy Research Working Paper 5111. 2009. http://wwwwds.worldbank.org/servlet/WDSContentServer/WDSP/IB/2009/11/03/000158349_20091103112908/Rendered/ PDF/WPS5111.pdf (accessed October 3, 2011).

19. Organisation for Economic Co-operation and Development. The Paris Declaration on Aid Effectiveness and the Accra Agenda for Action: 2005/2008. http://www.oecd.org/dataoecd/11/41/34428351.pdf (accessed October 3, 2011).

20. Fisk NM, Atun R. Market failure and the poverty of new drugs in maternal health. *PLoS Medicine* 2008; 5(1): e22.

21. Brookings Institution Global Health Financing Initiative. Debt2Health: Debt conversion for the Global Fund to Fight AIDS, Tuberculosis, and Malaria. Snapshot Series. Washington, D.C.; 2008.

22. Ketkar S, Ratha D, eds. Innovative financing for development. The World Bank. Washington, D.C.; 2009.

23. Hecht R, Palriwala A, Rao A. Innovative financing for global health. A moment for expanded U.S. engagement? A Report of the CSIS Global Health Policy Center. Washington, DC, 2010.

24. Sandor E, Scott S, Benn J. Innovative financing to fund development: progress and prospects. DCD Issues Brief. Organisation for Economic Co-operation and Development. 2009. http://www.oecd.org/dataoecd/56/47/44087344.pdf (accessed October 3, 2011).

25. Product Red 2006. Global fund private sector partnerships: resource mobilization overview. The Global Fund, June 2006. http://www.google.com/url?sa=t&source=web&cd=3&ved=0CCMQFjAC&url=http%3A%2F%2Fwww.theglobalfund.org%2Fdocuments%2Fpartnership_forum%2FPartnershipForum_2006Day1ResourceMobilisation_Presentation_en%2F&rct=j&q=product%20red%20%2B%20global%20fund%20%2B%202006&ei=TZAUToT6HIbu0gGbrfSWDg&usg=AFQjCNHuOLaLSF7h_NgT8Iye_w_pWrtlUQ&sig2=i--_P0_B90PZfyOXvYjd0g&cad=rja (accessed October 3, 2011).

26. Partnership for Maternal, Newborn and Child Health. The PMNCH 2011 Report. World Health Organization. 2011. http://www.who.int/pmnch/en/

27. Partnership for Maternal, Newborn and Child Health. Press Release: The next frontier in women's health. World Health Organization. 2011. http://www.who.int/pmnch/media/membernews/2011/20110919_integrating_ncds_pr/en/index.html (accessed October 3, 2011).

28. U.S. Department of State. Pink Ribbon Red Ribbon. 2011. http://www.state.gov/r/pa/prs/ps/2011/09/172244.htm (accessed October 3, 2011).

29. Atun RA, McKee M, Coker R, Gurol-Urganci I. Health systems' responses to 25 years of HIV in Europe: Inequities persist and challenges remain. Health Policy. 2008; 86(2-3):181-94.

30. Ullrich A, Ott JJ, Vitoria M, Martin-Moreno JM, Atun R. Long-term care of AIDS and non-communicable diseases. Lancet 2011; 377: 639-640.

31. Atun R, Bataringaya J. Building a durable response to HIV/AIDS: implications for health systems. Journal of Acquired Immune Deficiency Syndromes 2011; 57 (Suppl 2); S91-S95.

32. Stover J, Korenromp EL, Blakley M, et al. Long-term costs and health impact of continued Global Fund support for antiretroviral therapy. PLoS ONE 2011; 6(6): e21048.

33. Institute for Health Metrics and Evaluation, 2010.

34. Rasschaert F, Pirard M, Philips MP, et al. Positive spill-over effects of ART scale up on wider health systems development: evidence from Ethiopia and Malawi. Journal of the International AIDS Society 2011; 14(Suppl 1):S3.

35. Shakarishvili G, Lansang MA, Mitta V, et al. Health systems strengthening: a common classification and framework for investment analysis. Health Policy and Planning 2011; 26(4): 316-326.

36. World Health Organization. World Health Statistics, 2011. Geneva, Switzerland; World Health Organization. 2011. http://www.who.int/whosis/whostat/EN_WHS2011_Full.pdf (accessed October 3, 2011).

37. World Health Organization. The World Health Report 2010. Health systems financing: the path to universal coverage. Geneva, Switzerland; World Health Organization. 2010.

38. World Health Organization. The World Health Report 2000. Health systems: improving performance 2000. Geneva, Switzerland; World Health Organization. 2000.

39. Knaul F, Arreola-Ornelas H, Mendez-Carniado O, et al. Evidence is good for your health system: policy reform to remedy catastrophic and impoverishing health spending in Mexico. Lancet. 2006;368(9549):1828-41.

40. World Health Organization. World Health Statistics, 2011.

41. Mahal A, Karan A, Engelgau M. The economic implications of non-communicable disease for India. Health, Nutrition and Population Discussion Paper: World Bank. 2010. http://siteresources.worldbank.org/HEALTHNUTRITIONANDPOPULATION/Resources/281627-1095698140167/ EconomicImplicationsofNCDforIndia.pdf (accessed October 3, 2011).

42. Engelgau M, K Okamoto, K Navaratne, Gopalan S. Prevention and control of selected chronic NCDs in Sri Lanka: policy options and action plan. Health, Nutrition and Population Discussion Paper: World Bank. 2010. http://siteresources.worldbank.org/HEALTHNUTRITIONANDPOPULATION/ Resources/281627-1095698140167/ NCDsSriLanka.pdf (accessed October 3, 2011).

43. Nikolic I, Stanciole A, Zaydman M. Chronic Emergency: Why NCDs matter. Health, Nutrition and Population Discussion Paper: World Bank. 2011. http://siteresources.worldbank.org/HEALTHNUTRITIONANDPOPULATION/ Resources/281627-1095698140167/ ChronicEmergencyWhy NCDsMatter.pdf (accessed October 3, 2011).

44. World Health Organization. The World Health Report 2010.

45. Knaul FM, Gonzalez-Pier E, Gomez-Dantes O et al. The quest for universal health coverage: Achieving social protection for all in Mexico. Lancet 2012; August 16.

46. The Lancet. A crucial juncture for health in Mexico. Lancet 2012; 380(76): July 14.

47. Sridhar D, Gostin LO, Yach D. Healthy governance. How the WHO can regain its relevance. Foreign Affairs 2012; May 24.

48. Gwatkin D, Ergo A. Universal health coverage: friend or foe of health equity? Lancet. 2010; 377(9784):2160-1.

49. Farmer P, Frenk J, Knaul FM et al., 2010.

50. Frenk J, Gómez-Dantés O, Knaul FM. The democratization of health in Mexico: financial innovations for universal coverage. World Health Organization. 2009;87:542-48.

51. Frenk J, González-Pier E, Gómez-Dantés O, Lezana MA, Knaul FM. Comprehensive reform to improve health system performance in Mexico. Lancet. 2006; 368: 1524-34.

52. Knaul FM, Frenk J. Health insurance in Mexico: achieving universal coverage through structural reform. Health Affairs, 2005; 24(6): 1467-1476.

53. Frenk J, González-Pier E, Gómez-Dantés O, et al., 2006.

54. Knaul F, Arreola-Ornelas H, Mendez-Carniado O, et al, 2006.

55. Knaul FM, Gonzalez Pier E, Gomez Dantes O et al, 2012.

56. Comisión Nacional de Protección Social en Salud. Informe de resultados. 2°. Semestre 2010. http://www.seguro-popular.gob.mx/images/contenidos/Informes_Resultados/Informe_Resultados_SPSS_2010.pdf (accessed October 3, 2011).

57. Frenk J, González-Pier E, Gómez-Dantés O, Lezana MA, Knaul FM. Comprehensive reform to improve health system performance in Mexico. Lancet 2006; 368: 1524-34.

58. Knaul FM, Gonzalez Pier E, Gomez Dantes O et al, 2012.

59. Knaul FM, Gonzalez Pier E, Gomez Dantes O et al, 2012.
60. Sepúlveda J, Bustreo F, Tapia R, et al. Improvement of child survival in Mexico: the diagonal approach. *Lancet* 2006; 368: 201727.
61. Comisión Nacional de Protección Social en Salud. Catalogo Universal de Servicios de Salud, 2010. CNPSS. México, D.F. http://www.seguropopular.gob.mx/images/contenidos/Causes/catalogo_2010.pdf (accessed October 3, 2011).
62. Comisión Nacional de Protección Social en Salud. Informe de resultados. 2°. Semestre 2010. http://www.seguro-popular.gob.mx/images/contenidos/Informes_Resultados/Informe_Resultados_SPSS_2010.pdf (accessed October 3, 2011).
63. Diario Oficial de la Federación. Norma Oficial Mexicana NOM-010-SSA2-1993, Para la prevención y control de la infección por virus de la inmunodeficiencia humana. DOF 21-06-2000. http://www.salud.gob.mx/unidades/cdi/nom/010ssa23.html (accessed October 3, 2011).
64. Diario Oficial de la Federación. Norma Oficial Mexicana NOM-041-SSA2-2002, Para la prevención, diagnóstico, tratamiento, control y vigilancia epidemiológica del cáncer de mama. DOF 17-09-2003. http://www.salud.gob.mx/unidades/cdi/nom/041ssa202.html (accessed October 3, 2011).
65. Knaul FM, Gonzalez Pier E, Gomez Dantes O et al, 2012.
66. King G, Gakidou E, Imai K, et al. Public policy for the poor? A randomised assessment of the Mexican universal health insurance programme. *Lancet* 2009: 373(9673), 1447-1454.
67. Knaul FM, Gonzalez Pier E, Gomez Dantes O et al, 2012.
68. Bleich SN, Cutler DM, Adams AS, Lozano R, Murray CJL.Impact of insurance and supply of health professionals on coverage of treatment for hypertension in Mexico: population based study. *British Medical Journal* 2007; 335: 875-8.
69. Pérez-Cuevas R, Doubova SV, Zapata-Tarrés MM et al. Scaling up Cancer Care for Children Without Medical Insurance in Developing Countries: The Case of Mexico. *Pediatric Blood and Cancer* 2012; August 8.
70. Presidency of the Republic [Presidencia de la República]. HPV vaccine to be applied in 2012 [En 2012 se aplicará la vacuna contra el papiloma humano]. http://www.presidencia.gob.mx/2011/08/a–partir–de–enero–de–2012–se–vacunara–contra–vph–a–todas–las–ninas–de–9–anos/ (accessed Mar 23, 2012).
71. Arce-Salinas C, Lara-Medina FU, Alvarado-Miranda A et al. Evaluation of breast cancer treatment at a tertiary-level institution with Popular Health Insurance in Mexico. *Journal of Clinical Research* 2012; 64(1): 9-16.
72. Piñeros M, Sánchez R, Cendales R, Perry F, Ocampo R. Patient delay among Colombian women with breast cancer. *Salud Publica Mexico* 2009;51:372-380.
73. Rivera DE, Cristancho A, González JC. Movilización Social para el Control del Cáncer en Colombia. Technical Document, Instituto Nacional de Cancerología. 2007. Bogotá.
74. República de Colombia, Ministerio de Protección Social, Instituto Nacional de Cancerología. Plan Nacional para el Control de Cáncer en Colombia 2010-2019. 2010. from http://cancer.gov.co (accessed October 3, 2011).
75. República de Colombia, Ministerio de Protección Social. Actualizaciones y aclaraciones al POS-C y POS-S 1994-2010. 2010. http://pos.gov.co (accessed October 3, 2011).
76. República de Colombia, Ministerio de Protección Social, Instituto Nacional de Cancerología. Atlas of Cancer Mortality in Colombia [Atlas de Mortalidad por Cáncer en Colombia]. 2010. http://cancer.gov.co (accessed October 3, 2011).
77. República de Colombia, Ministerio de Protección Social, Profamilia, Instituto Colombiano de Bienestar familiar. Encuesta Nacional de Demografía y Salud, 2010. 2011. Bogotá.
78. Guerrero, R. Financing Universal Enrollment to Social Health Insurance: Lessons Learned from Colombia. *Well-being and Social Policy*. 2008; 4(2): 75-98.
79. Giedion U, Villar M. Colombia's Universal Health Insurance System. Health Affairs. 2009;28(3): 853-863.
80. Giedion U, Panopolou G, Gomez-Fraga S. Financiamiento del desarrollo: Diseno y ajust de los planes explicitos de beneficios: el caso de Colombia y Mexico. Naciones Unidas, 2009.
81. República de Colombia, Ministerio de Protección Social. Actualizaciones y aclaraciones al POS-C y POS-S 1994- 2010. 2011. http://pos.gov.co (accessed January 3, 2012).
82. República de Colombia, Ministerio de Protección Social, Instituto Nacional de Cancerología. Plan Nacional para el Control de Cáncer en Colombia 2010-2019. 2010. http://cancer.gov.co (accessed October 3, 2011).
83. Velásquez-De Charry, L., G. Carrasquilla, et al. Equidad en el acceso al tratamiento para cáncer de mama en Colombia. Salud Publica de Mexico. 2009 ; 51(Suplememento 2): 246-253.
84. Defensoría del Pueblo. La tutela y el Derecho a la Salud 2006-2008. 2008. http://defensoria.org.co (accessed October 3, 2011).
85. National Social Security Council (CNSS), Law 87-01, Act establishing a Dominican Social Insurance System , Santo Domingo, Rep. Dominicana, 2010.
86. Rathe M. Arquitectura del Sistema de Salud dhe la Rep. Dominicana: A 10 años de su creación, Boletín mayo – junio, Fundación Plenitud, Santo Domingo, Rep. Dominicana, 2011.
87. Peña E, Muñoz L, González Pons C, Gil G. Situación y tendencia de las Neoplasias en República Dominicana al 2007. Epidemiología. 2009;17(2).
88. Rathe, Magdalena y Moliné, Alejandro, El Sistema de Salud de la República Dominicana. Revista Salud Pública de México, Vol 53, Suplemento 1, 2011.

89. Rathe, Magdalena, Salud y Equidad: Una Mirada al Financiamiento a la Salud en la República Dominicana, Macro International – PHR plus, Santo Domingo, República Dominicana, 2000.

90. Seinfeld J. Case study: Peru. Challenges to incorporating cancer in the new universal health insurance system. GTF.CCC Working Paper and Background Note Series No.4. Boston: Harvard Global Equity Initiative, 2011. http://gtfccc.harvard.edu/icb/icb.do?keyword=k69586&pageid=icb.page420088 (accessed August 12, 2012).

91. Shimeles A. Community based health insurance schemes in Africa: The case of Rwanda. Working Papers in Economics, No. 463. University of Gothenburg, 2010. http:i130.241.16.4/bitstream/2077/23064/1/gupea_2077_23064_1.pdf (accessed May 24, 2011).

92. Innovations in Health Systems. USAID Rwanda newsletter, March 2010. http://www.usaid.gov/rw/our_work/newsroom/newsletters/docs/healthsystemsstrengtheningissue.pdf (accessed October 3, 2011).

93. Logie DE, Rowson M, Ndagiji F. Innovations in Rwanda's health system: looking to the future. *Lancet* 2008; 372: 256-261.

94. Basinga P, Gertler PJ, Binagwaho A, Soucat ALB, Sturdy J, Vermeersch CM. Effect on maternal and child health services in Rwanda of payment to primary health-care providers for performance: an impact evaluation. Lancet. 2011; 377: 1421-28.

95. National health accounts Rwanda 2006 with HIV/AIDS, malaria, and reproductive health subaccounts. Kigali, Rwanda: Republic of Rwanda Ministry of Health; 2008.

96. Republic of Rwanda, Ministry of Finance and Economic Planning. Ministry of Health. 2006. Scaling up to achieve the health MDGs in Rwanda. A background study for the high-level forum meeting.

97. Logie DE, Rowson M, Ndagiji F., 2008.

98. Ministry of Health. Health sector strategic plan: July 2009-June 2012. Government of Rwanda: Ministry of Health, 2009.

99. Ibid.

100. Shimelas A, 2010.

101. Logie DE, Rowson M, Ndagiji F, 2008.

102. Antunes Fernandes A, Saksena P, Elovainio R, et al. Health financing systems review of Rwanda: options for universal coverage. World Health Organization and Ministry of Health, Republic of Rwanda. 2009.

103. Ibid.

104. Logie DE, Rowson M, Ndagiji F, 2008.

105. Diop F, Leighton C, Butera D. Health financing task force discussion paper: Policy crossroads for mutuelles and health financing in Rwanda. Washington DC: Health Financing Task Force: 2007, http://www.asivamosensalud.org/descargas/Paper_Dra_Amanda_Glassman.pdf (accessed May 24, 2011).

106. Chankova S, Sulzbach S, Diop F. Impact of mutual health organizations: evidence from West Africa. *Health Policy and Planning* 2008; 23: 264-276.

107. Diop F, Leighton C, Butera D, 2007.

108. Binagwaho A, Wagner CM, Gatera M, Karema C, Nutt CT, Ngabo F. Achieving high coverage in Rwanda's national human papillomavirus vaccination programme. *Bulletin of the World Health Organization* 2012; 90: 623-8.

109. Cheng TM. Cancer prevention policy in Taiwan: Policy implications for global health. GTF.CCC Working Paper and Background Note Series No.5. Boston: Harvard Global Equity Initiative, 2011. http://gtfccc.harvard.edu/icb/icb.do?keyword=k69586&pageid=icb.page420088 (accessed August 12, 2012).

110. Bureau of Health Promotion, Department of Health, Taiwan. Cancer Screening (Colon Cancer, Oral Cancer, Cervical Cancer, Breast Cancer) (in Chinese). http://www.bhp.doh.gov.tw/BHPnet/Portal/Them.aspx?No=201007080002 (accessed October 3 2011).

111. Bureau of Health Promotion, Department of Health, Taiwan. Cancer Incidents and Ranking Published by the Department of Health 2008, April 13, 2011 (in Chinese).

112. Cheng TM. Taiwan's new national health insurance program: genesis and experience so far. *Health Affairs* 2003; 22(3): 61-76.

113. Cheng SH, Chiang TL. Disparity of medical care utilization among different health insurance schemes in Taiwan. *Social Science and Medicine* 1998, 47:613-620.

114. Bureau of National Health Insurance, Department of Health. Universal health coverage. May 2012. http://www.nhi.gov.tw/Resource/webdata/21717_1_20120808UniversalHealthCoverage.pdf (accessed on August 12, 2012).

115. Cheng, Tsung-Mei. Lessons from Taiwan's universal national health insurance: a conversation with Taiwan's health minister Ching-Chuang Yeh. *Health Affairs* 2009; 28(4):1040-1.

116. Department of Health. 2010 National Health Expenditure Statistics. Department of Health, Executive Yuan, Taiwan, updated July 20, 2012.

117. Okma KGH, Crivelli L (Eds.). Six Countries, Six Reform Models: The Healthcare Reform Experience Of Israel, The Netherlands, New Zealand, Singapore, Switzerland And Taiwan. Hackensack, NJ: World Scientific Publishing, 2010.

118. Cheng TM. Taiwan province of China's experience with universal health coverage. In Clements B, Coady D, Gupta (Eds.). The Economics of Public Health Care Reform in Advanced and Emerging Economies. Washington, D.C.: International Monetary Fund, 2012.

119. Cheng, TM, 2009.

120. Ibid

121. Ibid

122. Ibid

123. NT$70 roughly is US$2.42 (as of August 5 2011 US$1 = NT$29.75).

124. Bureau of Health Promotion, Department of Health, Taiwan. 2011 Budget for Tobacco Prevention and Health Promotion Fund of the Bureau of Health Promotion, Department of Health (in Chinese).

125. Porter ME, Baron JF. Koo Foundation Sun Yat-Sen Cancer Center: Breast Cancer Care in Taiwan (TN). Harvard Business School Teaching Note 710-465.

126. Chiou, S. Report on the 2007 Cancer Registry. Bureau of Health Promotion, Department of Health, Taiwan, 2009 (in Chinese).

127. Ministry of Health, China, Field working meeting for improving coverage and treatment capacity for childhood ALL and congenital heart defects in rural areas. June 25, 2010 (recorded documentation) http://www.hebei.gov.cn/article/20100625/1478725.htm (accessed August 12, 2012).

128. Arogya Sri Community Health Insurance Scheme for Below Poverty Line Families in Mahaboobnagar, Anantapur, and Srikakulam Districts. Health, Medical and Family Welfare Department. Government of Adhra Pradesh, 2007. httpi/dme.ap.nic.in/insurance/Bid.pdf (accessed September 11, 2011).

129. Aarogysari Health Care Trust: Quality Medicare for the Unreached. 2011. https://www.aarogyasri.org/ASRI/index.jsp (accessed October 3, 2011).

130. Mahal A, Karan A, Engelgau M, 2009.

131. Mehta A, Bhatia A, and A. Chatterjee (Eds.) Improving health and education service delivery in India through public-private partnerships. Public-Private Partnerships Knowledge Series. Phillipines: Asian Development Bank, 2010.

132. Swarup A, Jain N. India: Rashtriya Swasthya Bima Yojana. In Special Unit for South-South Cooperation. Sharing Innovative Experience. Volume 18. Successful Social Protection Floor Experiences. United Nations Development Program, Special Unit for South-South Cooperation, International Labour Organization, 2011.

133. Ibid.

134. High-Level Expert Group for Universal Coverage. High-Level Expert Group Report on Universal Coverage for India. Submitted to Planning Commission of India, New Delhi, November, 2011

135. Regional de cobertura efectiva. México D.F. 2010.

Chapter 9

EVIDENCE FOR DECISION-MAKING: STRENGTHENING HEALTH INFORMATION SYSTEMS AND THE RESEARCH BASE

Nancy Keating, Elena Kouri, Julie R. Gralow,
Kathy Cahill, Jo Anne Zujewski, Peggy Porter,
Gustavo Nigenda, Rifat Atun, Felicia Marie Knaul

Key messages

- Health information systems and research are essential inputs for effective decision-making on cancer care and control (CCC), yet both are lacking in low and middle income countries (LMICs).

- Evidence obtained through the study of the heterogeneous populations of LMICs would expand knowledge about cancer in ways that will help both rich and poor countries and their populations alike.

- Most of the components that permit the application of a complete framework for implementation of science and that comprise essential research and evidence around CCC are lacking in LMICs.

- Specific, high-priority areas of research include: cancer genetics and biology, epidemiological studies on cancer incidence and prevalence, clinical and health system research to provide information on factors influencing effective uptake of cancer services and new interventions and to understand optimal system designs for delivering cost-effective cancer services

• Although population-based cancer registries are essential for monitoring cancer incidence and control, only a few LMICs have been able to establish them, thus population coverage is very low.

• Data for generating evidence on cancer causes, treatment, and outcomes can be drawn from several sources, yet all tend to have limitations. These sources of data need to be strengthened and can serve, not only for CCC, but also for many other areas of health and healthcare as part of a diagonal approach to building health information systems (HIS).

• Building capacity in data collection and maintenance, in HIS and in research are essential to strengthen the evidence base for decision making in CCC.

• Local policy and academic institutions can and have played important roles in capacity-building for HIS, and research in cancer and CCC in LMICs.

• Institutions in high income countries can provide and channel financial support, but more importantly, they can participate in joint learning initiatives that build capacity globally.

• Converting information into decision-making requires uptake by national and global policy makers, which requires making evidence on CCC more easily adaptable and linking it to health system performance, closing the relevance-excellence gap.

• Both global and national frameworks for monitoring need to be developed. These frameworks can be effective in strengthening CCC, especially as part of broader efforts around noncommunicable diseases (NCDs) and chronic illnesses.

• National cancer plans should stress the need for investment in translation of evidence into policy, including the establishment of frameworks for monitoring and surveillance to assess health system performance data on CCC.

9.i Introduction

High quality and timely evidence is critical for improved CCC, and for closing the cancer divide. Both global and local evidence is necessary for decision-makers to inform efficient allocation of resources among competing priorities, to enhance accountability, and to introduce policy change.[1,2]

Yet, most LMICs lack the necessary HIS, analytic capacity, and research to generate the evidence needed for improved decision-making on cancer.[3,4] In most LMICs, less than 1% of national budgets are devoted to health research, with smaller amounts invested in HIS.

Although by 2010, almost US$ 514 million from domestic and external donor sources have been invested to strengthen health information systems in LMICs, these investments are far below the funding needed to establish systems that regularly provide relevant and reliable data.[5] Although substantial funding has been provided to LMICs through the Global Fund and GAVI,[6] these investments have benefited information systems for HIV, tuberculosis, malaria, and immunization, but not strengthened mainstream HIS.

This chapter reviews the areas of research and evidence that could be most important for building global knowledge and improving decision-making in LMICs for CCC. The chapter then identifies the main requirements for, and impediments to, producing this evidence; namely core data inputs for developing HIS for CCC, capacity to produce and analyze data, and strong institutions to promote these activities. The chapter concludes with a discussion of the translation of evidence into decision-making, especially through global initiatives that promote transparency via frameworks that measure progress in countries.

9.ii Priority Areas for research to strengthen the evidence base

Implementation science involves integration of scientific evidence, practice, and policy to improve the impact of research on cancer outcomes, and to promote health across individual, organizational, and community levels. The most complete framework for the continuum of multidisciplinary translation research builds on previous characterization efforts in genomics and other areas in healthcare and prevention.[7] The continuum includes four phases of translation research that revolve around the development of evidence-based guidelines. Phase 1 translation research seeks to move a basic genome-based discovery into a candidate health application (e.g., genetic test/intervention). Phase 2 translation research assesses the value of a genomic application for health practice leading to the development of evidence-based guidelines. Phase 3 translation research attempts to move evidence-based guidelines into health practice through delivery, dissemination, and diffusion research. Phase 4 translation research seeks to evaluate the "real world" health outcomes of an application in practice. Because the development of evidence-based guidelines is a moving target, the types of translation research can overlap and provide feedback loops to allow integration of new knowledge.

Most of the components that permit the application of a complete framework for implementation of science and that comprise essential research and evidence around CCC are lacking in LMICs. Yet, evidence obtained through the study of the heterogeneous populations of LMICs would expand knowledge about cancer in ways that will help both rich and poor countries and populations alike.

Most cancer research is conducted in high income countries, so global knowledge is skewed towards these populations and their specific cancers.[8] Consequently, much remains to be learned about cancer in LMICs, and this knowledge will also shed light on the nature of, and response to, cancer in high-income populations.

Specific, high-priority areas of research include: cancer genetics and biology, epidemiological studies on cancer incidence and prevalence, clinical research and health system research to provide information on factors influencing effective uptake of cancer services and new interventions. This will help us understand optimal system designs for delivering cost-effective cancer services. We briefly discuss examples related to cancer genetics and biology, as well as clinical and health systems research.

Cancer genetics and biology are especially important areas for basic research in LMICs, as there are likely to be fundamental differences in cancer etiology both between and within countries. Much remains to be learned about etiologies of the cancers that are more common in LMICs, especially cancers associated with infection.[9]

Consider, for example, the study of Kaposi sarcoma. Whether an individual develops the disease depends upon a number of co-factors, including but not necessarily limited to immunosuppresion with HIV. Other co-factors may play a role, so the study of heterogeneous populations where Kaposi sarcoma is common sheds light on this question. In most of sub-Saharan Africa, KSHV/HHV-8 seroprevalence reaches rates of approximately 50% to 60% of the population and Kaposi sarcoma is endemic. Molecular analysis of tumor tissues of lymphomas in East Africa suggests that in endemic regions, KSHV/HHV-8 is predominantly associated with KS, independent of HIV status. Immunophenotypic and molecular data seem to suggest 2 different mechanisms of viral infection are at work in lymphoid cells. Data confirm that KSHV/HHV-8 is involved in the neoplastic transformation of only certain types of lymphoma, probably in relation to their precursor infected cell. This evidence suggests that the maturation stage of KSHV/HHV-8–positive B cells as well as the type of viral infection may well determine the morphological, phenotypic, and clinical characteristics of KSHV/HHV-8–associated lymphomas.[10] These data assist in understanding why several southern European countries, and in particular, Italy and Greece, have a higher KSHV/HHV-8 seroprevalence rate in the general population. However, only a small proportion of immunocompetent individuals develop KSHV/HHV-8–associated malignancies, in comparison to immunocompromised individuals.

Another example where evidence in LMICs can inform global policy, especially for underserved populations, is efficacy of specific clinical or public health interventions. Consider for example vaccination against cervical cancer. A standard three-dose regimen of either Cervarix (the bivalent HPV16/18 vaccine with AS04 adjuvant produced by GlaxoSmithKline) or Gardasil (the quadrivalent HPV6/11/16/18 vaccine manufactured by Merck) prevents HPV16 and HPV18 infections and related cervical precancers among unexposed women. However, the cost of these regimens and logistical difficulties associated with administering three doses over 6 months make it extremely challenging to vaccinate preadolescent and young adult women in many low income settings.[11] Even in high income countries, vaccine programs often do not successfully administer all three doses. To provide additional options for vaccination in resource-constrained settings, investigators evaluated the vaccine efficacy of fewer than three doses of the HPV16/18 vaccine Cervarix in the Costa Rica Vaccine Trial.[12] This non-randomized analysis suggests that two doses of the HPV16/18 vaccine, and perhaps even one dose, are as protective as three doses. If these data are confirmed in future, randomized trials, and vaccination with fewer than three doses were to retain the high efficacy of the standard regimen, the ability to vaccinate more women for the same cost could translate into a significant public health benefit in underserved areas.

Even if a health intervention is proven efficacious in a controlled setting, its translation and application to a population faces a host of additional demand and supply side barriers. Health systems research across the CCC continuum provides much needed evidence and can inform decision-making in LMICs as well as the design of programs in underserved populations globally. Using both quantitative and qualitative methods of inquiry makes it possible to explore how contextual (e.g. socio-cultural, political, and economic), demand (e.g. stigma, gender discrimination, and lack of knowledge), and supply factors influence uptake of innovations and equitable access to high quality and responsive services.[13,14] This type of research can provide evidence that is essential to designing effective interventions that can address or work around these barriers. An example from research on barriers to early detection of breast cancer is provided in Text Box 9.1.

In LMICs where there is limited health systems research, it is especially important to understand health systems performance and how investments for cancer control are translated into service delivery and health outcomes. Yet, outside of interventions to reduce risk factors and some evidence around screening,[15-17] very little program evaluation research focused on chronic illness or cancer has been done in LMICs. Multi-method research can be used to explore how investments in CCC can be used effectively to strengthen health system functions through a diagonal approach (Chapter 4).[18,19]

Economic analysis can be a particularly useful contribution to CCC and can build on overall health systems research. National Health Accounts, for example, can be further developed into disease specific "sub accounts" for cancer. Another area for priority research is cost and cost-benefit analysis of interventions for CCC, as this evidence is particularly useful for decision-makers who have to prioritize how scarce resources are allocated.[20,21] There is an opportunity to expand cost-benefit analyses to key interventions for cancer control in LMICs. However, undertaking such analyses will require substantial investment to develop appropriate human resource capacity, including mechanisms which enable the use of the results of cost-benefit analyses in prioritization decisions. The World Health Organization Choosing Interventions that are Cost-Effective (WHO-CHOICE) program uses standardized tools to assemble databases on the cost, impact on population health, and cost-effectiveness of key health interventions, including indoor air pollution and tobacco use, as well as treatment and detection of breast, cervical, and colorectal cancers.[22]

Text Box 9.1
Increasing awareness and enhancing early detection of breast cancer in Gaza strip[23]

Rola Shaheen

Breast cancer is the most common cancer and the leading cause of death among women living in Gaza, one of the most densely populated cities in the world, with a population of 1.4 million living in a total area of 360 square kilometers (139 sq mi). Five-year survival rates are as low as 30-40% and are attributable to factors such as late-stage presentation, aggressive forms of breast cancer in Arab women, and young age at diagnosis.

The lack of resources for screening, diagnosis, and treatment pose severe challenges, which are exacerbated by ignorance about the disease and a lack of financial protection for women with cancer. Further, women residing in Gaza face the added barrier of fearing for their safety while travelling to medical facilities.

The very low breast cancer screening rate is likely the result of economic and institutional barriers, as well as societal and cultural barriers. A program was designed to assess women's understanding of breast cancer, use of screening mammography, and barriers to screening to guide the development of a comprehensive educational effort to target healthcare providers and their patients. This program had four stages: 1) a survey to identify barriers and opportunities; 2) development of education materials; 3) implementation of interventions; and 4) measurement of the impact of education and intervention.

In 2009, women living in Gaza, or from Gaza and living in other countries, were surveyed. These women expressed interest in obtaining appropriate care, including mammography. The key barriers to breast cancer screening that they identified included lack of information, education, and access to good, quality, affordable services in locations that could be safely reached. Religion and culture were not seen as direct barriers to breast cancer screening.

In phase two, the study team developed educational materials for physicians and patients about barriers to screening, breast cancer risk factors, and methods to increase compliance with screening. These materials helped facilitate training for local Palestinian healthcare providers in multidisciplinary aspects of breast cancer, including exposure to breast imaging, medical and surgical oncology, and breast pathology.

In April 2010, a booklet on breast cancer screening and a kit were published in Gaza with support for printing from CARE International. The third stage of the project involves training local healthcare providers. Recognizing the importance of evaluation research for refinement and scale-up, the fourth phase includes research to measure the impact of educational intervention on the attitudes of local physicians and their patients.

9.iii Strengthening data and health information systems for CCC

Robust HIS are needed to systematically capture evidence for effectively designing, monitoring, and updating global and national cancer planning and programs. Both global and national frameworks for monitoring need to be developed, as these convert data that can be used for decision-making into HIS.

The data that are the backbone of a robust HIS need to be gathered from multiple sources, including cancer registries, clinical records, laboratory investigations (especially those for tumor specimens), registration and licensing of drug use, infrastructure surveys, administrative records, and evaluations of outcomes. Yet, all data sources have limitations that need addressing before they can be used widely to generate the much needed evidence for expanding high quality and user responsive CCC. These data sources and examples of their uses are summarized in Table 9.1.

Table 9.1

Data on cancer causes, epidemiology, treatment, and outcomes.

Data Source	Uses	Limitations
Cancer registry data	• Crucial for understanding cancer incidence and mortality (descriptive epidemiology). • Distribution of staging to ascertain effect of screening programs. • Treatment data to assess access to effective treatment regimens. • Evaluation of public health interventions (e.g., screening or vaccination).	• Most registries do not have data on staging of cancer at diagnosis and treatments used. When available, data are incomplete.
Clinical trials	• Critical for establishing the potential impact of a prevention, screening, treatment, or supportive care intervention in a specific population.	• Though time consuming and costly, results may not be readily generalized to other populations or other settings with the same population.
Tumor specimens	• Understand biological and genetic variation in cancers among different populations, including germ line and somatic mutations. • Can potentially be linked to cancer registries and other data bases to link genotype with phenotype expression although data control and privacy concerns make this challenging.	• Depending on storage requirements, may be costly to collect, store and study.
Clinical data from medical records and pathology reports	• Understand treatments used and variance from evidence based guidelines. • Understand relative effectiveness of treatments in different populations or patient sub groups with specific tumor characteristics.	• Time consuming and costly to collect data. • Data from a single institution cannot be generalized. • Data from medical records requires good documentation and record storage.
Equipment licensing and registration data	• Availability of services that are registered or licensed, such as radiation equipment, controlled substances,[24,25] and mammography facilities.	• Can measure availability, but not access to these services.
Surveys	• National, population-based, health surveys – sometimes longitudinal: to understand behavior, attitudes and risks, and for resource mapping (human resources, infrastructure, health workforce skill sets). • Patient surveys to learn about understanding of disease, values and preferences, treatments, experiences with care, quality of life, and symptom control. • Hospital surveys about availability of services, including specialists. • Surveys of medical personnel about knowledge, beliefs, and practice patterns.	• Need statistically representative samples. • Can be challenging to identify generalized populations. • Low response rates can introduce bias. • Respondents' reports are subject to measurement error. • Often not comparable or available as a time series.
Administrative data from insurance claims or service encounter	• Understand resource mapping, patterns of service access, and care provided.	• Data not accessible in many LMICs, and when available, may be only for a particular subgroup (e.g. social security beneficiaries).

Cancer registry data are the primary source of information regarding cancer incidence and mortality and an essential building block for a strong HIS, as well as for developing a research and evidence base and evaluating the impact of health services and programs. Cancer registries are also crucial for developing national cancer plans. For this reason, strengthening cancer registry data should be considered a global, public good, and is singled out in this chapter as a particularly important input for expanding evidence for CCC.

Despite their importance, a serious challenge to developing a CCC evidence base globally, or for developing regions and LMICs, is the fact that only 8% of the world population lives in countries with regional or national cancer registries that meet the high standards of completeness and validity. These are mostly high and middle income regions and are represented in the International Agency for Research on Cancer (IARC)'s Cancer Incidence on Five Continents (CI5).[26] Figure 9.1 identifies countries with a national (dark grey), or at least one regional (light grey), population-based cancer registry with data of sufficient quality for inclusion in CI5.

Figure 9.1
Countries with Population-Based Cancer Registries

■ National Cancer Registry
■ 1 or More Regional Cancer Registries

Source: Curado MP, Edwards B, Shin HR, Strom H, Feray J, Heanue M. Cancer Incidence in Five Continents, Vol. IX. Lyon, France: International Agency for Research on Cancer: IARC Scientific Publications No. 160; 2007.

Indeed, the vast majority (80% in 2006) of the world's population is not covered by any population-based cancer registries. Registration is particularly sparse in Asia (8% of the total population) and in Africa (11%). Despite these severe limitations, IARC produces a global database of cancer incidence and mortality −GLOBOCAN− that has been widely used for both research and policy-making.[27,28] These estimates are based on cancer registry data when available. For the 75 countries where no data are available on cancer incidence, existing global estimates are based on modeling of mortality data (41 countries), or data from neighboring populations.

To be considered of high quality, registries must identify reliable sources of data, achieve centralized data capture, and establish data validation procedures and quality control measures.[29] The quality of cancer registry data depends on the completeness of case documentation, the validity or accuracy of the recorded data, and its timeliness.[30-32] Yet, it is important to recognize that registry data that can provide evidence for cancer planning can be generated from regional registries that cover only certain parts of a country. Indeed, these are preferable to national registries that offer limited data if the regional registries are high quality and comprehensive (population-based with a defined residential capture area representative of the population at risk). This is the case in the United States where the SEER (Surveillance, Epidemiology, End Results) registry covers just over 25% of the population.[33]

Establishing and improving cancer registries should be a high priority for expanding CCC capacity in LMICs. It is relatively low-cost, results can be obtained quickly, and international sources of funding may be available. Support for establishing and strengthening registries should take into account the needs for ongoing commitment to data collection, capacity building, including data management, privacy issues, and the capability to convert the data into evidence – components which are often lacking in LMICs.

A number of countries have successfully collaborated with academic and governmental organizations to establish cancer registries. Text Box 9.2 highlights two countries that have used national and international partnerships to establish cancer registries and improve local capacity.

Text Box 9.2
Leveraging collaborations to establish cancer registries in LMICs: Examples from Colombia and Uganda

Some countries have successfully established cancer registries by collaborating directly with academic institutions. One such registry is the Cancer Registry in Cali, Colombia, the first and longest-running population-based cancer registry in Latin America, which covers a population of 1.8 million people. The registry was established in 1962, through the Department of Pathology of Del Valle University, and has continued uninterrupted operations ever since.

The National Cancer Institute in the US provided training and guidance, and assisted with securing the initial funding for the registry – a $3,000 grant for "high risk projects" from the Fuller Foundation, and a small US surplus grant for scientific purposes in other countries.[34] Since its inception, the registry has been financed and maintained by an academic institution, the Del Valle University, with a small budgetary allocation.[35] Supplemental funding for the registry is provided by government health agencies, although the university provides most of the funding and support.

Data from the Cali Cancer Registry have been published in seven volumes of CI5, a tribute to the data's quality and completeness.[36] Data from the Cali Cancer Registry have guided targeted interventions that have led to improved outcomes. For example, high incidence rates of cervical cancer prompted national screening programs. Screening successfully led to a shift in stage at diagnosis, with lower rates of invasive cervical cancers and more identification of in situ cancers.[37] In 1998, the Cali Cancer Registry participated in the creation of a new population-based cancer registry, in the southern city of Pasto. The Pasto Cancer Registry covers a population of 350,000, and is the second population-based registry in Colombia.

Another model for developing a cancer registry utilizes existing cancer institutions as the starting point. The Kampala Cancer Registry in Uganda is an example of such a program, having obtained substantial initial support from the Uganda Cancer Institute. Similar to the Cali Cancer Registry, the Kampala Cancer Registry also receives assistance *from a university. The Kampala Cancer Registry was established in the Department of Pathology of Makerere University in 1951, and is the oldest population-based cancer registry in Africa.[38] The registry stopped capturing cases in 1978 because of political instability, but resumed registration in 1989, and has been in operation consistently since then. The registry's catchment area is Kyadondo County (population 1.2 million, in 1998), which includes the capital city of Kampala as well as neighboring urban and semi-urban areas.[39,40]*

Cancer cases are reported to the Kampala Cancer Registry by a university hospital with an oncology program and a radiation facility, and by four other hospitals and three private pathology laboratories. Data collection is supported by CANREG software from IARC. In the mid 1990s, cancer registration was approximately 90% complete.[41] Kampala Cancer Registry data have been published in Volumes I, VII, VIII, and IX of CI5.[42] Efforts to expand cancer registration in Uganda to the national level have been impeded by a lack of financing. Population-based cancer registries were started in the West Nile district of Kuluva and at Ishaka Hospital, but both closed due to the lack of funds.[43]

9.iv Capacity-building

Improving capacity around HIS and research in LMICs is essential to expanding CCC. This is necessary not only to improve data collection, but also to convert data into evidence for building knowledge and for decision making.

Inter-disciplinary, collaborative, and multi-institutional groups need to form within LMICs to collectively promote and undertake the evidence-building that is required in all areas of cancer research. These groups should bridge the gap between cancer and health systems research through a diagonal approach to capacity-building by drawing on existing HISs and research capacity, thereby maximizing the use of limited resources and infrastructure.[44] The experience in building HIS for HIV/AIDS and other infectious diseases in LMICs demonstrates the importance of working diagonally in ways that build system-wide platforms for information and research capacity.

Experiences with other diseases also suggest that investments should be targeted to national public health institutes or research institutions (Text Box 9.3). These are the local institutions that can provide the necessary infrastructure for building information systems and conducting research on cancer, as well as helping in the development of national cancer plans, health promotion campaigns, delivery of screening and prevention programs, training, and dissemination of evidence to other stakeholders such as civil society.[45] The International Association of National Public Health Institutes, for example, which is dedicated to improving public health capacity through developing partnerships with members globally, could prove to be an important facilitator, as was the case with HIV/AIDS.

In the case of CCC, as in many other areas of health, local academic and policy-oriented institutions may be best positioned to undertake data collection, research, and to manage HIS, often through collaboration across academic, governmental, and private institutions.[46] Partnerships between local and global institutions can be very effective, if global research agendas are balanced with local needs.[47,48]

Text Box 9.3
International, multi-institutional partnerships for capacity-building in cancer research: Uganda Program on Cancer and Infectious Disease[49]

Corey Casper

To conduct the most efficient and meaningful research on infection-related cancers, and to increase the potential impact on these diseases, scientists from the Fred Hutchinson Cancer Research Center (FHCRC) in the US partnered with the Uganda Cancer Institute (UCI) in Kampala, in 2004, to form the UPCID. The program has three core components: research, capacity-building, and care delivery.

The Uganda Program on Cancer and Infectious Disease (UPCID) research projects aim to clarify and answer the fundamental questions that could lead to comprehensive prevention and treatment for infection-related malignancies. One of the research areas being pursued is the characterization of the natural history of progression, from primary acquisition of viral oncogenes to the establishment of chronic infection and the eventual development of malignancies. A striking feature of infection-related cancers is that more than 70% of persons throughout the world are infected with at least one pathogen that can cause cancer, but less than 0.1% will ever develop cancer. Collaborative research is taking place between scientists at the UCI and FHCRC, investigating the pathophysiology of tumorigenesis, and simultaneously discovering and validating blood- and saliva-based biomarkers to identify individuals at highest risk for developing cancer. Another example is research on novel therapies and care delivery methods specific to infection-associated cancers. These new therapies are intended to target the etiologic infectious agent, leading to reduced toxicity, increased efficacy, and lower cost. Each of the methods under evaluation could result in new prevention and treatment strategies that could be used in both resource-rich and resource-poor settings.

The lack of personnel trained in cancer research, care delivery, and education is among the greatest challenges faced by UPCID, as the few with expertise must simultaneously conduct cutting-edge research and provide patient care, as well as provide administrative leadership. Still, and thanks in great part to strong training initiatives, substantial progress has been made over the first five years of UPCID (Chapter 6). More than a dozen research projects are well under way at the research clinic, with work to date elucidating the pathogenesis, diagnosis, and treatment of Kaposi sarcoma and lymphoma, the two most common cancers in sub-Saharan Africa.[50-53]

Bilateral research funding that catalyzes academic institutions, research organizations, and professional associations could be especially effective in building local capacity. Academic institutions both within and outside of LMICs should encourage staff exchanges and steer faculty and students to global health and cancer training research opportunities. The Fogarty International Center, part of the US National Institutes of Health, supports research and capacity-building in global health with a focus on LMICs. Research training programs address priority areas including NCDs and cancer. Two-thirds of grants support research training with a focus on providing grants directly to institutions in LMICs. The new National Cancer Institute's (NCI) Center for Global Health in the US will also undertake and support training to build research capacity, generating opportunities for synergies and collaboration within NIH and with institutions based in LMICs.[54]

Several regionally focused initiatives dedicate significant resources to capacity building, and offer opportunities for expansion should resources be available. The International Network for Cancer Treatment and Research (INCTR), for example, has been operating globally for more than two decades, with a focus on research and an extensive network of professionals in both high and lower income regions.[55]

In the global arena, IARC is a major contributor to research and HIS capacity-building, and this role could be expanded if additional resources became available. As discussed above, IARC provides resources to develop cancer registries globally, including training programs for establishing and improving cancer registration, particularly in LMICs. IARC has also developed the CANREG4 Software, a configurable computer program for cancer registration used by 140 registries in 75 countries. IARC provides ongoing support to maintain CANREG4 and hosts the International Association of Cancer Registries, a professional society dedicated to fostering the aims and activities of cancer registries worldwide.[56]

Cognizant that many LMICs lack graduate training in chronic disease epidemiology, IARC hosts training courses and supports exchanges and awards for scientists. In addition, IARC provides fellowships to support epidemiology training and serve as a resource for IARC's work on registries and population-based research. Of the 500 fellowships awarded to junior scientists since 1966, approximately 85% returned to their home countries upon completion of their training, and more than 80% remain active in cancer research.[57]

As discussed above, evaluation and health systems research –areas where capacity building is especially important– have been largely neglected. More collaboration between high income countries and LMICs, including commitment from the NCI Center for Global Health, would help catalyze this research.[58] Because of the challenges and costs of this research, it cannot be undertaken for all interventions or in all settings. Thus, available research should be generalized whenever possible, and results should be shared widely and disseminated globally. A global forum, initiated and sustained through a collaboration of academic and global institutions including IARC, UICC and inter-institutional networks such as the GTF.CCC, for collecting, vetting, sharing, and projecting results and lessons learned from implementation would be a valuable catalyst and complement to national research efforts. This forum could provide opportunities for face-to-face interaction as well as exchange of information on an ongoing and virtual basis, for training local research staff to establish a research core, provide input into study design, and recommend data collection tools and instruments for research projects. Such a forum could be a major area of work for the NCI Center for Global Health.[59]

Additionally, it is useful to bring together young researchers from LMICs with established researchers in projects that provide training in best practices. One example of this in clinical oncology has been developed through ASCO. This is further discussed in Chapter 10 of this volume.

A few examples of international collaborations have been analyzed and the results disseminated. For example, the St. Jude International Outreach Program has been quite effective in establishing a series of interactive platforms that promote capacity building and bridge clinical and implementation research. (Text box 9.4)

Text Box 9.4
Strengthening collaboration for implementation and evaluation research

The St. Jude International Outreach Twinning Program in Pediatric Oncology is an impressive example of a program that has dedicated substantial resources to implementation research in LMICs and to sharing lessons learned. This program "twins" hospitals in LMICs with St. Jude to provide more comprehensive and informed pediatric oncology care. To date, the program has more than 20 participating countries and hospitals. The St. Jude's team has published a series of research articles in leading professional journals, along with more open-access reports describing improvements in pediatric cancer care at the "twin" hospitals.[60-65] Resources have been dedicated to making this information available in several languages, including Spanish and Portuguese. Perhaps of greatest importance is that as part of the dedication to sharing information with the worldwide medical community, in 2002, St. Jude launched Cure4Kids, a comprehensive online resource dedicated to supporting the care of children with cancer and other catastrophic diseases. Cure4Kids (www.Cure4Kids. org) has more than 24,000 registered users in more than 175 countries.[66] One of the many important lessons learned and shared is that dedicated funding from the host hospital has been essential to developing a sustainable and expansive program. St. Jude dedicates 1-2% of its annual income to the IOP program.

Breast Cancer Program at Tikur Anbessa Hospital, in Addis Ababa: The pilot Breast Cancer Program at Tikur Anbessa Hospital in Addis Ababa, Ethiopia, offers another example of a collaborative cancer initiative in a developing country. This program also has a strong implementation research component and an emphasis on reporting and sharing results and lessons learned. In 2005, AstraZeneca began sponsoring a comprehensive program at the hospital to help build local capacity in the management of breast cancer, the second most common cancer among young women in the country. The objectives of the program were to strengthen human resource capacity, technical competency and advocacy, and to improve access to breast cancer treatment.[67] When the Ethiopia Breast Cancer Program started, the entire country had only one cancer specialist, with no mammography, no easy access to chemotherapy or hormonal agents, and no national treatment protocols.[68]

The program focused on strengthening diagnosis and treatment capabilities at Tikur Anbessa Hospital by developing treatment guidelines, improving the patient referral system, raising awareness of services available among healthcare workers, providing training for other physicians in Ethiopia, and setting up an institution-based cancer registry. This model, which started as a small, targeted pilot, has evolved into an effective collaboration with the Ministry of Health and the Ethiopian Cancer Association.[69] One direct measurable patient outcome of this program reduced time between diagnosis and surgery, from 12-18 months in 2006 to 3-6 months in 2009.[70]

Despite its modest size, this innovative, single-site initiative has had broader reach. All of the guidelines and reporting forms developed under this program have been distributed to all university and regional hospitals in Ethiopia. Anastrazole and tamoxifen can now be dispensed at other hospitals to lighten the travel burden for some patients, and oncologists from Tikur Anbessa now travel to other hospitals to train local doctors in breast cancer treatment and care. As a group, the researchers and clinicians involved in this program have also been quite effective at disseminating their findings in the literature.[71-73]

9.v Opportunities for global and national uptake

Health information systems and research are essential inputs for effective decision-making for CCC, yet both are lacking in LMICs. This is recognized in the Declaration of the High-Level Meeting of the UN General Assembly on the Prevention and Control of NCDs, which highlights the importance of research and innovation and the need for greater investment in science and technology. It also emphasizes the need to translate research into knowledge and action.

The declaration does not establish a set of specific targets or a formula to measure, monitor, or evaluate progress. Instead, it tasks WHO with developing a comprehensive global monitoring framework and recommendations for a set of voluntary global targets for the prevention and control of NCDs. As is discussed in Chapter 10, an overall global target for reducing NCDs by 25% by 2025 was accepted during the World Health Assembly of 2012.

Measurable health system performance targets directly related to cancer are needed to develop global and national frameworks for monitoring progress, including suitable metrics for evaluating health system performance.[74] These must be disease-specific, yet also integrated into HIS and broad health systems.

Academic, research, donor, and national and international agencies should work together to ensure that these targets and measures are developed. Existing frameworks demonstrate that global monitoring and surveillance promotes accountability, which helps ensure that national targets are achieved.

Lessons learned from frameworks for accountability on investment in women's and children's health can, and should, be applied to cancer and NCDs.[75] Global efforts to monitor fulfillment by countries of the terms set out in the Convention on the Rights of the Child provide useful lessons.[76] Work related to the Millennium Development Goals has analyzed commitments to advance the global strategy on women's and children's health, and a special Commission on Information and Accountability produced a series of concrete recommendations.[77] To ensure global oversight an Expert Review Group of external advisors reports regularly to the UN Secretary General.[78]

Translating information into evidence and then into decision-making on CCC requires uptake by policy makers to close the relevance-excellence gap.[79] The cancer research community must be engaged in this process, particularly in highlighting priorities.[80] National cancer plans should stress the need for investment in translation of evidence into policy, including the establishment of frameworks for monitoring and surveillance to assess health system performance in CCC.

References

1. Hanna T, Kangolle A. Cancer control in developing countries: using health data and health services research to measure and improve access, quality and efficiency. *BMC International Health and Human Rights* 2010;10(1):24.

2. Mellstedt H. Cancer initiatives in developing countries. *Annals of Oncology* 2006; 17(Suppl 8):viii24-viii31.

3. Global Forum for Health Research. About: 10/90 gap. Global Forum for Health Research. 2011. http://www.globalforumhealth.org/about/1090-gap/ (accessed October 5, 2011).

4. Annan KA. Challenge to the world's scientists. *Science.* 2003; 299:1485.

5. Health Metrics Network. Building Momentum and Saving Lives. Health Metrics Network. Results Report 2010. Geneva: World Health Organization, 2010.

6. Shakarishvili G, Lansang MA, Mitta V, et al. Health systems strengthening: a common classification and framework for investment analysis. *Health Policy Plan* 2010; 26(4): 316-26.

7. Khoury MJ, Gwinn M, Yoon PW et al. The continuum of translation research in genomic medicine: how can we accelerate the appropriate integration of human genome discoveries into health care and disease prevention? *Genetics in Medicine* 2007; 9: 665-74.

8. Mellstedt H, 2006.

9. Ibid.

10. Lazzi S, Bellan C, Amato T, et al. Kaposi's sarcoma –associated herpesvirus/human herpesvirus 8 infection in reactive lymphoid tissues: a model for KSHV/HHV-8– related lymphomas? *Human Pathology* 2006; 37(1): 23-31.

11. Goldie SJ, O'Shea M, Diaz M, et al. Benefits, cost requirements and cost-effectiveness of the HPV16,18 vaccine for cervical cancer prevention in developing countries: policy implications. *Reproductive Health Matters* 2008; 16(32):86-96.

12. Winstead ER. HPV Vaccine Study in Costa Rica Yields Insights on Cancer Prevention. *National Cancer Institute Bulletin* 2011; 8(18). http://www.cancer.gov/ncicancerbulletin/092011/page2 (accessed July 4, 2012).

13. Atun R, de Jongh T, Secci F, et al. Integration of targeted health interventions into health systems: a conceptual framework for analysis. *Health Policy Plan* 2010; 25: 104-11.

14. World Health Organization. The World Health Report 2000 - Health systems: improving performance. Geneva, Switzerland: World Health Organization, 2000.

15. Sepúlveda C, Prado R. Effective cervical cytology screening programmes in middle -income countries: the Chilean experience. *Cancer Detection and Prevention* 2005; 29(5):405-11.

16. Deerasamee S, Srivatanakul P, Sriplung H, et al. Monitoring and evaluation of a model demonstration project for the control of cervical cancer in Nakhon Phanom province, Thailand. *Asian Pacific Journal of Cancer Prevention* 2007; 8(4): 547-56.

17. Sosa-Rubí SG, Walker D, Serván E. Performance of mammography and Papanicolaou among rural women in Mexico. *Salud Pública de México* 2009; 51(suppl.2):s236-45.

18. Sepúlveda J, Bustreo F, Tapia R, et al. Improvement of child survival in Mexico: the diagonal approach. *Lancet* 2006; 368(9551): 2017-27.

19. Frenk J. Bridging the divide: global lessons from evidence-based health policy in Mexico. *Lancet* 2006; 369(9539): 954-61.

20. Valencia-Mendoza A, Sánchez-González G, Bautista-Arredondo S, et al. Cost-effectiveness of breast cancer screening policies in Mexico. *Salud Pública de México* 2009; 51(Supl.2).

21. Groot MT, Baltussen R, Uyl-de Groot CA, et al. Costs and health effects of breast cancer interventions in epidemiologically different regions of Africa, North America, and Asia. *Breast Journal* 2006;12(1):81.

22. World Health Organization. Choosing interventions that are cost effective (WHO-CHOICE). World Health Organization. 2005. http://www.who.int/choice/en/ (accessed October 6, 2011).

23. Shaheen R, Slanetz P, Raza S, Rosen M. Barriers and opportunities for early detection of breast cancer in Gaza women. *Breast* 2011; 20(2):s30-s4

24. Pain and Policy Studies Group. Opioid consumption data overview. Pain and Policy Studies, University

25. International Narcotics Control Board. Narcotic drugs – technical reports. International Narcotics Control Board. 2011. http://www.incb.org/incb/narcotic_drugs_reports.html (accessed April 30, 2011).

26. Curado MP, Edwards B, Shin HR, Strom H, Feray J, Heanue M. Cancer Incidence in Five Continents, Vol. IX. Lyon, France: International Agency for Research on Cancer: IARC Scientific Publications No. 160; 2007.

27. International Agency for Research on Cancer. GLOBOCAN 2008: Cancer incidence and mortality worldwide in 2008. International Agency for Research on Cancer. 2011. http://globocan.iarc.fr/ (accessed October 5, 2011).

28. Ferlay J, Shin HR, Bray F, et al. GLOBOCAN 2008, Cancer Incidence and Mortality Worldwide: IARC Cancer Base No.10. Lyon, France: International Agency for Research on Cancer; 2010. http://globocan.iarc.fr (accessed October 5, 2011).

29. Akhtar F, Pheby DFH. Cancer research and registration: presenting a case for population-based cancer registries in Pakistan. *Pakistan Journal of Medical Research* 2004; 43(1):39-44.

30. Parkin DM, Chen VW, Ferlay J, et al. Comparability and quality control in cancer registration. IARC Technical Report No. 19. Lyon, France: International Agency for Research on Cancer, 1994.

31. Bray F, Parkin DM. Evaluation of data quality in the cancer registry: principles and methods. Part I: comparability, validity, and timeliness. *European Journal of Cancer* 2009; 45:747-55.

32. Parkin DM, Bray F. Evaluation of data quality in the cancer registry: principles and methods. part II. completeness. *European Journal of Cancer* 2009; 45:756-64.

33. Surveillance, Epidemiology, and End Results (SEER) Program of the National Cancer Institute. Overview of the SEER program. National Cancer Institute. 2011. http://seer.cancer.gov/about/overview.html (accessed October 6, 2011).

34. Fontham ETH. A conversation with Pelayo Correa. *Epidemiology* 2010;21(1):154-7.

35. Universidad del Valle, School of Medicine, Department of Pathology. Cali Cancer Registry. Universidad del Valle. 2011. http://rpcc.univalle.edu.co/es/index.php (accessed October 6, 2011).

36. Curado MP, Edwards B, Shin HR, et al, 2007.

37. Fontham ETH. A conversation with Pelayo Correa. *Epidemiology* 2010;21(1):154-7.

38. Davies JN. The pattern of African cancer in Uganda. *East African Medical Journal* 1961; 38:486-91.

39. Parkin DM, Wabinga H, Nambooze S. Completeness in an African cancer registry. *Cancer Causes Control* 2001; 12:147-52.

40. Gondos A, Brenner H, Wabinga H, et al. Cancer survival in Kampala, Uganda. *British Journal of Cancer* 2005; 95: 1808-12.

41. Parkin DM, Wabinga H, Nambooze S, 2001.

42. Ibid.

43. Orem J, Wabinga H. The roles of national cancer research institutions in evolving a comprehensive cancer control program in a developing country: experience from Uganda. *Oncology* 2009; 77:272-80.

44. World Health Organization Maximizing Positive Synergies Collaborative Group. An assessment of interactions between global health initiatives and country health systems. *Lancet* 2009;373(9681):2137-69.

45. Frieden T, Koplan J. Stronger national public health institutes for global health. *Lancet* 2010; 376(9754): 1721-2.

46. Mellstedt H, 2006.

47. Council on Health Research for Development. Health research: getting the priorities right. Policy Brief No 2004.1. Geneva.Switzerland: Council on Health Research for Development, 2004. httpi/www.cohred.org/publications/library-and-archive/health_research_gett_1_211/ (accessed October 6, 2011).

48. Mellstedt H, 2006.

49. Casper C, Sessle E, Phipps W, Yager J, Corey L, Orem J. Uganda Program on Cancer and Infectious Diseases. GTF. CCC Working Paper Series, Paper No. 2, Harvard Global Equity Initiative, 2011.

50. Bateganya MH, Stanaway J, Brentlinger PE, et al. Predictors of survival after a diagnosis of non-Hodgkin lymphoma in a resource-limited setting: A retrospective study on the impact of HIV infection and its treatment. *Journal of Acquired Immune Deficiency Syndromes* 2011; 56(4):312-9.

51. Nguyen H, Okuku F, Ssewankambo F, et al. AIDS-associated Kaposi sarcoma in Uganda: response to treatment with highly active antiretroviral therapy and chemotherapy. *Infectious Agents and Cancer* 2009; 4(Suppl 2):O5.

52. Casper C. The increasing burden of HIV-associated malignancies in resource-limited regions. *Annual Review of Medicine* 2010; 62:157-70.

53. Phipps W, Sewankambo F, Nguyen H, et al. Gender differences in clinical presentation and outcomes of epidemic Kaposi sarcoma in Uganda. *PLoS ONE.* 2010; 5(11):e13936.

54. Varmus H, Trimble EL. Integrating cancer control into global health. *Science Translational Medicine* 2011; 3(101):28.

55. International Network for Cancer Treatment and Research. Cancer Registration. International Network for Cancer Treatment and Research. 2011. http://www.inctr.org/programs/cancer-registration/ (accessed October 5, 2011).

56. International Association of Cancer Registries. About IACR: History and aims of the association. International Association of Cancer Registries. 2011. http://www.iacr.com.fr/ (accessed October 5, 2011).

57. International Agency for Research on Cancer. Education and Training: IARC Fellowships for Cancer Research. International Agency for Research on Cancer. 2011. http://www.iarc.fr/en/education-training/index.php (accessed October 6, 2011).

58. Varmus H, Trimble EL, 2011.

59. Ibid.

60. Wilimas JA, Wilson MW, Haik BG, et al. Development of retinoblastoma programs in Central America. *Pediatric Blood & Cancer* 2009;53(1):42-6.

61. Ribeiro R, Pui CH. Treatment of acute lymphoblastic leukemia in low-and middle -income countries: Challenges and opportunities. *Leukemia & Lymphoma* 2008;49(3):373-6.

62. Rivera GK, Quintana J, Villarroel M, et al. Transfer of complex frontline anticancer therapy to a developing country: The St. Jude osteosarcoma experience in Chile. *Pediatric Blood & Cancer* 2008; 50(6):1143-6.

63. Rodriguez-Galindo C, Wilson MW, Chantada G, et al. Retinoblastoma: one world, one vision. *Pediatrics* 2008;122(3): e763-e71.

64. Leander C, Fu LC, Peña A, et al. Impact of an education program on late diagnosis of retinoblastoma in Honduras. *Pediatric Blood & Cancer* 2007; 49(6):817-9.

65. Howard SC, Pui CH, Ribeiro RC. Components of cure: treatment of acute lymphoblastic leukemia in Indonesia and other low -income countries. *Pediatric Blood & Cancer* 2008;51(6):719-21.

66. St. Jude Children's Research Hospital. About International Outreach. St. Jude Children's Research Hospital. 2011. http://www.stjude.org/stjude/v/ index.jsp?vgnextoid=2f166f9523e70110VgnVCM1000001e0215acRCRD&vgnext channel=e4le6fa0a9118010VgnVCM1000000e2015acRCRD (accessed October 6, 2011).

67. Dye TD, Bogale S, Hobden C, et al. Complex care systems in developing countries: breast cancer patient navigation in Ethiopia. *Cancer* 2010; 116(3):577-85.

68. International Federation of Pharmaceutical Manufacturers and Associations. Resources: Partnerships Directory. International Federation of Pharmaceutical Manufacturers and Associations. 2010. http://www.ifpma.org/resources/partnerships-directory.html (accessed October 6, 2011).

69. Reeler A, Sikora K, Solomon B. Overcoming challenges of cancer treatment programmes in developing countries: a sustainable breast cancer initiative in Ethiopia. *Clinical Oncology* 2008; 20(2):191-8.

70. Ibid.

71. Ibid.

72. Reeler A, Qiao Y, Dare L, et al. Women's cancers in developing countries: from research to an integrated health systems approach. *Asian Pacific Journal of Cancer Prevention* 2009; 10:519-26.

73. CanTreat International. Access to cancer treatment in low- and middle -income countries: An essential part of global cancer control. Shenzhen, China: 2010. 1-23.

74. Samb B, Desai N, Nishtar S, et al. Prevention and management of chronic disease: a litmus test for health-systems strengthening in low -income and middle -income countries. *Lancet* 2010; 376(9754):1785-97.

75. Time for action in New York on non-communicable diseases. *Lancet* 2011; 378(9795):961.

76. UNICEF. Convention on the Rights of the Child: Monitoring the fulfillment of States obligations. World Health Organization. 2011. http://www.unicef.org/crc/index_30210.html (accessed October 6, 2011).

77. Partnership for Maternal, Newborn and Child Health. The PMNCH 2011 Report: Analyzing Commitments to Advance the Global Strategy for Women's and Children's Health. World Health Organization. 2011. http://www.who.int/pmnch/topics/part_publications/PMNCH_Report_2011_-_29_09_2011_full.pdf (accessed October 4, 2011).

78. Every Woman Every Child. Expert Review Group Members. World Health Organization. 2011. http://everywomaneverychild.org/resources/independent-expert-review-group/expert-review-group-members. (accessed October 6, 2011)

79. Frenk J, Knaul F, Gómez-Dantés O. Closing the relevance-excellence gap in health research: the use of evidence in Mexican health reform. In Matlin S (Ed.). Global Forum Update on Research for Health, p. 48-53. London: Pro-Brook Publishing, 2005. Pro-book London.

80. Wild CP. The role of cancer research in noncommunicable disease control. *Journal of the National Cancer Institute* 2012; 104(14): 1051-8.

CHAPTER 10

STRENGTHENING STEWARDSHIP AND LEADERSHIP TO EXPAND ACCESS TO CANCER CARE AND CONTROL

Felicia Marie Knaul, George Alleyne, Rifat Atun,
Flavia Bustreo, Julie R. Gralow, Mary Gospodarowicz,
Peter Piot, Doug Pyle, Julio Frenk

Key messages

- As highlighted in the Political Declaration of the 2011 High-level Meeting of the United Nations (UNHLM) General Assembly on the Prevention and Control of Noncommunicable Diseases (Ncds), national and global institutions, and especially the World Health Organization (WHO), must be strengthened to provide more effective stewardship and to produce essential global and national public goods.

- Time-bound targets, in addition to the overall 25% by 2025 reduction in premature mortality from NCDs, should be developed, built into country and global strategies, and matched with strong monitoring and accountability frameworks. The Declaration of the UNHLM on NCDs requests that WHO establish a framework by 2012 and encourages national governments to do the same by 2013.

- WHO and the International Agency for Research on Cancer (IARC) are the lead UN institutions on cancer care and control (CCC) and they require a renewed and strengthened agenda that focuses on producing global public goods. Resources must be made available to enable both institutions to implement this agenda. Among UN institutions outside of health, the International Atomic Energy Agency's (IAEA) efforts around CCC are noteworthy.

- Multilateral agencies, such as the World Bank, as well as bilateral agencies have been largely absent from CCC and need to be engaged.

- Private sector engagement has been limited and should be significantly stepped up in order to successfully expand access to CCC.

- An independent multi-agency, multi-stakeholder, multisectoral partnership of experts and leaders should be established.

- National multisectoral, multi-stakeholder commissions should be put in place to help move forward expanded CCC activities at country level.

- The global cancer arena has expanded significantly over the past decades. The world is poised to launch all-inclusive, multisectoral and multi-stakeholder global and national cancer movements.

- Activities around CCC can spur global and national responses to the challenge of NCDs and chronic illness.

10.i Introduction

That cancer has received limited attention in low and middle income countries (LMICs) in the global health sphere should come as no surprise given the lack of active, consistent, and coordinated leadership at local and international levels. Consequently, in global health and within the global cancer community there is limited commitment to raising awareness, increasing financing, and improving access to CCC in LMICs. Strong stewardship and leadership are essential to reverse this unacceptable situation and mobilize global and country-level stakeholders, given the current opportunities to save lives to achieve the recommendations outlined in other chapters of this volume and to implement the strategies set forth in the Declaration of the UNHLM on NCDs.

This chapter first briefly reviews the stewardship function in health specific to CCC. It then discusses the current national and global landscape of CCC stakeholders, including illustrative country examples. The last sections propose a set of actions for key actors to enhance CCC in LMICs through multisectoral and multi-stakeholder action, seizing the propitious moment provided by the UNHLM on Ncds and the global awareness that this has produced.

10.ii Stewardship in health and CCC

Ministries of health play a critical role as the stewards of national health systems, as well as collectively in global health by participating in the governing bodies of international agencies. Effective fulfillment of this stewardship role requires inclusion and empowerment of all key cancer stakeholders, and especially the affected groups, while ensuring that the Paris and Accra Principles of country ownership are consistently upheld.[1]

Stewardship and leadership in the cancer arena necessarily requires effective engagement of stakeholders from within and outside the health sector. Yet in LMICs, stewardship and leadership of health systems and the capacity of ministries of health to effectively interact with other sectors is often weak.[2]

Text Box 10.1
Stewardship

Stewardship —the leadership of global, national, and sub-national health systems— is considered the most important health system function, as it influences all other health system functions.

National stewardship of health involves the provision of strategic direction for all players in the health system, as well as those who work outside of the system and can influence the health sector (e.g. finance, agriculture, environment). Stewardship activities include: generating and disseminating information and evidence; promoting and implementing the results of research; budgeting and allocating resources across health priorities; and, consensus-building and agenda-setting in order to define and implement national health policy. Establishing norms and regulations and eliciting compliance are especially important and have particular applications to certain aspects of cancer treatment as controlled inputs and substances are used (e.g. opioids, radiation therapy).[3]

Globally, stewardship involves the production and dissemination of public goods that are important to health systems, but usually are not produced by individual countries.[4-7] Global stewardship includes: production of knowledge that benefits all countries; production and monitoring of global frameworks for action (e.g. Millennium Development Goals and WHO Framework Convention on Tobacco Control, which are particularly important in cancer prevention and control); controlling the cross-border spread of disease, behavioral risk factors (e.g. through WHO Framework Convention on Tobacco Control), and environmental hazards; development of harmonized norms and standards for use by countries; regulation of international transactions including service provision and global risks; global solidarity for health financing (e.g. UNITAID); consensus-building and agenda-setting for global health actions (such as the UNHLM on NCDs); and actions to determine, implement, and monitor global policies to enhance access to effective medicines (e.g. Doha Declaration on Trade-related Aspects of Intellectual Property Rights [TRIPS]).[8,9]

A critical step in improving stewardship capacity is to produce a national or population-based cancer plan that incorporates and engages all constituencies and establishes measureable goals and methods of accountability. The process for creating national plans should be derived from multisectoral commissions that are led by ministries of health, but include representation of all stakeholders involved with CCC in-country, especially civil society and affected groups.

National cancer, health, and development plans are stewardship roadmaps that target national and global priorities. Aligning and perfecting national plans for specific diseases, health, and development produces an integrated mapping for stewardship. A national cancer plan provides strategic direction for all activities and actors specific to cancer. As with other NCDs and chronic illness, CCC should be mainstreamed into national health and development plans through the national cancer plan.

Still, many LMICs have yet to include cancer in their national health plans, few have plans specific to cancer, and even fewer have established comprehensive cancer plans that identify candidate cancers and compelling opportunities to set priorities. Countries that do have plans tend to cover only cervical and breast cancer, or tobacco. A survey by WHO in 2001 covering 167 countries showed that only half of these countries had national cancer plans; in Africa the figure was only 15%.[10]

Based on a review of 20 LMICs covering all regions, only a third had national cancer control strategies and/or programs in place. More than half had policies or programs specifically on cervical and/or breast cancer, but only about a quarter had national tobacco control programs. Only four countries had in existence or were in the process of drafting overall NCD policies, plans or programs.

WHO and other global agencies such as the International Agency for Research on Cancer (IARC) can provide useful guidance and support for developing and integrating national cancer plans into broader national health plans. The WHO framework for National Cancer Plan Development is one example.[11]

10.iii Stewardship and leadership for CCC: Building global and local stakeholder networks

The number and types of players, and their ability to voice opinions, affect policy, and provide core financing have expanded significantly over the past decades.[12] Indeed, internationally agreed upon principles of aid effectiveness, as well as strategy documents from international organizations, stress the need to foster broad dialogue as part of country ownership.[13,14]

Thus, CCC requires the mobilization and engagement of a wide range of stakeholders at the local and global level. These stakeholders span all levels of government (including legislators), patient groups and communities affected by the disease, multilateral development and financing institutions, normative and technical agencies, bilateral agencies, civil society organizations, research institutions, philanthropic institutions, and the private sector.[15] In turn, effective stewardship and leadership for CCC must draw on the energies of all of these global and local players to establish networks for effective dialogue and to foster country ownership.[16,17]

Yet, many of the global and local actors who can and should be more involved in guaranteeing the provision of CCC have stayed out of this arena. Cancer has been neglected, or at least under-recognized, in priority setting in global health –an error of ignorance– in favor of an emphasis on investment in communicable disease, in addition to the traditional investments in maternal and child, sexual and reproductive health. Even the organizations working on sexual, reproductive and women's health have tended to neglect women's cancers as a priority, despite the burden of cervical and breast cancer in LMICs.[18-20] Similarly, childhood cancer, and in fact all childhood NCDs, are missing from the child health agenda of international agencies such as UNICEF.[21]

Stakeholders involved in CCC have, in turn, fragmented efforts. They have focused narrowly and on specific cancers, with few linkages to other cancers, diseases, or health system actors or goals. Even the strongest civil society institutions working on cancer tend to be highly specific and lack broadly based networks to catalyze health system approaches to expanding access to CCC. Unlike academic circles, there is little knowledge sharing and collaboration between various societies and organizations.

This fragmentation underscores the importance of establishing multisectoral, multi-stakeholder forums to support, pressure, and guide governments and global organizations. As discussed below, several global forums exist, and these need to be strengthened, harnessed, and made more inclusive and better linked to work with global, multilateral, and bilateral agencies to promote a healthy feedback of knowledge, consensus-building, development of public goods, and policy making.[22]

10.iv The myriad of players in global and national CCC

This mapping builds on earlier analyses[23] and focuses on the leading global and national institutions working in the cancer arena to identify the depth and breadth of potential local (Text Box 10.2 on the example of Jordan) and global participants. This includes cancer-specific, other-disease focused, broader health, and development oriented institutions that should and could be more effectively and comprehensively mobilized.[24] These actors are discussed in turn, with a set of recommendations for their effective mobilization for CCC.

Locally propagated efforts that are entrenched in country contexts are proliferating at a rapid pace in LMICs. They range from initiatives by academics and professional associations to patient advocacy groups and philanthropic foundations. Several examples, including the African Organization for Research and Training in Cancer (AORTIC), Africa Oxford Cancer Foundation (AfrOx), Brazilian Federation of Philanthropic Breast Health Institutions (FEMAMA), and King Hussein Cancer Foundation and Center are mentioned in forthcoming sections of this chapter. Further, regional and bilateral initiatives have begun working globally and a few are discussed in the text that follows. Still, these constitute a small sample of the plethora of work being conducted globally.

A more complete mapping of both the global and national players in CCC, with their respective roles, will be useful to guide stewards and leaders in strengthening their capacity for cancer control.[25] The development of a repository of information on projects and programs should be considered a high-priority future project as it will significantly contribute to achieving an efficacious global exchange and collaboration.

Global health efforts focused on infectious diseases and reproductive health have created successful models for healthcare interventions in LMICs, established health delivery infrastructure in these regions, and trained global health experts throughout the world. Improvements in HIV, malaria, tuberculosis and maternal/child mortality have involved coordinated approaches in capacity building, health systems strengthening, novel approaches to drug pricing and procurement, implementation science, innovative healthcare financing, and basic, translational and clinical research. Successful incorporation of cancer into the global health agenda requires the balance and perspective of understanding the spectrum of global health issues and priorities. The field of global oncology could substantially benefit from formal opportunities for regular interaction and collaboration with global health experts and the broader global health community. Increased synergy across disciplines and areas of expertise could accelerate advances in both global health and cancer, and more rapidly achieve the goal of reducing cancer incidence and mortality throughout the world.

Another future project, to further coordinate efforts, is the creation of a Society for Global Health and Cancer to unite the cancer and global health communities and complement and catalyze ongoing activities in the field of global cancer. While multiple oncology societies exist, many with global representation in oncology, a Society for Global Health and Cancer could uniquely serve to unite the broader global health community to optimize efforts in combating cancer in LMICs. Such a society could provide a foundation and focal point for the open exchange of scientific knowledge and experience across disciplines, and the promotion of research and training opportunities in this field. Key stakeholders would include specialty societies representing diverse areas of expertise in oncology and other global health fields, academic institutions with global health departments, non-governmental organizations, and governmental agencies invested in this issue, including national cancer centers.

Text Box 10.2

Mapping of the CCC Arena in Jordan
Afsan Bhadelia, Imad Treish, Zaid Bitar

Actor	Role	Prospective
	Key National Actors	
Ministry of Health (MoH)	**Current** • Provide regulatory mechanisms around healthcare overall. • Allocate government resources to cancer within healthcare budget. • Manage cancer registry. • Provide primary, secondary and tertiary healthcare services through: 57 comprehensive healthcare centers, 368 primary healthcare centers and 29 hospitals. • Provide variable cancer care across facilities; chemotherapy administered only in Al-Bashir Hospital.	**Prospective** • Intends to develop national CCC plan or strategy to enhance registry. • Intends to establish National Cancer Institute (NCI) to strengthen and standardize care across the country, conduct cancer surveillance, manage research and training; KHCC has the potential to be designated responsibility of an NCI.
King Hussein Foundation and Center (KHCF/C)	**Current** • Largest cancer care provider (not-for-profit) and cancer specific non-governmental organization in Jordan. • Treats majority of new and ongoing cancer patients in the country annually. • Only comprehensive cancer care provider in Jordan and Middle East with accreditation front the Joint Commission as disease-specific cancer center. • Regional hub for training and complex treatments, including bone marrow transplants. • Only facility aside from the military with authority to import essential drugs for cancer treatment that are otherwise not available in Jordan. • Largest insurer providing affordable cancer treatment coverage to residents of Jordan. • Through various endowments and charitable funds, provides funding for treatment of indigent patients who do not have insurance and are not able to obtain any other coverage. • Strong projects and technology (P&T) committee that examines pharmacoeconomics of cancer medications and has authority to conduct formulary managment/approvals. • KHCC is a WHO regional collaborative center.	**Prospective** • Model facility of high quality cancer care within in the country to help upgrade standards for both government and non-governmental providers. • Expand the number of patients covered by KHCF's insurance program (known as Health Care Program). • Expand the pharmacoeconomics unit to include other health economic decision-making and advocate for MoH to adopt KHCC recommendations on national formulary.

Text Box 10.2

Mapping of the CCC Arena in Jordan (continued)
Afsan Bhadelia, Imad Treish, Zaid Bitar

Actor	Role
Key National Actors	
Jordan Breast Cancer Program	• Established under the leadership and support of KHCC/F with the directive of MoH. • Coordinates and conducts national screening program for breast cancer, particularly advocacy and capacity building efforts for provision of related services comprehensive services for the early detection and screening of breast cancer.[26]
King Abdullah University Hospital	• One of two main teaching hospitals with range of cancer care capacity and primary coverage of patients in the Irbid region.
Royal Medical Services	• 11 hospitals for active and retired military and security personnel, and their families. • Independent budget and insurance scheme. • Cancer care provided in varying degrees across facilities, and one facility where chemotherapy is administered.
Other private providers	• 59 hospitals, majority are affiliated with the Private Hospitals Association of Jordan. • Limited cancer care provided in varying degrees across facilities, including primary care clinics.
NGOs and charities	• Serve specific catchment areas and underprivileged populations.
United Nations Relief and Works Agency	• Operates 23 health centers providing primary and preventive healthcare services. • Serves as point of referral for cancer care at governmental and private facilities.
Joint Procurement Directorate	• Negotiates and conducts national drug procurement, including oncology drugs. • Procurement based on WHO List of Essential Medicines.
Other Stakeholders	
Middle East Cancer Consortium	• Partnership between United States and MoHs in Cyprus, Egypt, Israel, Jordan, and the Palestinian Authority to reduce the incidence and impact of cancer in the Middle East through the solicitation and support of collaborative research; limited activity in Jordan currently.[27]
US-Middle East Partnership for Breast Cancer Awareness and Research	• Public-private partnership between the US State Department, Susan G. Komen for the Cure® and countries in the Middle East region, including Jordan, to raise awareness. • Transitioning into an independent, regional entity.

WORLD HEALTH ORGANIZATION

WHO is the international health agency responsible for providing global public goods in health, including those for CCC, and in promoting global action on cancer and other NCDs.

The WHO Framework Convention for Tobacco Control, with 168 signatories and arguably the world's most important legal instrument against cancer has been effectively used for policy change in many countries, exemplifying the global reach and influence of the institution.[28]

Given its mandate as the global normative agency for health, WHO should strengthen its leadership role in CCC. Yet, WHO allocates few resources to this area, largely focused on country-level work and with too little emphasis placed on core global public goods. For example, the process of approving essential drugs lacks personnel, leading to bottlenecks in CCC.

WHO should lead international and local efforts to forge internal links among disease-specific programs by applying a diagonal approach to health systems strengthening.[29] For example, by providing leadership to catalyze dialogue among HIV/AIDS and NCD groups to identify areas of common linkages in prevention, treatment, and care.

Obvious, and to date underexploited, links also exist with sexual and reproductive, women's, maternal, newborn, children's, and community health activities. Encouraging steps have been taken to facilitate more interaction through a cross-cluster working group on breast and cervical cancer established in 2011 by the Family, Women's and Children's Health Cluster.[30-32] The first product of the working group has been an updated version of **Comprehensive cervical cancer control: a guide to essential practice**, which will be ready by the end of 2012. In addition, the 2013 WHO Bulletin will dedicate a full theme issue to the topic of women's health beyond reproduction, with a clear focus on the intersection between NCDs and women's health, and where cancer, particularly with breast and cervical cancer as the subject of analysis.[33]

Another important area of work is metrics and evidence building. Promising work is being undertaken on cost-effectiveness analysis that is producing evidence that can be used for policymaking.[34-37] For example, the WHO NCD action plan will develop a package of essential CCC interventions for primary healthcare.

Yet, many platforms for global advocacy are underutilized. For example, the role of the Goodwill Ambassador for Global Cancer Control could be developed into a more effective instrument for consensus building.[38] Also, the WHO regional offices can and should play an expanded role. Existing programs, such as the Pan American Health Organization (PAHO) funds for purchasing and procuring drugs and vaccines, could be expanded to include cancer. Looking internally for solutions is not sufficient. To strengthen its work on cancer and other Ncds, WHO must enlist the many potential partners that populate the global health and cancer arena. The UNHLM provides opportunities for this to happen, and the Declaration mandates the continuation and intensification of WHO's work on cancer and Ncds.

INTERNATIONAL AGENCY FOR RESEARCH ON CANCER (IARC)

UNAIDS and IARC are the only disease-specific agencies in the UN system. Cancer is thus the only NCD represented by an institution within the multilateral system. Yet, the potential of IARC to produce global public goods for CCC is underutilized.

Given the tremendous amount of research undertaken in governmental and academic institutions around the globe, IARC can reposition itself to play a more active role in data provision, training, monitoring and evaluation. It is well positioned to generate and disseminate more effectively a range of global public goods for CCC.

IARC could play a major role in strengthening the stewardship of national governments and promoting uptake of evidence by focusing and expanding support to countries for cancer registries, promoting government efforts to develop registries and core evidence, becoming a global repository and clearinghouse of knowledge, and developing in-house and in-country program evaluation capacity. New areas of opportunity for IARC in support of WHO include: providing evidence for guideline development; identifying and disseminating lessons on implementing CCC; integrating data on cost-effectiveness of interventions; disseminating latest research results; and, implementing programs and evaluation in LMICs. Increasing IARC's engagement in implementation science would accelerate progress in improving cancer control.

IARC can be pivotal in developing the cancer components of the monitoring and accountability framework of the Declaration of the UNHLM. Further, the institution is well positioned to produce a global cancer observatory that, on an annual basis, could monitor and follow up on progress of countries against the global and national targets that will be established as a result of the UNHLM.

Text Box 10.3
IARC

IARC, founded in 1965 through a resolution of the World Health Assembly, is located in Lyon, France. IARC is considered a part of WHO and follows the general governing rules of the UN family, but it is led by its own governing bodies. IARC's Governing Council is composed of representatives of 22 participating countries and the Director-General of WHO, and its research program is reviewed by a Scientific Council. IARC's member countries, primarily high income, provide most of the financing for the work of the institution.

IARC's mission and objective are focused on coordinating and conducting research on the causes of human cancer and carcinogenesis, developing scientific strategies for cancer prevention and control, promoting international collaboration in cancer research, and producing evidence-based science for global cancer control policies.

Within this mandate, IARC has been able to contribute significantly to the global public goods in evidence and information, both within and across countries. In particular, the agency is the repository of the GLOBOCAN cancer registry database and the producer of global, harmonized, comparative data from these registries.

UNITED NATIONS SYSTEM

By calling the HLM, the UN effectively generated tremendous activity around cancer and other NCDs. Moving forward, the leadership role of the UN is crucial for follow-through on the HLM Declaration and to ensure that each UN agency take part in implementation of the provisions under the guidance and leadership of WHO.

The mandates of many UN agencies, such as the International Labour Organization (ILO), United Nations Entity for Gender Equality and the Empowerment of Women (UN Women), United Nations Population Fund (UPFPA), United Nations Children's Fund (UNICEF), United Nations Environment Programme (UNEP), and Joint United Nations Programme on HIV and AIDS (UNAIDS), include programs that could be used for expanding CCC and meeting the challenge of NCDs. Yet, these linkages remain underexploited.

IAEA deserves special mention as its work in the cancer arena stands out among the UN institutions outside of health.[39] Through the Programme of Action for Cancer Therapy (PACT), IAEA has focused financial, advocacy, and technical resources on expanding access to radiation therapy and nuclear medicine. Further, the agency has adopted a broad, development-oriented approach and undertakes research and publication on solutions to the inequities in access to overall CCC.[40,41] Dating back to 1980, IAEA's work in cancer can serve as an example for other international agencies.

The UN should focus resources as a global steward in mobilizing donors –bilateral, multilateral, foundations, and private philanthropy– for cancer and NCDs. The successful strategies applied around Every Woman Every Child provide a useful framework and are discussed in greater depth in Chapter 8 of this volume.[42] Global stewardship to produce resources is especially important given that donor support did not emerge with the UNHLM on NCDs and the extant failure to mobilize global financing to meet the challenge of cancer beyond the basic risk factors and tobacco control.

THE GLOBAL FUND TO FIGHT AIDS, TUBERCULOSIS AND MALARIA

The Global Fund offers significant potential for expanding CCC because the organization has been effective in rapidly channeling large amounts of disease-specific resources to LMICs. Its investments in health systems potentially benefit CCC and other NCDs, yet this opportunity remains unexploited.

As discussed in Chapter 8, the Global Fund Strategy for 2011-15 proposes to maximize the impact of its investments beyond AIDS, tuberculosis and malaria, particularly for women and children.[43] Still, to date the institution has failed to develop meaningful strategies to invest effectively in health systems beyond a narrow set of interventions.

WORLD BANK, REGIONAL DEVELOPMENT BANKS, BILATERAL AGENCIES AND THE ORGANIZATION FOR ECONOMIC CO-OPERATION AND DEVELOPMENT

The multilateral financial institutions have not been very active in financing activities around NCDs, although recent reports have highlighted the importance of expanding existing health portfolios to include chronic diseases.[44] As a major investor in health systems, the World Bank, in particular, can play an important role in financing a more coherent response to NCDs, including cancer. A key area is the development of global public goods that will expand CCC in LMICs, including financing large-scale demonstration initiatives and their independent evaluations.

The regional development banks could also be very effective by financing programs that include strong evaluation components. Further, these institutions are well situated to facilitate regional cooperation and public goods.

With the exception of tobacco control, bilateral agencies have mostly shied away from supporting work on cancer, and more generally on NCDs. A few have even expressed their concern that undue focus on NCDs or chronic illness would detract from efforts towards achieving Millennium Development Goals (MDGs). National and global stewards and leaders must continue to work with the bilaterals to demonstrate the benefits of investing in health systems that will help achieve MDGs while benefiting NCDs, and at the same time help alleviate poverty.

The Organisation for Economic Co-operation and Development (OECD) could play an enhanced role in global CCC. Their work to date on NCDs and strengthening health systems, particularly in identifying the most cost-effective strategies, could be of use not only for the middle income countries that are now members, but also to provide lessons for LMICs.

CIVIL SOCIETY

Civil society –both global and local– is instrumental in galvanizing action in health and other social sectors. Its independence from government permits civil society to undertake unfettered advocacy to achieve equity and human rights.

The global HIV/AIDS response provides an excellent example of what can be achieved through concerted efforts by civil society. Advocacy from civil society, often driven by patients, was instrumental in catalyzing a special session of the UN General Assembly in 2000 and in creating global institutions to fight AIDS. Another example of the patient-driven advocacy movement can be found in tobacco control.[45]

In the United States, advocacy from civil society on cancer has fueled a generation of work, started by leaders like Mary Lasker who generated strong momentum around cancer and more recently around breast cancer.[46-49] Indeed, the cancer civil society network in high income countries is among the strongest of all the NCD networks and is empowered by the voices of patients, survivors, and their families. This presents both an opportunity and a responsibility to learn from these experiences in high income countries and to support the development of similar civil society action around cancer and other NCDs in LMICs.

Several civil society organizations based in the US and Europe have global outreach. For example, the American Cancer Society, founded in 1913 as the American Society for the Control of Cancer, now works globally.[50,51] Two of the strongest civil society agencies working in cancer in the US recently expanded their work to the global arena. LIVESTRONG began to work internationally in 2008 and has developed an important focus on global advocacy, concentrating on reducing stigma and promoting awareness.[52] Susan G. Komen for the Cure (SGKC), a US voice and force in breast cancer, began global work in 2007 with training in 16 countries. In 2010, global work expanded with the launch of the Komen Global Health Alliance in support of women's cancers and as part of the larger women's health agenda.[53] The Pink Ribbon Red Ribbon initiative, launched in 2011 by the George W. Bush Institute, the US President's Emergency Plan for AIDS Relief (PEPFAR), UNAIDs, and SGKC, is an innovative example of applying the diagonal approach by linking women's cancers and HIV/AIDS.[54]

Civil society organizations working on cancer in LMICs are increasingly active and politically involved. Many countries have at least one civil society organization dedicated to cancer issues, and several have institutions that focus specifically on childhood or breast cancer. However, these organizations, often established by those affected by cancer, tend to lack technical or health policy expertise and struggle to find financial stability and a niche from which to influence policy.[55] They would therefore benefit from stronger links to academics working on research and policy as well as to the private sector.

Yet, civil society organizations and other actors, including the private sector, often work in isolation in LMICs, frequently unaware of each other's efforts even in the same parts of the world. Strengthening and expanding communication on the growing number of endeavors in LMICs is critical to effectively expand CCC. There is a need for a global repository of information on initiatives designed to expand access to CCC and thus accelerate progress in implementing change. Indeed, collaborative efforts led by The Union for International Cancer Control (UICC) and American Society of Clinical Oncology (ASCO) are now underway to respond to this need by undertaking a mapping of existing and ongoing CCC initiatives and programs in LMICs. In the area of pediatric oncology, Oncopedia provides an example of an effective platform.

Text Box 10.4
**Eastern Europe/Central Asia breast cancer education,
outreach and advocacy: Connecting the United States,
Eastern Europe, and Central Asia
to improve women's health**

Ksenia Koon, Julie R. Gralow, Tanya Soldak, Jo Anne Zujewski

Breast cancer outreach in Eastern Europe and Central Asia (EECA) has been challenging due to a climate of limited social and political acceptance, as well as restricted funding. However, a series of biennial EECA breast cancer education, outreach, and advocacy summits have provided a forum for the exchange of ideas and perspectives. The EECA Summits bring together patient advocates, NGOs, healthcare providers, academics, researchers, government officials, policy makers, the media, and the pharmaceutical industry to address this challenge. This collaboration - involving stakeholders from the US and EECA- dates back to 1997, with a USAID -funded project in Ukraine.

The breast cancer peer-support volunteer movement known as the Amazonka Federation was established in Ukraine in the late 1990s thanks to a USAID-funded project coordinated by PATH, that included consultancy by faculty of the University of Washington Schools of Medicine and Nursing and the Fred Hutchinson Cancer Research Center. When the project was initiated, cancer carried so much stigma that doctors often did not inform patients of the diagnosis. Afraid or ashamed of breast cancer diagnosis, women did not talk about it with doctors, friends, family, or peers. Cancer support groups were almost unheard of, and psychological support to cancer patients was very limited.

In 1997, PATH began to provide patients and doctors with accurate, up-to-date information, including patient education materials. The project introduced the idea that women could help each other and invited breast cancer survivors from the US to take part in seminars in Ukraine. Inspired by this interaction, Ukrainian cancer survivors organized support groups across the country and established the Amazonka Federation that now includes chapters in the majority of the 25 Ukrainian regions. In October 2001, breast cancer survivors, family members, and healthcare providers gathered in the streets of Kyiv for the first "March for Life and Hope," now an annual event.

Fifteen years later, in 2003, the University of Washington, the Seattle Cancer Care Alliance, and the Fred Hutchinson Cancer Research Center implemented a second stage of work and coordinated an EECA Breast Cancer Education, Outreach and Advocacy Summit to share the lessons learned in Ukraine. This event, held in Vilnius, Lithuania and co-hosted by Nedelsk (Do Not Delay), provided a forum to foster regional dialogue around breast cancer issues.

The success of the first conference led to the creation of a biennial EECA Summit series rotating among countries (2005 in Kyiv in partnership with the Amazonkas; 2007 in Minsk with "In Rays of Hope" and the US Embassy; 2009 in Bishkek, Kyrgyzstan with "Ergene," the Kyrgyz Parliament, the Kyrgyz Ministry of Health, and the Kyrgyz National Cancer Institute; in 2011, in Vilnius, Lithuania with Nedelsk). Tbilisi, Georgia has been selected as the 2013 summit site.

There has been much progress in the participating countries since the first summit, though barriers to effective cancer care and the breast cancer movement remain. Participation has increased to include representation from Romania, Russia, Kaliningrad (Russia), Moldova, Poland, Estonia, Georgia, Kazakhstan, Tajikistan, and Uzbekistan, as well as the host countries. Important strategic partners have included Susan G. Komen for the Cure, the US National Cancer Institute, and the Resource and Policy Exchange, in addition to local breast cancer NGOs.

The EECA Summits provide unique forums for the exchange of perspectives, resources, and strategies. Advocates have become increasingly willing to publicly acknowledge their fights with breast cancer and play important roles in furthering public education and influencing policy. The summits have also stimulated cooperation and broadened partnerships between countries. The ongoing exchange of ideas and enhanced communication generated through these summits help achieve sustainable improvements in breast cancer and the health and status of women throughout EECA.

Text Box 10.5
Femama: Promoting policy change in Brazil
through civil society[56]

Maira Caleffi

Femama brings together civil society organizations and focuses on dissemination of information, as well as ensuring access to quality care (access to mammograms, reducing the time between diagnosis and the initiation of appropriate treatment), and advocacy for policy change in Brazil. The organization has successfully promoted multisectoral strategies to develop a national policy to address breast cancer, involving government, medical professionals, and the population in general.

Femama led a successful movement to pass legislation that resulted in the 2008 Brazil Federal Law 11.664. This law addresses the health of women in a comprehensive manner, encompassing the prevention, detection, and treatment of breast and cervical cancer. It ensures the availability of mammography to all women over 40 years of age.

In March of 2011, Brazil released a National Program for Control of Breast and Cervical Cancer. With respect to breast cancer, the objectives include guaranteeing increased access to examinations for early detection, improving quality of care for all Brazilian women, and creating a working group to implement the National Program of Quality in Mammography. The policies of Femama were incorporated into this national program.

Femama recognizes that much of its work must involve engaging society in the formulation of public policy and encouraging political participation. Promoting altruism and volunteer work has helped to generate a sense of civic responsibility and a powerful grassroots movement.

The Union for International Cancer Control is a global umbrella, civil society organization that dates back to 1933 and has a unique and important role to play in global stewardship and as a leader of the civil society movement.[57] The member organizations of UICC offer a glimpse into the range, depth, and complexity of institutions that span the globe in cancer (Text Box 10.6).

Further, UICC is a founding member of the NCD Alliance and led civil society in the cancer work for the UNHLM on NCDs.[58] This effective leadership by UICC in an important global setting demonstrates the potential of this organization to represent civil society cancer organizations in the future and to build bridges to groups that offer joint platforms, including the MCH, SRH, and HIV/AIDS communities, as well as agencies working to strengthen health systems.

Text Box 10.6
The Union for International Cancer Control (UICC)

Founded in 1933 and based in Geneva, UICC unites more than 470 member organizations engaged in cancer control, representing more than 125 countries. It has a broad mandate that extends to all facets of the CCC continuum.[59] UICC members span professional societies, cancer control bodies, advocacy organizations, patient and survivor organizations, and corporate industry partners. With such broad membership, UICC is well positioned as a steward of global advocacy on cancer.

Thus, UICC provides the entire cancer community with a platform from which to coordinate and mobilize civil society globally and nationally. For this platform to reach its full potential, it must be strengthened, expanded, and aligned to be able to respond effectively to current opportunities.

The World Cancer Declaration –a live, sign-on document, developed and managed by UICC– has proven an effective advocacy tool and offers a good stage for global CCC efforts. If expanded, it could also serve as a base upon which to build a set of measurable goals for global CCC. The Declaration could be a point of departure for undertaking a global observatory led by the civil society or "watched" by, for and from civil society for monitoring global and national CCC efforts.

Through an annual progress report based on measurable goals, UICC could turn existing efforts around the Declaration into powerful tools for civil society to bring about change. A Global Cancer Watch with a scorecard could include reflections and indicators of progress on civil society itself, as well as other sectors. An observatory could be generated to serve as a clearinghouse for information on organizations investing in or implementing programs on cancer in LMICs.

PROFESSIONAL ASSOCIATIONS AND RESEARCH INSTITUTIONS

Professional associations, which bring together global, regional, and local networks, can exert significant influence on health policy in their home countries and beyond, such as the International Federation of Gynecology and Obstetrics (FIGO), which brings together professional societies of obstetricians and gynecologists from member societies in 124 countries.[60]

Local physician associations operate in most LMICs, along with associations of nurses, social workers and other health professionals. Many have sub-specialty associations that include oncologists. In Mexico, for example, an active association of oncologists (Sociedad Mexicana de Oncología) dates back to 1951 and has a number of sub-specialty groups, such as the Asociación Mexicana de Mastología.[61,62]

Professional association networks have been created around global CCC, including several based in LMICs. These include the African Organization for Research and Training in Cancer (AORTIC) founded in 1983, the Sociedad Latinoamericana y del Caribe de Oncología Médica founded in 2003,[63] and more recently the Federación de Sociedades Latinoamericanas de Cáncer.[64]

Professional associations in high income countries have also expanded their participation in global cancer. For example, the International Network for Cancer Treatment and Research, established in 1988, has membership in 50 countries.[65,66] The International Society of Pediatric Oncology, founded in the late 1960s, now has more than 1150 members.[67]

Over the past decade, international professional associations, such as the ASCO and the European Society of Medical Oncology (ESMO), have significantly increased the scope and scale of their international work in response to requests from their members, though much needs to be done to utilize the expertise of ASCO to strengthen global advocacy by working with other stakeholders, such as UICC. Many other professional organizations have international activities, but these typically focus on training and capacity building with limited engagement in effective global advocacy around CCC.

Text Box 10.7
ASCO's evolving engagement in global cancer control

Since its first meeting in November 1964, ASCO —today with more than 30,000 members around the world— has been committed to working globally.[68] Unlike most American medical societies at the time, ASCO chose from the start to make membership in the society equally available to clinicians around the world.[69]

In the mid-to-late 1990s, as the international membership of ASCO grew exponentially and the ASCO Annual Meeting became a global conference, an International Affairs Task Force, comprised of members from around the world, was installed and ASCO started sponsoring and endorsing international oncology conferences.[70,71]

By 2000, one out of every four ASCO members was based outside of the US, and international members became increasingly active in governance.[72] Today, a third of ASCO's members —more than 9,000 oncologists from 120 countries— practice outside the United States, as do a majority of the attendees to the ASCO Annual Meeting.

ASCO has accelerated the development of programs to address oncology workforce issues in less developed countries. In 2002, ASCO offered its first International Development and Education Awards (IDEAs) that today support the mentoring and professional development of young oncologists in 42 LMICs. This was followed in 2004 by the launch of the Multidisciplinary Cancer Management Course, which has to date delivered training on cancer management principles to more than 2,000 clinicians in low and middle income countries. ASCO and the European Society of Medical Oncology also jointly developed recommendations for the training of medical oncologists globally.[73]

Since 2009, ASCO has launched several new programs in critical areas, including: the International Clinical Trials Workshop to train clinicians in economically emerging countries in international research skills and standards; the Long-term International Fellowship to support research collaborations between ASCO members; the IDEA for Palliative Care Award for oncologists from LMICs; the partnership with the UICC on the Global Access to Pain Initiative to advocate for access to pain medications in sub-Saharan countries; and the International Cancer Corps program to pair ASCO members with cancer centers in LMICs.[74] These programs have generated strong support and interest from the ASCO membership –both international and domestic– and several ASCO members recently published ambitious proposals for the society to further expand its contributions to cancer control in LMICs.[75]

There is an increasing amount of research and academic literature on global health and cancer, and a growing number of researchers based in high income countries are forming groups and strengthening their international work in cancer.

A systematic literature review on cancer in LMICs between 1990 and 2010 (using Medline, Embase, EBSCO, Web of Science and Google Scholar Publications with English abstract) showed a substantial increase in the number of publications on the subject. Between 2005 and 2010, 458 articles were published in academic journals – more than the total number of publications produced between 1990-2005. For example, Lancet and Lancet Oncology have published 66 articles on cancer in LMICs over the past two decades: 12 between 1990 and 2000, 24 between 2001-2005, and 35 between 2006-2010.[76] Further, journals such as The Oncologist are significantly expanding their work in global cancer.

Following the pivotal studies by the Institute of Medicine (IOM) of the US National Academies of Medicine,[77] several important studies have been financed and produced by civil society groups working with academia.[78-80] Indeed, the IOM recommendation that the academic community active in global health extend its work beyond the traditional areas of focus to include CCC has been taken up. The UNHLM on NCDs provided the impetus for this work and catalyzed a host of additional publications, particularly in academic and policy journals.[81]

Academic institutions from high income countries have expanded their activities in global health and cancer. For example, the Africa Oxford Cancer Foundation (AfrOx) was established in 2007 by leading researchers, politicians, and individuals from the private sector to encourage international collaboration to support improved cancer care in Africa.[82] The Breast Health Global Initiative, founded and led by the Fred Hutchinson Cancer Research Center and largely funded by Susan G. Komen for the Cure, develops and endeavors to implement best practices and guidelines in countries with limited resources.[83] The Fred Hutchinson Cancer Research Center is also actively working with partners in Uganda in the production of research.[84]

A particularly promising initiative is the Center on Global Health launched in 2011 by the National Cancer Institute of the US. This center offers both fresh perspectives on and resources for CCC in LMICs. It plans a broad research agenda that encompasses health systems strengthening and monitoring program effectiveness.[85] The Center can also play a key role in broadening work in global health to look beyond traditional targets around communicable disease, basic nutrition and reproductive health.

New interdisciplinary and inter-institutional networks of civil society organizations, academics, healthcare providers, and leaders from the private sector are emerging and engaging in advocacy, knowledge generation and dissemination activities to expand CCC in LMICs. CanTreat, for example, is an informal network dedicated to identifying treatment solutions.[86]

The Global Task Force on Expanded Access to Cancer Care and Control in Developing Countries (GTF.CCC), the entity that produced this volume through the Harvard Global Equity Initiative, brings together leaders from the cancer care and global health communities based at public and private institutions around the globe and with expertise that spans advocacy, research, clinical care, population health services, and government. Initially convened through Harvard University institutions and now jointly led with the Fred Hutchinson Cancer Research Center, GTF.CCC links a substantial group of leaders, many of whom had not previously engaged in work related to cancer.[87] The academic base of this network engages a wide range of participants, including national governments, international agencies, civil society, and the private sector.

PRIVATE SECTOR ENGAGEMENT

Effective mobilization of the private sector and its full involvement in developing solutions for CCC in LMICs requires global and national stewardship to establish meaningful dialogue and interaction with industries. This should extend both to companies directly involved in healthcare (such as pharmaceutical, diagnostics and medical device companies), as well as industries that can influence CCC, including food and beverage companies, the telecommunications sector, and marketing and media firms.

The private sector can play an important role in promoting workplace health and developing solutions to expand insurance to cover cancer. The formal private sector employs millions of staff globally and purchases health insurance for a large number of workers in high and middle income countries. Associations of small businesses and informal sector trades and professions can also participate as consumers of healthcare and insurance.

The private sector can assume a more proactive role in shaping the global strategies to expand access to care by creating new business models and proposing innovative, affordable, and scalable solutions to cancer care and treatment in LMICs. This includes, yet goes far beyond, developing and supplying inputs or achieving better prices for drugs and harnessing the potential of shared value.[88] Frugal innovations in packaging treatments, innovations in delivery, training of health professionals, appropriate marketing of products, and supporting demonstration products are a subset of areas for increased private sector activity. Further, public-private partnerships have proved especially useful in implementing innovative solutions for financing and delivery of healthcare.

Yet, few venues exist where the private sector can collectively address the challenge of scaling up access to CCC. The World Economic Forum offers a unique platform for these interactions, but other neutral spaces that can support ongoing multistakeholder, inter-industry and results-driven dialogue should be identified. Universities, especially business schools and departments working on global health, can offer important opportunities to promote effective dialogue between the private sector and the diversity of stakeholders that operate in CCC in LMICs. Cognizant of this opportunity to generate platforms for dialogue, the GTF.CCC includes an active Private Sector Engagement Group.

Text Box 10.8
An integrated partnership in Rwanda: Comprehensive National Cervical Cancer Prevention Program and the Rwanda Task Force on Expanded Access to CCC

Afsan Bhadelia

On April 26, 2011, the Government of Rwanda (GOR), through a public-private partnership with Merck and Qiagen, launched a Comprehensive National Cervical Cancer Prevention Program – the first in Africa and therefore an incredible feat.[89-91] This is also the first such collaboration of its kind and was initially announced by Merck and Qiagen at the 2009 Annual Meeting of the Clinton Global Initiative as one of thirteen commitments to empower girls and women.[92] This public-private partnership could serve as a model and pave the way for other countries in Africa where the HPV vaccine is direly needed to close the cancer divide – 93% of cervical cancer deaths are in LMICs, especially low income countries.

Between 2011 and 2014, Merck plans to donate 2 million doses of the HPV vaccine GARDASIL to vaccinate girls between the ages of 12 and 15. Qiagen is supplying 250,000 HPV DNA tests to screen women aged 35 through 45 at no cost along with equipment and training to administer the test.[93] Both companies have committed to making these latest technologies available to Rwandan women during the donation period. In addition, through partnership and negotiation with the GOR, the companies also committed to developing a sustainable strategy for ongoing vaccination and screening. This contributes to a larger initiative by the GOR for developing and implementing a National Strategic Plan for the Prevention, Control, and Management of Cervical Cancer, incorporating strategies for prevention, early detection, diagnosis and treatment, palliative care, and policy and advocacy.

Factors that have been critical to advancing action on cervical cancer in Rwanda include a very successful national program, within which more than 90% of children are vaccinated against 9 diseases. Rwanda has also benefited from champions within each of the partner entities, particularly within the GOR,[94-96] good governance, political support to form public-private partnerships, local ownership, willingness of industry partners to back commitments with donations, and a pledge of reduced and tiered pricing over the long-term. Transparency in negotiations and accountability helped foster an environment of mutual interest, which laid a foundation and provided incentives for a sustainable public-private partnership. However, even with the reduced prices of the vaccine and screening test after the initial 3 years, financial barriers to maintaining a national program exist.[97]

One of most interesting aspects of this program is the way the GOR has used this program as a catalyst for broader activities in CCC. The initiative has been integrated into health system strengthening and the primary sector through women and health programs in a truly holis-

tic and comprehensive approach. Also, the GOR is moving forward with much broader programs on early detection and treatment of cancer. With development partners, the GOR is developing a population-based cancer registry.[98] Further, the launch of the cervical cancer program has been a mechanism for integrating awareness and early detection of breast cancer into the primary healthcare system with a focus on MCH, SRH and HIV/AIDS programs. Innovative treatment programs working with civil society (Partners In Health and WE-ACTx) and hospitals based in high income countries (Dana Farber Cancer Institute and Brigham and Women's Hospital) are being extended (Chapter 6). The momentum around the public-private partnership on cervical cancer and an on-going recognition of the growing overall cancer burden by the GOR led to the simultaneous announcement of the Rwanda Task Force on Expanded Access to Cancer Care and Control. This multistakeholder group is working in collaboration with the GTF.CCC, and is lead by the Rwanda Medical Professional Associations working with GOR. Among other activities, these associations will help develop the Rwanda national cancer plan and serve as an external group for monitoring progress.

10.v Beyond the Declaration: Action to address the global cancer and NCD burden

In global health, long periods of inattention to specific issues or diseases are often followed by sudden, unpredictable, and sometimes fleeting bursts of policy attention.[99] These constitute opportune moments to forge global movements through advocacy and activism and for international priority setting.[100]

The UNHLM on NCDs, with participation by heads of state and governments and the active involvement of civil society, academia, and the private sector, provides just such an opportune moment. The Declaration positions NCDs as an economic as well as a health priority for the development agenda.[101]

Yet, it lacks specific, time-bound national and global targets and contains no overall goal for reducing preventable deaths. The Declaration proposes voluntary targets, missing the opportunity to hold donors and countries accountable. Further, the Declaration acknowledges that the resources devoted to NCDs are not commensurate with the magnitude of the problem, but there are no commitments to increase these resources.[102,103]

Advocacy and research since the UNHLM have contributed to convincing governments to commit to measurable goals. Indeed, the WHO recommendation for a 25% reduction in premature deaths from NCDs by 2025 was adopted as a voluntary, overarching target by the World Health Assembly in May of 2012. Still, the specific targets that would make this overall goal attainable were not agreed upon and continue to be the subject of international negotiation.[104]

The Declaration calls for a report by 2014 on the progress achieved globally and at the country level in realizing the commitments. This provides the opportunity to put in place an independent, transparent and robust system for global monitoring and accountability – ideally aligned with the Accountability Commission on Women's and Children's Health. Ideally, there would be a single framework that takes into account all global health priorities, including NCDs.[105]

Effective advocacy for multisectoral action for NCDs will require leveraging global institutions and national health systems and mobilizing all spheres of public policy and the many stakeholders in the global CCC arena, including the private sector. Further, it will be important to reach institutions that operate from outside the health arena yet enact policies that affect CCC and other NCDs – such as trade, environment, labor, fiscal policy, agriculture, and education[106] – to create "a whole-of-government and a whole-of-society" effort.[107]

The Declaration requests the Secretary General of the UN, through WHO, to work in consultation with Member States, all relevant UN bodies, and international organizations to produce and submit proposals for multi-sectoral action on NCDs through partnerships.

Despite its limitations, the UNHLM on NCDs generated new groupings for stewardship and governance in cancer and other chronic and NCDs.[108-110] The NCD Alliance continues to be a much welcome example of a grouping with more than 900 disease-specific organizations in 170 countries coordinating their efforts to speak with a unified voice.[111] Similarly, meetings leading up to the UNHLM, such as the First Global Ministerial Conference on Healthy Lifestyles and Noncommunicable Diseases (Moscow, April 2011), provided for development of multistakeholder forums.[112]

The Declaration requests the Secretary General of the UN, through WHO, to work in consultation with Member States, all relevant UN bodies, and international organizations to produce and submit proposals for multi-sectoral action on NCDs through partnerships. Yet, much remains to be done if the opportune moment created by the UNHLM is to be effectively capitalized upon. This includes endorsing the call to establish an independent multi-agency, multi-stakeholder, intersectoral task force of experts and leaders[113,114] to ensure effective financing of health systems to address global health priorities that remain inadequately addressed –including mental illness– and work to build bridges with the communicable disease communities.

UICC and IARC can make important contributions to this group or its secretariat. Further, as an interdisciplinary, intersectoral model, GTF.CCC offers a useful framework for establishing multistakeholder groupings in individual countries to expand advocacy, produce evidence and strengthen governmental programs around cancer.

The new partnerships that are being formed across institutions and in global health and cancer, coupled with the empowerment of cancer survivors, suggest that the cancer arena is poised for rapid expansion if better and more appropriate leadership and stewardship is made available. This will require closer collaboration among the many players that populate the cancer arena and engagement with governments and the private sector to defragment initiatives and develop a cohesive global response.

The cancer community can and should seize the window of opportunity created by the UNHLM to work as a unified force and play a leadership role to galvanize awareness, interest, and action around cancer and NCDs. This will entail establishing multisectoral, multistakeholder, national, and global platforms and partnerships to expand access to all aspects of CCC while benefiting other chronic diseases.[115]

References

1. OECD. The Paris Declaration on Aid Effectiveness and the Accra Agenda for Action. 2010. http://www.oecd.org/dataoecd/11/41/34428351.pdf (accessed August 8, 2011).

2. Balabanova D, McKee M, Mills A, Walt G, Haines A. What can global health institutions do to help strengthen health systems in low income countries? *Health Research Policy and Systems* 2010; 8(1):1-11.

3. World Health Organization. Everybody's business: Strengthening health systems to improve health outcomes. Geneva: World Health Organization; 2007.

4. Atun R, Weil DEC, Eang MT, Mwakyusa D. Health-system strengthening and tuberculosis control. *Lancet* 2010; 375(9732):2169-78.

5. World Health Organization. World Health Report 2010: Health systems financing: the path to universal coverage. World Health Organization. 2010.

6. World Health Organization. Everybody's business: Strengthening health systems to improve health outcomes. Geneva: World Health Organization. 2007.

7. WHO Commission on Macroeconomics and Health. Working Group 2. Global public goods for health: the report of Working Group 2 of the Commission on Macroeconomics and Health. World Health Organization. 2002.

8. Jamison D, Frenk J, Knaul F. International collective action in health: objectives, functions, and rationale. *Lancet* 1998; 351(9101):514-7.

9. Moon S, Szlezák NA, Michaud CM, et al. The global health system: lessons for a stronger institutional framework. *PLoS Medicine* 2010; 7(1):1-6.

10. World Health Organization. Assessment of national capacity for noncommunicable disease prevention and control. The report of a global survey. 2001. Geneva, WHO. http://whqlibdoc.who.int/hq/2001/WHO_MNC_01.2.pdf (accessed August 9, 2011).

11. World Health Organization. Cancer control: knowledge into action: WHO guide for effective programmes; Module 1. Planning. Switzerland: World Health Organization. 2006.

12. WHO Commission on Macroeconomics and Health. Working Group 2. Global public goods for health: the report of Working Group 2 of the Commission on Macroeconomics and Health. WHO. 2002.

13. OECD. The Paris Declaration on Aid Effectiveness and the Accra Agenda for Action. 2010. http://www.oecd.org/dataoecd/11/41/34428351.pdf (accessed August 8, 2011).

14. World Health Organization. Everybody's business: Strengthening health systems to improve health outcomes. Geneva: World Health Organization. 2007.

15. WHO Commission on Macroeconomics and Health. Working Group 2. Global public goods for health: the report of Working Group 2 of the Commission on Macroeconomics and Health. WHO. 2002.

16. Organisation for Economic Co-operation and Development (OECD). The Paris Declaration on Aid Effectiveness and the Accra Agenda for Action. 2010. http://www.oecd.org/dataoecd/11/41/34428351.pdf (accessed August 8, 2011).

17. World Health Organization. Everybody's business: Strengthening health systems to improve health outcomes. Geneva: World Health Organization. 2007.

18. Berer M. Integration of sexual and reproductive health services: a health sector priority. *Reproductive Health Matters* 2003; 11(21):6-15.

19. Integrating Cancer Care and Control with Women and Health: Identifying Platforms, Synergies and Opportunities for Action 2011 March 10-11, 2011; Harvard University, Boston, MA; 2011.

20. Bustreo F, Knaul FM, Bhadelia A et al. Women's health beyond reproduction: meeting the challenges. *WHO Bulletin* 2012; 90(7): 477-556.

21. The NCD Alliance. A focus on children and non-communicable diseases (NCDs). Prepared by the Child-focused Working Group of the NCD Alliance. Geneva, 2011. http://ncdalliance.org/sites/default/files/resource_files/20110627_A_Focus_on_Children_&_NCDs_FINAL_2.pdf (accessed August 1, 2012).

22. Frenk J, Knaul F, Gómez-Dantés O. Global Forum update on research for health. 2004: Pro-Brook Publishing; 2004.

23. Sloan FA, Gelband H. (Eds) Cancer control opportunities in low-and middle-income countries. Washington DC: National Academy of Press; 2007.

24. Knaul F, Cahill K, Bhadelia A. Institutions with direct and indirect involvement in CCC. GTF.CCC Working Paper and Background Note Series, Harvard Global Equity Initiative, Forthcoming, 2011.

25. Reich M. Political mapping of health policy: a guide for managing the political dimensions of health policy. Boston: Harvard School of Public Health. 1994.

26. Jordan Breast Cancer Program. About us. 2011. http://www.jbcp.jo/node/11 (accessed August 8, 2011).

27. Middle East Cancer Consortium (MECC). About. 2010. http://mecc.cancer.gov/about.html (accessed August 8, 2011).

28. World Health Organization. WHO Framework Convention on Tobacco Control. Informal working group on the draft protocol to eliminate illicit trade in tobacco products. World Health Organization. 2011. http://www.who.int/fctc/en/ (accessed August 8, 2011).

29. World Health Organization. Everybody's business: Strengthening health systems to improve health outcomes. P.35. Geneva: World Health Organization; 2007.

30. Knaul F, Bustreo F, Ha E, Langer A. Breast cancer: why link early detection to reproductive health interventions in developing countries? *Salud Pública de México* 2009; 51(2):220-7.

31. US Department of State. Pink Ribbon Red Ribbon Overview. Office of Electronic Information US State Department. 2011. http://www.state.gov/r/pa/prs/ps/2011/09/172244.htm (accessed October 22, 2011).

32. Flavia B et al, 2012.

33. Flavia B et al 2012.

34. World Health Organization. Choosing Interventions that are Cost Effective (WHO-CHOICE). WHO-CHOICE Interventions. World Health Organization. 2011. http://www.who.int/choice/interventions/en/ (accessed October 22, 2011).

35. Ginsberg GM, Lauer JA, Zelle A, Baeten S, Baltussen R. Cost effectiveness of strategies to combat breast, cervical, and colorectal cancer in sub-Saharan Africa and South East Asia: mathematical modelling study. *British Medical Journal* 2012; 344:e614.

36. Salomon JA, Carvalho N, Gutiérrez-Delgado C, Orozco R, Mancuso A, Hogan DR, Lee D, Murakami Y, Sridharan L, Medina-Mora ME, González-Pier E. Intervention strategies to reduce the burden of non-communicable diseases in Mexico: cost effectiveness analysis. *British Medical Journal* 2012; 344:e355.

37. Ortegón M, LimS, Chisholm D, Mendis S. Cost effectiveness of strategies to combat cardiovascular disease, diabetes, and tobacco use in sub-Saharan Africa and South East. *British Medical Journal* 2012; 344.

38. World Health Organization. Programmes and Projects: Nancy Goodman Brinker, Goodwill Ambassador for Cancer Control. World Health Organization. 2011. http://www.who.int/goodwill_ambassadors/nancy_brinker/en/index.html (accessed August 8, 2011).

39. Sloan FA, Gelband H (Eds.), 2007.

40. IAEA. Inequity in cancer care: a global perspective. Vienna, Switzerland; IAEA. 2011.

41. IAEA. Supporting comprehensive cancer control programmes: IAEA and cancer control. IAEA. 2010. http://cancer.iaea.org/whoarewe.asp#content (accessed August 8, 2011).

42. Jamison D, Frenk J, Knaul F, 1998.

43. Global Fund to Fight AIDS, Tuberculosis, and Malaria. Twenty-third board meeting. Geneva, Switzerland, 11-12 May, 2011.

44. Nikolic IA, Stanciole AE, Zaydman M. Health, Nutrition and Population (HNP) Discussion Paper: Chronic Emergency: Why NCDs Matter. The International Bank for Reconstruction and Development. World Bank. 2011.

45. Sloan FA, Gelband H (Eds.), 2007.

46. Enserink M. A Push to Fight Cancer in the Developing World. *Science* 2011; 331(6024):1548-50.

47. Mukherjee S. The emperor of all maladies: a biography of cancer. New York: Scribner; 2010.

48. Brinker NG. Promise Me: How a Sister's Love Launched the Global Movement to End Breast Cancer. Crown Archetype: New York. 2010.

49. Lasker Foundation. Home. 2011. http://www.laskerfoundation.org/ (accessed August 8, 2011).

50. American Cancer Society. Our History. American Cancer Society. 2011. http://www.cancer.org/AboutUs/WhoWeAre/our-history (accessed October 22, 2011).

51. American Cancer Society. Global Programs: Advancing the Global Fight Against Cancer. American Cancer Society. 2011. http://www.cancer.org/aboutus/globalhealth/ (accessed August 8 2011).

52. Neal, C., Beckjord, E., Rechis, R., & Schaeffer, J. (2010). Cancer stigma and silence around the world: A LIVESTRONG report. Austin, TX: LIVESTRONG. Available at http://livestrong.org/pdfs/3-0/LSGlobalResearchReport. (accessed October 23, 2011).

53. Susan G. Komen for the Cure. Press Release: Susan G. Komen for the Cure and World Health Leaders Launch Global Women's Health Initiative. June 8, 2010. http://ww5.komen.org/KomenNewsArticle.aspx?id=6442452157 (accessed August 8, 2011).

54. US Department of State. Pink Ribbon Red Ribbon Overview. Office of Electronic Information US State Department. 2011. http://www.state. gov/t/pa/prs/ps/2011/09/172244.htm (accessed October 22, 2011).

55. Durstine A, Leitman E. Building a Latin American cancer patient advocacy movement: Latin American cancer NGO regional overview. *Salud Publica de Mexico*. 2009; 52(Supplement 2).

56. Femama. Homepage. Femama. 2011. http://www.femama.org.br/novo/ (accessed October 23, 2011).

57. Sloan FA, Gelband H (Eds.), 2007.

58. Union for International Cancer Control. UN Summit on NCDs – Political Declaration. Union for International Cancer Control. 2011. http://www.uicc.org/node/9103 (accessed October 23, 2011).

59. Union for International Cancer Control. Union for International Cancer Control: Home. Union for International Cancer Control. 2011. http://www.laskerfoundation.org/ (accessed August 8, 2011).

60. International Federation of Gynecology and Obstetrics. (FIGO). International Federation of Gynecology and Obstetrics. Home. FIGO. 2011. http://www.figo.org/ (accessed August 8 2011).

61. Sociedad Mexicana de Oncologia A.C.. Sociedad Mexicana de Oncologia A.C. Quienes Somos: Historia. SMeO. 2011. http://www.smeo.org.mx/quienessomos/historia.php (accessed October 22, 2011).

62. Asociacion Mexicana de Mastologia A.C. Inicio. Asociacion Mexicana de Mastologia A.C. 2011. http://www.mastologia.org.mx/ (accessed October 22, 2011).

63. Sociedad Latinoamericanan y del Caribe de Oncología Médica (SLACOM). Acerca de SLACOM. SLACOM. 2011. http://www.slacom.org/acerca_historia.php (accessed October 22, 2011).

64. Federación Latinoamerica de Sociedades de Cancerlogía (FLASCA). Bienvenido a FLASCA. FLASCA. 2011. http://www.flasca.com/ (accessed October 22, 2011).

65. Personal communication, email with Ian McGrath and Elisabeth Dupont, INCTR (March 8, 2011).

66. Sloan FA, Gelband H (Eds.), 2007.

67. International Society of Pediatric Oncology (SIOP). About SIOP. SIOP. 2011. http://www.siop.nl/about-siop/ (accessed October 22, 2011).

68. American Society of Clinical Oncologists. Exploring ASCO's Roots: American Society of Clinical Oncology. 2003. American Society of Clinical Oncologists. http://www.asco.org/ascov2/About+ASCO/ASCO+Information/ASCO+History/History+Article+Series/Exploring+ASCO's+Roots (accessed October 22, 2011).

69. Ibid.

70. Ibid.

71. American Society of Clinical Oncologists. The ASCO Annual Meeting. 2004. American Society of Clinical Oncologists. http://www.asco.org/ASCOv2/About+ASCO/ASCO+Information/ASCO+History/History+Article+Series/The+ASCO+Annual+Meeting (accessed October 22, 2011).

72. American Society of Clinical Oncologists. ASCO's Founders Shared Vision for Future of Cancer Treatment. 2004. American Society of Clinical Oncologists. http://www.asco.org/ASCOv2/About+ASCO/ASCO+Information/ASCO+History/History+Article+Series/ASCO %27s+Founders+S hared+Vision+for+Future+of+Cancer+Treatment (accessed October 22, 2011).

73. Hansen H, Bajorin DF, Muss HB, Purkalne G, Schrijvers D, Stahel R. Recommendations for a global core curriculum in medical oncology. Annals of Oncology 2004; 15(11);1603-12.

74. American Society of Clinical Oncologists. International Affairs. 2011. American Society of Clinical Oncologists. http://www.asco.org/ASCOv2/About+ASCO/International+Affairs (accessed October 22, 2011).

75. Patel JD, Galsky MD, Chagpar AB, Pyle D, Loehrer Sr PJ. Role of American Society of Clinical Oncology in low- and middle- income countries. Journal of Clinical Oncology 2011; 29(30): 3097-3102.

76. Aguilar Rivera AM. Literature review on cancer and developing countries (1990-2010). GTF.CCC Working Paper and Background Note Series, No. 9, Harvard Global Equity Initiative, 2012.

77. Sloan FA, Gelband H (Eds.), 2007.

78. Beaulieu N, Bloom D, Bloom R, Stein R. Breakaway: the global burden of cancer–challenges and opportunities. Economist Intelligence Unit. 2009.

79. John R, Ross H. Global Economic Cost of Cancer Report. American Cancer Society. 2010.

80. Bloom DE, Cafiero ET, Jané-Llopis E, et al. The Global Economic Burden of Non-communicable Diseases. Geneva, Switzerland: World Economic Forum. 2011. http://www3.weforum.org/docs/WEF_Harvard_HE_GlobalEconomicBurdenNonCommunicableDiseases_2011.pdf (accessed October 23, 2011).

81. Alleyne G, Basu S, Stuckler D. Who's Afraid of Noncommunicable Diseases? Raising Awareness of the Effects of Noncommunicable Diseases on Global Health. Journal of Health Communication. 2011; 16(suppl 2):82-93.

82. Afrox. Improving cancer care in Africa: Our history. AfrOx. 2011. http://www.afrox.org/9/our-history (accessed October 22, 2011)

83. Breast Health Global Initiative. Background. Breast Health Global Initiative. 2011. http://portal.bhgi.org/Pages/Background.aspx (accessed October 22, 2011).

84. Casper C, Sessle E, Phipps W, Yager J, Corey L, and Orem J. Uganda Program on Cancer and Infectious Diseases. GTF.CCC Working Paper Series, Paper No. 2, Harvard Global Equity Initiative, 2011.

85. Varmus T, Trimble EL. Integrating Cancer Control into Global Health. Science Translational Medicine 2011; 3(101):101.

86. CanTreat International. Access to cancer treatment in low- and middle-income countries. An essential part of global cancer control; 2010.

87. Global Task Force on Expanded Access to Cancer Care and Control in Developing Countries. About Us. 2011. (accessed August 8 2011). http://gtfccc.harvard.edu

88. Porter ME, Kramer MR. Creating shared value – how to reinvent capitalism – and unleash a wave of innovation and growth. Harvard Business Review. January-February 2011.

89. CSR Press Release. Rwanda, Merck and QIAGEN Launch Africa's First Comprehensive Cervical Cancer Prevention Program Incorporating Both HPV Vaccination and HPV Testing. CSR Wires. April 25, 2011. http://www.csrwire.com/press_releases/32078-Rwanda-Merck-and-QIAGENLaunch-Africa-s-First-Comprehensive-Cervical-Cancer-Prevention-Program-Incorporating-Both-HPV-Vaccination-and-HPV-Testing. (accessed October 22, 2011).

90. Lancet. Financing HPV vaccination in developing countries. Lancet 2011; 377(9777):1544.

91. QIAGEN. First-of-its kind collaboration between QIAGEN and Merck will address cervical cancer in developing countries. QIAGEN. 2011. http://www.qiagen.com/jump/090923.aspx (accessed October 22, 2011).

92. Clinton Global Initiative. Corporations, NGOs, and Foundations Announce 13 New Commitments to Empower Girls and Women at the Fifth Annual Meeting of the Clinton Global Initiative. 2009. http://press.clintonglobalinitiative.org/press_releases/corporations-ngos-and-foundations-announce13-new-commitments-to-empower-girls-and-women-at-the-fifth-annual-meeting-of-the-clinton-global-initiative/. (accessed October 22, 2011).

93. CSR Press Release. Rwanda, Merck and QIAGEN Launch Africa's First Comprehensive Cervical Cancer Prevention Program Incorporating Both HPV Vaccination and HPV Testing. CSR Wires. April 25, 2011. http://www.csrwire.com/press_releases/32078-Rwanda-Merck-and-QIAGENLaunch-Africa-s-First-Comprehensive-Cervical-Cancer-Prevention-Program-Incorporating-Both-HPV-Vaccination-and-HPV-Testing. (accessed October 22, 2011).

94. Kabeera E. PM Makuza opens Cancer Summit. The New Times. April 29, 2011. http://www.newtimes.co.rw/index.php?issue=14609&article=40642. (accessed October 22, 2011).

95. Kagire E. First Lady to launch anti-Cervical Cancer campaign. The New Times. April 26, 2011. http://www.newtimes.co.rw/index.php?issue=14607&article=40573. (accessed October 22, 2011).

96. Muson E. First Lady leads campaign against Cervical Cancer. The New Times. April 27, 2011. http://www.newtimes.co.rw/index.php?issue=14608&article=40601. (accessed October 22, 2011).

97. Lancet. Financing HPV vaccination in developing countries. Lancet 2011;377(9777):1544.

98. Anastos, K. Rwanda's Population-Based Cancer Registry. Presentation at Women's Cancer Summit in Rwanda, April 28, 2011.

99. Moon S, Szlezak NA, Michaud CM, et al., 2010.

100. Fidler D. Architecture amidst anarchy: global health's quest for governance. Global Health 2007; 1(1):1-17.

101. Beaglehole R, Bonita R, Horton R, et al. Priority actions for the non-communicable disease crisis. Lancet 2011; 377(9775):1438-47.

102. Ibid.

103. Union for International Cancer Control. UN Summit on NCDs – Political Declaration. Union for International Cancer Control. 2011. http://www.uicc.org/node/9103 (accessed October 23, 2011).

104. Gulland A. World leaders agree to cut deaths from non-communicable diseases by a quarter by 2025 BMJ 2012; 344:e3768.

105. Beaglehole R, Bonita R, Horton R, et al., 2011.

106. Nishtar S, Jané-Llopis E. A global coordinating platform for noncommunicable diseases. Journal of Health Communication 2011; 16(Suppl 2):201-5

107. United Nations General Assembly. Draft political declaration of the high-level meeting on the prevention and control of non-communicable diseases. September 9, 2011. http://www.un.org/en/ga/ncdmeeting2011/pdf/NCD_draft_political_declaration.pdf (accessed October 22, 2011).

108. Alleyne G, Stuckler D, Alwan A. The hope and the promise of the UN Resolution on non-communicable diseases. Globalization and Health. 2010; 6(15).

109. WHA. A61.8 Prevention and control of noncommunicable diseases: implementation of the global strategy. Sixty-first World Health Assembly: World Health Organization; 2008.

110. World Health Organization. Towards implementation of UN General Assembly resolution A/RES/64/265 "Prevention and control of non-communicable diseases". Geneva, Switzerland; 2010 July 23 2010.

111. Beaglehole R, Bonita R, Horton R, et al., 2011.

112. World Health Organization. First global ministerial conference on healthy lifestyles and noncommunicable disease control. 2011. http://www.who.int/nmh/events/moscow_ncds_2011/en/ (accessed October 11, 2011).

113. Beaglehole R, Bonita R, Horton R, et al., 2011.

114. The NCD Alliance. NCD Global Framework: Delivering the Outcomes from the UN High-Level Meeting. http://ncdalliance.org/global-ncd-framework-campaign (accessed June 24th, 2012).

115. Institute of Medicine. The U.S. Commitment to Global Health: Recommendations for the New Administration. Washington, DC: National Academies of Press. 2009.

APPENDIX

GLOBAL TASK FORCE ON EXPANDED ACCESS TO CANCER CARE AND CONTROL IN DEVELOPING COUNTRIES
As of August 20, 2012

LEADERSHIP

HONORARY CO-PRESIDENTS

Her Royal Highness Princess Dina Mired
Director-General, King Hussein Cancer Foundation
Honorary Chairperson, Jordan Breast Cancer Program
Hashemite Kingdom of Jordan

Lance Armstrong
Founder
LIVESTRONG
Lance Armstrong Foundation

CO-CHAIRPERSONS

Julio Frenk, MD, MPH, PhD
Dean of the Faculty, Harvard School of Public Health
T&G Angelopoulos Professor of Public Health and International Development,
Harvard School of Public Health and Harvard Kennedy School
Former Minister of Health, Mexico

Lawrence Corey, MD
President and Director, Fred Hutchinson Cancer Research Center
Head, Virology Division, Department of Laboratory Medicine, University of Washington
Professor, Medicine and Laboratory Medicine, University of Washington

SECRETARIAT CO-DIRECTORS

Felicia Marie Knaul, MA, PhD
Director, Harvard Global Equity Initiative
Associate Professor of Medicine, Harvard Medical School
Founder, "Tómatelo a Pecho, A.C."

Julie R. Gralow, MD
Director, Breast Medical Oncology, Seattle Cancer Care Alliance
Jill Bennett Endowed Professor of Breast Cancer, University of Washington School of Medicine
Full Member, Fred Hutchinson Cancer Research Center

MEMBERS

Sir George Alleyne
OCC, MD, FRCP, FACP (Hon.), DSc (Hon.)
Director Emeritus, Pan American Health Organization
Chancellor, University of the West Indies
Adjunct Professor, Bloomberg School of Public Health, Johns Hopkins University

Rifat Atun
MBBS, MRCGP, MBA, DIC, MFPHM
Professor of International Health Management, Imperial College London

Seth Berkley, MD
Chief Executive Officer, GAVI Alliance

Agnes Binagwaho, MD
Minister of Health, Rwanda
Senior Lecturer, Department of Global Health and Social Medicine,
Harvard Medical School

Flavia Bustreo, MD, MSc
Assistant Director-General, Family, Women's and Children's Health,
World Health Organization

Lincoln C. Chen, MPH, MD
President, China Medical Board

Salomón Chertorivski Woldenberg, MPP
Minister of Health, Mexico

Lord Nigel Crisp, KCB
Chair, Sightsavers International
Senior Fellow, Institute for Healthcare Improvement
Distinguished Visiting Fellow, Harvard School of Public Health
Honorary Professor, London School of Hygiene and Tropical Medicine
Honorary Fellow, St. John's College, Cambridge

Paul Farmer, MD, PhD
Kolokotrones University Professor and Chair,
Department of Global Health and Social Medicine, Harvard Medical School
Chief, Division of Global Health Equity, Brigham and Women's Hospital
United Nations Deputy Special Envoy for Haiti
Co-founder, Partners In Health

Sir Richard Feachem, KBE, FREng, DSc(Med), PhD
Director, Global Health Group, University of California, San Francisco
Professor of Global Health, University of California, San Francisco and Berkeley
Former Executive Director, Global Fund to Fight AIDS, Tuberculosis and Malaria

Roger Glass, MD, MPH, PhD
Director, Fogarty International Center, National Institutes of Health
Associate Director for Global Health Research, National Institutes of Health

Mary Gospodarowicz, MD, FRCPC, FRCR
Medical Director, Cancer Program, Princess Margaret Hospital
Professor and Chair, Department of Radiation Oncology, University of Toronto
President-Elect, Union for International Cancer Control

Sanjay Gupta, MD
Chief Medical Correspondent, Health and Medical Unit, CNN
Assistant Professor of Neurosurgery, Emory University School of Medicine
Associate Chief of Neurosurgery, Emory University Hospital and Grady Memorial Hospital

David Kerr
CBE, MA, MD, DSc, FRCP (Glas, Edin & Lon), FRCGP (Hon.), FMedSci
President, European Society of Medical Oncology
Professor of Cancer Medicine, University of Oxford
Adjunct Professor of Medicine, Weill Cornell Medical College

Ana Langer, MD
Professor of the Practice of Public Health, Harvard School of Public Health
Coordinator of the Dean's Special Initiative in Women and Health,
Department of Global Health and Population, Harvard School of Public Health

Julian Lob-Levyt, MD, MSC
Senior Vice President, DAI
Managing Director of DAI Europe, DAI
Member, International AIDS Vaccine Initiative

Anthony MBewu, MD
Visiting Professor in Cardiology and Internal Medicine, University of Cape Town

Martin J. Murphy, MD
Chief Executive Officer, CEO Roundtable on Cancer
Chairman of the Board and Chief Executive Officer, AlphaMed Consulting

Elizabeth G. Nabel, MD
President, Brigham and Women's Hospital

Peter Piot, MD, PhD
Director, London School of Hygiene and Tropical Medicine
Former Executive Director, UNAIDS and Under-Secretary-General of the United Nations

Jonathan D. Quick, MD, MPH
President and Chief Executive Officer, Management Sciences for Health
Associate Scientist, Department of Global Health and Social Medicine, Harvard Medical School

Olivier Raynaud, MD
Senior Director, Global Health and Healthcare Sector, World Economic Forum

K. Srinath Reddy, MD, DM
President, Public Health Foundation of India
Incoming President, World Heart Federation

Jeffrey D. Sachs, PhD
Director, Earth Institute, Columbia University
Quetelet Professor of Sustainable Development
and Professor of Health Policy and Management, Columbia University
Special Advisor to United Nations Secretary-General Ban Ki-moon

John R. Seffrin, PhD
Chief Executive Office, American Cancer Society

Jaime Sepúlveda, MD, MPH, DrSc
Executive Director, Global Health Sciences, University of California, San Francisco

Lawrence Shulman, MD
Chief Medical Officer and Senior Vice-President, Medical Affairs, Dana-Farber Cancer Institute
GTF.CCC co-Chair, 2009-2011

George W. Sledge, Jr., MD
Former President, American Society of Clinical Oncology
Ballvé-Lantero Professor of Oncology, Indiana University
Professor of Medicine and Pathology, Indiana University
Co-Director of the Indiana University Simon Cancer Center Breast Program

Sandra M. Swain, MD
President, American Society of Clinical Oncology
Medical Director, Washington Cancer Institute

Christopher A. Viehbacher, CPA
Chief Executive Officer, Sanofi
Chairman, Genzyme
Chairman, CEO Roundtable on Cancer

SECRETARIAT
Harvard Global Equity Initiative

Felicia Marie Knaul, MA, PhD
Director, Harvard Global Equity Initiative
Associate Professor of Medicine, Harvard Medical School
Founder, "Cáncer de mama: Tómatelo a Pecho"

Gustavo Nigenda, PhD
Research Director, Harvard Global Equity Initiative

Afsan Bhadelia, MS
Research Associate and former Research Director, Harvard Global Equity Initiative

Maja Pleic, MA
Research Assistant, Harvard Global Equity Initiative

Kathy Cahill, MPH
Senior Advisor, Global Task Force
on Expanded Access to Cancer Care and Control in Developing Countries

Amy Judd, MS
Senior Advisor, Global Task Force
on Expanded Access to Cancer Care and Control in Developing Countries
Director, Program Development, Division of Global Health Equity, Brigham & Women's Hospital

TECHNICAL ADVISORY COMMITTEE
AS OF AUGUST 20, 2012

Hans-Olov Adami, MD, PhD
Chair, Department of Epidemiology, Harvard School of Public Health
Professor, Department of Epidemiology, Harvard School of Public Health

Cary Adams, MBA, BSc
Chief Executive Officer, Union for International Cancer Control (UICC)

Clement Adebamowo, BMChB (Hons), FWACS, FACS, ScD
Associate Professor, Department of Epidemiology and Preventive Medicine,
University of Maryland School of Medicine
Associate Professor, Institute of Human Virology, University of Maryland
Director, Office of Strategic Information and Research, Institute of Human Virology, Nigeria

Cinzia Catafalmo Akbaraly
Founder and President, Foundation Akbaraly

Samia Al-Amoudi, MBBCH, CABOG
CEO and Founder, Sheikh Mohammed Hussein Al-Amoudi Center of Excellence in Breast Cancer
Chairwoman and Scientific Chair, Women's Health Rights
Associate Professor and Consultant Obstetrician Gynecologist, King Abdulaziz University, Saudi Arabia

Benjamin Anderson, MD
Chairman and Director, Breast Health Global Initiative
Professor of Surgery, University of Washington School of Medicine
Full Member, Division of Public Health Sciences, Fred Hutchinson Cancer Research Center
Director, Breast Health Clinic, Breast Care and Cancer Research Program, Seattle Cancer Care Alliance

Jon Kim Andrus, MD
Deputy Director, Pan American Health Organization
Professor, Center for Global Health, George Washington University Medical Center

Kate Armstrong, BMed, DCH, MPH
Founder & President, Caring & Living as Neighbours (CLAN)
Chair, NCD Alliance Child-focused Working Group

Hector Arreola, MSc
Coordinator of Economic Research, Health and Competitiveness, Mexican Health Foundation

Rashid Bashshur, MS, PhD
Director of Telemedicine, University of Michigan Health System
Professor Emeritus of Health Management and Policy, University of Michigan School of Public Health

Zaid Bitar, BSc
Head, International Development Department, King Hussein Cancer Foundation

Dmitry Borisov, PhD
Executive Director, Non-commercial Partnership Equal Right to Life
Chairman, Public Council for Protection of Patients' Rights,
Administration of Federal Service on Surveillance in Healthcare and Social Development, Moscow

Gene Bukhman, MD, PhD
Assistant Professor of Medicine and Assistant Professor of Global Health and Social Medicine,
Harvard Medical School
Attending Physician, Brigham and Women's Hospital and VA Boston Healthcare System
Director of Program in Global Noncommunicable Disease and Social Change, Harvard Medical School
Cardiology Director, Partners In Health,

Maira Caleffi, MD, PhD
President, Federação de Instituições Filantrópicas de Apoio à Saúde da Mama (FEMAMA)

Corey Casper, MD, MPH
Associate Professor of Medicine, Epidemiology and Global Health, University of Washington
Associate Member, Vaccine and Infectious Disease, Public Health Sciences, and Clinical Research Divisions,
and Director, UCI/Hutchinson Center Cancer Alliance, Fred Hutchinson Cancer Research Center
Medical Director, Infection Control at Seattle Cancer Care Alliance
Assistant Director, CFAR Director, Scientific Program on AIDS-Associated Malignancies
and Infections (AAIMs)

Dov Chernichovsky, MA, PhD
Professor, Department of Health Systems Management, Ben-Gurion University of the Negev
Research Associate, National Bureau of Economic Research
Head, Health Team, Taub Center for the Study of Social Policy, Israel

James F. Cleary, MD
Associate Professor of Medicine (Medical Oncology),
University of Wisconsin School of Medicine and Public Health
Director, Palliative Care Service, University of Wisconsin Hospital and Clinics
Academic Medical Director, Hospice Care Inc.

Téa Collins, MD, MPH, MPA, DrPH
Executive Director, The NCD Alliance

David Cutler, PhD
Otto Eckstein Professor of Applied Economics, Harvard University

Alessandra Durstine, MS, MBA
Vice President for Regional Strategies, International Division, American Cancer Society

Barbara Ferrer, PhD, MPH, MEd
Executive Director, Boston Public Health Commission

Lindsay Frazier, MD, ScM
Attending Physician, Dana Farber Cancer Institute
Associate Professor, Department of Pediatrics, Harvard Medical School
Associate Professor, Department of Epidemiology, Harvard School of Public Health

Emmanuela Gakidou, MSc, PhD
Associate Professor of Global Health, University of Washington
Director, Education and Training, Institute for Health Metrics and Evaluation,
University of Washington

Amanda Glassman, MSc
Director of Global Health Policy and Research Fellow, Center for Global Development

Ramiro Guerrero, MSc
Director, PROESA – Centro de Estudios en Protección Social y Economía de la Salud

Susan Higman, PhD, MA
Director, Research & Analysis, Global Health Council

Michelle D. Holmes, MD, DrPH
Associate Professor of Medicine, Harvard Medical School
Associate Physician, Brigham and Women's Hospital
Associate Professor of Epidemiology, Harvard School of Public Health

David Hunter, MBBS, MPH, ScD
Dean for Academic Affairs, Harvard School of Public Health
Vincent L. Gregory Professor in Cancer Prevention, Department of Epidemiology and Nutrition,
Harvard School of Public Health

Mercedes Juan, MD
Executive President, Mexican Health Foundation

Amy Judd, MS
Director, Program Development, Division of Global Health Equity, Brigham & Women's Hospital

Nancy Keating, MD, MPH
Associate Professor, Department of Health Care Policy, Harvard Medical School
Associate Physician, Division of General Internal Medicine, Brigham and Women's Hospital

Niranjan Konduri, MS (Pharm), MPH, CHA
Senior Program Associate, Technical Strategy and Quality, Center for Pharmaceutical Management,
Management Sciences for Health

Eric L. Krakauer, MD, PhD
Director, International Programs, Center for Palliative Care
Assistant Professor of Medicine and of Global Health & Social Medicine, Harvard Medical School
Associate Physician, Palliative Care Unit, Massachusetts General Hospital

Pablo Kuri Morales, MD, MSc
Undersecretary for Prevention and Health Promotion, Ministry of Health, Mexico
Professor, Faculty of Medicine, National University of Mexico

Eduardo Lazcano-Ponce, MD, DrSc
Director of the Center for Population Health Research, National Institute of Public Health, Mexico

Constance Lehman, MD, PhD
Medical Director of Imaging, Seattle Cancer Care Alliance
Professor and Vice Chair of Radiology, University of Washington School of Medicine
Joint Associate Member, Public Health Sciences Division, Fred Hutchinson Cancer Research Center

H. Kim Lyerly, MD
George Barth Geller Professor of Cancer Research, Duke University
Director, Duke Comprehensive Cancer Center

Ian Magrath, DSc (Med), FRCP, FRCPath
President, Medical & Scientific Director, International Network for Cancer Research and Treatment
Adjunct Professor of Pediatrics, Uniformed Services University of the Health Sciences

Alejandro Mohar, MD, ScD
General Director, National Cancer Institute of Mexico

Claire Neal, MPH, CHES
Senior Director for Mission, Lance Armstrong Foundation

Rachel Nugent, PhD
Senior Research Scientist and Associate Professor, Department of Global Health, University of Washington

Meg O'Brien, PhD
Director, Global Access to Pain Relief Initiative, Union for International Cancer Control (UICC) and the American Cancer Society (ACS)

Olufunmilayo Olopade, MD, FACP
Professor of Medicine and Human Genetics, University of Chicago Medicine
Director, Cancer Risk Clinic, University of Chicago Medicine

Jesús Zacarías Villarreal Pérez, MD
Secretary of Health, Ministry of Health of Nuevo León, Mexico

Alfonso Petersen, MD
Technical Secretary, National Council of Health, Mexico

Peggy Porter, MD
Full Member, Division of Human Biology and Public Health Services, Fred Hutchinson Cancer Research Center
Co-Head, Women's Cancer Research Program, Fred Hutchinson Cancer Research Center
Professor, Pathology, University of Washington

Doug Pyle, MBA
Senior Director, International Affairs, American Society of Clinical Oncology

Johanna Ralston, MA, MS
Chief Executive Officer, World Heart Federation

Magdalena Rathe, MA
Executive Director, Fundacion Plenitud
Coordinator, Dominican Health Observatory (OSRD)
Coordinator, Network of Health Accounts of the Americas (REDACS)

Anne Reeler, PhD
Chief Technical Officer, Axios International

Raul Ribiero, MD
Member, St. Jude Faculty, St. Jude Children's Research Hospital
Director, International Outreach Program, St. Jude Children's Research Hospital
Director, Leukemia / Lymphoma Division, Oncology Department, St. Jude Children's Research Hospital
Associate Director for Outreach Program, Cancer Center, St. Jude Children's Research Hospital

Carlos Rodriguez-Galindo, MD
Director, Solid Tumor Program, Pediatric Oncology, Dana-Farber Cancer Institute
Associate Professor, Department of Pediatrics, Harvard Medical School
Medical Director, Pediatric Oncology Clinical Trials, Dana-Farber/Children's Hospital Cancer Center

Isabelle Romieu, MD, MPH, ScD
Head, Section on Nutrition and Metabolism, International Agency for Research on Cancer

Joanna Rubinstein, DDS, PhD
Chief of Staff to Jeffrey Sachs, The Earth Institute, Columbia University
Director of the Center for Global Health and Economic Development, The Earth Institute,
Columbia University

María del Rocío Sáenz Madrigal, MPH, MD
Vice President, Consultores en Desarrollo, Sociedad y Administración
Professor, School of Public Health, University of Costa Rica

Gloria Inés Sánchez, MSc, PhD
Coordinator, Infection and Cancer, University of Antioquia
Associate Professor, Faculty of Medicine, University of Antioquia

Miriam Schneidman
Lead Health Specialist & Cluster Leader, Africa Region, The World Bank

Nina Schwalbe, MPH
Managing Director, Global Alliance for Vaccines and Immunization

Rola Shaheen, MD, FRCPC
Chief of Radiology and Director of Women's Imaging, Harrington Memorial Hospital
Instructor in Radiology, Harvard Medical School

Isabel dos Santos Silva, MD, MSc, PhD
Head, Department of Non-communicable Disease Epidemiology,
London School of Hygiene and Tropical Medicine
Professor of Epidemiology, London School of Hygiene and Tropical Medicine

Tatiana Soldak, MD
Director of Programs, The Resource and Policy Exchange

Cristina Stefan, MD, PhD
Head, Hematology and Oncology, Department of Pediatrics and Child Health,
Stellenbosch University, Cape Town

Jeffrey Sturchio, PhD
Senior Partner, Rabin Martin
Former President and CEO, Global Health Council

Edward L. Trimble, MD, MPH
Director, National Cancer Institute (NCI) Center for Global Health

Vivien Davis Tsu, PhD, MPH
Director, HPV Vaccines Project, PATH
Associate Director, Reproductive Health, PATH
Affiliate Professor, Epidemiology, School of Public Health,
University of Washington

Jesús Zacarías Villarreal Pérez, MD
Secretary of Health, State of Nuevo León, Mexico

Anita K. Wagner, PharmD, MPH, DrPH
Assistant Professor, Department of Population Medicine,
Harvard Medical School and Harvard Pilgrim Health Care Institute
Member, Drug Policy Research Group and WHO Collaborating Center in Pharmaceutical Policy,
Department of Population Medicine, Harvard Medical School and Harvard Pilgrim Health Care Institute

Jo Anne Zujewski, MD
Head, Breast Cancer Therapeutics,
Clinical Investigation Branch of the Cancer Therapy Evaluation Program,
National Cancer Institute

An initiative promoted by: